FIGHTING GRAND CORRUPTION

Grand corruption – systemic, large-scale, and top-down misappropriation of public resources for private gain – remains a pervasive problem around the world. It affects the ability of governments to educate, feed, and care for their people. It undermines human rights, perpetuates impunity, and erodes trust in government and the judiciary. It strengthens disgruntlement, authoritarianism, and insurgency. Corruption, however, is not a static force. In this work, Naomi Roht-Arriaza explores how corruption has changed and how new anti-corruption thinking, especially in Latin America, centers human rights, victims' access to justice, and reparations. Roht-Arriaza shows how activists have used outside pressure and support for local actors – where state institutions have been captured – and foregrounds anti-corruption considerations in dealing with transitional justice and atrocity crimes. Written with engaging stories and examples, this book will appeal to lawyers, scholars of Latin America, and anyone else interested in fighting kleptocrats with the goal of reclaiming the common good.

Naomi Roht-Arriaza is Distinguished Professor of Law (emerita) and Sullivan Professor at the University of California School of Law, San Francisco, where she taught international human rights, international law and torts for almost thirty years. She is the author of *The Pinochet Effect* (2005) and *Impunity and Human Rights in International Law and Practice* (1995) and coauthor of *The International Legal System: Cases and Materials* (6th, 7th and 8th eds.). She is the president of the Board of the Due Process of Law Foundation and on the coordinating committee of the UNCAC Coalition.

Fighting Grand Corruption

TRANSNATIONAL AND HUMAN RIGHTS APPROACHES IN LATIN AMERICA AND BEYOND

NAOMI ROHT-ARRIAZA
University of California School of Law, San Francisco

CAMBRIDGE
UNIVERSITY PRESS

CAMBRIDGE
UNIVERSITY PRESS

Shaftesbury Road, Cambridge CB2 8EA, United Kingdom

One Liberty Plaza, 20th Floor, New York, NY 10006, USA

477 Williamstown Road, Port Melbourne, VIC 3207, Australia

314–321, 3rd Floor, Plot 3, Splendor Forum, Jasola District Centre, New Delhi – 110025, India

103 Penang Road, #05–06/07, Visioncrest Commercial, Singapore 238467

Cambridge University Press is part of Cambridge University Press & Assessment, a department of the University of Cambridge.

We share the University's mission to contribute to society through the pursuit of education, learning and research at the highest international levels of excellence.

www.cambridge.org
Information on this title: www.cambridge.org/9781009550581

DOI: 10.1017/9781009550574

When citing this work, please include a reference to the DOI 10.1017/9781009550574

First published 2025

A catalogue record for this publication is available from the British Library

Library of Congress Cataloging-in-Publication Data
NAMES: Roht-Arriaza, Naomi, author.
TITLE: Fighting grand corruption : transnational and human rights approaches in Latin America and beyond / Naomi Roht-Arriaza, University of California School of Law, San Francisco.
DESCRIPTION: Cambridge [United Kingdom] ; New York : Cambridge University Press, 2025. | Includes bibliographical references and index.
IDENTIFIERS: LCCN 2024050122 | ISBN 9781009550581 (hardback) | ISBN 9781009550574 (ebook)
SUBJECTS: LCSH: Corruption – Law and legislation – Latin America. | Corruption – Latin America – Prevention. | International law and human rights – Latin America. | Human rights – Latin America.
CLASSIFICATION: LCC KG966.M57 R64 2025 | DDC 345.8/02323–dc23/eng/20241022
LC record available at https://lccn.loc.gov/2024050122

ISBN 978-1-009-55058-1 Hardback
ISBN 978-1-009-55061-1 Paperback

This book is dedicated to my grandkids, that they may grow up in a better world. And to Gil, gracias, amor –ya sabés. *And to all the courageous journalists, lawyers, thinkers, and activists who keep on fighting, in Latin America and everywhere, to stem the tide of grand corruption and hold fast to a vision of the common good.*

Berkeley, California
September 2024

Contents

Acknowledgments

Many people helped educate me about the links between corruption and human rights; others sent me cases and laws and pointed out places where both anti-corruption and human rights practice needed changing. I am particularly grateful to Katya Salazar, Úrsula Indacochea, Ramiro Orías, and the rest of the staff at Due Process of Law Foundation for nudging me into taking on the topic; to Santiago Martínez for cowriting an earlier version of Chapter 9 on Venezuela with me; to the fabulous people at the numerous chapters of Transparency International and other national anti-corruption organizations who helped me brainstorm and pointed out cases to look at, especially Gillian Dell, Paula Fierro, Karina Kalpschtrej, Adriana Greaves and Estefania Medina, Carlos Guerrero, and Sara Bimbeuf; to Vivian Newman Pont, Marcie Mersky, and Daniela Cepeda Cuadrado, who commented on parts of the manuscript; to my colleagues on the Coordinating Committee and staff of the UNCAC Coalition and on its Working Groups, for sharing materials and brainstorming, and especially to Betina Pasteknik for pulling together the database on victims' access to courts; to Giulia Marchi for excellent research assistance and conducting the interview with Davida Pati of Libera; to Jonathan Escobar Valencia for excellent research assistance and letting me vent about El Salvador; and to Michael Burke for sharing his vast knowledge of the UNCAC and of US law. Special thanks to Victoria Valdés for struggling with the index – never a fun job. Thanks to the staffs of Insight Crime, the Organized Crime and Corruption Reporting Project, and El Faro for independent investigative journalism – where would we be without it? And not least, thanks to my husband for putting up with me through yet another period when I was buried in a manuscript.

Thanks, above all, to all the people I interviewed over the last three years, who enriched my understanding and grounded me in actual practice. Some of them did not want their names used – but you know who you are. Of course, where I understood wrong, those mistakes are all mine. And my sincere thanks, finally, to the human rights, environmental and anti-corruption academics, activists, lawyers, scientists, politicians, journalists, and plain old ordinary folks who refuse to stop dreaming of a better world, where human rights are respected, people have dignified livelihoods, businesses and judicial systems serve their communities, and public service is an honor and a responsibility, not an opportunity for plunder. In particular, to the Guatemalan protesters of August to December 2023, examples of determination and dignity.

PART I

SETTING THE STAGE: INTERNATIONAL AND TRANSNATIONAL LAW AND POLICIES

1

The Grand Corruption Problem

1.1 INTRODUCTION

In October 2023, protesters shut down highways across Guatemala. Farmers left their fields, joined by students, market vendors, factory workers, storekeepers, and even police. The protests were centered in the long-marginalized indigenous communities of the highlands, led by ancestral authorities who had mostly not been national political actors. Community groups organized food brigades for the protesters, while doctors and nurses made sure those needing medical attention got through the barricades. Eventually, the protesters set up a two-month long sit-in in the heart of the capital, with towns and villages sending delegations to take a turn at the barricades.

The immediate target of their ire: the country's Attorney General, her deputies, and a corrupt judge, who were using spurious investigations and prosecutions to try to keep Bernardo Arévalo from taking office. Arévalo campaigned on an anti-corruption platform with a new political party and was the long-shot winner of August 2023 elections. But the demonstrators were clear that this was not about partisan politics. It was about protecting democracy and fighting corruption. And those on the highways were quite clear about the connection between the two. "The corrupt people stole the money, that's why we have no school. Now they want to steal our election, so they can keep doing it," said one protester. It was clear to them that there is a link among corruption, democracy, and human rights.

Guatemala had become a prime – but by no means the only – example of the phenomenon I deal with in this book: high-level, massive corruption that infected state institutions and channeled the resources of the state into private gain. I will explain later how this phenomenon came about, but Guatemalans talk about it as the "pact of the corrupt," a toxic stew of organized crime, sectors of the military and the economic elite, and political officials who take turns looting the state. The result is worse health and education outcomes (Guatemala has the sixth worst child malnutrition rate in the world, for example), increasing economic polarization and growing out-migration of people who can no longer make a living at home and see no prospects of help.

I came to write this book after many years thinking, writing, teaching, and consulting on what countries coming out of dictatorship or armed conflict can do to avoid it happening again. That work focused on Latin American experiences over the last forty years. I studied truth commissions, helped prepare trials, trained civil society groups, and wrote about the design of reparations programs for survivors of gross violations of human rights and about the reforms needed to create so-called guarantees of nonrepetition. These kinds of measures, eventually known as transitional justice, became a stock part of the UN peacebuilding repertoire.

And yet, by the mid-2000s, it became clear to me that very little justice – transitional or otherwise – was possible in countries increasingly controlled by kleptocrats or mired in large-scale, systemic corruption. Judicial selection processes, often reformed in the first days of a post-armed conflict or post-repressive regime, were now cesspools of influence peddling and payoffs. The courts provided impunity for the powerful, whether for massacres or malfeasance. As I checked with my friends and colleagues in the Latin American countries where I have worked the most, they coincided in noting that a new, more virulent strain of corruption had taken over a significant part of the state. It was affecting not only their work in favor of human rights and justice but also that of colleagues working on environmental and climate protection, development, inequality, or pretty much any vision of a common good.

I began investigating what this new phenomenon looked like and where it came from. Corruption has always been part of everyday life in most parts of Latin America – you pay extra to get a phone line installed quickly, a traffic ticket not written, a coveted job, hospital bed, or grade – but this was different. This was the wholesale takeover of the centers of power – executive, legislative, judicial, local government, and media – by actors whose professed commitment to the public good had been replaced by a commitment to private gain, to use state resources on behalf of themselves, their family and close associates, and their political parties. In this, they were abetted by some private sector actors and by international enablers, from development banks to lawyers, consultants, accountants, and real estate brokers in the United States, Europe, and other capital-receiving countries.

My investigations coincided with an uptick in interest in the links between corruption and human rights among academics, civil society organizations, human rights institutions, and anti-corruption campaigners. We were all seeing the same thing: Corruption, especially large-scale, systemic corruption, is affecting the full range of human rights. Most obviously, corruption undermines economic, social, and cultural rights such as education, health care, and housing; if the money for these things is stolen by the minister in charge, or if the cement for low-income housing is substandard because the contract was the product of a bribe and so the house falls with the first storm of the year, that will impact the provision of education, health, and housing. If licenses, permits, public contracts, land titles, environmental approvals, or tax exemptions can be bought and sold with a bribe, those unable to pay up will see their standard of living, and often their property, impacted. But political and civil rights are also at risk. If political corruption means that only certain parties get financing or that some candidates can pay off electoral authorities, then the population's ability to choose their leaders is meaningless. If news media can be bribed to silence some views while allowing others to speak, freedom of the press is at issue. And if journalists, lawyers and judges, local land or environmental activists, or whistleblowers are subject to threats, imprisonment, inhumane treatment, and even death for their anti-corruption work, that violates the basic guarantees of life, liberty, and freedom from cruel treatment that are at the core of human rights.

What's more, large-scale, systemic corruption is insulating a small coterie in many countries from any kind of accountability, whether legal, political, or international. And in turn human rights violations are perpetuating and deepening the corruption problem, making it dangerous to discuss. But once we agree that these two areas of study, advocacy, and activism are linked, what next? How does that recognition change what both human rights and anti-corruption practitioners do? How does it change what the communities affected by both rights violations and corrupt practices can do to defend themselves and implement positive change? And how can the lessons learned through decades of anti-impunity work around grave human rights violations be useful to a new generation of anti-impunity activists and advocates? This book is an effort to answer these questions.

I start by defining my terms: What do I mean by corruption, and in particular grand corruption and kleptocracy? How has the change in the nature of the problem come about, and how has the field of anti-corruption work changed in response? On the human rights side, similar questions arise: How have traditional notions of human rights changed, and what does that mean for the intersection of the two concerns? I explain my focus on Latin America (with some necessary excursions elsewhere) and recall some historical examples of the ties between corruption and human rights. I end with some initial thoughts about why all this matters and about the structure of the chapters that follow.

1.2 WHAT IS CORRUPTION ANYWAY? AND HOW HAS IT CHANGED?

Like many writers before me, I struggled with how to define what I'm concerned about. It's actually a wicked stew of related issues: corruption, especially large-scale and systemic fraud, theft, and bribery, but also the corruption of political systems to respond to the highest bidder and abandon any pretense of serving the common good, and of judicial and other accountability systems to create impunity for the powerful across the board. It is also the increasingly massive intervention of organized crime that has diversified its businesses and markets way beyond drugs and allied with corrupt state and private economic actors in ever more pervasive and damaging ways. It is also connected to the conversation in the private sector about how to maintain a social license to operate, through environmental, social, and governance (including anti-corruption) compliance metrics and efforts. And, more broadly still, it is a reflection of the ethical challenges of a form of capitalism steeped in rising inequality, a lack of formal job opportunities for the young (especially in poor countries), environmental and climate collapse, and a "winner-takes-all" mentality that destroys community, poisons politics, and erodes shared values. Given all that, any single framework seems inadequate. I have chosen to label what I am talking about as "grand corruption," but it is a poor stand-in for the combination of these related phenomena.

Because corruption is notoriously hard to define precisely, most laws do not even try, opting instead for a list of specific acts, like bribery or embezzlement, that can be more easily broken down into elements. The most general definition is "the abuse of entrusted power for private gain." The entrusted power could be public service, but also private sector leadership, and entrustment could be formal or de facto. That spans a lot but can be divided into different subspecies: political corruption, corrupt public contracting, private-sector bribery, and the like. Corruption is also sometimes defined as a subset of illegal financial flows, a designation that also includes money laundering and tax evasion.

For our purposes, the most important distinction is between administrative corruption (a small bribe in exchange for a permit or a service, for example) and grand corruption. Administrative corruption is easiest to see as it is visible in peoples' everyday lives and so has until recently been the focus of most anti-corruption research and programming. The United Nations Convention Against Corruption (UNCAC) differentiates "corruption involving vast quantities of assets" from others. UNCAC-related expert groups have issued detailed recommendations on how to deal with this type of corruption,[1] some of which I take up below. Of course, the two types are connected, as part of the bribe to a cop or housing inspector is often paid upward, to a country's leaders, and those leaders turn a blind eye (or worse) to skimming by subordinates. The issue is not just about scale, but it is about a qualitatively different nature.

Transparency International defines grand corruption as "a systematic or well-organized plan of action involving high-ranking public officials that causes serious harm, such as serious human rights violations."[2] Sarah Chayes writes in the same vein that in nearly five dozen countries worldwide (it is probably more now), corruption can no longer be understood simply as bad acts of individuals. Rather, it is the operating system of sophisticated networks that crosses national and sectoral boundaries in its effort to maximize benefits for its members.[3] These networks are woven among the public, private, and criminal sectors, as well as external parties and institutions that interact with the political economy of a given country.[4]

Grand corruption, when it focuses on the link to political power, has also been called "kleptocracy." According to a recent publication by the US Agency for International Development (USAID), "[t]he most entrenched form of corruption, kleptocracy involves misappropriating the wealth of the nation and abusing it not only for personal gain but also to maintain political power."[5] The concept emphasizes the role of political leaders and senior heads of state. For Oliver Burroughs, "[k]leptocracy, the supercharged form of corruption [...] is the dark side of globalization." For Burroughs, offshore finance, where an asset like a Eurobond was legally outside the jurisdiction in which it was physically present, is what made it possible for crooked businesspeople and dictators to stash their cash, usually in a way that is tax free and untraceable.[6]

The idea of "state capture" highlights the political aspects of this process of appropriation of power. State capture was recognized as a problem back in the late 1990s, in the context of post-Soviet transition. At the time, it was seen as a problem of a few big firms having outsize and exclusive influence on state policies that affected them. The solution was to open up economies to competition and free trade.[7] More recently, Eduardo Salcedo and Luis Garay-Salamanca explain, "State capture has usually been conceived as a form of large-scale corruption that weakens a country's economic structure because it distorts the formulation of laws, norms, decrees, rules and regulations."[8] Elizabeth David-Barrett writes,

> A defining aspect of state capture is control over legislation and public policy: [t]he elites have expanded the scope of state capture to [...] the implementation of policy, through state organs such as state-owned enterprises, the

> bureaucracy and quasi-independent regulatory agencies, and the accountability ecosystem [...] such as the judiciary and the comptroller's office, as well as broader civil society, including the media.[9]

This presupposes that the state is not a monolithic entity but consists of several centers of power that are in a constant process of cooperation and competition and that relate to others, such as private enterprise, organized crime, political parties, and various international structures; therefore, different parts of the state can be captured to varying degrees or by different forces. In any case, state capture involves using political mechanisms to favor the economic interests of a small group of people while creating impunity for their actions. Jimena Reyes draws distinctions between kleptocracy and state capture: Kleptocracy is used to describe dictatorial regimes, while state capture through corruption can include democratic (but dysfunctional) ones. States can be partially captured, and state capture can be by third parties, not necessarily the leader(s) who plunder the state, while kleptocracy refers to total capture by crooked leaders.[10]

In its most virulent form, this phenomenon is not just about state capture, but the reconfiguration of the state itself for the benefit of the groups that have captured it. "At a sophisticated and complex level of State Capture, such as the Co-opted Reconfiguration of the State, not only is sustained economic benefit pursued, but at that stage, the co-opter aims to accompany the economic benefit with political power, legal impunity and social legitimacy."[11] This implies taking over state institutions and using them for the benefit of the co-opter, and at the same time, weakening the mechanisms of control, accountability, transparency, and citizen opposition. One of the main results of this process is a culture of impunity, where the powerful are not subject to sanction or punishment, and victims find themselves with no redress.

In these situations, political elites or organized crime do not simply bribe or threaten public officials to achieve their ends through the old "plata o plomo (silver or lead)" trope. The legal and illegal (and a "gray" sector in between), the private and the public, are intertwined; they are connected by family, schooling, or other personal and professional ties, and their alliances and disputes may vary over time or by region.[12] Corrupt schemes can originate at any point on this triangle.

1.3 CORRUPTION AND ORGANIZED CRIME

There's considerable, but not total, overlap between corruption and organized crime: Corruption doesn't always involve organized crime, but the latter always involves the former on some scale.

If ideas around the capture and reconfiguration of the State begin from the perspective of state actors, theories of criminal governance start from the actions of illicit groups, especially organized crime, and from a concern with the control of territory and the monopoly of force. Definitions of organized crime foreground numerosity (three or more persons), continuity over time, acting in concert (although no particular formal structure or roles are needed), and acting in order to obtain, directly or indirectly, financial or other material benefit.[13] These characteristics make organized crime more pernicious, and dangerous, than ordinary crime.

While most people think about organized crime in terms of drug production and smuggling, in recent years organized criminal enterprises have expanded to a wide range of illegal and quasi-legal businesses, including human, organ, and wildlife trafficking, gasoline theft, illegal logging, mining, and fisheries, waste disposal, and financial services, among others. They are often in shifting alliances with "legitimate" private businesses.

Scholars of national security and the use of violence observe that nonstate armed groups of various kinds challenge the state's monopoly on the use of coercion, sometimes sharing and sometimes disputing power. They use control of territory, economic sectors, and violence to regulate social order, including through the creation of formal or informal governance and justice institutions.[14] Criminal governance can occur at different scales, from a neighborhood to vast regions of a country, and can create "gray areas" where various state and nonstate groups overlap.[15] In some cases, territorial control can entail extortion and protection rackets, limits on access to neighborhoods and on livelihoods that radically affect community dynamics. Given the lack of either employment or protection alternatives, this control can entail a measure of popular support, especially where a hegemonic group keeps levels of violence relatively low and provides services that the absent state does not. The nexus between these illicit actors and the state makes them both allied protagonists and sometime competitors. It can help explain various phenomena, including Mexican cartels, Brazilian militias, and paramilitary groups in Colombia or Central American gangs.

A variant on this idea is that of "organized corruption," that is, the marriage of organized crime and systemic corruption "which creates a crooked ecosystem that enriches and protects those with access to power." It is "not only about systemic illicit financial gains and undue influence in decision-making, but also the systemic buying and influencing of social support to gain or maintain political and economic power."[16] This kind of organized corruption helps explain, for instance, the penetration of organized crime into judicial and oversight bodies.

Where these theoretical explanations coincide is in their analytic methodology. To understand the interpenetration of individuals, organizations, and sectors requires disentangling macrocriminal or "socio-political illicit networks."[17] The study of social networks helps to understand where the nodes concentrating power are located, who is connected to whom, how the visible and the invisible, the legal and the illegal are related. Similarly, it shifts the focus from individual figures (e.g., the "kingpins" of criminal organizations) to their connections and the interrelationship among structures and networks. These mapping studies can be done by country, by sector and by institution, using network analysis and large data sets to understand the ways in which macrocriminality manifests.[18]

Differences among countries may suggest that one theory works better than another in explaining the particularities. Thus, for example, the kleptocracy approach might be more useful in Venezuela, where there is a centralized effort by the regime to concentrate and order criminal and economic powers around itself,[19] while in Mexico, decentralized dynamics in different states, or even municipalities, and different configurations of criminal cartels, authorities, and economic elites could make a criminal governance approach more useful.

1.4 PRECURSORS IN LATIN AMERICA

I have focused my research mostly (although not exclusively) on Latin America. In part, because it's the region I know best, and where this set of problems is at the top of national agendas. I have, however, occasionally ventured into other continents where I think the experiences of a particular country bear valuable lessons. Nor have I been exhaustive even in the Americas, although I have tried to illustrate with stories from various countries in the region. I could have chosen other countries, including Peru, Bolivia, Paraguay, Nicaragua, and Ecuador, to illustrate variations on these themes.

I also focused on Latin America because there's a long history of intertwined anti-corruption and human rights agendas. At least since Iberians crossed the ocean more than 500 years ago to the Americas, the predominant economic model has been clientelist, patriarchal, and extractivist. Independence from colonial powers did little to change the extreme concentration of land and wealth, and the region continues to be one of the world's most unequal. The list of former high-ranking public officials formally charged (at home or abroad) with corruption includes nearly twenty former presidents as well as government ministers and other leaders in Venezuela, Peru, Guatemala, Colombia, Mexico, Brazil, Paraguay, Guyana, Argentina, Ecuador, Colombia, Chile, the Dominican Republic, Haiti, and even relatively squeaky-clean Uruguay and

Costa Rica. No wonder people are fed up. Even if most investigations didn't lead to a final conviction, and even if some were on shaky ground, that's still a lot of leaders.

Some of the most notorious human rights-related cases of the 1990s were also systemic corruption cases. Take the poster child of military dictatorship in the 1970s, Augusto Pinochet. Pinochet boasted that "not a leaf moved in Chile without me knowing it"; he headed a secret police that killed more than five thousand people and tortured tens of thousands. Yet a sizeable part of the Chilean population supported him, even after he left power and despite persistent rumors of arms deals and financial scandals involving his son. It was only when, as the result of a 2002 US Senate inquiry into money laundering by Washington, DC-based Riggs Bank, investigators found that Riggs had set up offshore accounts for Pinochet and his family worth some $20 million, an amount far greater than the general's salary and legitimate businesses. When he died in 2013, Pinochet was under indictment for tax evasion and embezzlement as well as enforced disappearance. Right-wing parties, more disturbed by self-dealing than by torture, distanced themselves from his legacy and much (but not all) of his fan base vanished.

In neighboring Peru, a similar thing happened a couple of decades later. Former President Alberto Fujimori and his spy chief, Vladimir Montesinos, had run Peru from 1990 to 2000. They used extrajudicial killings, forced disappearances and torture to defeat an armed insurgency and silence political opponents, including college professors, student activists and others. Montesinos was variously known as "Rasputin, Darth Vader, Torquemada and Cardinal Richelieu," in the words of a 1997 US Army intelligence report released under the Freedom of Information Act and reported by Frontline. At one point he worked simultaneously for the CIA and the Medellín cartel, a balancing act that was no doubt hard to maintain.[20] He was brought down due to his habit of secretly videotaping meetings, including those where he bribed officials, journalists and business leaders, presumably in order to blackmail them later. One of the videos, showing him bribing a congressman, eventually leaked, and the "Vladi-videos" became a national scandal that brought down the Fujimori government. Fujimori fled to Japan, and from there faxed in his resignation. A few years later he chose to visit Chile, and the Peruvian government asked for his extradition. He was extradited and eventually convicted in 2009 for running a death squad in two separate massacres; he served over a dozen years of a twenty-five-year sentence before being released on health grounds.

Shortly thereafter, the pair were tried for corruption offenses: phone tapping of the opposition; bribing members of Congress; embezzlement of state funds for illegal purposes; and the transfer of $15 million in public funds to Montesinos. Montesinos fled to Venezuela, where despite his plastic surgery he was arrested in June 2001 with the help of the FBI. Investigators discovered some $210 million in secret offshore accounts; an additional $600 million was found in 2015 in Panama. Montesinos was charged with influence peddling, abuse of authority, fraud, coercion, corruption, illicit enrichment, money laundering, drug and arms trafficking, extortion, bribery, forced disappearances, torture, murder, harboring a criminal, embezzlement, and illegal wiretapping. He was convicted multiple times, the latest in 2023, and will spend decades in prison. Some, but by no means all the stolen money, was returned to Peru.

Argentina also combined horrific human rights violations and corruption, especially among the armed forces and police in charge of arresting and forcibly disappearing real or suspected dissidents. Where the families of those detained had money, the abductors would demand titles to property or bank accounts in order to release prisoners (which rarely happened) or even to give the families a chance to say goodbye. In the case of Conrado Gomez, a supposed financier of the left-wing Montoneros, Navy Admiral Massera and four subordinates were accused of stealing properties, almost a million dollars and prize racehorses from Gómez, registering them in the name of fake companies controlled by Massera. Massera was later convicted of being the mastermind behind hundreds of forced disappearances and torture in the Naval Academy School (ESMA). Another torturer, Ricardo Cavallo, started his business with funds extorted from families of the missing. He eventually turned his experience forging documents in the ESMA to good use: he became a purveyor of drivers' licenses to governments. That was before he got arrested in Mexico on a Spanish arrest warrant, extradited to Spain, then re-extradited to Argentina to stand trial for his human rights-related crimes.[21]

In El Salvador, a decade-long armed conflict followed longer decades of military domination and repression of land reform movements. During that time, according to the New York Times,

> [a]n officer taking command of one of the three regional brigades had at his disposal a vast system of patronage and graft, with countless opportunities for enrichment. Colonels leased troops as guards or laborers to local businessmen, or even, in some cases, as hired killers to insure labor peace. And there was always money to be siphoned off from the base's payroll and food budgets.

Commanders created "ghost soldiers" who didn't exist but were nonetheless on the payroll, their salaries siphoned off. They created their own institutions, including a military social security fund and a shopping mall, and invested in land and fishing fleets. As a result, the military became the largest source of cash in the country – and the author of tens of thousands of deaths of civilians, including Jesuit priests, US nuns, and (in one famous massacre) over 600 children.[22] Unlike the previous examples, very little has been done about either human rights violations or military corruption.

I could say something similar about military intelligence officers in Guatemala, but I'll tell that story in Chapter 3.

The return to formal democracy did not diminish corruption. In many ways it exacerbated it as politicians scrambled to finance their campaigns by any means necessary, and waves of privatization and decentralization followed, a process I describe in Chapter 8. In the best-known example, in 2015, investigators in Brazil and the US discovered the sprawling bribery scheme known as Odebrecht. From a modest investigation into black market dollar-changers operating from car washes and gas stations in Brazil (hence the name "car wash" or Lava Jato given the investigation), it found evidence of bribes paid to the national oil company Petrobras. From there, the investigation soon expanded – and kept expanding. Eventually, it transpired that Odebrecht had bribed about 600 politicians and public servants in ten Latin American countries and two African ones to win bids for large infrastructure projects, and to renegotiate the projects at higher prices after winning them.

All this violated the US Foreign Corrupt Practices Act (FCPA), which gave the US jurisdiction because the company had used US banks and other US entities for the transactions. The Swiss also had jurisdiction because some of the funds were laundered through Swiss entities. On December 21, 2016, seventy-seven current and former Odebrecht executives signed plea agreements with the US Department of Justice and with the Swiss and Brazilian prosecuting authorities in exchange for reduced sentences. As part of the plea deal, the executives detailed corruption schemes involving USD$778 million in bribes paid to generate $3.6 billion in gross profits. It was one of the largest transnational corruption scandals ever.

Odebrecht created a separate branch dedicated to bribery, influence peddling and money laundering, with its own budget and a staff that reported directly to the CEO.[23] Once a payment was approved, this DSO paid through a network of shell companies and offshore bank accounts in multiple countries, set up precisely for this purpose. The company got contracts mostly by manipulating the technical or subjective criteria so that Odebrecht seemed like the most qualified (or the only qualified) bidder, even in a competitive tender.[24] Bribes went to politicians to create tailored requirements, or to heads of agencies – whoever the decisionmakers were. Once the contract was signed, bribes allowed its renegotiation to add on additional work, including whole new projects, without rebidding or scrutinizing the new terms.

These shenanigans surely made some government officials very rich and filled Odebrecht's coffers with the inflated prices and extra work. But who was harmed? Why wasn't this a victimless crime?

That depends on what happened to the projects at issue, and on what the bribe recipients did with the funds. In Brazil, as well as in Ecuador and elsewhere, much of the bribe money went into financing political campaigns. This wasn't a left or right ideological issue – *everybody* took bribes. Campaign finance was opaque, and legislators could easily change parties in most places, which made bribing more efficient. The private sector bribers got access and contracts, the politicians got fat campaign coffers and mansions, and the rest of the country got … cynical. As others have noted, political corruption breeds populism, instability and extremisms of various kinds, as ordinary people decide that the system is rigged. The result in Brazil was Bolsonaro.

Odebrecht was an infrastructure company, so it built what should have been useful things, like roads, airports, dams and ports. But as a result of bribes, the projects received little to no scrutiny or, worse, bribes ensured that they would go ahead despite serious economic, environmental, engineering and social concerns. Moreover, projects were quietly sliced and diced into component parts as part of the contract renegotiations, so that outside observers had no sense of the full scope.

Some of the work was particularly controversial. The Belo Monte dam in Brazil opened in 2016. Situated on the Xingu River in Pará state, it is the fourth largest hydroelectric dam in the world. Odebrecht was one of three key members of the construction consortium that built the dam. Environmental groups charged that the project had been pushed through despite studies showing that the river was not suitable and increasingly affected by climate change, and Amazonian indigenous groups protested that they would be severely harmed by changes to water quality and fishing grounds. When the Lava Jato corruption scandal broke, Otávio Marques de Azevedo, the former president of Andrade Gutierrez (Odebrecht's partner) admitted in a plea bargain that the companies had paid extensive bribes to the ruling party and its allies to get the contract. Which explained how the project was greenlighted despite the known adverse effects.[25] By 2020, the profits had been made, but the dam was producing at most half the electricity that had been promised, and at times – due to low water levels and high winds – almost no electricity at all.[26] Meanwhile, some 20,000 people were displaced. According to Daniela Silva, one of those forced out: "Belo Monte pushed the people into misery.

It ripped us out of our homes, and it didn't give us any tools to rebuild our lives."[27] Silva today works to protect and defend the Amazon basin.

Dams were not the only problematic projects. Roads built through heretofore virgin strands of forest populated largely by indigenous groups uninterested in being "found" by modern life brought settlers, miners and loggers. Construction projects in remote areas, greenlighted only due to bribes and influence-peddling, brought urban problems like prostitution and alcoholism. On the other hand, sometimes the problem was that the proposed project was never finished, a long-promised bridge or highway left half done, a subway system contracted for but not delivered. Not only the benefits never arrived, but all the time and costs of getting to a contract were wasted, and the projects were rarely rebid. In Venezuela, for instance, only nine of thirty-three projects were ever finished.

The Odebrecht scandals set off massive anti-corruption demonstrations in several countries, and led to arrests and trials in Brazil and elsewhere. The former Comptroller General of Ecuador was tried in Miami for taking a $10 million bribe from the company. In Colombia, former presidents Santos and Uribe have been connected to the scandal. In August 2023 charges including bribe-taking and money laundering were leveled against sixty people in Colombia, including public and private officials and contractors.[28] In Peru, at least five former presidents were caught up in investigations around bribe-taking and money laundering; one, Alan García, shot himself as the law closed in. (The last two presidents are also being investigated for corruption, including a collection of expensive jewelry discovered because journalists observed a series of fancy watches worn during press conferences.)

In Brazil, the corruption conviction against then- (and current) President Lula da Silva was annulled on contested grounds of collusion between prosecutors and the investigating judge, leading to legal questions about whether the convictions of other defendants were valid and a loss of credibility in the investigation.[29] By May 2023, the Brazilian Supreme Court had annulled several of the convictions on due process grounds, including that of Marcelo Odebrecht.

1.5 METHODOLOGY AND STRUCTURE OF THE BOOK

These precedents make it easy to understand why a human rights-based approach to combatting corruption makes intuitive sense to many people in the region. Latin America isn't just the site of some of the largest and most brazen scandals associated with organized crime and grand corruption. It's also characterized by vibrant social movements that have fought against impunity for rights violations for decades and have seen the connection to corrupt actors up close. It's that link between human rights and corruption that makes the issue real, and important, to ordinary people. It's the link that allows the strengths of human rights (and environmental) advocacy in the region to be applied in new areas, and also brings the advantages of anti-corruption law to bear where it can be useful. And therefore, it's the link that can mobilize resources, stir outrage, and unleash imagination, in the courts, the legislatures, the investigative bodies, and the streets. At least, that's my hope.

One of the consequences of a state partially or totally in the throes of grand corruption is that none of the usual mechanisms for combatting it work well. The courts are captured, so is the legislature, the media is bought off or muzzled. The kind of first-generation anti-corruption independent commissions, prosecutors or specialized courts under these conditions tend to be defanged or even turned into instruments for pursuing political enemies or opposition activists. Ostensible corruption-fighting becomes yet another instrument of the corrupt. The laws may be exemplary, but in practice they are twisted to perpetuate the system. What, then, can be done?

This book looks at two potential responses, both of them admittedly partial. First, within countries, bringing in outside voices and actors from civil society – not just state prosecutors – to bolster efforts at prevention and accountability, and to allow for stolen assets to be returned to the people they were stolen from, through asset recovery or reparations. Civil society has been fundamental to improvements in accountability for rights violations, including but by no means limited to criminal trials. That experience can be useful in anti-corruption efforts.

Second, turning to actors outside the country to open up space, pressure recalcitrant kleptocrats and make it harder for them to enjoy the fruits of kleptocracy. This too is a time-honored tradition in the human rights sphere. As Kathryn Sikkink and others have noted,[30] when domestic rights advocates in the 1970s were stymied by repressive governments, they turned to the UN and regional human rights bodies. The governments professed their commitment to human rights, which opened up spaces for activist networks to hold them to their word, creating a spiral of increasing rights observance. This same approach is increasingly visible in the tactics of the global anti-corruption movement, as I discuss in several chapters.

I wrote the book based on a combination of official documents, court decisions, reports and other desk research, and interviews with a variety of actors. Some of those interviews took place at international anti-corruption or human rights conferences, and others on trips to the region in 2022 and 2023. All the translations are mine. I have tried to intersperse attention to legal arguments and evolution with the stories of some of the people who bring law to life. A couple of the chapters use material from my earlier academic articles, cited at the beginning of the chapters. I focused on international as well as domestic law and institutions, since by nature grand corruption is a transnational problem that will not be solved by any single country. Money moves around too fast, and the networks moving it – from transnational business to organized crime syndicates to enablers – operate across borders. But it's also true that international law mostly remains pieces of paper until it's carried into reality by national governments, courts, and civil society. I try here to look at both, and at how they intersect and influence each other.

I look first at the state of international treaty law in the intersections of anti-corruption, human rights and the environment, with a focus on an emerging convergence among them. I explore three ways that the links have been theorized: Corruption as context and cause of other rights violations, procedural principles of human rights applied to corruption, and corruption as itself a stand-alone violation of human rights. I then turn to recent transnational efforts that implicate both anti-corruption and human rights concerns. I look first at international support for domestic prosecutions, as pioneered by the Commission Against Impunity in Guatemala and its short-lived cousins in Honduras and El Salvador. I then turn to the use of visa and financial "smart" sanctions against individuals and companies for either human rights or corruption-related abuses by the US, the UK, Canada, Australia and the European Union. I conclude by looking at other potential sources of pressure on governments unable or unwilling to combat grand corruption, including extraterritorial prosecution and forfeiture actions, market-based incentives and greater scrutiny from international lenders. (I leave discussion of a proposed International Anti-Corruption Court to Chapter 10).

The next part of the book, pulls apart what it might mean to "put victims at the center" of anti-corruption work. I consider the complexities of defining who is a victim (if it's not just the state), and how victims can conceptualize and prove the harms suffered, be represented in official proceedings of various sorts, and establish the appropriate causal connection. In doing so, I ask how the corpus of human rights law on the rights of victims might (or might not) be applicable to corruption cases, and trace efforts to do so in the region. I then consider the issue of reparations for victims of corruption. I look first at asset recovery of funds found abroad and returned to the home state, as the UNCAC demands. I ask how victim communities, and the public generally, can play a constructive role in recovery, return and repurposing of assets, using experiences to date as a guide. I then look at national experiences with reparation, as broadly defined in human rights law, and ask whether those experiences can, or should, be adapted in a corruption context.

The next set of chapters take up specific areas of human rights practice and ask how a focus on corruption, especially grand corruption, would benefit them. I look first at transitions away from dictatorship or armed conflict. I ask why, despite extensive efforts to come to terms with the past and create the conditions for nonrepetition, so many paradigmatic examples of transition ended up with a serious corruption problem. I look at four countries: Guatemala, South Africa, Tunisia and Colombia. I do realize that two of these are not Latin American, but I included South Africa because it became the poster child for a successful transition, while Tunisia went the furthest to date to try to combine human rights and anti-corruption actions in the wake of the Arab Spring. Guatemala and Colombia's experiences are a generation apart. I then turn to how a corruption lens can be useful for atrocity crimes like genocide, war crimes and especially crimes against humanity. I posit that it can help clarify and strengthen proof of several elements of the crimes, and consider the options available for operationalizing such a lens. I use Venezuela and Mexico to illustrate my points.

A concluding chapter summarizes some of the lessons learned regarding the borrowing from human rights law and its application to grand corruption. I summarize some of the limitations of current anti-corruption law, and look forward. I consider here the proposals for an International Anti-Corruption Court. I then take up objections to a focus on human rights and corruption, including the dangers of defining those affected as victims, of politization and "lawfare," and of spreading limited resources too thin. And I end by connecting the anti-corruption and human rights agendas to current efforts to bolster citizen security, protect the planet, and fight inequality and antidemocratic backsliding in the region.

The fight to tame grand corruption and uphold human rights will require tenacity, imagination and new alliances. This book is dedicated to the new generations of activists and advocates inside and outside government trying to wage that fight under adverse circumstances today.

2

Treaty Law on Corruption and Human Rights

Convergence and Gaps

As I started researching, I began trying to understand how to better combat the more potent brand of systemic corruption, with its dire consequences for human rights, that I was seeing in scandals like Odebrecht. I wanted to know whether infusing more anti-corruption law and policy into human rights law (and, in places, into environmental law) and vice versa, could make both of them more potent. This was especially important given the continuing weaknesses, misuses and loopholes of law in general, and international law in particular, in an era of increasing authoritarianism, democratic backsliding, and rampant inequality. I found that there are ways in which, indeed, ideas and mechanisms in each body of law can complement and strengthen the other. To understand how, I start with brief summaries of the evolution of anti-corruption law – in its international and national aspects – and of human rights law. I next take up ways in which the two areas of law converge around general procedural norms that largely mirror what has been called a human rights-based approach, including accountability, transparency, participation, and protection. I conclude by asking whether it would be useful to envision a stand-alone right to be free of corruption, and how a focus on systemic or grand corruption might help.

2.1 THE EVOLUTION OF ANTI-CORRUPTION LAW

Most of anti-corruption law was created using an earlier paradigm, focused on bribe-givers and on individual wrongdoers who were an exception to generally law-abiding officials and private actors. Indeed, during one period in the 1960s and beyond corruption was often seen as a positive, a way of "greasing the wheels" of otherwise inefficient (mostly non-Western) societies.[1] A series of corporate scandals involving bribes to foreign officials in Chile and elsewhere led the US Congress to pass the 1977 Foreign Corrupt Practices Act.

The Act penalizes bribe-giving (but until 2023 not taking) by US citizens and companies and foreigners acting with some tie to the US. Business entities complained that the US would lose competitive advantage if its companies had to act ethically while its competitors did not; this led the US to push for a global treaty.

Twenty years later, the 1997 Organisation for Economic Co-operation and Development (OECD) Anti-Bribery Convention was signed. It applies to all OECD countries, while others can opt in. At the same time, James Wolfensohn, president of the World Bank from 1995 to 2005, emphasized the negative effects of corruption on development and tried to move the Bank toward combatting it in its loan portfolio. And in the Americas, the Inter-American Convention Against Corruption became the first in a series of regional treaties, including two in Europe (one criminal and one civil, in 1999), the 2003 African Union Convention on Preventing and Combating Corruption, the Economic Community of West African States Protocol on the Fight against Corruption, the Southern African Development Community Protocol against Corruption, and the Arab Convention to Fight Corruption of 2010. In the African Union, an Advisory Board Against Corruption frames dialogues and promotes model legislation, while the Inter-American Convention created a Follow-Up Mechanism for the Implementation of the Inter-American Convention against Corruption which reviews domestic legislation in thirty-four countries in the Americas and recommends measures to strengthen domestic anti-corruption frameworks. Among other provisions, these treaties create prevention obligations, commit states to criminalizing specific acts of corruption such as active, passive or transnational bribery or illicit enrichment, and contain sections on cooperation among states, including for purposes of extradition. As in many treaties, states are obligated to ensure that their domestic laws match the requirements of the treaty but there is little or no international monitoring or consequences for noncompliance.

The Council of Europe's twin Criminal and Civil Conventions on Corruption are an exception, in that they create a monitoring and peer review body (known as GRECO) that requires states to periodically submit reports, followed by a visit from experts of other member states, who ask about implementation, suggest reforms, and check on compliance with recommendations.[2] The peer review model, as we'll see, has become part of the implementation toolbox of both anti-corruption and human rights regimes.

The 2003 United Nations Convention Against Corruption (UNCAC) was a game changer. Almost every country in the world has ratified it. The Convention follows the same structure as the earlier regional treaties: prevention, criminalization, transborder cooperation among civil and criminal authorities. For the first time, the treaty provides an asset recovery framework for freezing, confiscation, and return to the country from where the assets were stolen. It sets up a conference of states parties that is to meet regularly, and leaves open the possibility of a periodic peer review mechanism on how states are implementing its provisions (the review mechanism was later created, but has a number of limitations on its effectiveness).

The requirement to criminalize bribery in every state's national law now extends to both giving and receiving something of value except when the bribe-taker is a foreign official, when it's optional. The treaty also requires criminalization of money laundering and obstruction of justice in corruption cases and embezzlement by a public official. Beyond that, it's up to each state to decide whether or not to outlaw other types of corrupt acts like undue influence, abuse of functions and illicit enrichment by public officials, as well as various offenses committed by private actors. Despite its innovations, the UNCAC has few mandatory provisions and lots of "where possible" and "according to domestic law," limitations no doubt necessary to gain agreement from wildly different states, some with their own corruption issues. Its procedures allow some marginal participation by civil society, but much less than in human rights or environmental international forums. States almost always act by least-common-denominator consensus, and agree not to criticize each other (or allow NGOs to do so) by name in their conferences and reviews.

This makes it difficult to pin down how well actual implementation and use of UNCAC is going. In 2017, the UN Office on Drugs and Crime published the results of the first round of peer review of the parties, which focused on criminalization and law enforcement cooperation.[3] The review found that, while most parties had taken at least some steps to translate the treaty to domestic law, there were significant gaps even among the mandatory provisions. These included how to define "public official" and nonmaterial benefits broadly, and incorporating the giving (not just receiving) of bribes, especially of foreign public officials, as an offense. There were also problems in defining obstruction of justice, in the scope of money laundering, and in holding corporate entities criminally liable. And that's just the mandatory provisions. With respect to the nonmandatory ones, few jurisdictions have criminalized receiving bribes from foreign public officials, trading in influence or illicit enrichment (this last often because of concerns over the use of presumptions and effects on the presumption of innocence). There were also problems reported regarding the scope of immunities, limits on asset confiscation, and protection of witnesses and whistleblowers. On the other hand, one positive result of the implementation review process was increased communication and cooperation among agencies within each state as well as sharing of good practices across borders. Latin American countries did better on anti-illicit enrichment measures and pausing statutes of limitations while the alleged offender was in office, but worse on translating influence trading and private sector bribery into domestic law.[4]

UNCAC turned twenty years old in 2023. It is on its second cycle of peer reviews. Not surprisingly, getting through reviews of almost 200 countries is taking a long time. There's a Working Group on Asset Recovery, one on Prevention, and a group dedicated to the review process. Each meeting of the Conference of States Parties (CoSP) results in resolutions, which generally recommend good practices and call attention to the need to do more in specified areas. I attended the 10th CoSP, which saw a lot of late night, bleary-eyed delegate meetings to hammer out language despite persistent (and often inexplicable) opposition from a handful of states, NGO-led side events where people from all over talked about the challenges facing them, and resolutions on things like creating registers of the real owners of shell corporations, protecting whistleblowers and making public procurement processes more transparent.

Other treaties touch on related issues. The UN Convention against Transnational Organized Crime (UNTOC or Palermo Convention) defines its subject as organized criminal groups, which operate across borders and are made up of three or more persons who over a period of time act in concert to commit serious crimes, in order to obtain a financial or other material benefit. The treaty requires states to criminalize agreements or conspiracies to commit serious crimes, money laundering, corruption and related offenses, allow for confiscation of the proceeds of crime, provide protection and compensation for victims and cooperation among states. Recent meetings under both treaties have stressed the links between corruption and organized crime; the two conventions share a secretariat in the UN Office of Drugs and Crime in Vienna.

Anti-money laundering (and terrorist financing) rules are the subject of the Financial Action Task Force (FATF), a collaboration among finance ministries that maintains influential Recommendations and its own system of periodic mutual evaluations or peer review. Although technically a nonbinding non-treaty, FATF recommendations are backed by a system of blacklisting, which can lead to economic sanctions, and greylisting, which leads to increased international scrutiny and a need to enact reforms within a limited time. In many ways, FATF exercises more real power than many "binding" treaty regimes.[5]

The field of national anti-corruption work is too vast to summarize here. Over the years, it has included anti-corruption commissions, anti-corruption courts, anti-corruption campaigns, and a thousand other efforts large and small, with mixed results that seem to depend as much on the political context and the individuals involved as on the design of the institution. As the extent of the problem has come into clearer focus, civil society groups have pushed to strengthen the anti-corruption legal and regulatory regimes to make prevention, accountability, and redress more robust. On the prevention side, they have championed mechanisms of open public contracting, limits on no-bid contracts and contract modifications, and open government – putting corruption-prone activity online where journalists and activists can find it. They have insisted that the real owners of bank accounts, property and other wealth be identifiable through beneficial ownership registries, ideally open to journalists and researchers as well as prosecutors, judges and auditors, that limit the ability to hide dirty money beneath layers of shell companies. So far, major sites of company registry like the US and the EU have agreed to create these registries but not to open them beyond government authorities.[6] They have pushed for extending the anti-money laundering rules that apply to banks to real estate sellers, attorneys, asset managers and other enablers of kleptocracy, especially in countries like the US and the UK where much dirty money is stashed.[7] And they have insisted that journalists, activists and whistleblowers enjoy robust protections against retaliation. These measures would go some ways toward making it more difficult for kleptocrats to enjoy the fruits of large-scale corruption.

The anti-corruption regime is slowly and haltingly starting to recognize the link between corruption and human rights. The Political Declaration[8] adopted at the 2021 Special Session of the United Nations General Assembly Against Corruption (UNGASS Declaration) expressed concern "about the negative impact that all forms of corruption, including the solicitation of undue advantages, can have on access to basic services and the enjoyment of all human rights, and recognize that it can exacerbate poverty and inequality and may disproportionately affect the most disadvantaged individuals in society," and pledged "to prevent and combat corruption and strengthen international cooperation in a manner consistent with our obligations with regard to and respect for all human rights, justice, democracy and the rule of law at all levels." Several CoSP resolutions, including from the 7th (Res. 7/2, 2017), 8th (Res. 8/11, 2019) and 10th (Res. 10/1) CoSPs, use variants on this language.

Within the UNCAC regime itself, there have been intimations of a new openness to thinking about links to human rights, but not a lot of concrete applications. Starting with the linkage between development and anti-corruption recognized in the Fifth Conference of the Parties,[9] the references to human rights have become a stock part of the introductory clauses of each year's resolutions, with little follow-through in the operative paragraphs. For example, Res. 6/6 (2015) (echoed in Res. 9/6 (2021) and 10/3 (2023)), "*Stressing* that preventive measures are one of the most effective means of countering corruption and of avoiding its negative impact on the enjoyment of human rights."[10] Or this, in a 2015 resolution on education: "[…]investing in anti-corruption education and enhancing professional capacities are effective ways to contribute to achieving sustainable development, safeguarding human rights and strengthening the rule of law."

So far, the repeated references do not seem to have translated into concrete cross-fertilizations. However, there are some encouraging signs: A side event at CoSP 10 in 2023 highlighted how a human rights approach would be useful in evaluating state compliance with obligations under the UNCAC Review Mechanism. UNODC has said that it will produce a brief on the interlinkages by 2025, just in time for the 75th anniversary of the Universal Declaration of Human Rights.[11]

2.2 CHANGES IN INTERNATIONAL HUMAN RIGHTS LAW

Like anti-corruption law, human rights law is based on a series of near-universal treaties and "soft law," with implementation mostly left to national bodies. The international machinery, a few decades older, also centers monitoring, public and private condemnation of violations by other states, and more recently peer review. While human rights as a concept go back millennia, the modern human rights corpus of laws and institutions dates from the twentieth century, especially the treaties drafted after the World War II. Those treaties include covenants on civil and political rights and on economic, social and cultural rights, and eventually a dozen or so more specialized treaties on specific vulnerable groups or specific human rights-related crimes. Each one set up an implementation mechanism, usually including an expert committee to evaluate state reports on their progress in carrying out the treaty, to issue general comments on what specific provisions mean, and under certain circumstances to recommend action in individual cases. "Special rapporteurs" and independent experts acted as experts to look into and report back on problematic countries or themes of interest. Starting in 2005, all states also reported periodically to a peer review mechanism (Universal Periodic Review), where other states could ask questions and suggest reforms. Regional treaties and a welter of "soft law" guidelines, principles, declarations, and resolutions round out the system.

In its first few decades, human rights law and advocacy focused largely on violations of basic physical integrity, civil and political rights, including torture, summary executions, enforced disappearances and mass killings. By 1993, states in the Vienna Declaration had agreed that economic and social rights were just as important as civil and political ones, but in practice, they weren't. Violations were committed by state agents, or at most by private individuals closely connected to the state or where the state was complicit.

By the 2000s, that started to change. One change involved clarifying the ways in which states could be held liable for violations of international law, even those involving private individuals, paramilitaries or corporations.

The human rights treaties contained language creating rights for individuals (and, occasionally groups) and corresponding duties on governments (and occasionally others). The jurisprudence of regional human rights courts and UN quasi-judicial bodies increasingly talked in terms of a range of duties. Duty-bearers are required not only to respect rights in their own actions, but to protect/ensure/secure and fulfil rights. Respecting rights is largely a negative obligation (don't torture, don't shut down newspapers), but protecting, ensuring, securing and fulfilling have positive aspects that require states to actively regulate private actors, prohibit rights-violating conduct, investigate, prosecute and redress violations, and create the architecture to prevent repetition. These obligations can be immediate or progressive, but backsliding is generally not allowed, and all rights are covered.

Thus, for instance, a failure to prevent or adequately investigate grand corruption (even if the underlying crimes cannot yet be proved) could itself be a violation of state's obligations under Article 2.1 of the International Covenant on Civil and Political Rights (obligation to ensure rights), Article 2.1 of the International Covenant on Economic, Social and Cultural Rights (especially the requirement to "achieve progressively"), Article 1.1 of the American Convention on Human Rights (ensure rights), or Article 1 of the European Convention for the Protection of Human Rights and Fundamental Freedoms (secure rights). The obligation to prevent does not mean that the state must succeed in preventing all crime, but where it is aware of a high risk of violations, it must take reasonable legal, political, administrative and cultural measures to counter the risk. The obligation is one of due diligence. This obligation has been important, for example, in cases involving violence against women or environmental harms.

Beyond obligations to prevent, investigate, prosecute and repair, these positive obligations extend the situations in which private conduct could be attributable to the state for purposes of making the state liable for the violations.

In countries of the global south like India, South Africa and Argentina, domestic courts used human rights law to enforce rights to food and water, housing and social welfare. Increased attention to the accountability of corporations, especially transnational enterprises, in rights violations led to the UN's Global Compact, followed by the Guiding Principles on Business and Human Rights. The latter set in motion the widespread institution of due diligence structures within corporate entities, aimed at analyzing and mitigating human rights, environmental and social risks created by business ventures (or at least going through the motions). Due diligence was also spurred in part by government offers of leniency in corruption-related cases in the US (and eventually elsewhere) if entities could show their efforts to comply with the law. Eventually, these voluntary initiatives led to mandatory due diligence and disclosure laws, especially in Europe and certain US states. Negotiations began on a binding treaty on corporate behavior. That attention also encompassed greater recognition of growing economic and social inequality as a driver of threats to rights and democratic practices, and of the role of private actors in these threats. All this activity brought rights and anti-corruption campaigners closer.

It also brought new attention to economic violations and social and environmental harm. Critiques of rights discourse and practice focused on the neglect of economic and social rights, and of widening inequality, as a reason for the felt limitations of a rights-based paradigm in the face of burgeoning authoritarianism. The traditional tools of the human rights movement – naming and shaming, passing resolutions, strategic litigation – worked less well against governments that had systematically dismantled potential checks and balances, destroyed the independence of the judiciary, prosecutors' and auditors' offices, threatened or bought off legislatures and the media, and often wrapped themselves in populist rhetoric to do it all. Cocooned in impunity, cushioned by assets safely hidden abroad, and often unencumbered by electoral threats, the leaders of these governments just didn't care much. Rights advocates, spurred by the 2008 meltdown of financial institutions and the lack of accountability for their actions, began to look more broadly at tax policy, anti-poverty policies, and other macroeconomic factors.

The climate and biodiversity crises led to a similar reevaluation of environmental law and its relationship to human rights. As noted below, the Inter-American Court of Human Rights in 2017 finally accepted the direct justiciability of ESC rights, and in a 2021 Advisory Opinion it recognized the right to a healthy environment under the American Convention.[12] The UN Human Rights Council resolution 48/13 recognized that a clean, healthy and sustainable environment is a human right in 2021, followed by the General Assembly. Activists in these fields began to adopt the critiques of economic orthodoxy that social justice advocates, especially in the global South, had long espoused. This brought them closer to anti-corruption campaigners.

The 2015 Sustainable Development Goals developed by the UN General Assembly included governance objectives. Most of the SDGs are about various aspects of development, including clean water, combating hunger, poverty and ill health, gender equality – 17 in all. SDG 16 has the mind-numbing title "Promote peaceful and inclusive societies for sustainable development, provide access to justice for all and build effective, accountable and inclusive institutions at all levels." It's important because, for the first time, sustainable development is linked to justice and governance. Relevant targets include: "by 2030, significantly reduce illicit financial and arms flows, strengthen the recovery and return of stolen assets and combat all forms of organized crime"; "substantially reduce corruption and bribery in all their forms," and "ensure public access to information."[13] States are supposed to come up with national plans to implement the SDGs, and many have done so. The SDGs also have a list of indicators, but in the case of corruption the indicators are focused on how many people and businesses have been asked for a bribe, a poor estimator of high-level or grand corruption. In 2021, the Report of the High Level Panel on International Financial Accountability, Transparency and Integrity for Achieving the 2030 Agenda looked at ways to limit illicit financial flows, including those stemming from corruption and money laundering, in the context of a lack of progress in meeting the SDGs.[14]

2.3 CORRUPTION AS CONTEXT, CAUSE, AND CONSEQUENCE OF RIGHTS VIOLATIONS

Anti-corruption, human rights and environment concerns are beginning to come together in the statements and concerns of the separate treaty bodies, secretariats, resolutions and workstreams. Although these are still siloed in many aspects, and although the cultures of New York (UN headquarters), Geneva (where the human rights bodies are based) and Vienna (where the anti-corruption and anti-organized crime secretariats live) are very different, there has been some movement at both a global and regional level. For the most part, initial efforts have seen corruption as causing other rights violations, as context explaining or aggravating such violations, or, conversely, as a consequence of other rights violations (lack of freedom of expression, for example). Advocates follow and contribute to these movements toward convergence because they change the language in which the problems are described and so help change the public imaginary, create new avenues for advocacy and public denunciation, and provide support (and some protection) for domestic efforts in governments and the private sector.

The human rights bodies have led the way. This isn't surprising since they are much more open to civil society input and rely on independent experts rather than just government diplomats to investigate problems and recommend solutions. An early effort, in 2006, resulted in a conference on anti-corruption measures, good governance and human rights; other reports and resolutions followed. Much of the effort was driven by African countries incensed that former dictator's stolen millions were sitting in bank vaults and government coffers in rich countries. They focused on asset recovery and return of stolen monies to the countries from whence they were stolen. The result was, in part, the Asset Recovery chapter (chapter V) of the UNCAC, but there were also parallel efforts in the Human Rights Council and the UN General Assembly.

A study by the Human Rights Council's Advisory Committee sums up the usefulness of a human rights approach:

> ... [A] human rights-based approach to asset recovery implies that communities in the country where illicit funds originate may be recognized as rights holders and thereby enabled as key actors in processes and decisions that affect them, rather than being passive recipients. Framing the repatriation of funds as a human rights issue, therefore, portrays the countries bearing the frozen assets as duty bearers toward the countries of origin, with an obligation to help the rights holders to pursue their human rights claims.[15]

The UN Human Rights Council, a political body, has repeatedly addressed the links between corruption and the ability to realize rights, especially ESC rights, asset recovery, good governance, and the right to development.[16] The resolutions and discussions have balanced a view of corruption as limited mostly to bribery and embezzlement, and a broader view that tax evasion, transfer pricing and other practices by individuals and companies should also be encompassed. In part, this reflects a north-south difference in emphasis, with the global South interested in the financial drain of corporate tax evasion, while the North focuses on public officials. Most recently, the Office of the High Commissioner for Human Rights has increased its staffing and attention to corruption as a human rights issue, with an emphasis on economic, social and cultural rights. A report to the Human Rights Council is due in 2024. UN treaty bodies and experts have noted links between corruption and rights violations, and states have recommended anti-corruption measures as part of the Universal Periodic Review.

Regional bodies have also picked up the subject, albeit in a fragmented and as yet nonoperational manner. The Inter-American Commission addressed the subject in 2017 and 2021 in the context of Guatemala,[17] and again more generally in 2018.[18] In 2019, the Inter-American Commission on Human Rights issued a groundbreaking report on Corruption and Human Rights.[19] It recognized that states, as part of their legal obligation to ensure and protect as well as respect rights, needed to both prevent and respond to corruption, protect witnesses and those who report corrupt acts and provide effective remedies for victims of corruption.

With regard to individual cases, in 2015 the Commission found Guatemala to have violated the human rights of the family Ramirez Escobar, whose sons Osmin and J. R., aged seven and eighteen months at the time, were taken away from their parents, put into a home for orphans, and eventually adopted by two families in the United States. The Commission called out the corruption at the root of intercountry adoptions in Guatemala, providing great detail as to the illegal nature of many such adoptions and the link to both transnational organized crime and corrupt officials. However, this was provided only as context; in its discussion of legal violations, the Commission focused on other aspects of the case, and recommended only that the state take the necessary measures to punish those responsible and bring the law and practice up to international standards.[20]

When the case came before the Inter-American Court, it held that corruption negatively affects the whole of society, that it "undermines the confidence of the population in the government and, over time, in the democratic order and rule of law."[21] It went on to denounce the organized crime structures that had run illegal adoption rackets, the weaknesses in Guatemala's institutions and laws that allowed complicity by the state, and the vulnerability of the victims and their families due to their extreme poverty. Here, too, corrupt adoption rings served as explanation and context, but the actual reparations focused only on the two concrete victims.

The Court has referred to corrupt practices in other contexts as well: The lack of adequate consultation between indigenous groups and oil companies trying to use their land, due to corrupt practices aimed at dividing the community (Sarayaku v. Ecuador[22]); killings of journalists due to investigative reporting on corruption and organized crime (Carvajal v. Colombia[23]); and killings of environmental activists for the same reason (Luna López v. Honduras[24]). In all these cases, the corrupt acts were background and context.

At the end of 2023, the Court addressed corruption directly, in a case involving a whistleblower. In Viteri Ungaretti y Otros v. Ecuador,[25] Viteri was a Navy officer assigned as a military attaché in London. He publicly denounced that several contracts signed by his office appeared to be the result of bribery and misappropriation, with a corresponding loss to the national treasury. For his trouble, he was removed from his post, arrested four times, ostracized, given a dead-end desk job and threatened. The threats and hostility got so bad that when he returned to Ecuador, he left his children to London with their grandmother. He eventually quit the Navy, and he and his wife fled back to London. Criminal proceedings against those allegedly responsible were dismissed, even though the Comptroller found that money was indeed missing.

The Court found the state responsible for violations of freedom of thought and expression, personal liberty, political rights, labor rights, freedom of movement and residence, protection of the family and (with respect to his children) the rights of the child. The state was ordered to pay damages, to publish the decision, to protect Viteri and his family if they chose to return, and to apologize to the victims in a public ceremony.

The Court began by recognizing the link between corruption and a wide range of rights violations. It pointed out that corruption in public or private service providers especially affects vulnerable groups, including minorities, indigenous groups, migrant workers, disabled persons, refugees, prisoners, women, children, and the elderly and poor.[26] Human rights are an important part of combatting corruption, especially the rights to seek, receive and impart information, to participate in public affairs, and the right to a fair trial with due process guarantees before a competent, independent and impartial court; complaints or accusations of corruption are especially protected speech.[27] Therefore, the state should provide adequate internal and external channels to facilitate and incentivize complaints about corrupt acts and protect the complainants. The Court went on to spell out the minimum conditions for these whistleblower channels. It did not, however, characterize corruption as of itself a rights violation, rather than the precipitating context for the violation of a range of existing rights.

The African Human Rights system, in principle, pays particular attention to corruption. The African Charter on Human and Peoples' Rights requires lawful recovery and compensation for "spoliation."[28] When the African Union decided to add a Protocol creating a criminal chamber to the African Court of Justice and Human Rights, it included corruption "when of a serious nature affecting the stability of a state, region or the Union" as one of the crimes, alongside crimes against humanity and war crimes. Corruption is broadly defined, including unjust enrichment, bribery, embezzlement and influence peddling.[29] Nonetheless, as a matter of caselaw African regional human rights bodies have been reluctant to take on the issue, seeing it as something for national authorities to deal with.

In a 2010 case, a Nigerian NGO sued Nigeria and its Universal Basic Education Commission in the ECOWAS Court for failing to provide basic education in ten Nigerian states due to high-level corruption and impunity, which led to shortages of funds.[30] The plaintiffs alleged violations of the right to education, the right of the people not to be dispossessed of their wealth and natural resources and the right of the people to economic and social development. The Court found that

> [t]here must be a clear linkage between the acts of corruption and a denial of the right to education. In a vast country like Nigeria, with her massive resources, one can hardly say that an isolated act of corruption contained in a report will have such devastating consequence as a denial of the right to education, even though as earlier pointed out it has a negative impact on education.

Responding to the allegation that the corruption was not isolated at all but systemic, the Court refused to engage, holding that a single report with allegations was insufficient, and that only domestic criminal trials could provide proof of large-scale corruption. And, of course, such trials had not been held. The ECOWAS court never addressed the question of why this might be so.

The Council of Europe recognized the link between human rights and corruption at least as far back as 1999. In the Civil Law Convention on Corruption, the preamble reads: "[e]mphasising that corruption represents a major threat to the rule of law, democracy and human rights, fairness and social justice, hinders economic development and endangers the proper and fair functioning of market economies."[31] The European Court of Human Rights has also largely referred to corruption as a background condition in cases involving journalists like Khadija Ismayilova, whom the government of Azerbaijan imprisoned and sanctioned because of her anti-corruption investigations,[32] or in cases of anti-corruption officials being fired. In a case involving human trafficking linked to the death of the victim, it found that the state should have investigated police corruption and used the Palermo Protocol on Trafficking to inform its decision.[33] It has not to date taken up corruption as itself a rights violation.

The European Parliament went beyond previous efforts in 2022. Its recommendation of February 2022 calls on the EU institutions to

> acknowledge the linkage between corruption and human rights and that corruption is an enormous obstacle to the enjoyment of all human rights; adopt, therefore, a human rights-based approach in the fight against corruption, with victims of corruption placed at its core, and place the fight against corruption at the front and centre of all EU efforts and policies promoting human rights, democracy and the rule of law around the world; address corruption as a global phenomenon requiring effective anti-corruption institutions, prevention mechanisms and an international regulatory framework, as well as asset recovery and criminal prosecution within the EU; initiate work on an internationally-recognised definition of corruption, using the UNCAC as a guideline; recognise that fighting corruption requires

> concerted global action and greater collaboration between anti-corruption and human rights specialists [...][34]

The recommendation also refers to the need to align EU external finance and aid with a human rights-based approach to corruption, to advance discussions about an international infrastructure to combat large-scale corruption and impunity, to tackle political corruption and that affecting the environment, and to set up EU-wide mandatory due diligence procedures for business.

2.4 A HUMAN RIGHTS-BASED APPROACH TO GRAND CORRUPTION

One way to conceptualize the relationships between corruption and human rights is to focus on common principles and procedural norms informed by human rights law and practice. The components of a human rights-based approach (HRBA) have been discussed in the context of development and development assistance over the last several decades.[35] This approach imbues both issue areas with common guidelines for how to be effective, and uses global human rights law as a standard to which policies should conform, but does not in itself require characterizing corruption as a human rights violation. Several themes overlap: transparency, participation, accountability, and protection of the vulnerable.

2.4.1 *Transparency*

One of the central tenets of human rights, environmental and anti-corruption work is the old adage that "sunlight is the best disinfectant." Making information available to journalists, researchers, and civil society groups in addition to government agencies and prosecutors on governmental decisions, corporate ownership, activities and donations, and other subjects of public interest is key to all three areas. In the human rights area, Article 19 of the Civil and Political Rights Covenant provides that "Everyone shall have the right to freedom of expression; this right shall include freedom to seek, receive and impart information and ideas of all kinds, regardless of frontiers, either orally, in writing or in print, in the form of art, or through any other media of his choice." The right may be subject to restrictions, but only if provided by law and necessary for respect of the rights or reputations of others, for the protection of national security or of public order (ordre public), or of public health or morals. The UNCAC's Article 13(d) has almost identical language regarding respecting, promoting and protecting the freedom to seek, receive, publish and disseminate information concerning corruption, subject to almost identical restrictions. Articles 7(4) and 10 of UNCAC require states to "enhance transparency in [] public administration," although subject to national law. Article 8(5) suggests that states implement asset declarations for public officials, but only where appropriate and in accordance with national law.

In General Comment 34, the Human Rights Committee specified that access to information legislation should limit fees for access, provide timely responses and explain the reasons for withheld information, with an appeals mechanism. Regional human rights treaties also contain provisions on access to information.[36] The Council of Europe Convention on Access to Official Documents (Trømso Convention) entered into force in 2020, but so far only fifteen states have ratified it. The Inter-American Court of Human Rights established in Claude Reyes et al. v. Chile[37] that Article 13 of the Convention protects the right of all individuals to ask for access to public information as a basic human right.

The 2021 General Assembly Special Session on Corruption (UNGASS Declaration) also commits states to increasing transparency "including by adopting appropriate and necessary procedures or regulations and designating and enhancing bodies responsible for facilitating access to information, as well as through the use of digital tools, open data and Internet-based portals to help make information more accessible." In practice, uptake of this provision has been mixed: Many countries, for example, have not responded to requests to make public their self-evaluations on compliance with the treaty. Both human rights and environmental instruments contain greater detail, which might be helpful to fill out the meaning of these UNCAC provisions.

The most detailed provisions on access to public information come from the environmental area. The 1992 Río Declaration[38] recognizes the right to access to information and participation in public decision-making. Two regional conventions elaborate: the UNECE Convention on Access to Information, Public Participation in Decision-making and Access to Justice in Environmental Matters (Aarhus Convention) came into force in 2001[39] and the Escazú Regional Agreement on Access to Information, Public Participation and Justice in Environmental Matters in Latin America and the Caribbean, which came into force twenty years later, in 2021. Both contain much more elaborate provisions on access to information, albeit limited to environmental matters broadly defined.

2.4.2 *Participation and Empowerment*

Under a HRBA, people should participate in decisions that will affect them, and should be empowered to claim their rights. People are not passive beneficiaries of charity but rather active rights-holders entitled to enforce their rights against states and other duty-holders. This implies attention to ensuring that people understand their rights, and to protecting the ability of those vulnerable to rights violations to seek redress. In human rights law, participation rights span freedoms of expression, assembly and association, to vote and stand for office, to free, prior and informed consent when policies or actions affect indigenous peoples, and specific attention to the disability, language, poverty or gender-based biases that may limit participation. Here too, the Escazú treaty provides the most detailed language. Article 7 on public participation requires "open" and "inclusive" participation in decision-making processes, revisions, reexaminations or updates with respect to projects and activities or matters of public interest. Participation is to be encouraged and facilitated from the early stages of a decision, organized within a reasonable timeframe, with delineated and publicized procedures for the public to present observations. Moreover, it should be adapted to the social, economic, cultural, geographical and gender characteristics of the public and consider the special needs of vulnerable populations.[40]

On the anti-corruption side, the UNCAC's Article 13 requires states to "take appropriate measures … to promote the active participation of individuals and groups outside the public sector, such as civil society, non-governmental organizations and community-based organizations, in the prevention of and the fight against corruption […]." Most of the specific measures suggested refer to access to information, as we've seen. The article incorporates standard human rights treaty language regarding freedom of expression but says nothing about ensuring participation of vulnerable groups. A 2023 resolution for the first time focuses on gender and anti-corruption.[41] States should also "enable the views and concerns of victims to be presented and considered at appropriate stages of criminal proceedings" as required by UNCAC Article 32(5), and should provide for victims to obtain remedy (this is the subject of Chapter 5).

2.4.3 *Accountability*

Accountability under a HRBA requires monitoring and due diligence to avoid violations, and avenues for effective remedy. In both human rights and anti-corruption work, the fight against impunity and the obligation of due diligence are central.

Both human rights violators and corrupt actors tend to be powerful people who can use the levers of power to be able to get away with their crimes. Control over courts and prosecutors, changes in legislation and regulation, and the use of threats and violence to silence and intimidate critics make it harder to fight back against both grand corruption and human rights abuses.

The most detailed definition of impunity comes from the UN Set of Principles for The Protection and Promotion of Human Rights Through Action to Combat Impunity[42]:

> "Impunity" means the impossibility, de jure or de facto, of bringing the perpetrators of violations to account – whether in criminal, civil, administrative or disciplinary proceedings -since they are not subject to any inquiry that might lead to their being accused, arrested, tried and, if found guilty, sentenced to appropriate penalties, and to making reparations to their victims.

This definition could apply equally to grand corruption.

Judicial integrity and independence is the subject of numerous human rights treaties, starting with Article 14 of the Civil and Political Rights Covenant and its expert interpretation in General Comment 32 (2007).[43] The 1985 UN Basic Principles on the Independence of the Judiciary[44] and the 2002 Bangalore Principles on Judicial Conduct[45] set out standards for judicial action. Starting in 1994, the UN Human Rights Council has maintained a Special Rapporteur (expert) on the Independence of Judges and Lawyers, who reports periodically to the Council on threats to judicial and legal systems.[46] A host of private standards complements and details the relevant obligations of states and of judicial and prosecutorial entities.

In the human rights area, the creation of international, hybrid or internationalized courts, the use of extraterritorial jurisdiction to prosecute offenders (and sometimes sue them for damages) when their home state will not, the creation of an international trust fund for victims of the gravest crimes, and regional human rights court decisions that provide some measure of redress for victims have allowed activists to bypass captured or implicated states. Moreover, legal theories pioneered by regional and national courts help compensate for the difficulties investigating complex conspiracies and networks (on statutes of limitations or indirect liability, for example) and to limit amnesties and pardons in cases of crimes prohibited by international law. The UNCAC also has provisions on some of these issues (see, e.g., Article 29 on generous statutes of limitations and Article 30 on prosecutions consistent with the gravity of the offenses).

The UNCAC speaks specifically to corruption in the judiciary and prosecution services. Article 11 requires State Parties to "take measures to strengthen integrity and to prevent opportunities for corruption among members of the judiciary" and among prosecutors where they are not judicial officers. Integrity is broader than anti-corruption, focusing on the structural and political independence and accountability of the judicial sector.[47] A sizeable academic literature speaks to lessons learned in this area, yet a 2023 survey showed that less than half the foreign aid provided by European donors to support judicial reforms addresses corruption.[48] A human rights-based approach would apply anti-impunity standards, especially in the selection and discipline of the judiciary.[49]

Due diligence obligations apply both to the state and to private actors. For the state, due diligence and monitoring obligations spring from the general duty to ensure, protect and fulfill rights in human rights law. Due diligence obligations in the UNCAC are not mentioned with that term, but chapter II of the treaty (including setting up anti-corruption monitoring bodies, standards, and other types of preventative measures) puts such obligations on states. With respect to the private sector, an extensive discussion about the human rights obligations of business entities led to the UN Guiding Principles on Business and Human Rights.[50] The Guidelines specify the obligations of private entities to respect basic human rights in their operations, and to engage in prior assessment and ongoing monitoring to ensure compliance. The voluntary nature of the Guidelines has led some states and NGOs to propose a binding treaty on business and human rights, currently under discussion.[51] In the UNCAC context, there are few binding obligations to criminalize foreign private corrupt acts, and prevention measures in Article 12 are left largely to the states' discretion. They should include enhanced auditing standards and may include codes of conduct. Despite the lack of detailed binding obligations dealing with private entities, in practice a large number of business organizations have developed standards, codes of conduct and internal controls covering environment, social/human rights, and governance/corruption, of varying degrees of effectiveness.

2.4.4 *Protection*

Whether from the perspective of human rights, environmental/climate protection or corruption, protection of the lives, livelihoods, reputation and freedom from arbitrary detention of researchers, journalists, and activists working in these areas is key. Whistleblowers and witnesses to crime need protection, but so do their families, civil society members and even, sometimes, prosecutors and judges going up against powerful and often ruthless defendants. Latin America has a particularly poor record in this regard, with by far the highest number of attacks on human rights, environmental and anti-corruption defenders of any region. Attacking defenders has a multiplier effect, intimidating whole communities, forcing them to flee or stay silent.

The UNCAC's Article 32 calls for the protection of witnesses, experts and victims and their families against potential retaliation or intimidation, but only while serving as a witness or giving testimony. Article 37 extends that protection to those who participate in a corruption-related crime and then cooperate with the authorities in investigation or prosecution. Unfortunately, experience has shown that most intimidation and attacks happen during investigation or even prior to complaints to the authorities; adequate protection during testimony, for example, has not stopped violence against potential witnesses in human rights-related cases. There's also a whistleblower protection provision (Article 33) but states need do no more than consider legally protecting them. A 2020 CoSP resolution focuses on what UNCAC terms "reporting persons," which means insiders providing information on corruption in their organization. It encourages states to protect these persons, allow them to report confidentially, directly to law enforcement and without reference to their possible motivations. It says nothing, however, about the broader group of outsiders working on corruption-related investigations or fighting corrupt projects. Many states have no law at all protecting whistleblowers. A 2023 resolution encourages states to "provide effective protection from potential retaliation or intimidation for those affected by corruption, as well as for witnesses and experts who give testimony … and, as appropriate, for their relatives and other persons close to them."[52]

The Escazú Treaty has a section on protection of environmental defenders that requires states to "guarantee a safe and enabling environment for persons, groups and organizations that promote and defend human rights in environmental matters, so that they are able to act free from threat, restriction and insecurity."[53] States must also prevent, investigate and punish attacks against them. This would cover those denouncing corruption related to the environment, but not more generally.

The UN's General Assembly in 1999 passed the Declaration on the Right and Responsibility of Individuals, Groups and Organs of Society to Promote and Protect Universally Recognized Human Rights and Fundamental Freedoms[54] which (although it's not obvious from the name) is known as the Human Rights Defenders Declaration. It reminds governments that people have the right to form associations and groups, to complain about public officials, attend hearings, access information, speak freely and obtain a remedy when harmed. The general statements in the Declaration have been given concrete and detailed form in the Esperanza Protocol, a civil society initiative focused on investigation of threats against defenders.[55]

The Special Rapporteur on Human Rights Defenders in December 2021 issued a report on human rights defenders working against corruption.[56] She called on states to recognize those working against corruption, including lawyers, journalists, academics, gender-based activists and those working at the local level as human rights defenders, and to take measures to protect them.

She added specific recommendations on whistleblowers, legal harassment, and the need for the UNCAC review process to allow civil society participation in order to better protect defenders.

2.5 IS THERE A HUMAN RIGHT TO BE FREE OF CORRUPTION?

There is broad agreement that corruption, especially grand corruption, violates a wide range of existing human rights. The predominant view of human rights courts, and many scholars, has been that it is enough to focus on the violation of existing human rights, using corruption to explain the genesis, cause or context of the violation. Remedy would therefore focus on the state's responsibility to reestablish the underlying right – to a school, to health, to employment, to freedom of expression – through reparations, declaration or injunction. But the underlying corrupt acts themselves would remain a matter for domestic criminal, civil or administrative law.

While the HRBA detailed above provides some guidelines and procedural convergence around human rights and corruption, they remain at a high level of generality. Some scholars have gone further, and posited that corruption is itself a freestanding violation of human rights and should be recognized as such.[57] Doing so would permit those harmed to hold the state itself accountable for its failure to adequately ensure or protect rights, in particular to investigate, prosecute, remedy and prevent corruption. That approach would strengthen and complement UNCAC's focus on the state obligation to criminalize – but not per se to effectively investigate, prosecute or redress – illegal behaviors.[58] Anne Peters concludes that "[t]he framing of corruption not only as a human rights issue but even as a potential human rights violation can contribute to closing the implementation gap of the international anti-corruption instruments and can usefully complement the predominant criminal law-based approach."[59]

Moreover, this would mean that a state would incur state responsibility not just for the acts of its own officials – permitted or ultra vires or not – but also would have to put in place regulatory structures to ensure that private actors upheld the right, which would help fill the existing gaps with regards to private sector corruption and bring anti-corruption squarely within the due diligence frameworks of the Guiding Principles on Business and Human Rights.

Here, as elsewhere, the trajectory of the right to a clean, healthy, and sustainable environment as a human right sheds light on the difference recognition as a stand-alone right might make. As with the right to be free from corruption, the first step was recognizing the multiple links between environmental degradation and violations of established human rights. Some of the same difficulties with regard to causal nexus and state attribution that have bedeviled discussions of corruption and human rights also made recognition of the right to environment difficult. Over the years since 1972, as mentioned above, the content was fleshed out to include substantive obligations (to clean air, safe climate and water, healthy food and the like) and procedural obligations to access to information, participation, and access to justice. The Inter-American Court of Human Rights recognized the right in 2017, and in 2021, the UN Human Rights Council did so.[60] In 2022 the UN General Assembly followed suit, recognizing a stand-alone right.[61]

With respect to corruption, scholars have suggested that such a right could be found in common Article 1 to the basic human rights covenants (ICCPR and ICESCR), which holds that peoples may freely dispose of their natural wealth and resources, and may not be deprived of their own means of subsistence.[62] Other authors find it in Article 2(1) of the IECSCR which requires states to take steps to the maximum of available resources to respect, promote and fulfill the rights therein, and to some extent in the anti-discrimination provisions of most human rights treaties.[63] A freestanding right could be established through a protocol to existing treaties,[64] through a strategy culminating in Human Rights Council and General Assembly resolutions, or through an incremental approach that would depend on national court decisions, encourage the creation of a new Special Rapporteur on the subject along with establishing reporting obligations under existing treaties and the Universal Periodic Review.

The drawbacks of this approach include states' reluctance to create new rights and to pay for their upkeep given already-stretched resources, the relative failure of most "third generation" rights (with the exception, as noted above, of a right to environment) to provide practical improvements in rights observance, and the enormous effort that would be needed by civil society to enshrine a new stand-alone right.[65] There are also thorny – if perhaps manageable – problems of definition: If human rights bodies use the UNCAC list of mandatory crimes to define corruption, it's a limited and partial list of behaviors, but if they include other potential crimes, state obligations will vary from one state to another depending on internal legislation. How would extraterritorial state responsibility be dealt with where most systemic corruption involves more than one state, and is there a danger that human rights law would prove more restrictive than existing anti-corruption law? Moreover, no society is totally free of corruption of one sort or another. What would a minimum standard for compliance look like? Here perhaps a restriction to grand, pervasive or systemic corruption that affects the rights of large numbers of persons might make for easier application of a stand-alone right.

In the Latin American context, a stand-alone right to be free of (systemic, large-scale, grand) corruption would allow anti-corruption treaties to be treated like human rights treaties, which often (although not always) have a superior status to ordinary laws and become part of a "constitutional bloc" that national judges and officials must apply as domestic law through the doctrine of constitutional control.[66] Some national courts in the region have moved in the direction of recognizing such a stand-alone right to be free of corruption. In Mexico, there have been a number of intermediate-level decisions decided under the constitutional review (*amparo*) of lower court decisions not to investigate irregular practices by state officials. In a 2016 administrative law case, the court said:

> the Constitution recognizes the fundamental rights to transparency, honor, and accountability with respect to public resources, [...] which translates to a fundamental right of individuals to live in an environment free of corruption in which all public officials carry out their jobs with enough honesty, transparency and openness to be able to have confidence in their work and their decisions.[67]

Subsequently, while denying standing to an association to represent victims in a criminal case (a story I tell in Chapter 5), a court found that there had been no violation of the human right to live in a corruption-free environment, implying that there is such a right.[68] Moreover, the Mexican states of Baja California and Tabasco recognize a right to be free of corruption.[69]

In a case involving an unsuccessful constitutional challenge to El Salvador's Civil Forfeiture Law, the Salvadoran Constitutional Chamber had to decide whether to use the Anti-Narcotics Convention, UNTOC and UNCAC as part of their constitutional analysis. Prior decisions said that human rights law, but not any and all treaty law, was relevant for constitutional interpretation. So the Court had to decide whether these were, in effect, human rights treaties. It answered affirmatively, in that "drugs, organized crime and corruption are objectionable conduct that produce direct and indirect violations of fundamental rights." It then listed, for each treaty, what the rights violations entailed. The Anti-Narcotics Convention aimed at protecting the right to health. The UN Convention on Organized Crime was relevant because organized crime affected rights including the right to life, security and physical integrity, to property (through extortion), to free movement, to education and a wide range of other rights. Finally, the UNCAC dealt fundamentally with equality, but also implicated the rights to free expression and to stand for election.[70] From there, the Court held that

> [a]cts of corruption are themselves direct or indirect violations of fundamental rights. Direct violations occur when a corrupt act entails lack of compliance with the obligations to respect, protect and fulfill fundamental

> rights [...] Indirect violations are consequences of the series of events generated by the corruption that, in the end, lead to the lack of compliance with [those] obligations.[71]

As we'll see, the Argentine criminal procedure code allows civil society groups to represent victims in cases of crimes against humanity or grave human rights violations. The provision was created for cases arising out of the 1970s–1980s "dirty war." Nonetheless, an anti-corruption group was permitted to represent victims because a federal court found that corruption was a grave human rights violation, since it implicated many different kinds of rights.

Costa Rica's constitution in Article 50 establishes the right to a "healthy environment." Its Supreme Court has interpreted this right to be far broader than nature conservation, locating it within "any sphere of human development."[72] The courts have then used this broad view to find that Article 50 recognizes a right to live in an environment free of corruption.[73] A number of cases recognize the right as diffuse, that is, belonging to the entire society. If there is a stand-alone right to a clean, healthy and sustainable environment, and environment is broadly defined to include the social and moral environment (as here), this provides another avenue leading to a right to be free of corruption.

There are also some cases from outside the region that recognize a stand-alone right to be free of corruption. The Indian Supreme Court[74] considered whether a public servant who had been fired after being convicted of corruption-related crimes could have the order of dismissal stayed while he appealed the conviction. The Court refused, stating: "Corruption is not only a punishable offence but also undermines human rights, indirectly violating them, and systematic corruption, is a human rights' violation in itself, as it leads to systematic economic crimes."

Thus, by the 2020s it was increasingly clear that simply recognizing the links, or using corruption as background or context was insufficient. In the same way that human rights advocates in the 1990s recognized that massive and systematic rights violations could not simply be dealt with on a case-by-case basis but required analysis of the connections among perpetrators and their networks and action against them on that basis, anti-corruption campaigners came to the same conclusions. And just as rights campaigners had turned to international mechanisms (courts, but also support for prosecutors' offices, truth commissions, and reparation trust funds) when it was clear that domestic institutions were unable or unwilling to do the job, so anti-corruption advocates began considering a range of additional options to strengthen international support for their efforts. I discuss some of these efforts in Chapters 3 and 4.

3

Transnational Approaches I

Sizing Up Guatemala's CICIG

One of the things that makes grand corruption so difficult to attack is that the usual solutions become part of the problem. Normally, allegations of bribery, embezzlement or the like would go to police, prosecutors and judges, but what if some or all are in league with corrupt politicians, shady businesses or organized crime groups (or all three)? Lobbying for better laws and appointments will encounter the same problem if the legislature or the executive is crooked. As we've seen, the international treaty architecture relies on states to prevent, criminalize and cooperate, but it largely assumes that the state is willing and able to do the job. What if it's not?

One answer might be international or mixed criminal courts, and I take up that option in Chapter 10. Another might be using the regional human rights courts or UN human rights bodies, as I described in Chapter 2. Here I consider other ways that outside actors could potentially influence the treatment of corrupt actors, especially in grand or systemic corruption cases. I focus first on long-term international assistance to domestic prosecutors, as exemplified by Guatemala's Commission Against Impunity (CICIG) and its variants.

3.1 ANTECEDENTS: HOW DID CORRUPT NETWORKS EMERGE FROM THE ARMED CONFLICT?

Helen Mack was worried. After thirty years of war in Guatemala, peace accords had been signed in 1996, but attacks on human rights activists continued. The human rights section of the peace accords committed the government to eradicate illegal armed groups and clandestine security apparatuses, but it hadn't happened, and violence was increasing. Now it wasn't openly the military doing the attacking, but journalists and activists were still being murdered by shadowy forces that seemed to be a mixture of current and former military intelligence officers, members of the Presidential Guard, organized crime bosses, and gangs. (I discuss the role of those forces in the emergence of a kleptocratic state in Chapter 8). One of those killed was Helen's sister Myrna, an anthropologist working with internally displaced communities, stabbed to death on the orders of an army colonel in 1990. The killing turned Helen from a businesswoman to a justice activist. To gain the benefits of peace, she thought, something more needed to be done.

> We were on the ground, so we felt how these [] groups were changing and taking advantage of their position of power, how they began spinning webs of corruption. In their continued evolution, they were also creating problems of governability .... As victims, we saw the lack of independent investigation and when it came to independent trials. So there was a convergence of interests around the fight against impunity, explained Helen Mack.[1]

Guatemala provides the clearest case of a direct line between the thirty-six years of repressive military governments and internal armed conflict and the emergence of the kind of profoundly corrupt and predatory state described in the previous chapters. Even the individuals involved are often the same. This chapter examines how the armed conflict and its aftermath set the stage for the emergence of grand corruption. It then turns to a novel use of international support for domestic prosecutions, the Commission Against Impunity in Guatemala, known as CICIG. During its tenure, CICIG successfully investigated and sometimes dismantled corrupt networks, but in the end, was unable to resist the forces arrayed against it. Nonetheless, it remains a model of international-national action worth studying.

Guatemala's armed conflict originated in the 1960s, shortly after a CIA-backed coup cut short efforts at democratic renewal and modernization. At its height in the early 1980s, it led to acts of genocide by the military against various Indigenous groups in the rural highlands; the toll of the conflict was over 200,000 dead, with some 40,000 forcibly disappeared. Peace agreements were signed between the military and a much-reduced insurgency in 1996.

As a result of the accords, Guatemala set up a Commission on Historical Clarification that looked into the causes and consequences of the war and publicly presented its report in 1998.[2] There was also a church-sponsored inquiry into what had happened.[3] A National Reparations Program started out with a broad set of goals, but ended up mostly issuing modest checks to some (but not all) victims of the armed conflict. An amnesty law covered both the guerrillas and the security forces but excluded genocide and other international crimes. Nonetheless, during the first fifteen years or so of the transition there were few prosecutions of either human rights violators or grand corruption. That changed by the 2010 decade, when judicial reform and independent attorneys general combined to permit some corruption as well as human rights-related cases to come to trial, involving soldiers and former ministers, generals and former dictator Efraín Ríos Montt.[4]

The informal power structures developed and nurtured during the war years were never squarely confronted in all these efforts, and so were able to survive and evolve. During those years the army developed its own institutions, including a bank and a pension fund, that concentrated capital in military hands, taught officers how to evade civilian financial oversight, and moved the military from being a servant of economic elites to being their equal, partner and competitor.[5] Military officers accumulated large land holdings in resource-rich, remote areas. The army also took control of customs, ports, immigration, infrastructure and other potentially lucrative pieces of the state, initially to control insurgents and arms flowing across borders. It soon became clear that these sites could be used for personal advantage. Rachel Schwartz describes the dynamic: a perception by counterinsurgent elites that an insurgent threat has increased (whether true or not) allowed the suspension of existing rules, increased the discretion (and insulation from accountability) of small groups of military intelligence officers, and discouraged monitoring of their activities.[6] Military intelligence officers who had worked together during the armed conflict retained control of customs, ports and other sites throughout the transition period, with little real oversight despite the advent of civilian governments in the 1990s. "With control of customs, they then controlled the flow of goods and services, and developed strong links to narcotics trafficking and other illicit activity. These criminal networks became deeply entrenched…"[7]

One criminal group, known as the Moreno network, focused in particular on customs fraud. It arose from the creation of an office known as Special Ministerial Services within the Ministry of Finance, staffed largely first by members of the president's military detail, known as the EMP, and then by those affiliated with the intelligence grouping known as the "Cofradía." These officers ran the place with a huge amount of discretion, creating their own rules. It wasn't long before they started using import and export duties as their private piggybank, underreporting customs duties and pocketing the difference, or disappearing entire shipping containers to pocket the missing tax payments; the merchandise would be unloaded on the side of the road and later sold.[8]

The leader of this smuggling group was formally arrested, others fired, and the group formally disbanded during the Arzú government (1996–2000), but the underlying power structures remained. Those involved in that network simply diversified their associates and efforts. They allied with a group of lawyers and judges to ensure continued impunity; expelled from government, they became informal advisors to then-President Portillo (convicted in 2014 in the US for laundering the proceeds of bribes from Taiwan using US banks),[9] and their allies took over the newly revamped tax authority. When a rival group of retired military officers used lax political finance and party rules to win election in 2011, they reestablished many of the same customs and tax fraud mechanisms as their predecessors. It was this group, headed by ex-General Perez Molina and his Vice President Roxana Baldetti, that implemented the La Linea customs fraud and others discussed below.

Demobilization led to the creation of numerous private security forces, bodyguard businesses and security-related consulting firms, which absorbed former soldiers but continued the oversupply of arms in the country and made continuing insecurity and crime lucrative. For example, Pedro Garcia Arredondo, the secret police chief who ordered the massacre of thirty-six people inside the Spanish Embassy in January 1980, ran his own security firm before his trial and conviction on massacre charges in 2015. So did Manuel Callejas y Callejas, the former intelligence chief and customs head (and key member of the Cofradía) widely known for his links to both corruption and organized crime.[10] (Like Arredondo, Callejas was eventually tripped up by his human rights-related crimes. He was convicted – by Judge Pablo Xitumul, whom we'll meet in Chapter 8 – of the enforced disappearance of fourteen-year-old Marco Antonio Molina Theissen in 2017).

The knowledge and ability to access remote areas where illegal landing strips, warehouses and labs were feasible made former military officers into attractive partners for smugglers of all sorts seeking new routes to the US border. The post-war transition occurred just when Central America became a favored transshipment route for drugs heading north from Colombia, and the military and former military were obvious partners. The empty spaces for drug production and transshipment had been facilitated by the forced displacement of population from the rural north and west during the war. Organized crime families with military connections then used cattle ranching (known as "narco-ganado") to launder money, control territory, and ship drugs.[11] Connections to drug and other illegal smuggling networks, in turn, allowed military intelligence to fund its clandestine activities off-budget. Drug money – oodles of it – could be used to finance political campaigns, to create alliances, and even to provide jobs or soccer fields to unemployed youth.

All this was facilitated by the lack of a thorough cleaning out of the military. The peace accords required a reduction in overall numbers, but allowed officers to keep their posts with little or no screening. The same was true of the police: although the most notorious units were disbanded and a new civilian police force was created, little vetting of the new forces' officers was done. The lines between military and policing functions were quickly erased as a wave of common crime fueled by too many guns and too few jobs overwhelmed the new, under-resourced police.

At the same time, under the first civilian governments, the phone company, the national airline, the post office, roads and dams were privatized, becoming sources of income for former military officers allied with outside capital; corruption scandals included overpriced helicopters purchased with kickbacks for top army brass and the president's brother.[12] One of the juiciest privatization targets was the port system, which had been the backbone of the Moreno network's racket and was now handed over to private firms on no-bid contracts, including a group connected to the network. Municipalities, now constitutionally guaranteed a percentage of the national budget, became newly ripe targets for takeover by mafias. And political parties, abetted by electoral laws that allowed legislative party-switching and provided immunity from prosecution to lawmakers, became both repositories of laundered funds and more enticing targets for quid pro quo politics.

The peace accords said little about judicial systems, although they did create a human rights ombudsman and separated the administrative and judicial functions of the courts. They recognized that: "The reform and modernization of the administration of justice should be geared to preventing the judiciary from producing or covering up a system of impunity and corruption."[13] They said nothing about other control functions of the state, including auditor, comptroller, or the tax authority. These failures of the transition were not remedied by transitional justice mechanisms. The Commission on Historical Clarification in Guatemala researched the reach of military intelligence units in repression, but their links to corruption and organized crime only became apparent later. The long lag time between armed conflict-related crimes and prosecutions meant that the deliberate undermining of legal systems was largely unchallenged for a long time. It took the creation of CICIG to confront these tendencies head on.

3.2 INTERNATIONAL SUPPORT FOR NATIONAL PROSECUTIONS: THE EMERGENCE OF CICIG

CICIG was, in the beginning, a civil society initiative aimed at dismantling networks like the Cofradía, who were threatening human rights and anti-impunity groups in the wake of the peace accords. Helen Mack found allies in the then-vice president and the head of the official human rights commission. They also found a receptive ear at the UN's Department of Political Affairs, where its Latin America head, Martha Doggett, had spent considerable time in next-door El Salvador. The UN had done technical assistance missions in the past, but any effort on Guatemala needed to be more ambitious. Doggett worked with a team to come up with a structure that both the UN and the Guatemalan government might be able to accept. The first incarnation of CICIG, known as CICIACS, created an independent international prosecutor appointed by the UN Secretary-General, who would work within the Prosecutors' Office. (Known as the Public Ministry or MP in Spanish, the MP is headed by the Attorney General and is technically independent of the government). Guatemala's Constitutional Court found that this structure violated the exclusive constitutional delegation of prosecutions to the MP and ruled it out. A revised structure was acceptable to the Constitutional Court, the legislature approved it, and the agreement between the United Nations and the government took effect in 2007.

CICIG was to "determine the existence of illegal security groups and clandestine security organizations, their structure, forms of operation, sources of financing, and possible relation to State entities or agents and other sectors that threaten civil and political rights in Guatemala, in conformity with the objectives of this Agreement."[14] It would collaborate with the State in the dismantling of these groups, promote the investigation, criminal prosecution, and punishment of crimes committed by their members, and recommend the adoption of public policies for eradicating such groups and preventing their reemergence. Given how deeply entwined these groups were with the state, this was not likely to be easy.

As noted in a 2016 report from Open Society Justice Initiative, the mandate was drafted with a reference to human rights to ensure that it would be superior to other domestic laws, and therefore a hostile Congress could not legislate to override its investigations. It was written to exclude cases from the recently concluded internal armed conflict, seen as a necessary concession to the military and its supporters. It also allowed the government to stress its usefulness as a way to fight organized crime, at least so long as there was some tie to state actors.[15]

To accomplish its goals, CICIG could not directly prosecute crimes, but it could initiate criminal complaints and do its own investigations, provide information to the MP, and act as a private prosecutor (*querellante adhesivo*) in criminal cases. This last attribute proved especially valuable, as it meant that Commission staff could get access to case files, present witnesses, and participate fully in proceedings. The Commission could subpoena documents, hire its own staff, file disciplinary complaints against public servants, and guarantee confidentiality to witnesses. It could also issue thematic reports and propose legislative or judicial reforms. On the other hand, the Commission could not compel testimony directly and depended on the MP, as the only party who could actually take cases to court.

The first CICIG Commissioner, Carlos Castresana, was a Spanish former judge and anti-corruption prosecutor who had, years earlier, been instrumental in opening cases in Spain against the Argentine generals who headed that country's state terrorism of the 1970s. (Those cases eventually were consolidated with the case against Chilean dictator Pinochet, which led to his arrest in London in 1998).[16] Castresana knew the region and had consulted for the UN on the CICIACS proposal, so he was well-placed to become Commissioner in 2007.

Castresana set up an office and established relationships with the press, the police, the MP, and civil society groups. He pushed for vetted and specially selected specialized police investigative and prosecutorial units that would become CICIG's partners, and was instrumental in proposing legislative reforms that made it easier to carry out complex criminal investigations. Together with Supreme Court Criminal Chamber head César Barrientos, he supported the 2009 creation of special "high-risk" courts that aimed to provide better security and support for judges and to concentrate risky or high-profile cases in the capital.[17] Those courts would prove to be key for moving human rights-related, organized crime and corruption cases forward. When the backlash came, some of their most effective judges would be attacked, isolated or forced into exile. But at first, the high-risk courts were a useful strategy for concentrating honest and competent judges without having to reform the entire judicial system.

Castresana struggled to find a unifying narrative for case selection, going after organized crime groups as well as former President Alfonso Portillo, who was accused of stealing US$15 million. "This lack of clarity about CICIG's purpose (to map the influence of criminal–political networks or assist the government in tackling organized crime groups) and scope (complete a few key paradigmatic cases or provoke major reform) would shadow the Commission across the arc of its first eight years," according to OSJI.[18] I would argue that this tension followed the Commission during its entire lifespan, although it later morphed into misgivings about too many cases and about a focus on financial crime not necessarily connected to the violent shadow networks that were the initial focus.

Castresana's big break came in a bizarre case that seemed made-for-TV (indeed, a movie and a "true crime" episode were eventually made). Rodrigo Rosenberg, a well-connected lawyer and businessman, was found shot one morning after going out bicycling in his neighborhood. He left behind a taped message accusing the then-President, Alvaro Colom, and his wife Sandra Torres of the killing, supposedly to cover up other killings and government-linked bank fraud. Rosenberg's message caused a media frenzy and political uproar in the country; Castresana had no choice but to promise a CICIG investigation. The fate of the Colom presidency rested on his findings.

Eight months later, CICIG revealed that, improbably, Rosenberg had ordered his own killing to bring down the presidential couple. He was depressed and had money troubles and had hired killers thinking his death would frame a president he hated. In this, he was abetted by some of the same shadowy networks that CICIG had been formed to expose and prosecute. CICIG took advantage of the MP's newly legislated abilities to use wiretaps, tracking devices, confidential informants, ballistics, and other non-witness based techniques in an investigation that showed off its powers and established its usefulness.

Castresana quit in 2010, after President Colóm decided to nominate a lawyer with notorious ties to organized crime to be the next Attorney General. It didn't help that Castresana's outspokenness had made him enemies in the judiciary as well as the elite and he faced a vicious media campaign accusing him of personal and professional improprieties. His resignation embarrassed Colom, leading him to withdraw the AG nomination and instead put forward Claudia Paz y Paz, a human rights and international criminal lawyer who had scored the highest qualifications of the six candidates presented. She would be key in reforming the Attorney General's office and leading high-profile human rights and organized crime cases. Soft-spoken, barely five feet tall with long curly dark hair, Paz y Paz was brilliant and determined; she became the face of the justice system. CICIG, under new Commissioner Francisco Dall'Anese, a Costa Rican anti-corruption jurist, kept a low profile and focused on strengthening the prosecutors' office. He was instrumental in helping prosecutors modernize investigative strategies and techniques and in supporting Paz y Paz's initiatives. He was criticized for inaction, but insisted that he was there to support the prosecutors, not give press conferences.

The next CICIG Commissioner was much more public and proactive. Beginning in late 2013, CICIG's new head was Ivan Velásquez, a former prosecutor and Supreme Court judge from Colombia. Velásquez was no stranger to thorny and violent politics when he arrived in Guatemala. He had, after all, been the chief prosecutor in Medellín during the height and aftermath of its drug wars in the 1990s. He had seen his investigators gunned down, his wife held in an elevator and threatened, and his case files mysteriously disappear. It wasn't just the drug cartels, but right-wing paramilitary groups that increasingly held sway throughout the region. He finally moved to Bogotá to become an assistant justice on the Supreme Court. By 2005, he was in charge of investigating the links between organized crime, paramilitary militias and political figures in Colombia, in a set of scandals known as *parapolítica* that reached as high as then-President Alvaro Uribe and dozens of ministers and Congresspeople.[19] (In 2022, Velásquez became Colombia's Defense Minister). He was thus well-positioned to understand how macrocriminal networks could penetrate and take over parts of the state, because he'd seen it happen in Colombia. He was also, to Guatemala's conservative elite and former military, a closet Communist for taking on the right-wing paramilitaries – and Uribe.

His office soon reoriented its strategy to focus on "illicit political-economic networks," described as encrusted in

> different spheres of the State apparatus and surrounding it, which have historically existed and over more than 30 years of democratic transition have infiltrated the spaces of political power to introduce their agenda of legal and illegal interests, converting the agenda of the State and public interest to its own ends, shaping political relations, the logic of political parties, forms of business dealings and contracting with the State.[20]

These structures operate between the public and private sectors, between the formal and informal. Leading politicians, public officials, members of the judiciary, lawyers, military personnel, business leaders are involved, where opportunistic relationships are established to commit crimes and their impunity is guaranteed. In other words, the structures behind grand corruption. In particular, CICIG, partnering with new Attorney General Thelma Aldana and the now-strengthened Attorney General's Special Unit on Impunity (FECI, for its Spanish initials), focused on dismantling political finance corruption and the links between politicians and organized crime, the takeover of state agencies such as customs and ports, and large-scale corrupt state procurement contracts. A second area of emphasis was on the judicial system, especially with respect to influence-peddling among judges and lawyers. To the MP and CICIG, dismantling these structures was simply following where the evidence led, but to opponents, this seemed like a big leap from the original mandate.

Some of CICIG's cases highlighted the links between corruption and human rights violations. The Genesis case involved fourteen members of a longtime crime family, the Mendozas, accused of stealing peasant lands in the northern Petén region through intimidation, trickery and violence, and then having corrupt notaries register the lands in the name of family members. Cases against the national health system focused on shady contracts with unqualified medical providers that led to the death and injury of patients;

for example, more than fifty patients died for lack of medical care when the kidney dialysis contract was given to an unknown company that botched the procedures. (That story is told in Chapter 5.)

CICIG's most impactful cases started with an importer (improbably code-named Meow-Meow) who was bribing port officials to let his shipping containers through. Prosecutors had wiretapped his phone as part of a previous investigation of illegal activity at ports. As CICIG and MP lawyers listened in and followed the suspects, they found a giant network of corruption that included false invoicing, fake customs duties, and bribes to let merchandise in or containers out. There was a parallel tax authority, a parallel port authority, and more. A big break came in 2014 when the private secretary of the vice president, up to his eyeballs in the scheme and with the law closing in on him, offered prosecutors information in exchange for leniency. He explained that the co-conspirators identified as "number 1" and "number 2" in intercepted communications were President Pérez Molina and Vice President Roxana Baldetti, who were the top of "La Linea" (as the case was called).

The case caused a political upheaval. Growing crowds demonstrated every Saturday outside the presidential palace demanding reforms and the government's resignation, in what was called a "Guatemalan spring." Even a large majority of the Chamber of Commerce supported an extension of CICIG's mandate, which the beleaguered president agreed to. The combination of legal jeopardy and popular fury worked: First the vice president, then the president, were forced to resign and later jailed awaiting trial on corruption charges; several properties, including houses and helicopters, were confiscated.[21]

And it didn't stop there. CICIG and MP joint investigations into the networks underlying La Linea found that illegal parallel structures to channel state resources into the hands of politicians permeated Guatemalan institutions. The TCQ case involved the port. The Construction and Cooptation case involved kickbacks, money laundering and illegal campaign financing stemming from construction contracts by the then-Minister of Communications (and perennial presidential candidate) Alejandro Sinibaldi and twenty-eight others. Sinibaldi fled the country, but in 2020 returned and turned himself in. According to his sworn testimony, Odebrecht (yes, the same company we met earlier) had paid a total of nearly $32 million to the president, vice president and every one of the 108 Congress members to get a $400 million contract for highway expansion.

The biggest case, known as State Cooptation, showed that starting in 2008, Pérez Molina and Baldetti had begun setting up front companies to receive and launder private funds, using them to illegally finance their political campaigns and to buy houses, farms, horse ranches, cars, and helicopters. Once they won the presidency, they put their cronies in charge of the operations of government (either openly or behind the scenes). Those cronies charged at least 10 percent in "monetary commercial incentives" (i.e., bribes) to do business with the state; the total takings were estimated at some US$71 million.[22] Some of the looted funds were then funneled directly to the president and vice president in the form of expensive "birthday presents."[23]

Still other cases seemed lifted from a magical realism novel. On March 23, 2015, Baldetti ferried reporters out to the middle of Lake Amatitlán, a highly polluted body of water near the capital. She announced a USD$20 million contract with an Israeli firm, Tarcis Engineering, to provide a substance that would clean up the lake. Soon after, she was charged with fraud and undue influence based on her work steering the contract to Tarcis, knowing that the supposedly cutting edge cleanup liquid was just a combination of salt, water and chlorine (plus herbs, according to some accounts); in typical Guatemalan tongue-in-cheek fashion, it was dubbed the "magic potion" case. The project description had been tailored so that Tarcis was the only bidder, no environmental impact statement was done, all the scientists consulted were skeptical, and the Israeli company had no track record that anyone could find; several officials (also later convicted) received considerable kickbacks from the deal. In October of 2018, High-Risk Court Judge Pablo Xitumul (whom we'll meet again later) sentenced Baldetti to fifteen years in prison.

By the time these cases came to court, though, the tide was turning against the Commission; the backlash was ferocious. The private sector associations, incensed by cases targeting their own for bribery (and not just corrupt politicians, which was more acceptable), spent heavily on a lobbying campaign in Washington to turn the Trump administration against CICIG. In this, they were abetted by self-proclaimed human rights advocate Bill Browder, whose Russian clients had been sentenced to prison by a court for buying fake Guatemalan passports. Browder decided CICIG was a Russian government plot, and sold this story to Senator Marco Rubio, who held hearings in Congress that highlighted the unproven claims of Russian involvement and helped break what until then had been a bipartisan US consensus supporting the Commission (including financially). The Commission realized the threat to its funding and support too late in the game. The private sector elite joined forces with then-President Jimmy Morales, a former comedian who had run on the slogan "not a thief, nor corrupt." The slogan became ironic when Morales' son and brother were accused of embezzling $35,000 years earlier, and he was investigated for large-scale illegal campaign finance; this quite naturally turned Morales against CICIG. He refused to extend the agreement with the UN and declared Iván Velásquez persona non grata. CICIG closed in 2019.

3.3 ACHIEVEMENTS AND LIMITATIONS OF CICIG AS A MODEL

The results of CICIG's work, while it lasted, were spectacular. CICIG investigated 124 cases, leading to more than 400 criminal convictions over 11 years – including heads of state, legislators, judges, and corporate executives – and dismantling some 70 criminal networks. CICIG uncovered corrupt networks involving former Presidents Alfonso Portillo, Otto Pérez Molina, Alvaro Arzú, and Jimmy Morales, along with leaders of other political parties, members of Congress, lawyers and judges, military officers, elite businessmen and organized crime groups engaging in human trafficking, drug smuggling, land grabbing, fraud in construction and health care contracting, and the like.

Beyond the statistics, CICIG helped change the way cases were investigated. It confirmed that modern investigative techniques could be more reliable than witness testimony and helped pass legislation that allowed for a wide range of such techniques. Starting under AG Paz y Paz, prosecutions went from a case-by case focus on individual crimes and defendants to a broader approach based in network analysis and patterns of macrocriminality, connecting the dots among actors and acts. CICIG's strategy, especially under Velásquez, focused on root causes: Campaign finance by organized crime and shady elites, corrupt state contracting and tax evasion, and guarantees of impunity through a captured judiciary. This implied changes in how both CICIG and the MP worked, with thematic investigations and large criminal and financial analysis sections.

Because only the MP could actually prosecute, a close relationship between the two institutions was imperative. CICIG had the unexpected advantage of good relationships with committed and competent Attorney Generals between 2009 and 2018. After a few initial hiccups, and despite debates over tactics or timing it worked closely with the MP, and especially with the anti-corruption section (known as FECI), headed between 2015 and 2021 by Juan Francisco Sandoval, whom we'll meet again. The close relationship had its downside, as Attorney General Aldana especially was seen as politically ambitious. This created suspicions about CICIG's political agenda and led it to take up small cases (including one against the then-president's son) that could have been easily left to the regular criminal system. CICIG also focused little on training of MP prosecutors and investigators in its casework, mostly keeping its investigations under wraps until advanced stages.

This no doubt was seen as necessary to protect security, but was also a lost opportunity to share knowledge.

Did CICIG's – and the MP's – prosecution strategy, especially in its last five years, invite the ferocious backlash that came, or was backlash inevitable? Probably a bit of both. Guatemala's elite was unaccustomed to (and furious about) being held to account. The choice, heavily encouraged by the US government, to go forward with elections in 2015 amid the upheaval of Pérez Molina's resignation without any reforms to the system of campaign finance, electoral law or judicial selection probably ensured antagonistic governments going forward; it also left the civic movement of 2015 divided, exhausted and dispirited. Retired military officers and their advocacy arm, the so-called Foundation Against Terrorism, wanted payback against judges and prosecutors for bringing human rights-related cases against high-ranking military officials, and made common cause with elites who felt unjustly persecuted by CICIG. So some degree of backlash was bound to happen.

I'm not suggesting that pulling its punches would have gotten CICIG an extended mandate, or avoided the vengeance exacted on those prosecutors and judges who remained after 2019. But once CICIG moved beyond organized crime, secret intelligence networks and public officials to investigate the recipients of crooked contracts and the bribers in the private sector (in the Construction, Odebrecht and other cases), what had been grudging respect for the Commissioner and even some quiet support for cleaning up government among the traditional elite became a united and militant front in opposition. It also didn't help that the MP, perhaps to show even-handedness or concerned that time was running out, went after center-left former President Colom but not his notoriously corrupt then-wife Sandra Torres, and after then-President Morales' family but not after much more substantial cases elsewhere. Moreover, the cases were sometimes too quickly pulled together to easily hold up in court, but those accused could spend years in preventive detention while the courts sorted it out. This too led to ranks closing against the Commission.

When I asked Ivan Velásquez about his strategy, he replied that he saw the risks but felt that he had little choice: It would have looked like political favoritism to move against some actors and not others (like the president's relatives) when evidence against them had already been made public. But favoritism is not the same as prioritization, and trying to divide your adversaries rather than unify them is a time-honored strategy. As many observers noted, sometimes the Commission was politically tone-deaf.

CICIG, and the MP, also found themselves stymied by the slow and byzantine workings of the courts. Early on, attacks on the judiciary by the first two

Commissioners, often with little evidence, set up an antagonistic relationship with many judges. After an initial 2009 raft of reforms, it proved impossible to change judicial selection processes that had become politicized or to rein in influence peddling. Once cases started coming from the MP, they were often sprawling and multifaceted, with dozens of defendants. As Miguel Angel Gálvez, one of the high-risk court judges told me: "the cases were like a fire-hose, we couldn't work with so much information. It would have been better to bring fewer, stronger cases." The courts, hobbled by antiquated procedures, never-ending constitutional interlocutory challenges, motions to recuse judges, and general desuetude, could never catch up, and the slow turning of the wheels of justice allowed its enemies to regroup. Some of CICIG's emblematic cases from 2015 have still not come to trial as of 2024, while many others have been sabotaged or abandoned by the current MP.

Unlike its casework, the policy and legislative work of CICIG by all accounts fell short. It had some early successes, including the new wiretap, protected witness, plea bargaining, and forensics laws. But it never developed an adequate lobbying strategy for an admittedly uncooperative Congress, which over the life of the Commission became even more hostile to its agenda. It published useful reports and suggestions but couldn't overcome legislative polarization and dysfunction to turn them into law. Building on years of work by civil society and professional organizations, it pushed unsuccessfully for constitutional reforms to tamp down malicious litigation and endless delays, for more respect for indigenous justice, and for changes in judicial selection processes. Of course, CICIG alone couldn't push these changes through, and there wasn't enough of a constituency in Congress to do so. But it also never figured out how to mobilize its considerable support among the population[24] to make the needed changes.

Finally, the Commission's relation to the UN was a source of tension from the beginning. It was created through a bilateral agreement between the UN and the government but was not set up to be a UN body. This meant that local CICIG investigators and personnel had no UN diplomatic immunity, and that the Commissioner hired and managed his own personnel, security (including counterintelligence), facilities and budget. This provided flexibility and nimbleness, and successful fundraising (mostly from the US and Europe) meant that the Commission was not dependent on UN resources. But it also meant that there were holes, and that everything depended on a single individual rather than an institution. The two-year mandate was not long enough to make real change, and so had to be extended over and over.[25] But not having a firm sunset date and exit plan and having to repeatedly seek government agreement (and foreign funding) created uncertainty and made it hard to recruit and retain good people. It also meant that there was no oversight of the Commissioner's decisions, even though the UN's reputation was on the line if things went terribly wrong. And it meant that, when the Commissioner or the CICIG as an institution were attacked, there was little the UN could do to support them beyond public handwringing.

After CICIG was forced out, a new Attorney General aligned with corrupt groups began dismantling the areas of the MP that had worked closely with CICIG or on human rights cases, bringing flimsy or downright nonsensical charges against her own prosecutors. A few, like Virginia Laparra, former CICIG Executive Claudia González or Orlando López, were prosecuted on spurious charges. More, including Sandoval, Aldana and several of the highest-profile judges fled the country, most decamping to Washington DC. Without CICIG to protect them, the people who had worked with the Commission, directly or in the MP, proved terribly vulnerable.

3.4 BEYOND CICIG

The CICIG example at its height spawned similar attempts in the region and elsewhere. In Honduras, the government, under heavy pressure due to massive anti-corruption protests, agreed with the Organization of American States (OAS) to set up a prosecutorial support mission known as the Mission to Support the Fight Against Corruption and Impunity in Honduras (MACCIH).[26] Unlike CICIG, the Honduran version could not initiate its own investigations or act as a private prosecutor because the figure of private prosecutor did not exist in Honduran law. It did help vet and set up a special anti-corruption unit (UFERCO) that took on massive frauds in the health service and president's office.[27] MACCIH lasted four years, but in 2020 the government refused to renew its mandate. Until the 2021 elections, the legislature then spent its time systematically dismantling the work of the UFERCO special prosecutors' office and making it more difficult to pursue cases against the powerful. These efforts included passing legislation to restrict access to information, granting immunity for legislators, making corruption investigations be subject to approval by a (captured) Comptrollers' Court, undermining and closing out MACCIH's investigations, and reducing penalties for corruption-related crimes.[28] President Xiomara Castro campaigned on a promise to create a new, UN-backed version, a CICIH. By 2024, such a Commission looks increasingly unlikely, although some of the worst legislation passed under her predecessor (eventually convicted in New York of drug trafficking charges) has now been repealed.

In El Salvador, President Nayib Bukele promised a Salvadoran version of CICIG, but once in power he put in place a defanged office capable only of advising the Attorney General. Nonetheless, even that proved too potent, as the CICIES began investigating his associates for COVID-related health care fraud. According to press reports, the Commission, at the president's invitation, began investigating deals, and found that Bukele's close collaborators had apparently overcharged for hospital upgrades, food packages, and surgical masks.[29] President Bukele dissolved the anti-impunity Commission after less than two years. In Ecuador and Mexico, a CICIG-like entity was proposed but never got off the ground. In Kosovo, the European Union Rule of Law Mission in Kosovo (EULEX) had some similar characteristics.

Despite CICIG's abrupt end, and the dismal state of Guatemala's justice system in 2024, it remains a model worth considering. According to a recent study, during its eleven years of existence, it plausibly prevented the occurrence of between 20,000 and 30,000 homicides,[30] reduced levels of violence, improved conviction rates, and changed the way ordinary people understood how corruption and human rights violations were intertwined. It provided hope that the corruption/impunity paradigm could be broken, and showed a new, better way to investigate large-scale, systemic corruption crimes. It made anti-impunity a popular concept and paved the way for the anti-corruption upsurge of 2023 (which I describe in Chapter 1). Of course, the exact circumstances that gave rise to CICIG are unlikely to repeat elsewhere. But with some changes, starting with those discussed earlier, international support for domestic prosecutors – or for other specialists, like forensic accountants, financial analysts or others – may well be part of future efforts to combat grand corruption.

4

Transnational Approaches II

Sanctions, Standards, and Third-Party States

Outside support for prosecutors is one of a number of ways to attack grand corruption when domestic institutions cannot do so alone. This chapter considers other ways of using outside pressure to impact the incentive structures that fuel the problem, especially when domestic avenues seem unproductive. I consider "smart" sanctions against individuals, pioneered by the Global Magnitsky Act in the US and its analogues elsewhere. I then look at pressure from public banks and from voluntary standards aimed at private behavior. Finally, I look at the advantages and pitfalls of national prosecutions where the underlying crimes occurred elsewhere, as in money laundering or organized crime prosecutions in money-receiving states.

4.1 CHANGING INDIVIDUAL AND CORPORATE BEHAVIOR: TARGETED SANCTIONS

Behind the corrupt acts that affect human rights are people and companies, with families and assets. With proper incentives, you can change their behavior without trials or punishment. That, at least, is the idea behind the targeted sanctions pioneered with respect to Russia and now employed globally in the US, the EU, Australia, and Canada.

Economic sanctions go back to antiquity, with the "Megarian Decree" that Athenian statesperson Pericles issued in 432 BC.[1] In more recent times, they have been seen as a preferable alternative to armed conflict, and therefore justifiable to deter state wrongdoing. But sanctions against countries are a blunt instrument, usually hurting both the people of the sanctioned state and those of the state imposing the sanctions.[2] They can often not do much to change the behavior of rulers, especially when those rulers need not worry about public pressure. In fact, broad economic sanctions can often benefit those in charge, who profit from the resulting black markets and sanctions-busting schemes.[3]

These critiques have been leveled against the broad US sanctions imposed in 2017 against Venezuela. In addition to bilateral sanctions, the UN Security Council can also impose countrywide as well as targeted sanctions for violations related to international peace and security, including arms-dealing.[4]

Criticism of statewide sanctions regimes led to a search for "smart sanctions": Noncriminal incentives that were more narrowly focused on the people causing the harm, rather than on innocent citizens of an offending state. These sanctions against specific persons would not necessarily or unduly damage relations with governments, while pressuring individuals to change their behavior. They were considered forward-looking, not punitive.

The issue came to a head with a death in custody. Sergei Magnitsky was a Russian accountant who uncovered a massive $230 million fraud committed by Russian government officials. When he reported the crime in November 2008, he was arrested, allegedly for tax evasion. While in custody, he was beaten, tortured and denied medical care, family visits and due legal process. He died in prison in November 2009 at the age of thirty-seven.[5] Magnitsky worked for Hermitage Capital, a foreign investment brokerage in Russia. The Chief Executive Officer of Hermitage Capital, William Browder (yes, the same one who helped sink CICIG) brought congressional attention to Magnitsky's story, which clearly illustrated that "corruption and human rights offences often go hand in hand."[6] In 2012, Congress passed the Sergei Magnitsky Act envisaging sanctions such as asset freezes, financial restrictions, and visa bans imposed by the US government against the persons responsible for Magnitsky's detention, abuse, or death.[7] Russia reacted with fury, banning adoptions of Russian children by American citizens.[8]

The 2012 law focused on Russia, but it retained language that manifested the importance of upholding respect for human rights globally, and underlined how "systemic corruption erodes trust and confidence in democratic institutions, the rule of law, and human rights protections."[9] Members of Congress hoped that future legislation would "disrupt the impunity and comfort that far too many international human rights violators currently enjoy and keep their tainted money out of our financial systems."[10] Several years of negotiations followed, with bipartisan support to expand the law globally and to cover corruption directly as well as corruption-related rights violations. Thus, from the beginning, the law married concerns about human rights and corruption.

According to Republican Representative Christopher Smith, the 2012 act was "a major step in freeing ourselves from aiding and abetting international perpetrators." The global version, he said, "marks the next step in taking a stand against their crimes."[11] He cited as an example Teodorin Obiang Mangue, son of the President of Equatorial Guinea, who lived in California and owned a

$35 million mansion in Malibu, with a golf course, two swimming pools, and a tennis court, as well as a multimillion-dollar collection of Michael Jackson memorabilia. People like him "should not be able to steal from foreign firms and their own people and then use those funds to live lavishly in our country," Mr. Smith said. "Similarly, those who torture and otherwise commit the worst human rights violations against others should not be welcomed here either." (I tell the story of efforts to seize Teodorín's ill-gotten gains in Chapter 6).

The 2016 Global Magnitsky Act applies worldwide. It authorizes, but does not require, the president to publish a list, and keep it updated, of "foreign persons" (both individuals and entities) that the president determines are responsible for torture, extrajudicial killings, "significant corruption" or other "gross violations of internationally recognized human rights committed against individuals seeking to promote human rights or to expose illegal activity carried out by government officials." The law authorizes financial sanctions, freezing any property held in the US and prohibiting US citizens or entities from entering into transactions with the "foreign person"; and visa restrictions, denying entry into the US and revoking any already-issued visa.

Executive Order 13818 further strengthened the Global Magnitsky framework in December 2017 (during the first Trump administration). It broadens the scope of the potentially sanctionable targets to foreign persons determined "to be responsible for or complicit in, or to have directly or indirectly engaged in, serious human rights abuse." The new language thus covers a variety of nonstate as well as state actors, aiding and abetting or other indirect participation, and a wider range of violations and victims. The Global Magnitsky Act was set to expire at the end of 2022, but President Biden signed its permanent reauthorization into law on April 8, 2022, using the broader definition in E.O. 13818.[12] By that time, 420 human rights abusers and corrupt actors had been sanctioned in 43 countries, according to Human Rights First.[13]

Because the sanctions are nonpunitive, the standard of proof in practice is lower than it would be for criminal activity. NGOs, Congressmembers or other states can submit information, and the Treasury Department will evaluate it based on a threshold of "reasonable belief based on credible information."[14] In response to concerns about potential misuse, a procedure exists for getting off the list based on either being listed unfairly or having changed the objectionable behavior.

Financial sanctions under Global Magnitsky also include visa sanctions, but the converse is not true. Three separate programs, run by the US State Department, can impose visa denials or retractions based on significant corruption or gross violations of human rights. The first, Section 7031(c) of the Foreign Operations and Related Programs Appropriations Act, covers current or former foreign government officials and their immediate family members. The State Department can choose whether or not to name the people sanctioned.[15] On the other hand, Section 212(a)(3)(C) of the Immigration and Nationality Act doesn't require any explicit tie to corruption or human rights, just "potentially serious adverse foreign policy consequences" if the person (or their family) is let in. Those sanctioned lose their visa, but their name never becomes public. These sanctions have most recently been used against antidemocratic actors in Guatemala and elsewhere.

Central America's close relationship to the US merited additional visa sanctions authority. In 2020, Rep. Norma Torres (who moved to the US from Guatemala when she was five) and Rep. Eliot Engel convinced Congress to pass the United States-Northern Triangle Enhanced Engagement Act. The Act aimed to address the root causes of migration from Central America by among other strategies, fighting corruption and strengthening democratic governance. It requires the State Department to publish a yearly list of corrupt and undemocratic actors from Guatemala, El Salvador, Honduras, and (as of 2022) Nicaragua. Those on the "Engel List" are ineligible for visas to the US. There is overlap among the different sanctions lists, although financial sanctions are considerably less common than visa denials.

Most of those listed under any of these sanctions were publicly defiant. "Why do I need a visa? I've already been to Disneyland," said one official. In private, some sanctions clearly do matter. For example, sanctions against over one hundred members of the Guatemalan Congress in December 2023 – although the names were not released, there was little doubt about most of their identities – were widely credited with tamping down efforts to impede the transfer of power to the elected president the following month.[16]

The wide discretion left to the US State Department about whether to publish the names of sanctioned entities, and what exactly "antidemocratic" means, are also problematic. At the least, public (but not private) sanctioning identifies those sanctioned as corrupt or human rights violators, which may have spinoff political or economic effects including some satisfaction for victims.[17] Financial sanctions keep these people from enjoying ill-gotten gains, or at least makes them spend time moving their money to less secure or lucrative jurisdictions.

4.1.1 *Global Magnitsky Equivalents Outside the US*

If the US maintains a strict sanctions regime, but other capital-receiving countries don't, then money will just shift around; those sanctioned will just go to Disneyland in Paris. Luckily, Canada, the European Union, the United

Kingdom and Australia have passed their own analogous acts, and incipient coordination mechanisms exist regarding multiple sanctions on individuals. In addition, Norway, the Baltic states, Kosovo, Jersey and Gibraltar have some version of targeted sanctions for corruption and human rights abuses.[18]

Canada's economic and financial sanctions target foreign nationals through the Justice for Victims of Corrupt Foreign Officials Act (Magnitsky Act). The Magnitsky Act was introduced in October 2017, with sanctions including asset freezes and confiscation, as well as economic sanctions on banking and property. It applies globally to foreign individuals responsible for extrajudicial killings, torture or other gross violations of human rights against whistleblowers or rights defenders, or public officials or their associates engaged or complicit in, or providing support for, significant acts of corruption.[19] These are defined as bribery, misappropriation, or money laundering, and "any act of corruption related to expropriation, government contracts or the extraction of natural resources."

Amendments in 2022 strengthened the asset-related provisions of the law, expanding Canada's power to seize and order the forfeiture of a broad range of real and personal property. A judge must confiscate frozen assets upon a determination, at the state's request, that they have been frozen and are owned, held, or controlled (directly or indirectly) by a relevant foreign national. The judge must give notice to those who have an interest in the property, although it's not clear if that extends to potential victims of the rights violations or corrupt acts.[20] As of December 2023, Canadian authorities had used the law seventy-three times.[21]

The European Union's restrictive measures against serious human rights violations and abuses were adopted in December 2020 under the EU Global Human Rights Sanctions Regime. The regulations do not bear Magnitsky's name, a decision taken to avoid making Russia feel that it was specifically targeted.[22] The legal framework is composed of two separate pieces of legislation, which were adopted simultaneously: the Council decision and the Council regulation.

The EU divides human rights abuses into two categories. The first involves "serious human rights violations and abuses." These include genocide, torture, slavery, extrajudicial killings, and arbitrary arrests. The second addresses abuses when they are widespread and systematic including human trafficking, abuses of freedoms of peaceful assembly, association, opinion and expression, religion, and belief. The scope of the first category is similar to that of the US, Canada and the UK laws, while the second category includes a much broader range of offenses that are not explicitly mentioned by the other jurisdictions. In May 2023 the European Commission introduced a proposed Directive on fighting corruption and an expansion of the sanctions regime to cover serious acts of corruption; as of 2024, these were still under debate, so the EU does not cover corruption-related sanctions.[23]

The UK's 2020 Global Human Rights Sanctions Regime can be used to impose sanctions for serious violations or abuses of three human rights when carried out by or on behalf of a foreign state: The right to life, the right not to be subjected to torture or cruel, inhuman or degrading treatment or punishment, and the right to be free from slavery, not to be held in servitude or required to perform forced or compulsory labor. The regulations specify that individuals and entities that participate in, assist in, are owned by, provide financial services to, or benefit from the sanctioned behavior or entities are covered. No one can deal with their funds or other economic resources – their assets are frozen.[24] They are also ineligible for visas. Corruption is dealt with separately: In the 2021 regulations[25] individuals and entities that engage in or otherwise are connected to serious corruption – defined narrowly as bribery or misappropriation of property – are subject to the same asset freeze and visa limits.

On December 8, 2021, Australia passed the Autonomous Sanctions Amendment (Magnitsky-style and Other Thematic Sanctions) Bill 2021. The new law enables the government to impose targeted financial sanctions and travel bans addressing: "the proliferation of weapon of mass destruction; threats to international peace and security; malicious cyber activity; serious violations or serious abuses of human rights; activities undermining good governance or the rule of law, including serious corruption; and serious violations of international humanitarian law."[26]

In practice, sanctioning decisions can be opaque, leading to charges of selectivity, and it can be unclear exactly what behavior, and what procedure, is required to lift the sanctions. There is also a tension, as Cecily Rose points out, between freezing sanctioned assets and returning them to the countries they were stolen from.[27] Foreign ministries can decide how aggressively they want to sanction as well as where to focus their efforts and can also shift in their openness to civil society input or reporting requirements. Certain regions, like South and Central Asia, and certain types of victims have been underrepresented.[28] While NGOs provide evidence, coordinate across countries and suggest appropriate targets, only a third of US sanctions originated in civil society recommendations, and the figures for the EU (13%) and UK (4%) are even lower. Visa sanctions, especially, have diminishing returns as those targeted find other venues for study, medical care, shopping, and business relations. Financial sanctions do bite, but governments are much more reluctant to impose them given both the administrative burden and the costs to its domestic financial institutions.

Multilateral targeted sanctions would increase that bite, but as of November 2022, "out of the 761 total unique perpetrators sanctioned by the U.S., Canada,

UK, and/or EU under their Magnitsky-style programs, only 11% have been sanctioned by at least one other jurisdiction under comparable mechanisms."[29] Sanctions for corrupt behavior are less likely to be multilateral than those for human rights violations; most such sanctions are imposed by the US. Part of the problem is that the legal language in each country is slightly different in scope, so translating the relevant facts into the legal grounds for sanctions in each place takes time.

Nor have sanctioning countries used the possibility of secondary sanctions to full effect. Secondary sanctions can be imposed on financial institutions or professional services providers who enable individuals who are subject to primary sanctions under Global Magnitsky or sister regimes to hide or move their money around, thus reducing the bite of the sanctions. According to a recent proposal, greater use of such secondary sanctions would improve overall compliance with financial sanctions and "disrupt the [relatively small] network of shady offshore enablers that facilitate corruption and money laundering."[30]

On the bright side, the US has begun using network analysis to sanction not just individual wrongdoing, but the associates, companies, enablers, and family members who are part of the same corrupt networks. The largest Global Magnitsky action to date involved some forty-five individuals and entities, including a media mogul, a gambling czar and several high-ranking government officials, all accused of bribery in Bulgaria.[31] Another action targeted illegal fishing networks in Asia, and resulted, among other effects, in a Chinese company being delisted from the NASDAQ stock exchange.[32]

Which brings us back to Guatemala. Juan Francisco Sandoval, the slight, serious, bespectacled head of the Anti-Corruption Bureau of the Guatemalan MP (known as FECI) worked closely with Ivan Velásquez at CICIG and brought many of the Commission's cases to court. When CICIG was shut down in 2019, he continued doing so, at least until new Attorney General Consuelo Porras decided to rid the MP of CICIG-related prosecutors and defang his unit. Sandoval at the time was deep into an investigation of bribery in the mining sector. According to him, a Russian-controlled mining company (headquartered in Switzerland) known as Solway wanted a new license to mine and export nickel from Izabal province, near Guatemalan's Caribbean coast. They also wanted their own port facility to export the nickel. He told me how his office found, based on an eyewitness report by a whistleblower, that the Russians (and one Kazakh) had met with then-president Giammattei on April 26, 2021. Three days later, a gift arrived at the president's home. It was a carpet, rolled up and full of money. Of course, it was dubbed the "magic carpet."[33]

A month after that, the mine got its long-delayed license.

The company's mine operations faced long-standing ferocious opposition from some local fishing and farming communities and sporadic accusations of land grabbing, environmental harm, violence by mine security personnel against villagers including rapes and the killing, forced disappearance, and arbitrary detention of community leaders. (A former army lieutenant colonel pleaded guilty to murdering a local teacher and activist in January 2021;[34] a civil suit against the mine's former owner continues in Canada.) Despite a fish-killing red tide apparently caused by nickel and chromium tailings in nearby Lake Izabal, the Guatemalan Mining Ministry had never seen a problem with the company's environmental impact analyses. Leaked documents from the mine detailed how mining authorities paid the police and local judges to harass and criminalize mine opponents, and pressured President Giammattei into imposing a state of emergency in the area to quell protests.[35] In 2020, the Constitutional Court (the country's highest court) ordered mine operations suspended due to the lack of proper consultation with local indigenous communities – the sham version was not good enough. Less than a year later, the president of that Court had been forced out of the country.

Apparently, the mine had worked to divide the communities, and to deny that they were impacting communal K'ekchi land. In December 2023, the Inter-American Court of Human Rights found otherwise, holding Guatemala liable for the lack of communal land rights and adequate consultation around the mine.[36] Leaked documents showed the company planning to pay police to evict people from their lands.

Sandoval's digging eventually led his boss, Porras, to try to close his cases and then to arrest him, in part on grounds that he took a copy of the case file with him to avoid destruction of the evidence. He narrowly escaped over the border to El Salvador, where he held a press conference about his initial findings on the "magic carpet." He too now lives outside Guatemala. In September 2021, Porras and her deputy were put on the "Engel List" for obstructing corruption investigations. In May 2022, the State Department designated Porras as a corrupt official, and denied her, her deputies and her immediate family visas to the United States under section 7031(c). According to the designation, Porras repeatedly obstructed investigations to protect her political allies and obtain unwarranted political favors. Porras brushed off the visa restrictions. In February 2024, the EU imposed its own visa sanctions on Porras, two deputies and a crooked judge. At the end of 2024, she was still in office.

More surprisingly, on November 18, 2022, the US Embassy in Guatemala announced that two mine executives (one Russian, one Belarussian) and three related corporate nickel mining entities – two associated with Solway and another, Mayaniquel, with Russian mining company TelfAg, were being sanctioned under Global Magnitsky. The financial sanctions were imposed on the individuals because they, and their companies "allegedly led multiple bribery schemes over several years involving politicians, judges, and government officials [and] conducted corrupt acts in furtherance of Russian influence peddling schemes by unlawfully giving cash payments to public officials in exchange for support for Russian mining interests."[37] Russian access to strategic minerals in the context of the Ukraine war may well also have made the US nervous and unhappy. Unlike the visa restrictions on Porras and other political figures, these sanctions had financial teeth, freezing the companies' assets in the US and prohibiting US businesses from dealing with them.

Solway reacted by firing the two sanctioned individuals and hiring US law firms to investigate the corruption allegations, while Mayaniquel insisted that even though they were innocent they were cooperating with US Treasury authorities. The sanctions apparently had more far-reaching effects: According to a mining industry website, Canadian mining company Bluestone Resources had been considering buying the Guatemalan mine, but pulled out after the sanctions were imposed. "We did not want to get in trouble with the US government," President and CEO Peter Hemstead said.[38] After an initial report cleared the company's leadership, the US removed the sanctions in September 2023. Perhaps as a condition, Solway soon hired former FBI director Louis Freeh to advise on compliance issues, including, according to Solway's attorney, improved anti-bribery and corruption policies.[39] Meanwhile, mining operations remained formally suspended awaiting a new license, although locals reported continuing activity in the area.

Other mine-related visa sanctions followed. On October 31, 2023 the State Department imposed visa sanctions on former Minister of Internal Security Gendri Rocael Reyes Mazariegos, former Energy and Mining Minister Alberto Pimentel Mata y Vice Mining Oscar Rafael Pérez Ramírez, all for bribery. Pimentel and Pérez were the officials responsible for creating fake "consultations" about the mine's plans (for which they received illicit payment) and for refusing to comply with the court decision to suspend its operations (among other shady natural resource-related deals), while Reyes was in charge of police who attacked protesters at the site. Financial sanctions on Pimentel followed in January 2024, for, among other things, rigging contracts, requesting bribes and accepting "large monthly payments to facilitate the acquisition of necessary permits and licenses for a private company operating in the energy and mining sector of Guatemala."[40]

On the same date, three days after leaving office, the US State Department imposed visa restrictions on former president Alejandro Giammattei and his three adult children for accepting bribes.[41]

Juan Francisco Sandoval thinks the most useful role of sanctions was sending a message to the Guatemalan government that made it pull back on attacking judges and the press. But what about private actors? Is this a success story, in that the sanctions on Solway cost it possible business advantages and made it change its behavior? Or is it a case where the US' pragmatic need for increased nickel production competed, and finally won, over a desire to hold corporate misfeasance to account? It's hard to know, since the detailed bases for imposing sanctions (or removing them) are not published. But it does underline that sanctions, in the end, are political, imposed or removed by states according to their interests, not just according to the severity of the underlying behavior.

4.2 USING THE COURTS OF THIRD-PARTY STATES

If internal accountability is blocked due to state capture or incapacity, expanding the use of national courts elsewhere to seek punishment of offenders and return of stolen funds might provide an alternative. In the context of massive human rights crimes, extraterritorial jurisdiction has been useful in allowing victims to tell their story, to make evidence public, to catalyze national justice processes, and (less often, admittedly) to convict and imprison offenders and provide reparation to their victims. I have written about how the case against Chilean dictator Pinochet in Spain helped consolidate and advance domestic cases; recent examples of universal jurisdiction-based human rights cases include Syrians and Iraqi Yazidi in Germany, or Salvadorans in Spain, Zimbabweans in South Africa, or Myanmar Rohingya in Argentina.[42] In human rights law, universal jurisdiction is mandatory under the Geneva Conventions in cases of grave breaches, and jurisdiction is also required under the Torture Convention and several anti-terrorism treaties when the offender is present in the territory and not extradited.[43]

The UNCAC requires a state to exercise jurisdiction over offenses listed in the Convention when they take place on its territory. It permits, but does not require, jurisdiction in cases where the alleged perpetrator is found in the state, no matter their nationality or the place where the crime occurred. However, most third-party investigations and prosecutions for UNCAC-listed crimes have been based not on the presence of the defendant but on a violation of a sanctions law, the use of the state's territory for the commission of part of the offense,[44] or on money laundering offenses.

Fallout from the looting of Venezuela's national oil company, known as PDVSA, and scandals involving currency manipulation, food and health care, and dozens of other corruption cases involving high-ranking state officials are spread around much of the world. The systemic and top-down nature of the corruption encompassed sending the proceeds to banks outside Venezuela. For example, just in the PDVSA cases, national courts in the US, Switzerland, Andorra, Spain, and Portugal have investigated and prosecuted based on assets found or actions taken in their jurisdiction. A website called Corruptometro[45] counts 254 cases in 30 countries worth US$64.6 billion in stolen assets as of 2024. None of these cases, as far as it's possible to tell, is based on universal jurisdiction, even where countries have a broad definition of applicable crimes. In part, this is because even though UNCAC allows it, most countries rely on domestic penal statutes to provide jurisdiction – and judges tend to interpret such statutes narrowly – as well as require a link to the underlying crime.

A good number of cases around Venezuelan assets are in Spain and Argentina. The Argentine cases are mostly about local firms bribing Venezuelan government officials for contracts. The US has the largest number of cases, including convictions of the former head of the Venezuelan Treasury Office and her spouse for laundering in the US the proceeds of bribes they received in relation to currency manipulation.[46] Another former Treasurer cut a deal with US authorities, and forfeited some $260 million in assets.[47] The Trump Justice Department charged high-ranking Venezuelan politicians and military leaders along with members of the Colombian FARC of participating in a "narco-terrorist" conspiracy to traffic drugs into the US.[48] Most are money laundering cases; the US asserts jurisdiction over the funds based on the use of US banks, wire transfers or other financial activity connected to the US to hide the proceeds of crime, even though the underlying corrupt conduct may have happened abroad. The bulk of these cases involve civil forfeiture of assets found in the US, although there are some criminal money laundering cases.

Money laundering civil forfeiture, with its expansive jurisdiction and civil (lesser) burden of proof, can be an important tool for freezing and confiscating funds when the territorial state has no interest in doing so. Courts can freeze, seize and confiscate assets that have been laundered, proceeds from money laundering or predicate offenses, instrumentalities used in or intended for use in the commission of these offenses, or property of corresponding value, so long as they don't prejudice the rights of bona fide third parties.[49] Unlike cases brought under universal jurisdiction, however, money laundering prosecution is a two-step process: The prosecuting entity must show that there is an underlying offense, and that it is connected to the funds or assets alleged to be laundered. The underlying offense varies: in some countries, any serious felony is good enough, whereas in others (like the US) there is a list of specified "predicate offenses." These include some but not all corruption crimes, murder and grievous bodily injury, trafficking, and in some instances environmental crimes.[50] It would be useful for capital-receiving states to make sure all UNCAC crimes are listed as both predicate offenses for money-laundering purposes and as offenses subject to universal jurisdiction, with a broad list of circumstances under which the jurisdiction is triggered.

Another possible avenue for third-party prosecutions would be to target bribe-offering officials in foreign states. As of 2024, the US penalizes both bribe-givers (through the FCPA) and bribe-solicitors, through the Foreign Extortion Prevention Act.[51] The act, passed with bipartisan support and as a result of proposals from civil society groups, makes it "unlawful for any foreign official or person selected to be a foreign official to corruptly demand, seek, receive, or accept, or agree to receive or accept, directly or indirectly" anything of value. It applies a broad definition of public official that includes, for the first time, senior foreign political figures acting in official or unofficial capacities and their immediate family members. Thus, it takes into account some of the ways in which money actually changes hands in kleptocratic states. It provides for jurisdiction if the bribe demand happened in the US, or was directed at US citizens or companies organized under US law or publicly traded in the US. It's not clear why a foreign state with a high-level corruption problem would agree to extradite its bribe-offering official to the US (especially since the penalties under FEPA are severe), so this may be most useful to publicize the names of alleged bribe-solicitors and keep them from traveling, as a complement to FCPA actions where the bribe-offering company seeks leniency and has kept good records, or when there is a change in the foreign government.

While use of third-party states' courts to punish and to confiscate ill-gotten gains has advantages, it is also open to the same complaints about neocolonialism and imperial overreach that plagued early discussions around universal jurisdiction. The jurisdictions bringing these cases are overwhelmingly those that receive the assets, which in most cases means developed, Western countries. Moreover, as we'll see, anti-money laundering prosecutors are not focused on, nor necessarily sympathetic to, the needs and agency of victims of these crimes rather than the integrity of their own financial system. Nonetheless, developing a strategy for collaboration between these prosecutors and civil society groups may, over time, bear fruit.

4.3 MARKET-BASED STANDARDS AND CERTIFICATION

Where systemic corruption on a large scale affects the integrity and credibility of state institutions, a possible response would involve bypassing the state and using market-based mechanisms to ensure transparency, accountability and compliance with anti-corruption, human rights (and other social and environmental) standards. Market-based signals primarily affect private companies that provide goods and services to consumers, but they can also affect the ability of both private and state agencies to obtain financing, insurance or access to markets.[52] These market-based mechanisms include international bodies like the Extractive Industries Transparency Initiative, composed of more than fifty countries and participating companies that agree to abide by (and demand of oil, gas and mining industries) a standard set of disclosure and civil engagement practices, including contract transparency; in 2021, EITI published a non-required guidance note on addressing corruption risks using the standards.[53]

They can also be private certification bodies, which attest to voluntary company compliance with a set of production and distribution practices that uphold specified environmental, social and/or governance outcomes. Certification schemes such as the Forest Stewardship Council (FSC) aim to obtain better prices for certified producers in exchange for their commitment to more sustainable land tenure, land use, labor and logging practices demonstrated by on-the-ground independent audits carried out by accredited auditors according to a list of standards. In theory, having to prove through periodic audits that they comply with national laws, treaties and regulations should result in fewer instances of large-scale corruption.

A 2013 study of the FSC[54] found that, while certification mattered for markets in low-corruption countries, it had little impact in places where corruption is endemic or systematic, in part because the certifiers rarely engaged with public officials in charge of granting concessions, permits and other approvals often subject to corruption, and could not easily evaluate when legislative and regulatory changes were driven by state capture. As of 2017, as a result of NGO complaints about inappropriate certifications as well as EU limits on imports of illegally sourced timber, FSC added specific anti-corruption provisions, including a corruption risk assessment in places where there's a high perception of corruption, and to "publicize a commitment not to offer or receive bribes in money or any other form of corruption, and […] comply with anti-corruption legislation [or] implement other anti-corruption measures proportionate to the scale and intensity of management activities and the risk of corruption."[55] There's also an ability for outsiders to complain about the conclusions of the audit procedure, but it's too soon to know how much this will be used.

Certification programs have often not been successful in reining in corrupt activities in their sector because they are voluntary and so problematic producers can simply withdraw when they're caught. That's what happened in 2015, when community leaders in Uyacali, in Peru's Amazon region, accused a palm oil producer named Plantaciones de Pucallpa of violating environmental laws and bribing public officials to oust small farmers from their land either at gunpoint or for pennies. They went to the industry's "sustainable palm oil" self-certifier, known as the Roundtable on Sustainable Palm Oil or RSPO, complaining that land grabbing and cutting down primary forests to create monoculture was hardly sustainable and violated their ancestral rights, something the RSPO standard prohibits. In response, the palm oil company changed its name – and pulled out of the RSPO. Moreover, NGO investigations of RSPO found that auditors often ignored or even colluded with problematic producers.[56] While the RSPO requires a prohibition on bribery, minimum transparency and compliance with UNCAC provisions, there seem to be few specifics or public cases of companies decertified due to corruption.

Nonetheless, if private standards and certification programs more explicitly connected environmental and social goals with preventing and responding to the specific types of corruption common in the sector, they could provide a useful tool to raise awareness and, in some cases, to affect the bottom line of producers in situations where government provides few checks.

4.4 THE ROLE OF INTERNATIONAL DEVELOPMENT BANKS AND AGENCIES

One tactic for fighting grand corruption has focused on enablers like real estate brokers, lawyers, import-export agents, and auditors.[57] But other enablers have largely escaped scrutiny and pressure on the corruption front: consulting/auditing firms (discussed in Chapter 8), and international and regional development banks. Development banks provide public, and access to private, financing of large-scale infrastructure and service projects as well as government budgets; they could put powerful pressure on recalcitrant governments and companies to clean up their act – or else. The big public international financial institutions all have admirable anti-fraud and anti-corruption policies on paper, including prevention, debarring, and contracting policies.[58] They also have safeguards and complaint mechanisms in place with respect to the environment, labor and human rights, but these are apparently not often cross-referenced with the integrity offices, leading to missed red flags. And both sets of policies tend to miss the big picture state capture issues.

Sometimes, entire international development banks can be captured. That was the case, according to a recent investigation by journalists,[59] with the Central American Bank for Economic Integration (CABEI), which provides almost half of the region's development finance. CABEI was known to have financed questionable projects in the region. Remember Odebrecht, the giant Brazilian infrastructure company embroiled in a huge corruption scandal? According to the investigation, Odebrecht paid off Guatemalan state officials (including former Minister Alejandro Sinibaldi, who was at one point indicted with help from CICIG) using millions of dollars from a CABEI loan (those implicated all deny it). We'll soon meet Berta Cáceres, the Honduran environmental and indigenous rights activist killed for her opposition to a dam project on the Gualcarque River, in Chapter 5. According to the report, "internal audits show that CABEI ignored numerous red flags about the dam, performed scant due diligence, and continued to back the project after a protester was killed, their co-investors backed out, and the bank received dozens of complaints from indigenous communities – before selling off the loan in 2019."[60] CABEI was also accused of financing highways to nowhere in Guatemala and Costa Rica, giving few-strings-attached policy loans to Honduras' notoriously corrupt electricity company and letting Salvadoran leader Nayib Bukele shift funds slated for COVID-19 recovery to his pet project – making Bitcoin El Salvador's legal currency. It financed Nicaragua's repressive Ortega/Murillo regime even after other banks wouldn't, ignoring warning signs and even building a fancy new headquarters in Managua. The bank and its leadership profited handsomely from the loans.

Even institutions like the International Finance Corporation (IFC) (whose performance standards on things like environmental assessment are followed in big projects worldwide) can miss or ignore obvious warning signs despite extensive "integrity" checks. The IFC is the private sector, market-rate lending arm of the World Bank, and the part of the Bank most Latin American countries use. According to a 2018 investigative report,[61] the IFC financed a Spanish corporation, Grup Maritim TCB, to build a new terminal for the TCQ port on Guatemala's Pacific Coast. It apparently got the contract in 2012 by agreeing to pay a US$30 million kickback to various Guatemalan government officials (although it actually paid out only US$12 million). The intermediary: Juan Carlos Monzón, whom we met earlier as private secretary to Vice President Roxana Baldetti at the center of the "La Linea" case. Monzón eventually told CICIG and prosecutors that the IFC gave Grup Maritim TCB a US$62 million loan and purchased US$7.7 million worth of shares in the company, thus acquiring a 15 percent stake in TCQ. The IFC also funded banks in Guatemala and Honduras caught in corruption scandals. In all, according to the investigation, "[o]f the US$850 million that the IFC has invested in the Central American region, including in shareholder equity and loans, US$240 million were invested in projects that are currently [in 2018] under investigation for corruption allegations." This despite an apparently robust due diligence process, including the ability to debar violators.[62]

Why might this happen, and how can it be avoided? In part, it seems like development banks and their cousins are still seeing corruption as largely episodic and aberrant rather than systematic and woven into macrocriminal networks that include both state and private actors. In particular, there is insufficient attention to state capture dynamics. For another, the banks tend to have separate safeguards and complaint policies for integrity and for environmental and social issues, with little civil society input into the former. And, as is true for national prosecutors entering into settlements, plea bargains or DPAs, there is a tendency to accept promises of compliance and due diligence plans of questionable companies at face value, rather than evaluating their effectiveness in systemically corrupt environments. For the banks to be part of the solution, that needs to change.

PART II

PUTTING VICTIMS AT THE CENTER OF ANTI-CORRUPTION WORK

5

Fraud on the River

*Victim Access to Corruption Proceedings**

They came for her late at night. She was at home, with a visiting Mexican fellow activist who played dead to survive. Berta Cáceres, a well-known indigenous rights and environmental activist, was killed in March 2016. The killers, some with ties to the military, had been sent by David Castillo, a former military intelligence operative turned erstwhile head of the energy company DESA. DESA, in turn, had connections to former ministers of justice and to the country's leading banking family. Its Agua Zarca dam was one of forty-nine hydroelectric projects that Berta Cáceres had denounced before her death. Not only was the project an environmental nightmare for the Lenca people and the sacred rivers that crisscrossed their territory, but there was something decidedly fishy about how it had been planned, permitted, and built. Castillo, DESA's head, was employed by the public electricity authority at the time the contract was signed. In an atmosphere of widespread corruption from the top down, a project backed by a well-known elite family won a contract to generate and sell electricity to the state without being on the list of approved bidders, without a valid environmental impact statement, and with a design apparently aimed at maximizing the haul from government coffers. For years, Cáceres had been trying to blow the whistle, apparently to no avail. Now she was dead.

The organization that Cáceres cofounded, the Civic Council of Popular and Indigenous Organizations (COPINH), vowed to seek justice for her killing, and to continue pushing for an end to destructive dam and other extractive projects on indigenous territory. The triggermen were quickly arrested and convicted, but those behind the killing stayed free. Only in July 2021, after an international expert investigation into the killing and continued pressure from supporters, was Castillo convicted of murder in the case; he was sentenced the following year to twenty-two years in prison, although in 2024 the case was still not finalized. Others suspected of bankrolling or abetting the murder remain at large.

Berta and COPINH early on brought their concerns to the Mission Against Impunity (MACCIH), a group of foreign prosecutors backed by the Organization of American States to support Honduras' beleaguered justice system in the wake of widespread anti-corruption protests in 2015. (I discuss MACCIH briefly in Chapter 3.) They thought there was no way the dam would have been built without corruption; in March 2019, MACCIH's affiliated Honduran prosecutors agreed, opening a case against sixteen defendants including the vice-minister for environment on grounds of fraud, abuse of authority, dereliction of duty, negotiations incompatible with the exercise of public functions, and document falsification.

Honduras, like many countries with a penal code tracing back to Napoleon, allows victims of crimes to participate in the criminal trial.[1] Victims get access to the case file, can bring their own evidence forward, and in many cases can cross-examine witnesses and defendants and address the court. If the defendant is found guilty, they can request damages based on a showing of the harm to them. This system benefits victims because the state provides the expertise and funds to investigate the crime, rather than leaving it up to the victim to file a separate civil case, which in many countries is expensive, has short statutes of limitations and often requires posting a bond.

In countries where the legal system is particularly prone to high-level political interference and lacks resources and independence, the system provides additional benefits. In some places, it allows victims to bypass a prosecutors' office, at least initially, to bring their complaint directly to a judge. Elsewhere, (and especially after 1990s procedural reforms throughout Latin America) the prosecutors' office serves as a gatekeeper, but once a case is opened, access to the case file and evidence and being able to present their own evidence and witnesses makes victims and their lawyers an important check on prosecutor inaction or mishandling of cases. In the cases involving torture, enforced disappearance and other grave rights violations, it has almost invariably been the victims who have propelled the cases forward. Given the well-known ties of recent Honduran governments to corruption and organized crime (for starters, former president Hernández was convicted in the US for drug trafficking in 2024), and the obstacles to judicial independence, the lawyers for COPINH wanted to keep a close eye on the case, now known as Fraud on the Gualcarque River. And they wanted their evidence of malfeasance to be part of the record.

The trial court accepted, in the face of a defense challenge, COPINH's right to be a civil party in the fraud case.[2] Defendants appealed. The Court of Appeals, in an August 28, 2019 decision,[3] agreed with the defendants that COPINH was not a proper civil party. They based the decision on two procedural provisions in national law. First, Article 17 of the Criminal Procedure Code defines victims as those directly affected, including the state and public and private entities; the family member of someone who has been killed; and the members of a commercial or civic organization with regard to the crimes that affect it and common owners of property with respect to their indivisible interests. The court assumed that only the civic organization provision applied, but then read it narrowly to refer only to commercial or property interests, which according to the court were not implicated here.

Second, the court noted that this is not a human rights violations case, where the victim and their family would have standing to intervene; they found that an indigenous rights treaty ratified by Honduras was merely "programmatic." Nor was the environmental harm to riparian communities enough, since remedying that harm was not the purpose of the lawsuit. The only protected interest was public faith in the administration of the state; the only victim, therefore, was the State.

5.1 WHO IS THE VICTIM OF GRAND CORRUPTION UNDER THE UNCAC?

The traditional answer in law to the question of who is a victim in grand corruption cases is everyone and no one. When state funds are misused or go missing, under this view at the most the State is the victim. Therefore, only the State has standing to sue for, or receive restitution of, the stolen assets. When the assets are found abroad, they should be repatriated to the state, and when proceedings are domestic, only the state is able to represent the interests of the people in proceedings – criminal or administrative – to recoup its losses. Until recently, this was the consensus.

That consensus, however, is slowly changing. In the last decade or so, activists and lawyers have begun to argue that it's not just states, but individuals and collectivities as well as society as a whole that suffer losses and need to be both represented and repaired in cases involving grand corruption. These arguments come in part from the experience of state capture and the difficulties in holding corrupt leaders and company officials to account, and in part from a history of human rights and humanitarian law development around the rights of victims that has begun to permeate other areas of law. Anti-corruption law has, to some extent, followed suit.

Legal developments on the corruption side began to change the perception of who was a victim, who had the right to participate in proceedings, and who was the subject of reparations. The Council of Europe's 1999 Civil Convention on Corruption was a precursor.[4] It provides that persons who suffer damages from corruption can bring civil claims, but never defined who that might be. It requires each party to "provide in its internal law for effective remedies for persons who have suffered damage as a result of acts of corruption, to enable them to defend their rights and interests, including the possibility of obtaining compensation for material damage, loss of profits and non-pecuniary loss." It allows suit against not just those who committed the corrupt act, but those who authorized or failed to take reasonable steps to prevent it. And it provides for state (civil) responsibility for corrupt acts by public officials that have caused damage, requires relatively generous statutes of limitation, and provides for periodic peer monitoring of its implementation.

The UN Convention on Organized Crime, in its Article 25, provides that each State Party "shall establish appropriate procedures to provide access to compensation and restitution for victims … and each State Party shall, subject to its domestic law, enable views and concerns of victims to be presented and considered at appropriate stages of criminal proceedings against offenders in a manner not prejudicial to the rights of the defence."[5]

The UNCAC also provides that victims of corruption have rights. A number of articles make clear that the state is not the only victim of corruption, and that those harmed have access and compensation rights. Article 13(1) sets out a policy of encouraging public participation by civil society and nongovernmental organizations in anti-corruption efforts.[6] The obligations in Articles 32 and 35 are "hard," (framed as "shall" unlike much of the Convention) although given the differences in national legal systems, the particulars are left to each state. Article 32(5) reads: "Each State Party shall, subject to its domestic law, enable the views and concerns of victims to be presented and considered at appropriate stages of criminal proceedings against offenders in a manner not prejudicial to the rights of the defence." Clearly, if the only victim of corruption offenses were the State, this article would be unnecessary, nor would it include the reference to "victims" in the plural. According to the drafting history, States contemplated individual, collective, and legal (corporate) victims. One early draft of the text read:

> 1. Each State Party shall ensure that its domestic legislation takes into account the need to combat corruption and provides, in particular, for effective remedies for persons whose rights and interests are affected by corruption in order to enable them, in accordance with the principles of their domestic law, to obtain compensation for damage suffered.
>
> 2. Each State Party shall, subject to its domestic law, allow the views and concerns of victims to be presented and considered at the appropriate stages of criminal proceedings against offenders without thereby undermining the rights of the defence.[7]

In the course of the negotiations, the concerns of the States Parties to the UNCAC about victims were so important that they led delegates to create a separate article, which subsequently became Article 35. Article 35 sets out a requirement that:

> [e]ach State Party shall take such measures as may be necessary, in accordance with principles of its domestic law, to ensure that entities or persons who have suffered damage as a result of an act of corruption have the right to initiate legal proceedings against those responsible for that damage in order to obtain compensation.[8]

The legal action referred to in Article 35 maybe civil or administrative, or it may form part of a criminal action; this flexibility was deemed necessary given the existence of different legal systems.

In the preparatory work for Article 35, there are other indications of its scope. States proposed, for example, that the compensation should cover "material damage, loss of profits and non-pecuniary losses."[9] It is impossible to think that a State, as such, could suffer the last two types of damage, especially non-pecuniary. This is also reflected in the Interpretative Note in Article 35, which specifies that "[t]he expression 'entities or persons' includes States as well as legal and natural persons." Finally, Article 57(3)(c), on asset recovery, requires states to "…give priority consideration to returning confiscated property to the requesting State Party, returning such property to its prior legitimate owners or compensating the victims of the crime." This makes clear that states are not the only entities entitled to recovered assets.

Taken together, these articles make clear that persons or entities other than the state are entitled to participate in proceedings, whether they be criminal, civil suits or administrative or constitutional actions. The provisions beg the question of how to define "victim" or "persons who have suffered damage." Perhaps understanding the difficulties in too strict a formulation given wide differences in national law, the preparatory drafts simply required that (i) damages have been caused to the person or entity and (ii) there is a causal link between the act of corruption and the damages.[10] How strictly a causation requirement should be construed, and whether it is subject to limits based on legal or proximate cause, or whether forms of alternative causation can apply have been the subject of debate ever since.

The UNCAC Working Group on Asset Recovery (WG) has issued a number of studies on "good practices for identifying victims of corruption and parameters for their compensation" based on self-reporting from states, as requested at the 6th CoSP. In its 2016 study,[11] the WG identified employers, shareholders, unsuccessful bidders, foreign states and society as a whole as potential victims. It detailed various mechanisms for allowing victims to sue, including class or collective actions, in criminal, civil or administrative proceedings. It listed as "good practice" having a wide range of options for victims to obtain compensation, allowing anti-corruption NGOs to participate in proceedings on behalf of victims, freezing assets to hold for compensation, and allowing fines to compensate victims. In a subsequent 2019 study, the WG added a section on how states have gone about distinguishing transfers of assets to others for purposes of hiding them or confusing ownership chains from transfers to bona fide third parties.[12] Other reports from UNODC[13] and the World Bank/StAR initiative[14] and the work of the UNCAC Coalition on visibilizing victims lay out options and good practices. But in reality, states have been reluctant to move forward with this agenda, despite a mention in the 2023 CoSP Atlanta Declaration of "the importance for States parties to consider, in appropriate cases, the impact of corruption offences on victims in their measures to prevent, investigate and prosecute corruption offences and further consider the participation and protection of victims in their domestic efforts to combat corruption, in accordance with the Convention and domestic law."[15]

5.2 THE DEFINITION(S) OF VICTIM IN INTERNATIONAL HUMAN RIGHTS LAW

Human rights groups and networks of family members of those massively killed and forcibly disappeared in the 1970s and 1980s Latin American dictatorships and civil wars have changed the legal landscape for anti-corruption campaigners. They were one of the driving forces behind the developing international law on the rights of victims to participate on an equal footing with defendants in criminal processes. Victims have rights, including the right to be heard, to demand the truth of what happened to them and their loved ones, and to reparation. The definitions developed in this context, involving powerful figures able to create impunity for themselves, have proven useful in anti-corruption efforts involving equally powerful figures.

Human rights treaties all include a right to a remedy. The Universal Declaration of Human Rights, proclaims that "[e]veryone has the right to an effective remedy by the competent national tribunals for acts violating the fundamental rights granted him by the constitution or by law."[16] Subsequent global and regional treaties reiterate the right to an effective remedy, including undoing, repairing and compensating for violations.[17] In addition to reiterated treaty provisions, widely accepted soft law elaborates on who is a victim and what remedies are due. The evolution of soft law began with the 1985 UN Declaration of Basic Principles of Justice for Victims of Crime and Abuse of Power.[18]

> Victims means persons who, individually or collectively, have suffered harm, including physical or mental injury, emotional suffering, economic loss or substantial impairment of their fundamental rights, through acts or omissions that are in violation of criminal laws operative within Member States, including those laws proscribing criminal abuse of power.[19]

In the context of human rights law, this was followed by the Basic Principles and Guidelines on the Right to a Remedy and Reparation for Victims of Gross Violations of International Human Rights Law and Serious Violations of International Humanitarian Law which uses an almost identical definition.[20]

The Inter-American human rights system has played a key role in broadening and specifying the definition of victim. In many countries in the region, the jurisprudence of the Inter-American system on victims is incorporated through the "constitutional bloc" into domestic law, while in others it is highly influential. The Rules of Procedure of the Inter-American Court of Human Rights, in its text in force since November 2009, defines in its Article 2 the "alleged victim" as "the person whose rights protected in the Convention or in another treaty of the inter-American system are alleged to have been violated."[21] Likewise, Article 35 establishes that to submit a case to the Court, the Inter-American Commission must comply with the identification of the alleged victims, and that when it is not possible to identify one or more alleged victims because there are mass or collective violations, the court will decide in due course whether to consider them victims.[22]

The jurisprudence of the Inter-American Court has progressively broadened the scope of the notion of victim and has recognized subjects who were not originally recognized as such.

For example, in the judgment handed down on November 19, 1999, in the *case of Villagrán Morales y Otros (Street Children) against Guatemala*, the Court recognized that the relatives of the minors who were tortured and murdered were also victims in their own right. Such relatives were subjected to cruel, inhuman, and degrading treatment as a result of the heinous crimes allegedly perpetrated against their children by state agents.[23]

The Court has also recognized the rights of indigenous communities as such, not just the rights of individual community members. In its 2016 pronouncement on the subject,[24] the Court held that legal persons like corporations are not entitled to rights under the American Convention on Human Rights, since Article 1.2 of the Convention only establishes rights for natural persons. However, the Court reiterated its recognition of indigenous and tribal communities as well as trade unions as subjects of rights as such. The Court stressed that the violation of those rights has a collective dimension and cannot be limited to effects on individuals.

The jurisprudence of the European Court of Human Rights is less expansive. The Court has consistently held that the Convention does not provide for the institution of an *actio popularis*.[25] Article 34 of the European Convention sets out the definition of victim as including the person or persons directly or indirectly affected by the alleged violation, either because it caused harm or because they have a valid and personal interest in seeing it brought to an end.[26] An association that merely represents the general interests or populations involved, rather than their interest in the specific dispute, does not qualify.[27] Nonetheless, as we'll see shortly, under specific circumstances associations can represent groups of victims.

On the political level, the European Parliament in 2022 recognized that "countries, communities, companies or individuals can become victims of corruption, particularly those involved in efforts to investigate, report, prosecute and try corruption, who are at heightened risk and in need of effective protection[…]"[28] It called on EU institutions to, among other things, "provide support for victims of corruption – individuals as well as communities – so that they can be identified and informed, participate in judicial proceedings and claim and receive compensation for damages caused."[29]

The advent of the International Criminal Court in 1998 also advanced the discussion of victims' rights. The Rome Statute governing the ICC defines victims broadly, as "natural persons who have suffered harm as a result of the commission of any crime within the jurisdiction of the Court."[30] The Rome Statute and its Rules of Procedure and Evidence contain extensive provisions regarding victims' participation at different stages of the proceedings,[31] and (for the first time in an international criminal proceeding) allow for court-ordered reparations.[32] According to the Court, this "reflects a growing recognition in international criminal law that there is a need to go beyond the notion of punitive justice, towards a solution which is more inclusive, encourages participation and recognizes the need to provide effective remedies for victims."[33] These innovations gave rise to a robust debate over the forms and extent to which victims could or should participate in criminal justice, especially in cases where impunity tends to be the norm.[34] It also led to a great deal of thinking about how to provide integral reparations where it was difficult to tie the wrongdoing to specific victims.[35]

In particular, the ICC had to confront the problem of large numbers of potential victims, physically located far from the Court and often unable to speak the Court's official languages. It created an Office of Public Counsel for Victims to represent the interests of victims in proceedings. Multiple victims can choose to be represented before the Court by a Common Legal Representative, so long as the victims share common interests.[36] Victims wanting to participate in proceedings can fill out a questionnaire and be assisted by a Victims Participation and Reparations Section.

Most countries now have some provision for the rights of victims in their national law, often driven by advocacy around domestic violence or terrorism offenses. These can be found in separate "rights of victims" laws, as part of criminal procedure codes, or (rarely) in sentencing guidelines for specific offenses. The range of rights provided to victims varies depending on the legal system, with civil law countries generally having some variant of civil complainant or private prosecutor, and common law countries having provisions for victims to be informed of decisions in the case (including plea bargains, deferred prosecutions, parole or abandonment of the case), to make their views known, and to address the court through victim impact statements before sentencing.[37] The rights of victims must generally be balanced against the due process rights of defendants and other national interests, like national security.

The definition of victim in national law is pretty general and not very illuminating. French law, for example, covers "those who have personally suffered damage directly caused by the offence," which the French Court of Cassation has interpreted in terrorism cases to include those attempting to interrupt or prevent the recurrence of the crime.[38] Canada's Victims Bill of Rights defines *victim* as a Canadian citizen or permanent resident or a person present in Canada "who has suffered physical or emotional harm, property damage or economic loss as the result of the commission or alleged commission of an offence."[39] Canada's recent law on Remediation Agreements (which allow deferred prosecution for bribery and other economic crimes) requires companies to try to identify victims, including where necessary foreign victims, or explain why they can't.[40]

The EU's April 2024 Directive on Asset Freezing and Confiscation (discussed more in Chapter 6) specifically recognizes

> that criminal activities can inflict great harm on victims, [so] it is essential to protect their rights, including the rights to compensation and restitution. Therefore, Member States should take appropriate measures to ensure that victims' claims to restitution and compensation against the person who is subject to a confiscation measure as a result of a criminal offence are taken into account in asset-tracing, freezing and confiscation proceedings, including in cross-border cases.[41]

In the UK, sentencing guidelines provide a broad view of harms specifically in corruption-related cases. They include "[s]erious detrimental effect on individuals (for example, by provision of substandard goods or services resulting from the corrupt behaviour), serious environmental impact, serious undermining of the proper function of local or national government, business or public services, and substantial actual or intended … loss."[42] However, despite this broad language most cases restrict the amount of damages to the amount of the bribe or gross profit.[43] Other UK precedents make it nearly impossible for foreign victims of corruption to participate in proceedings. Not even foreign states can participate as victims, and there is no provision for nonstate actors to present victim impact statements or otherwise outline the harm to them.

Moreover, UK courts have been downright hostile to damage claims involving large-scale corruption. Part of what makes overseas corruption so worthy of compensation is that powerful people often get away with the crimes through complex and secret chains of ownership, transactions, and effects. And yet, UK case law only awards compensation to victims after conviction in cases that are "simple and straightforward" and not in those "where there are real issues as to whether those to benefit have suffered any, and if so, what loss."[44] Thus, perversely, the cases least likely to allow damages requests are those where the bribery is global or widespread, where intermediaries are used, where there is no request from the state where the bribery took place, where there is no proof of an inflated contract or substandard performance, or where it's not clear to whom compensation should be paid. And yet, those are the cases most likely to cause widespread harm.

In the most recent iteration of this perverse result, the SFO (prosecutor) declined to propose, and the court refused to allow Nigeria to intervene as a victim in bribery proceedings against Glencore Corporation for its activities in five African countries. Glencore paid $318 million in fines and confiscated assets to the UK, but the court found that neither Nigeria nor anyone else had standing to request compensation. It was afraid that allowing "representations from the wide range of victims" would pose "a risk of deluging the criminal justice system."[45]

5.3 THE HONDURAN SUPREME COURT RULES

Victor Fernández, the Honduran lawyer for COPINH, was getting anxious. After filing a request to the Supreme Court for constitutional review (known as *amparo*) in November 2019, he had heard nothing. The trial date had been postponed for other reasons, but it was creeping nearer. Once the trial started, the *amparo* request would be moot, and COPINH would be frozen out.

Meanwhile, the situation in Honduras was worsening: the government had closed down the Mission Against Impunity and attacked the anti-corruption unit in the prosecutors' office. The Supreme Court had thrown out charges against ten of the sixteen defendants, and killings and harassment of human rights and environmental defenders continued.

At COPINH's request, international human rights legal groups, including Lawyers without Borders/Canada and Due Process of Law Foundation, filed amicus (friend of court) briefs and wrote repeatedly to the court stressing Honduras' obligations under the American Convention on Human Rights as well as the UN Convention on Corruption. As the day of trial approached with no resolution, COPINH and its supporters picketed the front of the anti-corruption court, calling for the voices of the victims to be heard. The first day of trial, and still no word from the court. The day was taken up with initial procedural and evidentiary skirmishes.

Then, finally, the Supreme Court ruled. For the victims.

The Court grounded its ruling in human rights law, not in the international law on anti-corruption.[46] In particular, it echoed COPINH's argument that ILO Convention 169 on indigenous rights, in particular the right to participation of indigenous peoples in decisions affecting their interests, applied here. It found that COPINH represented the Lenca and other indigenous peoples, who had concrete interests in water and collective property rights, and thus constituted "victims." It referenced the U.N. definition of "victim" as well as Article 8 of the American Convention on Human Rights establishing the right to access to justice, as well as the due process provisions of the Honduran constitution. Citing the Inter-American Court's Advisory Opinion 22/16, it distinguished COPINH from other associations and private entities because it represented an indigenous community. Moreover, the Court argued policy: allowing COPINH to fully participate in the case would not interfere with the administration of justice, but rather provide transparency and objectivity.[47]

It was a narrow ruling, based on the particular collective and territorial rights of the indigenous Lenca and carefully distinguishing the general right of legal entities to be classified as victims, no doubt with an eye toward future cases. The court did not engage with the "directness" of the victims at all. Despite the limits, Victor and his colleagues were pleased, especially with the recognition of collective indigenous rights. The trial court rewound the proceedings to the point when they had been excluded. Doing so allowed a replay, possibly including additional evidence, of pretrial decisions including the dismissal of charges against most of the defendants. The case then reopened against the six remaining defendants, including the head of the state energy company and the minister of natural resources. Three of the six were finally convicted of fraud and falsification of public documents in May 2024. The convictions stem, in part, from the fact that the head of the company constructing the dam was also involved with the electric utility and was therefore able to throw the contract to his company, and that the environmental data was falsified.[48] The victims can now present their proposals for reparations, since the defendants' appeals were exhausted in November 2024. Meanwhile, lawyers for Copinh have gone after the banks that financed the project, including the Dutch FMO and the public Central American Bank of Economic Integration (CABEI) discussed in Chapter 4.

When I asked Victor why they were able to win even in an adverse political and legal climate, he pointed to the broad and assertive indigenous social movement that backed them. "It's clear that there's a different quality to a case when the victims are there – the dam concession affected *their* forests and water. The victims, not the state, are the subjects, and they have a different moral weight." He also pointed out that in conditions of systemic corruption, anti-corruption courts are not exempt from pressure: "the anti-corruption court threw us out of the case, and the constitutional court let us back in."

5.4 AN EMERGING LATIN AMERICAN JURISPRUDENCE

The Fraud on the Gualquarque Dam case is one of a number of recent cases allowing victims to participate in corruption-related trials. Courts have taken two major routes to let victims in: directly linking their harm to the case, or allowing public interest groups focused on anti-corruption to act in the name of the victims, often where law allows representation of "diffuse interests" by such groups. Sometimes, there's an overlap between the two.

5.4.1 *Direct Harm to Victims*

In some corruption cases, the causal link between the corrupt acts and harm to specific plaintiffs is easy to make, and proximate cause is less problematic. The most straightforward involve bribes to judges or prosecutors that affect the outcome, and thus the rights and lives of the parties. Cases involving extortion, with consequent financial and nonpecuniary loss, also can easily be seen as "direct." Beyond that, these are generally cases where a separate tort (civil damages) case would be warranted, but where victims, especially in civil law systems, find it important to join the criminal case for corruption as private prosecutors, partie civile or complainants. This may be based on the need for access to information about the facts, or on a healthy suspicion of the prosecuting authorities (or both), as well as a desire to seek reparations in the fastest and least costly way.

A good example is the "*Once*" ("Eleven") case in Argentina. Leaders of the Ministry of Transportation in charge of running and maintaining commuter trains pocketed the train maintenance budget over several years, leading to dilapidated and unsafe trains. In February 2012, a train crashed, killing fifty-one people and injuring 789. The courts found the state officials guilty of fraudulent administration and sentenced two ex-Ministers of Transportation, among others, to prison.[49] The representatives of various classes of victims of the crash participated in the proceedings.

Another potential example comes from the IGSS/Pisa and IGSS/Chiquimula cases in Guatemala. High-ranking officials in the procurement and head offices of the state's public/private health service (known as IGSS), along with well-connected private operators, received a $2.5 million bribe from medical supply firms for a contract to provide kidney dialysis to some 530 patients.[50] The firms had no existing clinics, knowledge or experience of the procedure, and supplied faulty or inoperative dialysis machines and supplies that caused patients great pain. Infections increased 900 percent; some sixty people died. A group of patients, aided by two civil society groups, brought a criminal complaint. The fraud part of the complaint eventually led to over twenty indictments, including a well-connected son of a judge and a former military intelligence officer who was now head of the governing board of the IGSS. The issue of victims' participation arose when a group of eight former patients accepted the defendants' (inadequate) settlement offer and the lawyers for the victims quit. The trial court ruled that the remaining victims and their family members could not testify or otherwise participate in the proceedings because they had lost their representation, but an appeals court panel reversed, finding that due process required that they be able to present evidence. The defendants were initially convicted of fraud, but the convictions were overturned on appeal under conditions suggesting undue influence on the judges.[51] After the corruption investigation collapsed, family members of the victims tried to restart wrongful death investigations, but apparently to no avail.

Honduras boasts another instance where direct harm is relatively easy to establish. In the Pandora case, corrupt lawmakers and their allies established two phantom foundations to receive international funds, supposedly for agricultural development, especially crop diversification, rural schools and support of young rural mothers.[52] Instead, $11.7 million of the money went to illegally finance political campaigns.[53] Among those charged were former ministers, ex-functionaries of the Agriculture and Finance ministries, foundation heads and elite businessmen. The Honduran Supreme Court in 2020 closed the cases of twenty-two of the twenty-eight charged defendants.

Complainants from the specific municipalities and social groups that were supposed to receive the funds according to the projects financed, argued that they should have a claim as victims, since the diversion of the promised funds defeated their reasonable expectations and left them further impoverished, and their attempt to get redress led to threats, violence and attacks on their reputations, as well as increased youth migration. The Supreme Court, acting on a request from a peasant organization (but without touching on the standing issue) agreed to reopen the closed cases in April 2023,[54] but as of this writing the case is pending. (I'll come back to Pandora in the chapter dealing with reparations).

In these cases, the complainant can sue because of interests that are particular to them, as an individual or a group. They tend to be prevalent in certain fields, including health and land and environmental protection. In the health area, for instance, the COVID-19 pandemic turned up multiple instances of patients dying or getting sicker because the money for ventilators, vaccines or food for those stuck inside was stolen, or the price of medical supplies was jacked up outrageously as part of bribery or kickback schemes.[55] The families of those who died for lack of a stolen or inoperable ventilator or antiviral medication, but who otherwise more likely than not would have survived, should have a claim. In the environmental area, many cases look something like the Fraud on the Gualcarque case described above. Land is stolen using bribes to ministers, Congresspeople, notaries or land registrars, or hydroelectric, agribusiness, forestry or mining projects are approved based on collusion or payments to state officials to accept false documentation and invented "consultations." Those whose land, water, and resources are stolen or degraded through these practices should have an individual or collective claim.

In other cases, the difference between individual or group victims representing their own interests and those representing the more diffuse interests of taxpayers or society at large are less clear. A Mexican case involves bribes in highway construction contracts used to finance political campaigns in the State of Mexico. Senator Emilio Alvarez and Ana Riojas, a member of the federal Assembly, who initially brought the complaint, brought a writ of *amparo* seeking to correct a lower court decision denying them access to the case file as "victims." They cited the evolution of domestic and international law (including UNCAC) to facilitate greater access for victims to criminal proceedings. They pointed in particular to Article 20 of the constitution, which sets out the rights of victims, to Article 108 of the Criminal Procedure Code, and to Article 4 of the Victims Law of 2013, which reads: "direct victims are physical persons who have suffered economic, physical, emotional or general harm or detriment that endangers or harms their legal goods or rights as a result of the commission of a crime or a human rights violation recognized in the constitution or in ratified treaties."[56] Here, the relevant rights violation was the right to be free from corruption. At least one lower court had already agreed with the complainants on the broad scope of who constitutes a victim.[57]

The lower court here treated the issue as one of standing, and found that to seek case participation, the complainants had to show that their rights, or their individual or collective interests, had been affected. The generic interest of society was not enough, there had to be specific individual or group interests at stake.[58] The court then found that simply having denounced the illegal conduct to prosecuting authorities was not enough to convert the complainants into victims. They had not personally suffered physical harm, financial loss or negative impact on a fundamental right as a result of the defendants' alleged crimes – in any case, the entire society was affected.[59] This is a common argument against allowing victims into corruption proceedings, as we'll see in the Medellín, Colombia case involving maternal health and school lunches I discuss later.

The appeals panel disagreed.[60] They found that the definition of victim has changed in Mexican law over time, and that the post-2000 constitutional scheme contemplates a progressive definition of victim, giving victims an equal status to offenders, including with regard to participation in criminal proceedings. The Mexican Supreme Court had earlier found that victims can challenge a prosecutor's failure to indict through *amparo* proceedings, due to the right to reparations that accrues to victims if there is a guilty verdict.[61] The court here found that a broad reading of the rights of victims was necessary given expansive Inter-American jurisprudence and given the growing importance of collective or supra-individual claims. Thus the court used cases coming from human rights law and applied the concepts to corruption.

Once the court recognized collective claims, it was a small step to name the fight against corruption as such a claim, one that therefore any affected member of society could raise. The legislators, the court found, had not only filed a complaint: they had a specific interest in the use of public monies. The court imposed two limits: the complainant must be part of the affected community, and the complainant must actively file a complaint about the alleged wrongdoing.[62] As was true with the Honduran court, the court seemed to be looking for limiting factors to its otherwise very broad ruling. Here, those limiting requirements were easily met, and thus the two legislators were entitled, as victims, to copies of the case file and to full participation in the proceedings.

The Mexican Supreme Court has been of two minds about the issue, depending on the procedural posture of the case. On the one hand, in a case involving administrative proceedings rather than criminal prosecution, the Mexican Supreme Court found that 2016 reforms creating the General Law of Administrative Responsibilities as part of a package of anti-corruption laws changed the role of a complainant from that of a simple spectator to a central participant in the subsequent investigation and proceedings. It thus overruled its earlier negative jurisprudence, citing the Inter-American Commission on Human Rights and anti-corruption treaties to find that where the authorities decide not to open an administrative proceeding despite a complaint, this does not only affect the complainant's desire to see the irregularities investigated – and thus, corruption be effectively fought, as the constitutional reform intended – but also, at the same time, bars the complainant's ability to intervene actively in the proceeding as a third party, able to argue, present evidence and even disagree with decisions that determine the nonexistence of administrative responsibility. Thus, "it is through the complainants that the social controls ('una contraloría social') that overcome the State's inabilities to combat the phenomenon of corruption can be relied on." The complainant is different from a mere bystander and has standing to fully participate in the administrative proceedings against public employees.[63] However, because this is an administrative proceeding aimed at sanctioning the public servant, reparations for the complainant are not available.

Just a few months later, in May 2023, an appeals court hearing a case from Aguascalientes, unanimously upheld a local trial court, finding that "victims of corruption" could indeed participate as parties to the criminal case. The case involved the apparent embezzlement of 140 million pesos (USD $8.2 million) paid by the state legislature to dozens of nonexistent companies. When the legislators didn't investigate the matter, journalists and civil society groups complained to the Prosecutor.[64]

On the other hand, in a February 2023 *amparo* case, the Supreme Court decided that complainants were not per se victims under the Victims' Law and the Criminal Procedure Code. It was not enough to represent the public interest. The victim had to show that they have personally suffered a physical harm, financial loss or violations of their rights; collective victims are defined as groups, communities or organizations whose rights, interests or collective assets have been affected. The Court rejected arguments that the UNCAC provided standing for victims of corruption, finding that the relevant provisions either were not binding, were merely about "prevention," or did not require the ability to participate in a criminal proceeding in order to exercise their rights. Therefore, in Mexico, future arguments about victim standing cannot be based just on the UNCAC treaty or on having filed a complaint.

Because the jurisprudence is as yet unsettled, this decision does not yet create precedent binding on other courts.[65] Moreover, in spring 2024 the Mexican government passed a reform of the *amparo* law that could curtail judges' ability to affect collective interests.[66]

5.4.2 *Civil Society Organizations Representing Diffuse Interests*

A second way of managing victim participation is through their representation by organizations. Many countries' legislation allows public interest organizations standing to intervene in cases involving the interests they represent – including Argentina, Brazil, Ecuador, Peru, Chile, Costa Rica, El Salvador, Guatemala, Paraguay, Uruguay, Venezuela, and Bolivia.[67] Other countries have liberal standing requirements through the application of the ancient Roman principle known as *actio popularis*. Countries that follow this principle typically will allow "any person" to sue the government for its failure to uphold the law.[68] These cases differ from the previous ones because the organizations represent the interests at stake or the public interest, rather than the collective interests of their members (the way COPINH represents the Lenca people).

Thus, environmental organizations can represent the rights of those harmed by pollution or of natural features needing protection, consumer rights organizations the rights of consumers, and anti-corruption organizations can represent the interests of victims in corruption proceedings. The courts refer to collective harms (to a specific group as such) and diffuse harms (to society as a whole or undifferentiated subgroups of people).[69] While most of these laws are geared toward public interest or diffuse or collective interests generally, Argentina's (as of 2009) allows public interest representation in crimes against humanity and grave human rights cases. Costa Rica does so specifically in corruption cases. There, Article 70 of the Criminal Procedure Code defines victims as including "associations, foundations and others, in the crimes that affect collective or diffuse interests, so long as the objective of the group is directly related to those interests." Brazil allows public interest organizations to intervene when the prosecutors' office has not acted by the legal deadline; the prosecutor's office can take control of the case back at any time.

A number of countries allow standing for environmental organizations in cases involving protection of the environment, and such standing is encouraged in treaties like the Aarhus and Escazú agreements, as we saw in Chapter 2.[70] Indigenous peoples and local organizations also act as guardians of natural features like rivers and mountains in the emerging jurisprudence around the rights of nature, in which "legislatures, courts, or voters in [New Zealand], Australia, Colombia, Ecuador, Bangladesh, India, Uganda, and the U.S. have declared that rivers and other living systems have legal rights."[71]

Indeed, litigation around climate and environment may prove a fruitful source of inspiration and caselaw on diffuse interests, public interest standing, and the required causal connection between the corrupt acts and the harm. For example, in the *Neubauer* v. *Germany* case brought by young activists to push Germany to accelerate its climate-related emissions reductions, the court held that the fact that climate impacts will affect virtually all persons living in Germany did not prevent the young plaintiffs from being affected in their own right, and therefore meant that they had standing to sue.[72] Other courts have accepted the rights of children and of future generations as sufficient to confer standing in climate-related cases.[73]

The European Court of Human Rights, as we've seen, takes a narrow view of who is entitled to victim status. With regard to organizations, the Court has allowed standing only under certain circumstances. Where an association was formed specifically to defend the legal rights of its members in the dispute under consideration, the ECHR found that:

> the term "victim" in Article 34 must also be interpreted in an evolutive manner in the light of conditions in contemporary society. And indeed, in modern-day societies, when citizens are confronted with particularly complex administrative decisions, recourse to collective bodies such as associations is one of the accessible means, sometimes the only means, available to them whereby they can defend their particular interests effectively. Moreover, the standing of associations to bring legal proceedings in defence of their members' interests is recognized by the legislation of most European countries. That is precisely the situation that obtained in the present case. The Court cannot disregard that fact when interpreting the concept of "victim." Any other, excessively formalistic, interpretation of that concept would make protection of the rights guaranteed by the Convention ineffectual and illusory.[74]

Thus, associations and groups can be victims, but there must be a tight link between the association's purposes and the object of the litigation. Most recently, the Court found that an association formed to defend the human rights of its members against the threats arising from climate change in Switzerland (where a significant portion of members were older women particularly vulnerable to heat-related illnesses) had standing because it was "genuinely qualified and representative to act on behalf of those individuals who may arguably claim to be subject to specific threats or adverse effects of climate change on their life, health, well-being and quality of life as protected under the Convention," even though the individual victims themselves might not have victim status.[75]

The cases known as "Ill-Gotten Goods" (*Biens Mal Aquis*) in France gave new impetus to the push for organizational standing in corruption proceedings. In that case, the civil society organizations Transparency International and Sherpa denounced the political leaders of Equatorial Guinea, Congo, and Gabon and their families for their participation in acts of grand corruption connected with assets stolen from their countries and now located in France. The French Court of Cassation (the highest court in criminal matters) decided that organizations have standing to represent these interests, as they have been specifically affected as anti-corruption organizations. Article 2 of the French criminal procedure code requires a showing of damages to be classified as a victim and to be able to act in the criminal case. The acts of corruption reported were considered sufficient to generate personal and direct effects on the complainant organizations, and therefore to give them participation in the criminal trial even without specific authorization from the legislature.[76] Eventually, Teodorín Obiang, the son of Equatorial Guinea's president was stripped of his six-story Paris mansion (complete with disco, hammam and gold water taps), among other goods.[77]

Belgian law starting in 2019 allows NGOs to file cases when their corporate purpose is violated. The first case using this new provision involved a passport scam in the Democratic Republic of the Congo. Three NGOs, along with fifty-one individual victims, in 2020 joined an already-open investigation that had stalled out. Belgian company Semlex had apparently been a party to a kickback scheme that inflated the price of a passport for Congolese citizens, netting then-president Kabila and his cronies up to $35 million. Shortly thereafter, the new DRC government said it would not renew Semlex' contract.[78]

In Spain, "popular action" theoretically gives broad standing to reputable public interest groups to participate in cases that involve their interests. In human rights cases, including the investigations of the Argentine and Chilean militaries that resulted in the arrest of Chilean dictator Augusto Pinochet, such groups could persuade an investigating judge to move forward even without the support of the state prosecutor, at least at the time. However, in corruption cases, the Supreme Court has been more restrictive, making such popular actors in effect subordinate to the prosecutor.[79] Moreover, courts can require a bond to cover any future costs incurred; this understandably discourages potential complainants, especially nonprofits without big budgets. For example, the Spanish judge demanded a hefty bond in a case involving Nervis Villalobos, a former Venezuelan Vice-Minister of Energy apparently implicated in a multimillion-dollar embezzlement of funds from the national oil company who fled to Spain and eventually confronted criminal charges for money laundering. This made it impossible for a Spanish anti-corruption group to intervene, and the judge then proceeded to reject the most serious charges in the case.[80]

5.4.3 *Latin American Experiences with Diffuse Interests*

In Medellín, Colombia, a civic organization called Todos por Medellín (All for Medellín) was outraged to find that local officials were stealing funds from nutrition programs that serve poor and vulnerable communities. The former education secretary of Medellín, Alexandra Agudelo, and two more people are accused of embezzlement from a program, called "good beginnings," for pregnant and lactating women and preschool and school lunch programs for poor students. Over time, officials allegedly siphoned off US$6.2 million from these programs, replacing nutritious food with less healthy meals, reducing portions, serving spoiled food, neglecting family and group visits, and the like. The schoolchildren and their families, represented by Todos por Medellín and eighteen individual mothers, are complainants in the case. It is part of a larger set of complaints about corruption in school lunch programs; as of January 2022 the *Contraloría* (state auditor) was investigating 144 cases around the country of overcharging, kickbacks, undue influence, noncompetitive bidding, and other problems worth millions of dollars.[81]

"Long before we went to court, we started talking to people and other organizations and mapping local community actors. We had to build confidence," Juan David from Todos recounted. "We also started pulling together different datasets, using everything from overarching government plans to contracts, to surveys asking local people about how nutrition programs for their kids had changed. We held a march in front of the mayor's office holding empty plates, which got a lot of social media coverage."

Under the jurisprudence of the Colombian high courts, those harmed by a crime are a broader group than the "victim"; while the former have suffered some kind of harm as a result of the crime, the victim is the object of the criminal act. Both can be civil parties. Article 132 of Law 906 (2004) defines victim as a natural or legal person who individually or collectively has suffered some harm as a consequence of the action at issue. There needs to be a real, concrete and specific harm, which does not have to be pecuniary or property-based and can be exclusively concerned with obtaining justice or information. It is not enough to file a complaint about illegal action; individual or collective harm is required.[82] The Constitutional Court has found that the inhabitants of Bogotá were "abstract collective victims", in a case involving corruption in public works contracting in Bogotá.[83] In addition to participation in criminal cases, Colombia allows individuals and groups, including the Procuraduría (state attorney) to bring "popular actions" to take preventative action against potentially damaging government decisions, including those affecting diffuse interests.

On November 20, 2023, I listened to the hearing as the judges of the 10th Criminal Circuit Court of Medellín heard arguments in the case. The key issue was whether Todos por Medellín, and the mothers and children affected by the loss of funds, could be considered victims for purposes of participation in the proceedings and eventual reparations. The initial trial judge had ruled that they could. There was some doctrinal basis for this decision: in 2002, the Constitutional Court had ruled that in some cases, victims or those who had been harmed (*perjudicados*) might legitimately participate in a case even if the material damages were small, or the harm was diffuse, because they had an interest in establishing what happened and finding out who was responsible, and that constituted a real, concrete and direct interest. This was most likely to happen, the Court added, in cases involving crimes against public morality, the public purse, or collective rights. "The principle of dignity impedes that human beings … can be reduced to an economic calculus of their worth."[84]

Lawyers for the defendants objected. They argued that just because the organization had filed a complaint didn't make them direct or indirect victims, that the damages were unspecified, and that in any case Todos por Medellín had been formed months after the events at issue, and that was too late. Lawyers for the victims, the prosecutors' office and the Procuraduría (state attorney) supported the designation as victims of both the organization and the individual mothers. They told the judges that human rights law supported a broad definition of victim, that their participation was not based on filing the complaint but on concrete (if not yet proven), tangible and intangible harms that are specific to them. Both sides cited the public participation law,[85] which according to defendants created a limited list of public participation options in corruption cases, not including intervening in a criminal trial. According to the Todos por Medellín lawyer, the list was open-ended, included the ability to "make use of legal actions and petitions as needed to effectuate social control [over governmental action]," and the organization was acting as a "social auditor" (*veeduría*) able to intervene in public hearings in the cases and conditions set by law.

In February 2024, the court ruled against Todos por Medellín, finding that it would upset the balance between defense and prosecutor to have a third party involved, and that existing norms did not authorize the intervention. Therefore, the organization was unable to continue as part of the case.

In Argentina, the courts have held that civic anti-corruption organizations may access the case file so long as the subject matter is one related to their purpose and doing so does not implicate privacy concerns of the parties or reveal details of prosecutorial strategy. In a case popularly known as "Bribes in the Senate" the Argentine courts prosecuted former president de la Rúa and other high-ranking government officials for politically-related bribery.[86] Two anti-corruption NGOs petitioned to intervene, seeking access to the case file. The Buenos Aires federal court found that organizations defending collective interests are in a position analogous to those of an individual victim with respect to their legal interests. They are, at the least, potential victims of the crimes. Given that, regulations limiting access to the case file to prosecutors and parties were not absolute and had to give way to the interest in openness and public access that underlay Argentina's (then recent) procedural reforms. While not formally "complainants" with the ability to intervene, the groups could access the case file in order to provide a check on prosecutors. Their interest was limited to the court documents in the case and did not extend to personal information about the defendants.

A different Argentine case directly connects access for anti-corruption organizations to a human rights rationale. An anti-corruption group (Fundación Poder Ciudadano) acted as criminal complainant in a corruption case involving hundreds of phantom jobs that the La Plata National Technological University allegedly set up as part of a fake contract with the state. The defendants objected that the law only allows civil society groups to intervene as complainants in cases of crimes against humanity or grave human rights violations.[87] The law at issue deals with cases of death, torture and forced disappearance arising from the "dirty war," not with corruption, they argued. The trial court, and then the Federal Court of La Plata (2nd Chamber) disagreed, finding that since corruption affects a wide range of human rights including health, education, access to justice, dignified housing and the organization was set up to deal with corruption and would be affected, the requirements of the statute were met.[88] As a complainant, the organization could participate in the proceedings, call witnesses, and make sure that the case moved forward.

Poder Ciudadano now represents societal interests in three other cases. One involves the investigation of a high-ranking Buenos Aires official for illicit enrichment and money laundering based on his luxurious lifestyle. The same judge as in the earlier case allowed Poder Ciudadano into the case as a complainant, because crimes against public administration "affected the collective interests that the organization defends."[89] Other cases involve phantom jobs in the provincial legislature, and stealing from a jobs and social welfare program; It also tried to get admitted as *amicus curiae* (friend of the court) in a corruption case under initial investigation. The case involved kickbacks from sales to the Venezuelan government from Argentine firms; the trial judge had been trying to get information from Venezuelan authorities through mutual legal assistance, to no avail. Poder Ciudadano and Transparencia Venezuela, working together, created a dossier with the available information and tried to get it into the record informally. The judge, thanking the organizations for their work, accepted the information and named the organizations as "collaborators of the tribunal," able to provide otherwise unavailable information. (despite the informal path from Venezuela to him).[90]

In neighboring Chile, a clean government, anti-corruption organization, Fundación Ciudadano Inteligente (Intelligent Citizen Foundation), brought complaints against several lawmakers under the Chilean Criminal Procedure Code, which allows anyone to bring a criminal complaint if they are locally based, against crimes allegedly committed by a public official that affect personal rights guaranteed by the Constitution or that affect public probity.[91] One complaint targeted then-sitting senator Jaime Orpis. The gist of the complaint was that Orpis had taken bribes from a large fishing company, Corpesca, to the tune of $2 million Chilean pesos a month, which he used to finance his political campaign. In return, he used his seat on the relevant committee to insert pro-Corpesca provisions into the Fisheries Law then being discussed. A local judge accepted the Foundation's complaint, and active role in the criminal process, in August 2015.[92] Orpis was convicted in April 2021 and sentenced to five years and a day in prison, a fine and a prohibition on holding public office. The bribing corporation, Corpesca, was also convicted, fined, and ordered to publish part of the judicial decision detailing its crimes in a local newspaper.[93]

Peru, on paper, has a broad view of organizational standing. Article 94 of the Criminal Procedure Code defines the aggrieved person as anyone directly harmed by the crime or negatively affected by its consequences. The definition thus goes beyond those who are directly harmed to those who suffer economic, moral or other harm as a result of it; while the two are usually the same, this is not always so, and the courts have recognized that those who are injured or affected by a crime may become civil parties.[94] It goes on to consider organizational standing: Organizations may act as affected parties "in crimes affecting collective or diffuse interests that injure an indeterminate number of persons, or in offences included as international crimes in the international treaties approved and ratified by Peru," provided that their corporate purpose is directly linked to those interests and they have registered as organizations prior to when the alleged crime was committed.[95] The Constitutional Court of Peru has found that, indeed, the fight against corruption constitutes a diffuse interest, and that individual and diffuse interests can both be at stake in a given case.[96]

Nonetheless, in practice, it has been hard to get prosecutors and judges to allow organizational standing for anti-corruption groups. Take the Kuskachay Association, an established anti-corruption group that asked prosecutors under Article 94 to participate in a case involving extortion and bribe-seeking by local government. The diffuse interest at stake was that of effective public administration, and they met the requirements since they had suffered diffuse harm and were legally registered. The prosecutor refused, on grounds that only the State was a victim of corruption, and that the State's representatives were designated by law and were the only ones who could complain.

The Association went to the courts, but a first-instance court threw the case out on grounds that the investigation was still preliminary and so within the total control of the prosecutors' office. Review by an intermediate court, aided by several letters from international experts, led to a partial victory in August 2024. The court found that the organization could challenge the prosecutor's decision, but that the court couldn't directly tell prosecutors what to do at this stage of the proceedings, only order them to reevaluate the earlier denial. On the substance, the court used the distinction between the entity that owns the legal interest that has been harmed or put at risk, and whoever is affected or harmed by that unlawful act. The Association had indeed suffered harm, and its interest needed to be considered so that it could "contribute in good faith with clarification of the facts, which will substantially aid prosecutors' work," and therefore exclusion was a due process violation.[97]

Article 4 of the Mexican National Law for Victims provides that "groups, communities or social organizations can be considered as victims when they have been affected in their collective legal rights, interests, or assets resulting from the commission of a crime or violation of rights."[98] Nonetheless, despite the openness we saw earlier to individual complainants representing the public interest, Mexican courts have been less willing to accept organizations, especially in high-profile cases where the apparent purpose of the intervention is to avoid a sweetheart deal between defendants and prosecutors.

For example, the prosecution of former Veracruz governor Javier Duarte – believed to have stolen up to US$35 million and (at the least) allowed impunity for murders of journalists and others – resulted in a plea bargain that greatly reduced the charges and led to a relatively short nine-year sentence, given the gravity of the crimes. TOJIL, an anti-corruption NGO, claimed that the short sentence reflected a sweetheart deal based on bribes to prosecutors, and asked for an investigation. They also asked to be accorded victim status in that investigation. A lower court initially agreed, based on arguments similar to those above, but an appeals panel reversed by a vote of 2 to 1, the majority finding that the complainants had not shown that they had suffered any legally cognizable harm, that providing information was an adequate way of participating, that there was no right to live in a corruption-free society, and that a human rights organization could only claim victim status if its members had been harassed or threatened as a result of their actions.[99] For dissenting judge Lilia Mónica López

Benítez, human rights could be both individual and collective, and in the case of collective rights anyone harmed by their violation should have a right to sue. She cited Supreme Court jurisprudence on the evolving rights of victims in criminal cases, and argued that those broad rights applied to collective victims like those represented here. TOJIL has asked the Inter-American Commission on Human Rights to take the case; it is still studying admissibility.[100]

In another emblematic case, the prosecutors' office refused to let the same organization intervene in the criminal case against former PEMEX (Mexican oil company) official Enrique Lozoya for grand corruption, a case connected to the Odebrecht bribery scandal.[101]

In short, courts are slowing opening the door to claims by victims, based on human rights considerations, but are obviously concerned about opening the door too wide and are searching for limiting factors. These to date include specific treaty obligations (as with ILO 169) or status as complainants in the case, not just interested parties. How much of a limit these limiting factors actually become is still a work in progress. But the earlier vision of the state as the only victim has been left behind.

5.4.4 *Who Represents Civil Society? Law and Criteria*

Organizational standing begs the question: which organizations should qualify? After all, organizations run the gamut, from highly prestigious, competent and transparent to fly-by-night, "GONGOs" (government-backed fake organizations masquerading as civil society, sometimes known as "astroturf" groups) to NGOs backed by or allied with organized crime groups. On the other hand, if the government puts in place an accreditation process, won't it necessarily favor groups close to the government, or at the least not known as troublemakers for the party in power? Who is to choose, and based on what criteria? Who minds the minders?

France has pioneered an approach. French criminal procedure already had organizational standing for other interests as varied as animal rights, cultural heritage and the protection of the French language. As of 2016, the French Criminal Procedure Code provides that groups (including foundations recognized as being of public utility) in existence for at least five years, whose bylaws constitute them as fighting corruption, may be civil parties in cases involving statutes penalizing corruption, money laundering and electoral financing-related crimes. The Council of State is to fix the conditions under which they can participate.[102]

Accordingly, the government created an accreditation system that allows designated NGOs to directly refer corruption offenses to independent judges, without going through prosecutors. This accreditation has to be sought and may be renewed every three years by the Minister of Justice. Only three NGOs have held such an accreditation: the French branch of Transparency International, Anticor, and Sherpa. In 2023, the Paris Administrative Tribunal denied Anticor's reauthorization without explanation, despite (or perhaps because of) its extensive litigation on the subject, including a case involving the then-Minister of Justice. It took months of intense lobbying and media campaigns for the Prime Minister to override the decision and reinstate the authorization. Sherpa was also temporarily denied reaccreditation, which impeded it from acting in a major case where it had long been an intervenor.[103] Thus, although the five-year-in-existence requirement limits the number of suspect groups who might seek intervention to obtain access to the case file or torpedo a case, government accreditation can easily be manipulated to quash or pressure legitimate actors who become overly enthusiastic, or where an organization has internal disagreements that find their way into the public sphere.

The European Court of Human Rights, in the Swiss climate change case discussed above, set out criteria for an organization to have standing in climate change cases, many of which would be relevant more generally:

> the association in question must be: (a) lawfully established in the jurisdiction concerned or have standing to act there; (b) able to demonstrate that it pursues a dedicated purpose in accordance with its statutory objectives […]; and (c) able to demonstrate that it can be regarded as genuinely qualified and representative to act on behalf of members or other affected individuals within the jurisdiction […]. In this connection, the Court will have regard to such factors as the purpose for which the association was established, that it is of non-profit character, the nature and extent of its activities within the relevant jurisdiction, its membership and representativeness, its principles and transparency of governance and whether on the whole […],the grant of such standing is in the interests of the proper administration of justice.[104]

In Brazil, Article 5 of the LACP (law on public civil actions) establishes standing to file class actions for associations that are over one year old and whose objectives involve the protection of either public or social patrimony, the environment, consumers, economic order, open competition, the rights of racial, ethnic or religious groups, or artistic, aesthetic, historical, touristic, or scenic patrimony.[105] Peru restricts standing to organizations that existed before the events at issue took place.

Guidelines to promoting legitimacy of those representing collective interests in corruption cases, then, turn on a sustained period of activity before the events in question took place, formal identity as an anti-corruption group in the bylaws or articles of incorporation or association, and a determination that the group represents those interests in a concrete case. One might also look toward transparency in the organization's financing and donors, periodic outside evaluations of probity and the like, as ways of guaranteeing legitimacy and avoiding fake or questionable organizations getting access to sensitive files. To avoid excessive political or policy interference, governments might find ways to create distance between the accreditation function and political interests, delegating the process to an independent agency at a national or supranational level, making an appeals process both transparent and speedy, or making decisions less discretionary.

As we've seen, many organizations seek to participate or intervene in corruption cases because they want access to the proceedings and files and the ability to present evidence and to challenge decisions when they seem unwarranted. But victims generally also want representation in order to obtain reparations, whether in criminal, civil or administrative/forfeiture proceedings. This raises another set of complexities. In cases where organizations with expertise and interest in fighting corruption represent victims, should they be the ones to receive and/or distribute compensation for social harm? Should reparations be paid directly to the organization, on grounds that it has acted as a "private attorney general" and should be compensated for the time and risk involved, and to encourage others to weed out corruption? That is the theory, for example, behind citizen suits and False Claims Act cases in the United States. Are there specific rules needed to ensure that recoveries for victim representatives accrue to victims, at least in part, while also allowing organizational plaintiffs to recoup their costs and fees? Eventually, negotiations on these issues will be required.[106]

In the end, one reason states are reluctant to grant standing and access to victims is that they worry about having to pay reparations. I take up the issues involved in reparations in anti-corruption cases in Chapters 6 and 7.

6

Giving It Back

Transnational Asset Recovery and Repurposing

From a human rights perspective, remedying grand corruption requires getting the assets returned and used for the benefit of victims. It's not easy to do: of the $788 million that the Brazilian construction company Odebrecht paid in bribes, the company returned $184 million to the Dominican Republic as part of its plea bargain with the US, Brazil and Switzerland, and $19.5 million to Peru.[1] In addition, the Swiss found in their banks and returned $365 million to Brazil in 2019.[2] The US returned $686,000, proceeds from the sale of a Maryland house that former Peruvian president Alejandro Toledo bought in 2007 with his share of Odebrecht bribes.[3] Additional assets are still frozen in Panama, Mexico, Switzerland, Spain, Andorra and the UK, according to the World Bank's Stolen Asset Recovery (StAR) database. There's probably more waiting to be repatriated. Much of the money will never be found.

It's not surprising that crooks and kleptocrats would want to stash their loot in rich countries, with their more stable economies, investment and consumption opportunities, and bank and corporate secrecy. It's also not surprising that rich country banks and other enablers have wanted to keep their secretive but well-off customers happy, no matter how shady their money. Nor is it surprising that a wide range of actors has looked to recovered stolen assets as a source of funds to combat enormous challenges such as climate change, poverty, and disease outbreaks.

What perhaps surprises a bit more is how the asset return panorama has shifted over the last decade or two, driven by the end of the cold war, the activism of African countries and civil society groups, and anti-money laundering efforts triggered by the "wars" on drugs and terrorism. This shift has come in phases. At first, asset-receiving governments simply deposited any confiscated stolen assets or proceeds of bribery into their national treasuries, with no consideration for where the money had been stolen from. A second phase saw no-strings-attached returns to some of the source countries. A third and current phase involves the return of ill-gotten gains not only to the countries they were stolen from, but to specific uses in those countries aimed at the people who should have benefited from them in the first place. Internationally, a series of principles, experiments and innovations model what could be done to return stolen funds fairly and sustainably, as well as where some of the minefields lie. This chapter focuses on cross-border and international efforts, while the next one raises some of the debates and dilemmas of national reparations for grand corruption.

6.1 THE EVOLUTION OF CROSS-BORDER ASSET RECOVERY

Until recently, most stolen assets were shielded by bank secrecy laws in Switzerland and other financial havens and by governments who saw no objection (and maybe advantages) to dictators finding safe haven in their luxury enclaves. Moreover, the dictators had usually been supported – or even installed – by major powers, so criticizing their kleptocracy seemed at best impolite if not counterproductive. Fallen dictators routinely took their millions abroad, where they lived in golden exile. For the most part, their assets were never frozen, much less confiscated or returned. Fulgencio Batista of Cuba in 1959, Mobutu Sese Seko of Zaire (now the Democratic Republic of Congo) in 1979, and dozens of others took their millions with them. Some still do.

A set of notorious cases in the 1980s began to shine a light on the connected nature of corruption, human rights violations, and stolen assets stashed abroad. All three cases involved Switzerland, long the poster child of bank secrecy and complicity in plunder. Haitian dictator François Duvalier ("Papa Doc") passed the office of president (for life, starting in 1957), and much of his wealth, to his son Jean-Claude ("Baby Doc"), who finally fled Haiti in 1986 and took up residence in France after a wave of mass protests against his fifteen-year misrule. The new Haitian government asked Switzerland to freeze some of his millions while they produced evidence that the funds were ill-gotten, but never followed up. The Swiss government could do little without criminal charges filed in Haiti. By 2009 a Swiss trial court decided that, despite the lack of legal action, the frozen assets should be used for social or humanitarian projects to benefit the Haitian people, but the family objected. The Swiss Federal Supreme Court agreed with them, finding that without more evidence, $5.7 million had to be returned to the Duvaliers. The resulting outcry, especially after an earthquake devastated Haiti the next day, pressured the Swiss government to override the decision. Two legal problems in particular needed changing: the Swiss could only act on the basis of requests from Haiti, but what if the Haitian government was uninterested, overwhelmed or otherwise unable to pursue the stolen assets? Also, the statute of limitations on disposition of frozen assets was too short, given the difficulties in proving illicit origin when high officials were involved.

Ferdinand Marcos and his wife Imelda fled the Philippines for Hawaii, chased out in 1986 by the "people power" revolt after years of rights violations and embezzlement estimated as between $3.5 and $5 billion. The incoming reform administration created a Commission on Good Government (PCGG) to investigate the Marcos' corruption and try to get the stolen assets back. In addition to its work within the Philippines, the Commission almost immediately filed a request to freeze Marcos' assets in Switzerland. The Swiss government, embarrassed by the exposed complicity of Swiss banks with blatant looting, agreed. To confiscate the funds, however, Swiss law then required a criminal conviction from the national court of the country where the ill-gotten gains were stolen from, which became impossible after Marcos died in 1989. The law was finally changed (in 1995) to allow a civil judgment to suffice. In 2003, the Philippines Supreme Court found that the assets were subject to civil forfeiture since the couple could not have amassed the reported $680 million in Swiss banks on a civil servant's salary. The Swiss then returned the money, which was used to fund agrarian reform and reparations to victims of human rights violations.[4]

In 2011, the Arab spring uprisings in Egypt, Tunisia, and Libya also laid bare the shortcomings of the asset recovery regime. The Mubarak, Ben Ali and Khaddafi families all had assets abroad, and were widely believed to have stolen millions. The new governments requested return of the assets, but Swiss law again proved inadequate. Having learned from the Duvalier experience, the Swiss government proactively froze the assets of the former rulers involved and their entourages without waiting for requests for mutual legal assistance from the countries in question. It could only do so, however, as an emergency measure based on the government's constitutional right to safeguard Switzerland's interests.[5] The law was still not up to the task. The same problems that plagued early Swiss law were also true, to one degree or another, of other asset-holding states.

The question of what to do with the proceeds of corruption and organized crime became more urgent with the rise of anti-money laundering (and antiterrorist financing) laws, aimed at stopping drug profits from spreading into the rest of the economy. These laws required banks (but not others who dealt with potentially shady money) to "know their customer" and gave rise to treaties and, separately, a coordinating body (the Financial Assets Task Force or

FATF) that established anti-money laundering standards. Over time, more tainted money was confiscated and collected.

Another stream of potential assets came from companies and individuals accused of bribing foreign officials to swing business to them. The FCPA in the US, and analogous laws eventually framed by the OECD Anti-Bribery Convention, led to prosecutions of private bribe-givers. Very few of these cases, anywhere, ever went to trial – it was too hard, too expensive, too time-consuming. Instead, governments developed variants on abbreviated proceedings, deferred or conditional prosecution agreements, or other mechanisms that allowed companies to pay fines and settlements without trial, and often with limited acceptance of responsibility so long as they promised to do better in the future. The upshot was a growing revenue stream: some $25 billion in the US, considerably less elsewhere. But if the harm was not only to competitors but to the people of the country where the bribery took place, why should the US or the UK treasury keep the benefit, especially if their oversight of corporate activities had manifestly been inadequate? The discussion turned to repatriation and repurposing.

6.2 ANTI-CORRUPTION LAW ON ASSET RETURNS: UNCAC'S CHAPTER V

Early anti-corruption law focused on criminalization, not asset recovery or return. Neither the FCPA nor the 1997 OECD Bribery Convention mention the subject. The 2009 OECD Recommendation on Bribery of Foreign Officials has a single mention, tucked into the international cooperation section: "cooperate … [by] upon request, [the] provision of evidence, extradition, and the identification, freezing, seizure, confiscation and recovery of the proceeds of bribery of foreign public officials."[6] The 1996 Inter-American Convention against Corruption merely allows a state that confiscates the proceeds of corruption to share them with another state that helped in the investigation. The 2003 African Convention on Preventing and Combating Corruption talks about freezing, confiscation and repatriation of stolen assets, but without elaboration.

Chapter V of the 2003 UNCAC deals with asset recovery. It covers everything from "know your client" rules to investigations, freezes, confiscation and return of assets. The underlying conduct must be prohibited in UNCAC, and also be a crime for which confiscation is a penalty in both the sending and receiving states, carried out by public officials or private actors performing a public function (like executing a government contract).[7] But although it sets out different ways that assets can be returned and stresses cooperation among states, UNCAC for the most part assumes that the requesting state will take the initiative to get its money back. Assets must be finally (with no pending appeals) confiscated in the state where the asset is located, either through enforcement of an order of confiscation from the requesting state or confiscation in the host state on the requesting state's request. (Confiscation based on money laundering charges does not need a requesting state, however.)

UNCAC also works through an Open-Ended Intergovernmental Working Group on Asset Recovery, established at the first meeting of the parties.[8] In its latest reports, the Working Group found that challenges to implementing chapter V abounded, led by lack of legislation allowing the return of assets, their preservation during the return process, insufficient financial controls and inability to identify politically exposed persons, no provisions for non-conviction based forfeiture of assets, and no ability to give effect to foreign orders for confiscation.[9]

Article 57 provides for both mandatory and priority (but discretionary) asset returns. Under Article 57(a) and (b), returns are mandatory, but only if there's a final confiscation judgement from the requesting state. In addition, 57(a) only applies to embezzlement of public funds or laundering of such funds by a public official, while 57(b) covers a wider range of offenses, but only where the state requesting the return of confiscated assets can prove prior ownership or show pecuniary damages. In all other cases (and this includes situations in which the recovery action is initiated by the destination state or by a third party rather than by the state that suffered harm at the hands of corrupt officials) the Convention sets forth that states should "give priority consideration to returning confiscated property" to the requesting state, to prior legitimate owners or to compensation of the victims. The upshot is that most asset returns depend on voluntary agreements among states, usually through an informal Memorandum of Understanding. While states strive to act consistently with the spirit if not the letter of Article 57, some major asset returns have not followed its provisions but have relied solely on national law.

The UNCAC structure assumes that the state the assets were stolen from wants to get them back from the people who stole them, but that's not the case if the thieves or their family and friends still hold power (formally or informally), as in cases of grand corruption. Thus the requirement of a final confiscation order in the home state becomes problematic in cases of grand corruption except when those who stole the money are already gone from power. The requested state can waive the requirement where a final confiscation order cannot be obtained due to the death, flight or absence of the offender "or in other appropriate cases." These might include sweetheart deals, immunities or the lack of adequate laws, especially around non-conviction based confiscation.[10]

Discretionary return under 57(c) allows for self-initiated confiscation by the host state party. Assets located outside the territory of the host state can also be returned. Importantly for grand corruption cases, the United States (and a few other states) have broad forfeiture jurisdiction, including over assets located outside the US that are proceeds of foreign public corruption-related crimes and that used the US banking system to launder the funds. This was the basis, for example, for a return of funds stolen by former Nigerian president Sani Abacha and found in Jersey and the UK, sent to the US under an asset-sharing agreement, and then returned to Nigeria.[11]

In 2007, The World Bank and the UN Office on Drugs and Crime jointly created the StAR initiative to deny safe haven to stolen funds and encourage their timely return to legitimate owners. StAR works to improve coordination between financial centers and states requesting return of their money, to train prosecutors and regulators, and to affect policy debates on asset recovery within the context of the UNCAC. The US Justice Department chimed in with its own Kleptocracy Asset Recovery Initiative in 2010, and since then has beefed up its asset recovery operations, including through a special Ukraine/Russia focused taskforce (called Operation KleptoCapture), a rewards program, legal reform initiatives to make asset freezing and confiscation easier, and cooperation with allies including a REPO (Russian Elites, Proxies, and Oligarchs Task Force). Other countries have similar initiatives, many driven by sanctions against Russia.

All this set the stage for thinking not only about repatriation of stolen assets, but about the purposes and destinations of funds within the requesting states. Simply returning the money to the government in countries with long-standing systemic corruption, no questions asked, risks it being re-stolen or used to perpetuate in power the very people who set up the kleptocratic system. On the other hand, putting conditions on returning money is tricky, raising concerns about sovereignty as well as administrability. States have tried a number of strategies to balance these concerns, foremost among them specifying the uses of the returned funds, building in anti-corruption contracting and auditing rules for their use, and involving external actors and local civil society groups in distribution and monitoring. It's here that a human rights-based approach adds value.

6.3 SOFT LAW APPROACHES TO ASSET RECOVERY

The 2016 publication of the Panama Papers[12] showed that London, and British Territories such as Jersey and the Cayman Islands, were major centers for tax evasion and money laundering. Embarrassed, UK Prime Minister David

Cameron invited major leaders to a December 2017 anti-corruption summit, even while remarking privately to the Queen that two of the countries invited, Afghanistan and Nigeria, were "fantastically corrupt." (President Buhari of Nigeria, according to press reports when Cameron's remarks were leaked, agreed with that assessment).[13] Summit participants agreed to more transparency around beneficial ownership of companies and properties, greater scrutiny for lawyers, accountants and realtors, and to a Global Forum for Asset Recovery (GFAR) that, in Cameron's perhaps unintentionally ironic words, would focus on "getting stolen assets returned to people like President Buhari and President Ghani [of Afghanistan], so they can be reinvested in the future of their countries."[14]

As part of GFAR's implementation, governments along with the World Bank agreed to a statement of Principles for Disposition and Transfer of Confiscated Stolen Assets in Corruption Cases.[15] Among general calls for partnership between transferring and receiving countries, dialogue, transparency, accountability, and preclusion of benefits to offenders, the Principles contained several provisions relevant to the form and beneficiaries of asset return. Principle 5 reads: "Where possible, and without prejudice to identified victims, stolen assets recovered from corrupt officials should benefit the people of the nations harmed by the underlying corrupt conduct." Along the same lines, "consideration should also be given to encouraging actions which fulfill UNCAC principles of combating corruption, repairing the damage done by corruption, and achieving development goals." Most important for future actions, Principle 10 reads:

> To the extent appropriate and permitted by law, individuals and groups outside the public sector, such as civil society, non-governmental organizations and community-based organizations, should be encouraged to participate in the asset return process, including by helping to identify how harm can be remedied, contributing to decisions on return and disposition, and fostering transparency and accountability in the transfer, disposition and administration of recovered assets.

A coalition of European civil society groups subsequently proposed their own Principles for Responsible Asset Recovery in 2020.[16]

Starting in 2015, the African Union's Special Declaration on Illicit Financial Flows called for the return of stolen assets to fund the continent's development agenda, tying asset recovery to development programs. The 2020 Common African Position on Asset Recovery encompasses stolen artwork and natural resources as well as tax evasion, and stresses the need to investigate, preserve, manage, and return assets to African states. It proposes transparency, monitoring of return processes, and "ensuring greater involvement of civil society and the media in accountability processes, in accordance with domestic laws, and enhanced international coordination and cooperation in this area."[17]

The 2022 Recommended Principles on Human Rights and Asset Recovery from the UN Office of the High Commissioner for Human Rights details some of the links between anti-corruption and human rights, including shared underlying principles, the need for societal participation and remedy, due process for alleged offenders, and cooperation obligations of both requesting and requested states in asset recovery cases.[18] Two principles are particularly relevant here: Principle 7 states that [r]eceiving States should allocate returned assets in an accountable, transparent and participatory manner. Principle 8 specifies that receiving states should use such assets in a manner that contributes to the realization of human rights. In addition, the UN Independent Expert on the effects of foreign debt and other related international financial obligations of States pulled together a "Non-binding set of practical guidelines for efficient asset recovery" in 2023 that stresses that assets include not just the product of bribery or embezzlement but also of tax evasion and other such practices, and calls for states to apply "the underlying principles that underpin human rights: international cooperation and assistance; equity and non-discrimination; participation; and access to information" in freezing, confiscating, maintaining and returning stolen assets.[19]

6.4 NATIONAL LAW OF STATES WHERE ASSETS ARE OFTEN LOCATED

National laws in many states likely to hold stolen assets are moving toward greater accountability to the populations of the countries from where they were stolen in returning these assets, albeit slowly and hesitantly. Recent legal reforms in some places have aimed at implementing the GFAR Principles; for others, like France, reforms were triggered by the earlier inability to use the assets of people like Teodorín Obiang (the Equatorial Guinean heir and minister whose French assets were then in the process of being confiscated) for the benefit of Equatorial Guineans. Pressure built for better return mechanisms. Thus, a new generation of laws explicitly links returns to development programs, reparations or improvements in combatting impunity. They specify accountability and transparency measures, and seek to balance sovereignty, accountability and due process for putative asset owners. And, most importantly, they increasingly recognize the important role to be played by civil society groups in proposing and monitoring the use of funds. In other words, they are moving toward a human rights-based approach.

The UK, on paper, has extensive rules including 2018 General Principles to compensate overseas victims (including affected States) in bribery, corruption and economic crime cases.[20] The General Principles "aim to ensure that overseas victims of bribery, corruption and economic crime, are able to benefit from asset recovery proceedings and compensation orders made in England and Wales. Such victims could include affected states, organizations and individuals." They direct state prosecution authorities to consider the question of compensation and use all available mechanisms to get it, including confiscation, sentencing at a criminal trial, Deferred Prosecution Agreements, or support for civil cases. Prosecutors are to work with the Foreign and Home Offices, the UK aid agency and the treasury to identify potential victims of corruption, assess the case, obtain evidence, ensure a fair and transparent process, and "identify a suitable means by which compensation can be paid to avoid the risk of further corruption." A subsequent Guidance makes clear that authorities should consider these issues early in the case, and that to qualify for an award, victims will have to prove their identity, the amount and type(s) of harm, and that the harm resulted from the offense in question.

In England and Wales, these Principles were accompanied by a 2017 intergovernmental agreement, further modified in 2022. Known as the Principles for Transparent and Accountable Asset Return, the Principles suggest (but do not require) consultation with civil society organizations on

> the likelihood of funds being put to use as agreed by the central government and which organisations in the country may be best placed to deliver programmes or projects in the country if required. Domestic CSOs can provide a link between [the government] and CSOs in the recipient country, who may provide valuable insight into the circumstances of that country.[21]

The UK government requires that an agreement with the receiving country include provisions on how the money will be spent, due diligence regarding the receiving agency, and allows for the possibility that the funds can be directed to funding a project abroad rather than to the central treasury. It may also provide for third-party monitors on spending, including CSO monitors funded by the returned assets. Thus, the Principles attempt to balance the receiving country's sovereignty interests with the sending state's concern that the money not simply be stolen again. Of course, if the relevant prosecutors are overworked and underfunded (as by all accounts they are), and judges are unwilling to engage with asset return in complex cases (which they also are, as described in Chapter 5) then these provisions will remain nice words on paper.

In practice, it has been difficult to get money to victims even when assets are frozen or confiscated. According to an analysis by Spotlight on Corruption,[22] very few cases have actually applied these Principles. One impediment is the Proceeds of Crime Act[23] which requires a showing that the offender has benefited from their criminal conduct. But proving that the benefit arose from conduct that resulted in a conviction can be difficult. Civil forfeiture is also possible but has similar causation problems. Unexplained Wealth Orders, which reverse the burden of proof on whether funds are in fact of illegal origin, should make it easier to overcome these difficulties, but have not been very effective. In part, this is because they allow suspects to show that the wealth was generated legally under the laws of the country where the income arose, which is pretty easy to do if you (or your family or friends) control the levers of that state.[24]

France's Restitution Law 2021-1031 allows for return and repurposing of assets confiscated for corruption (but not before). French law allows foreign states to participate in confiscation proceedings in France or to ask for recognition of a judgment abroad. But what about cases (like Obiang's) where the foreign state has no interest in getting the assets back? In the past, the assets simply went to the French treasury. The new law, in Article XI, requires that the proceeds of the sale of assets confiscated from persons with a definitive conviction for corruption-related offenses "are returned, except for legal costs, at the most local level possible to the population of the foreign State concerned, where the court ruling concerned has established that the initial offence was committed by a person holding public authority of a foreign State."[25] According to a recent Redress report, "[t]he proceeds from the sale of the confiscated property are allocated to a specific State budget programme dedicated to the restitution of ill-gotten gains… The funds are ringfenced from the French government's general budget, and subject to Parliamentary oversight."[26]

If possible, the money is to be allocated in agreement with the government where the funds were originally stolen, but if that can't be done (or there are no diplomatic relations with that state) within two years, "the funding can be used for cooperation and development actions directly benefiting the populations concerned, particularly via actions where civil society organizations in the country concerned are counterparties, in accordance with best practices for transparency and traceability of the use of the funds."[27] There are provisions for local consultations on needs, for choosing partners, and for a monitoring committee, to meet quarterly, which includes representatives of both requesting and requested states, the implementing organization, and "one or more representatives of the local population in the country of origin, based on criteria of representativeness, independence and probity and on the sectors of activity of the cooperation and development actions." There are also transparency provisions for projects and audits, a commitment that no funds will go to any associate of a person whose assets were confiscated, and an ability to use some of the funds to train local monitors.

The EU in April 2024 updated a 2014 directive dealing with freezing and confiscation of assets related to organized crime.[28] The new directive recognizes some of the difficulties involved in tying assets to specific offenses, at least in the context of organized crime, and creates multiple pathways for freezing and compensation in response. It requires states to initiate asset-tracing as soon as an investigation is opened in cases where the offense likely will give rise to substantial economic benefit, and allows for immediate freezing of assets in danger of disappearing.[29] In addition to proceeds stemming from a criminal offense, the directive allows for "extended confiscation" in situations where "the offence committed is liable to give rise, directly or indirectly, to economic benefit, and where a national court is satisfied that the property is derived from criminal conduct." How should such a court decide? According to Article 14, "account shall be taken of all the circumstances of the case, [...] such as that the value of the property is disproportionate to the lawful income of the convicted person." Even without a conviction, Article 16 allows for confiscation of unexplained wealth "derived from criminal conduct committed within the framework of a criminal organization and that conduct is liable to give rise, directly or indirectly, to substantial economic benefit." The definition of a criminal organization is broad enough to encompass participants in a grand corruption scheme.[30] Evidence of unexplained wealth may include the discrepancy between lawful income and the value of the property, the lack of a plausible licit source of the property; or that the affected person is connected to people linked to a criminal organization. This loosens substantially the causal nexus required for confiscation. The rest of the directive obliges states to create asset recovery and asset management offices, plans and procedures, to cooperate with each other, and to gather statistics on asset recovery.

As we've seen, early cases involving Swiss banks set the stage for the emergence of a purpose-driven approach to asset return. In large part due to that experience, the Swiss Foreign Illicit Assets Act of 2016[31] considers situations where cooperation with the state authorities of the home state is inadvisable or impossible. It allows freezing assets over which foreign politically exposed persons or their close associates have power of disposal or are beneficial owners in two scenarios. First, in anticipation of future cooperation with a new government, assets may be frozen where the government or certain members of the government of the country of origin have lost power, or a change in power appears inexorable; the level of corruption in the country of origin is notoriously high; it appears likely that the assets were acquired through acts of corruption, criminal mismanagement or other felonies; or the safeguarding of Switzerland's interests requires the freezing of the assets. Second, assets may be frozen in situations of total or substantial collapse or impairment of the country's judicial system, or where cooperation proves impossible due to procedural shortcomings.[32] Such assets may be confiscated without a request from the home state.

Switzerland has also pioneered an approach to freezing and confiscation that creates a rebuttable presumption that assets are of illicit origin where

> the wealth of the individual who has the power of disposal over the assets or who is the beneficial owner thereof increased inordinately, facilitated by the exercise of a public function by a foreign politically exposed person, and the level of corruption in the country of origin or surrounding the foreign politically exposed person in question was notoriously high during his or her term of office.

"Inordinate" is defined as "a significant disproportion, inconsistent with ordinary experience and the prevailing circumstances in the country, between the income legitimately earned by the person with the power of disposal over the assets and the growth in that person's wealth."[33]

Regarding asset return, the law provides that restitution should be made "to improve the living conditions of the inhabitants of the country of origin, or to strengthen the rule of law in the country of origin and thus to contribute to the fight against impunity." Restitution should be done through the financing of programs of public interest, set out in agreements between Switzerland and the country the funds are returned to, or if that is not possible, the Swiss government may return the forfeited assets through international or national organizations. Agreements for asset return shall, "to the extent possible … include non-governmental organisations in the restitution process."[34]

The United States has repatriated the greatest amount of assets. The US generally uses both civil (non-conviction based) forfeiture, which gives *in rem* jurisdiction over assets located in the US, and criminal jurisdiction based on money laundering through the US financial system. Surprisingly, there is no mandatory set of rules about asset returns; indeed, the US Senate took the position that UNCAC implementation did not require further legislation on this point. Therefore, US actions are based on three programs not specific to foreign public corruption.[35] First, the Attorney General, through the Department of Justice's Kleptocracy Asset Recovery Initiative (a specialized prosecutors' unit focused on confiscation and return of stolen assets), has extremely broad discretion to transfer forfeited assets "to any foreign country which participated … in the … forfeiture of the property."[36] When the assets are going to a foreign country, the DoJ must cooperate with any other states involved and, when over $25 million is involved, must get approval from the State Department and notify Congress. This international sharing allows up to 100 percent (but usually up to half) of the forfeited assets to be returned to a foreign government as a reward for its collaboration in bringing the case to fruition.[37]

Second, the US Department of Justice can decide to order remission in cases where there is a direct pecuniary loss resulting from the crime, or restoration if there are court-mandated restitution orders, and can also "take other actions to protect the rights of innocent persons in civil or criminal forfeitures that are in the interest of justice and that are not inconsistent with the provisions of the statute."[38] Remission to private parties is most often used in private fraud or theft cases, and does not generally extend to indirect or consequential damages. In money laundering cases, remission may extend to the victims of the underlying crime. Remission to the government can be accomplished even where the assets have not, or could not be, confiscated in the requesting state. It can also be subject to conditions like disbursement in tranches, audits, or civil society monitoring, on a case-by-case basis.

In 2021, the Biden administration declared the fight against corruption to be a national security issue. Officials pledged to "hold accountable corrupt individuals, transnational criminal organizations, and their facilitators, including by, and where appropriate, identifying, freezing, and recovering stolen assets through increased information sharing and intelligence collection and analysis, criminal or civil enforcement actions, advisories, and sanctions or other authorities, and, where possible and appropriate, returning recovered assets for the benefit of the citizens harmed by corruption."[39] Despite this pledge, to date Congress has not taken up legislation to modernize and specify the terms of international asset return, so it remains case-by-case and discretionary.

Canada's laws on asset freezing, confiscation and recovery were passed in June 2022 as amendments to the existing Special Economic Measures Act (SEMA) and the Justice for Victims of Corrupt Foreign Officials Act (Sergei Magnitsky Law). It applies to

> circumstances where an international organization of states or association of states of which Canada is a member calls on its members to do so, a grave breach of international peace and security has occurred, gross and systematic human rights violations have been committed in a foreign state, or acts of significant corruption involving a national of a foreign state have been committed.

A judge may order property (broadly defined to include financial as well as real property) seized, frozen and, for the first time, eventually forfeited.

The law applies to individuals who "control" property (broadly defined), with no requirement that the property be tied to a specific criminal act.

> After consulting with the Minister of Finance and the Minister of Foreign Affairs, the Minister may … pay out … the net proceeds…, but only for any of the following purposes: (a) the reconstruction of a foreign state adversely affected by a grave breach of international peace and security; (b) the restoration of international peace and security; and (c) the compensation of victims of a grave breach of international peace and security, gross and systematic human rights violations or acts of significant corruption.

Under the Magnitsky Law, the "proceeds of forfeited property will only be paid out for the compensation of victims of gross human rights violations rather than the reconstruction of a foreign state or restoration of peace and security."[40] In December 2022 the law was used for the first time, to seize $26 million from Russian oligarch Roman Abramovich, to be used for the reconstruction of Ukraine.[41] While the seizure did not publicly specify which ground of SEMA was applied, Abramovich has long been accused of making his fortune through shady means, and of supporting Putin and his associates economically.[42]

Of course, some stolen asset havens have much less law on asset returns. And laws don't necessarily translate into practice. Most returns continue to be ad hoc and case-by-case despite the crop of recent laws. Confiscation of property that is tied to corruption elsewhere is still difficult to prove and problematic in national law, especially if the home state is uncooperative or unable to assist (even leaving aside due process concerns). Many countries, for instance, don't have a specific asset recovery agency that can help not only with seizure of assets but adequate administration and maintenance, or a civil forfeiture law, or well-funded and trained prosecutors interested and with the resources to pursue stolen funds.

6.5 RETURN AND REPURPOSING: FOUR MODELS

As we've seen, the current law and policy on returns of stolen assets specifies the intended uses of the assets to support human rights, rule of law or other social goods, and declares the intent to avoid having them re-stolen. Some precursors made specified uses for returned assets more palatable. In 2010, BAE Systems (a UK company) agreed to pay approximately US$37 million to settle a case of alleged bribery in the sale to Tanzania of an outdated and redundant military air traffic control system; the money went to bolster the country's education system. In a case involving payoffs to Kenyan and Mauritanian officials by a small UK printing company to obtain government contracts, the sentencing court declined to order compensation, saying that there was no official request from Kenya and no specific nexus to the crime. However, late in the case an anti-corruption campaigner wrote to the authorities asking that the funds obtained by fines and confiscation be used to benefit Kenyans. As a result, the UK prosecuting authority on its own decided to use some of the money to buy seven ambulances for use in Kenyan health centers and give additional funds to the World Bank to use for projects in Mauritania.[43]

Since then, asset returns have taken four paths: create a purpose-built entity in the country to receive, administer and monitor the funds; use government agencies but with outside (international or civil society) monitoring; rely on established international organizations; or use multilateral funds set up to receive and distribute confiscated assets. I consider these in turn.

6.5.1 *Purpose-built: The BOTA Foundation Example*

One of the more creative transnational asset recovery and repurposing examples comes from the Swiss-US prosecution of James Giffen and his company. Giffen ran an oil consulting business that advised the government of Kazakhstan on oil prospecting concessions. According to the US DoJ, Giffen and his company diverted about $70 million in fees from oil companies into his own secret accounts, and then used some of the money to bribe high-ranking Kazakh officials, including the then-president and prime minister, to keep throwing business his way. In 2003, Giffen was arrested and charged with violating the US Foreign Corrupt Practices Act. Swiss authorities also went after Giffen for money laundering. Eventually, Swiss and US investigators collaborated, finding the secret accounts as well as lots of expensive jewelry and other luxuries. Giffen eventually settled the case, leaving at least $84 million (plus interest) from his frozen Swiss bank account to be recovered. As part of the settlement, the federal court stipulated that the funds should not be returned directly to the Kazakh government for fear of re-stealing, but should be used for social benefit, and be disbursed by a third party with involvement of the World Bank.[44]

The Bank didn't want to take on the task directly, nor did the governments involved. Instead, they negotiated with the Kazakh government to create a new Kazakh nongovernmental organization, the BOTA Foundation.[45] The Foundation worked between 2009 and 2014 to "improve the lives of vulnerable children and youth suffering from poverty in Kazakhstan through investment in their health, education, and social welfare."[46] (The word "bota" means camel cub, appropriate for a child-centered mission.) After concluding that there was no local nongovernmental organization that could safely manage the amounts of money involved, the World Bank contracted two international development NGOs (IREX and Save the Children) to run it. With World Bank support, a governing Board composed of five independent Kazakhstanis and representatives of the US and Switzerland oversaw the Foundation's work over more than five years. The Kazakhstan government approved programs and budgets but did not control the funds, which were doled out twice a year by the Foundation's Board after evaluating the programs' performance. The foreign governments and the World Bank had to sign off on programs, which slowed everything down (and increased administrative costs) but also provided some assurance and legitimacy.

The Foundation established three programs: Conditional Cash Transfer, Social Service, and Tuition Assistance. The cash transfer program delivered regular cash payments amounting to about 30 percent of a minimum income to four categories of beneficiaries within poor households: those with preschool aged children, children with disabilities, women with infants up to the age of six months, and young people aged 16–19 who had completed school but not yet found employment. In exchange, the families had to participate in preschool education, health and training programs. By the end of the Foundation's life, it had served nearly 150,000 beneficiaries using local NGOs and volunteers. The social service component provided grants to local NGOs to work on maternal and child health, preschool education, child protection, and youth services programs. The tuition assistance program, as the name suggests, gave grants to cover tuition and living expenses for poor students at the Kazakhstani university of their choice; after 2011, it focused on ensuring that existing college students had the funds to actually graduate. Students were expected to remain in good standing and to do community service. Over the life of the Foundation, it gave out 841 grants.

Most reports agree that the BOTA Foundation was a qualified success: It served more people than originally planned, it kept kids in school and improved child welfare, it gave lots of local professionals exposure to effective social welfare programming, and it was done with tight controls and very few instances of corruption or conflicts of interest.[47] The choice of child and maternal welfare as the overarching goal made it hard to object to (or politicize) the Foundation's work, and in its operations it worked hard to balance regional and ethnic tensions. Over time, employment in Foundation-related programs shifted from majority-foreigner to majority

Kazakhstani. On the other hand, no domestic entity stepped up to lead, or to continue the work of the Foundation when the funds were spent, and there was no explicit government commitment to continue the programming; the US and Switzerland actually wanted the funds spent down as quickly as possible. There were also no funds allocated to support domestic anti-corruption or similar efforts.

Moreover, creating an entity from scratch, installing multiple audit and oversight systems, and mobilizing personnel and volunteers throughout the country – all without involvement by state agencies – was a monumental undertaking, not clearly replicable in many countries even given the availability of funds. The political circumstances were also somewhat unique: then-President Nazarbayev had insisted that the Swiss investigate a political rival's bank accounts but was caught when his own secret accounts surfaced. The US DoJ's investigation clearly tied him and other top leaders to the bribes, and Nazarbayev and his government wanted to rehabilitate their image to attract foreign investment. The World Bank, while refusing to administer the project, served as "honest broker" in part due to its then-president's desire to showcase innovative anti-corruption initiatives. All of which makes successful imitators more unlikely.

6.5.2 *Citizen Monitoring: The Abacha Funds and MANTRA*

The easiest way to return funds, of course, is simply to send them back to the state; the problem then is ensuring that they're not re-stolen or used for the pet vanity projects of those in power rather than aimed at the vulnerable. For example, Nigeria at one point lost about 40 percent of its natural wealth to corruption and corruption-related mismanagement,[48] which came out to about $40.9 billion lost through illicit financial flows between 2001 and 2010.[49] A series of governments embroiled in corruption has made it difficult to return assets even once they're found.

An early iteration of the return of looted assets from former Nigerian dictator Sani Abacha didn't leave much room for optimism. The US and UK had agreed to return some $155 million in looted assets stashed in the UK, but Nigeria wanted to give nearly $100 million of those funds to Kebbi state Governor Abubakar Bagudu.[50] Bagudu had years earlier been accused of laundering some $163 million in state funds (he returned the money and charges were dropped). The US objected, and the money stayed in the UK. The Swiss, however, returned money, initially without oversight or conditions. Between 2004 and 2010, some $700 million was returned to the Nigerian government, which promised to spend it on health, education, roads and other infrastructure. The money was folded into the regular budget; eventually, the World Bank was commissioned to monitor it, but had a hard time distinguishing returned assets from other money after the fact and so couldn't say how much of the funds had been spent. Unofficial monitors and the Bank both found that funds had been used to cover budget shortfalls on existing projects, and that half the proposed projects were never completed, suggesting misappropriation.[51]

A second tranche of funds recovered in the US and the UK (Jersey) was used to build three specific road and bridge infrastructure projects already approved by Parliament. A 2016 Memorandum of Understanding between the UK and Nigeria[52] declares that

> the Participants attach great importance to ensuring returned assets are used for the benefit of the people and that the Participants therefore decide that returned funds will be used in line with the budget of the Federal Republic of Nigeria for Projects that will impact on the poorest segment of society, and to improve access to justice for all Nigerians.

Nigeria committed to transparency in contracting, anti-corruption safeguards, and a monitoring body including federal government officers and CSO representatives with expertise in engineering, anti-corruption and anti-trafficking, to be chosen by the existing procurement authority. Nonetheless, observers worried about the integrity of the procurement system in a notoriously corruption-prone sector and the lack of consequences for noncompliance.[53]

The Rev. David Ugolor lives in Benin City near the Niger Delta, where he ministers to a congregation and is the executive director of a group focused on environmental and poverty-related issues in southern Nigeria. Ugolor is enthusiastic, crinkly eyed, gregarious, the type of person who seems to know everyone – and he knows a lot of people – on a first name basis. Since 1995, his organization (the Africa Network for Environment and Economic Justice, known as ANEEJ) has pushed for the repatriation of assets stolen by Nigerian government officials and their cronies, and for better international guidelines on how to avoid repeated misappropriation, improve transparency and accountability and focus asset returns on the poor. "When we started," he told me,

> we pushed for an MOU between the US and Nigerian governments that granted us access to contracts and plans for how to the money was to be used. We got access to some but not all. The government said that returned assets should go into a presidential discretionary fund and be distributed among different tribes and contractors, not based on victims' losses. So we decided to get more engaged.

The third tranche of returned funds totaled $322.5 million, the bulk of it Abacha's looted money found in Switzerland. Now, however, the US, UK and Swiss supported civil society proposals that the money should be spent on monthly cash transfers to poor and vulnerable people; the government agreed. It signed an agreement with ANEEJ to coordinate civil society monitoring of the disbursement. Thus, in 2018, the Monitoring of Recovered Assets in Nigeria through Transparency and Accountability (MANTRA) project was born. It eventually covered thirty-two Nigerian states and lasted through 2021.

MANTRA was funded by foreign aid and worked through a network of 118 civil society partners and 700 individual citizens on monitoring recovered funds across the country. It surveyed beneficiaries, followed up on complaints and verified data from state and federal officials. It found that the beneficiaries were indeed from the target population, but there were complaints that money was late and/or some had been skimmed off; these decreased over time. In addition, the project helped the government finalize regulations on dealing with returned assets, and occasionally intervened to ensure that monies were actually used for the poor: In Bayelsa State, for instance, returned assets initially budgeted for new judges' offices were assigned instead to the health sector.[54] All in all, the returned money benefited over a million people. The MANTRA model also included extensive media coverage, training of local groups to monitor government agencies, and lobbying for greater transparency of funds.

By assuming a monitoring but not planning or disbursement role, the civil society organizations gave up a measure of control over implementation in exchange for a lower administrative burden and responsiveness to government concerns about sovereignty and conditionality. This model only worked because there was adequate funding for the civil society monitoring portion and a strong civil society that could demand accountability, as well as a government keenly aware of the need for the country to clean up its image.

6.5.3 *Using Existing International Organizations: The Uzbekistan Return*

A third option uses existing UN and/or bilateral aid agencies to hold and employ funds from asset returns. There's a precursor here too: the £4.4 million (approximately US$5 million) recovered as a result of shady oil deals in Chad, one of the poorest countries in Africa. The wife of the deputy chief to the Chadian Mission in the US bought a block of shares in a Canadian oil company, which inflated in value under suspicious circumstances. The oil company paid a fine in Canadian proceedings, but in the UK, prosecution focused on the sale of the shares, and resulted (after much litigation) in an order to confiscate their value. The money was turned over to the UK's aid agency to be used for the people of Chad. In turn, the aid agency sent the bulk of the funds (£3.1 million) to UNICEF and the World Food Programme to fund nutrition and food assistance, while another £1.1 million went to COVID-related funding and £200,000 to the International Committee of the Red Cross for emergency assistance. According to the UK government, the funds benefited some 150,000 people, while minimizing the UK's administrative burden.[55]

A variant on this model governs the return of at least $131 million stolen from Uzbekistan by Gulnara Karimova, daughter of the country's former strongman. The funds were found and frozen in Switzerland in 2012, derived from bribes Karimova got for steering telecommunications contracts to certain companies. They are part of a much larger haul of at least $715 million still frozen in various jurisdictions, as criminal cases wind their way through the courts. (In 2022, a Swiss court refused to confiscate some $303 million, on grounds that although Karimova clearly had influence through her father, that didn't make her a "public official" under bribery law.)[56] In 2020, the two states signed an agreement that the return would be transparent and subject to monitoring, used to improve living conditions and invested in projects which support sustainable development, and would feature the "potential involvement of non-state actors."

As a result, the Swiss and Uzbeki governments agreed in 2022 to create a multiparty fund known as Uzbekistan Vision 2030 Fund for return of the money. The fund is governed by a management council of UN, Uzbek and Swiss representatives and administered by the UN Development Program. UNDP is disbursing the funds through UN agencies including the UN Population Fund, UNICEF, and the World Health Organization. The Fund includes a civil society council with mostly national members, whose job is to advise the management council. The money is to be used to advance the Sustainable Development Goals through "improving living conditions, strengthening the rule of law or fighting impunity."[57] The Fund, which began operations mid-2022, decided to focus at first on maternal and infant mortality and rebuilding schools. A strong anti-corruption component will be incorporated across all programs and projects.[58] It is specifically not to be used for large infrastructure projects or political proselytism, or for the benefit of those connected to the bribery.

While these provisions are clearly superior to either keeping the money in Switzerland or returning it without conditions (as France did early on with $10 million of the Karimova loot), they are also less detailed and less rigorous than the return of the Abacha funds. The aims of the fund and the monitoring provisions are quite general, and the UN has a checkered history of accountability for administering large amounts of money (see the billion-dollar 2005 Iraq oil for food scandal,[59] or the more recent corrupt practices at UNOPS,[60] for example) and high administrative overheads. The civil society advisory committee is apparently handpicked by the management committee (which means a preponderant role in practice for the Uzbek government, which knows the players better) and besides giving its opinion does not seem to have a monitoring or accountability role. Civil society groups have protested that project implementing agreements have not been made public, that the conflict of interest policy is inadequate, and that vague assurances about civil society involvement leave too much to a still-captured government.[61] The advantage is that no new bureaucracies need be put into place and so getting benefits to the target populations can be quicker and easier; the drawbacks include the possible confusion of foreign aid with restitution of assets (which according to the GFAR should be kept separate), and the potential lack of transparency and accountability. It is also possible that if this becomes a common practice it will negatively impact other sources of voluntary funding for the UN implementing agencies.

6.5.4 *Beneficial Trusts, International Criminal Tribunals, and Asset Return*

A fourth option might involve the creation of a trust fund where the beneficiaries are the people of the country whose assets were stolen, or a subset of them. A constructive trust could hold the assets for the benefit of the country's population, and return them according to either requests or proposals from local groups or a stipulated set of priorities agreed to by victims, CSOs, and states. Here, the experience of the international criminal tribunals might serve as a useful precedent.

After World War II, none of the defendants at the International Military Tribunal at Nuremberg lost their assets as part of the criminal sentence: In subsequent trials held by the occupying US military in Germany, the industrialist Alfred Krupp was ordered to forfeit property before trial, but the order was later rescinded.[62] As Daley Birkett has written, while subsequent international criminal tribunals have generally had the ability to impose fines and forfeitures and to seize assets, they've done it very few times. In part, the tribunals have been hobbled by a perception that they can only act where property-related crimes (like pillage) have been charged, or where there is a clear nexus between the assets and specific criminal conduct.

The International Criminal Court allows for a broader connection to the crimes: it contemplates both fines and "forfeiture of proceeds, property and assets derived directly or indirectly from that crime."[63] It can ask state parties to identify, trace, freeze and seize a suspect's assets, property or instrumentalities of crime at the pretrial stage, even without an arrest warrant, so long as the action is "in relation to investigations or prosecutions."[64] Despite the broader language, the ICC has done very little in this sphere. It has imposed a fine in two cases, one of which was reversed on appeal (on other grounds).

Most reparations paid to victims have come through the ICC-related Trust Fund for Victims. Confiscated assets and fines are to be deposited in the Trust Fund, but in practice this has happened rarely, in part because the ICC lacks resources to investigate defendants' wealth. In one of the few cases where a defendant had obvious wealth, the Court froze the assets, but then allowed the defendant to use them to pay his lawyers and returned the rest to him.[65] Only four cases had ordered reparations from defendants as of 2021, and in none have sizeable amounts been collected; most often, defendants have been found indigent. Rather, the Trust Fund has engaged in a range of reparatory activities both ordered by the Court and on its own initiative, funded by donations from member states and individuals. The Trust Fund was established by the ICC's Assembly of States Parties, and has a five-person Board (one member from each geographic region where the Court works), an Executive Director and a Secretariat.

The UN has a number of such voluntary Trust Funds, including for victims of torture, human trafficking and violence against women. They all suffer from insufficient funds from only a few countries to enact a broad mandate. An agreement to return assets could create a country-specific fund, a regional fund, or some combination. A trust fund could also look more like an escrow account, a place to park forfeited assets for distribution based on a negotiated set of instructions using a combination of existing guidelines, but where implementation would not have to be reinvented each time.

In the case of Venezuela, the UN set up a humanitarian fund using state assets that were frozen in the US, Europe and elsewhere as a result of country sanctions. When it became clear that Maduro would not be leaving power soon, the US and its allies proposed the fund as a way of ameliorating the desperate economic situation in Venezuela without giving the money directly to the government. Eventually, the Maduro government agreed. The $3 billion in Venezuelan assets currently frozen by sanctions overseas will finance programs in health, education, food security, and electricity.[66] The fund got caught up in issues around shielding creditors as well as in fluctuating political negotiations but started operating at the end of 2023.

The UN Fund relies on frozen state assets. A group of Venezuelan-Americans proposed in addition using assets confiscated in criminal or civil forfeiture proceedings from individuals associated with the Venezuelan government accused of corruption in US courts. There are over sixty such cases, and the amount of assets involved could top $1.5 billion. Legislation to create a Venezuela Reconstruction Fund is pending in the US Congress. It would use forfeited assets to support human rights, democracy promotion, independent media, and anti-corruption activities, including through support of civil society.[67] I asked María Alejandra of the Venezuelan Asset Recovery Initiative about why a separate fund was needed. "I believe the proceeds from corruption should be administered separately, to fulfil the GFAR principles, and because with a Fund that has to publicize its accounts we can effectively monitor them and exercise citizen accountability," she told me.[68]

6.5.5 *When No Return Is Possible*

Venezuela is one of a number of countries where (for now at least) money cannot be returned easily to the country it was stolen from – at least without it being stolen again. In the Equatorial Guinea context, for example, the funds confiscated from Teodorin Obiang in the US ended up donated to the international COVID-19 vaccine organization COVAX, to be used for the benefit of Equatorial Guineans, because the ministries and even non-governmental groups allowed to operate in the country were not independent of the ruling family.

One way of dealing with that problem would be to focus on refugees and diasporas. In cases of grand corruption, as we have seen, there are almost always accompanying economic disasters and pervasive human rights abuses. These cause significant outflows of people "voting with their feet" as well as more traditional refugees. As early as 1939, Sir Robert Jennings already attempted to establish the responsibility of refugee-generating States to pay for the costs of large numbers of refugees moving elsewhere, and refugee advocates have long looked to recovered assets as a possible source of funding for resettlement.[69] Especially in situations where there is no good way to send the funds home, creative uses outside the country might focus on the diaspora. In Equatorial Guinea, for example, Tutu Alicante and others have proposed using confiscated funds to pay for university and graduate study abroad for the next generation. More broadly, confiscated funds could support education, social services or livelihood generation for those forced to flee, thus providing a further incentive for states where stolen assets are located to act diligently. On the other hand, recovered stolen assets should not be used to avoid the international responsibilities of refugee-receiving states under existing international law.

Any distribution of funds on a large scale raises difficult issues about defining the target population, setting priorities, avoiding duplication of efforts, and ensuring effectiveness and accountability for the use of funds. These issues have arisen in national reparations efforts focused on war, forced labor, and other serious human rights violations. I take up the lessons learned from these efforts, and how they might apply to reparations in grand corruption cases, in Chapter 7.

7

Reparations for Victims of Grand Corruption

Applying a Human Rights Framework

The courtroom was full on August 20, 2020, for the sentencing of Arnoldo Medrano. For the last twenty-six years, Medrano had been the mayor of Chinautla, a municipality of some 140,000 in central Guatemala famous for its terracotta pottery. He was also, according to multiple corruption investigations into his family, the head of a criminal syndicate that doled out fake contracts and jobs and received kickbacks to the tune of at least $US67 million. Judge Pablo Xitumul read out the charges: fraud, money laundering and illicit association (what in the US would be called racketeering), including fake roadbuilding and housing schemes. He was sentenced to twenty-nine years in prison, a $3 million fine, and $8 million in civil damages. Fourteen other people were also convicted.

Judge Xitumul then did something unusual in a corruption prosecution. He declared that, according to Guatemalan law, reparations were to be "integral," which meant that they should include "the restoration of the right affected by the crime, which begins with recognizing the victim as a person who is the subject of rights [...] and also the available alternatives for their social reintegration [...] and, if applicable, the compensation of the harms stemming from the crime."[1] Therefore, he continued, they should include guarantees of nonrepetition. He ordered Medrano to affix a large plaque to a prominent location outside City Hall. It was to read: "the Town of Chinautla has zero tolerance for the corruption and impunity of public employees and officials."[2] In addition to the plaque, the former mayor was to publicly apologize in the town square to the people of Chinautla, promising never to do it again. The apology was to be videotaped and written and video versions were to be distributed to the local schools, media, and the Association of Municipal Governments. The local justice of the peace was to witness and confirm that these acts were carried out, with additional criminal charges to follow from noncompliance.

Pablo Xitumul is, admittedly, a rather unusual judge. Of Maya Ach'i heritage, he grew up dirt-poor in the countryside with eight siblings. He worked from a young age, and before becoming a lawyer had worked in a sawmill and a textile plant, as a bricklayer, and managing a McDonalds. He studied law because the late-afternoon classes allowed him to work during the day. He was a public defender before becoming a Justice of the Peace and eventually a judge. When the High-Risk Courts were organized to centralize sensitive cases (see Chapter 3) he jumped at the chance to join them.

Xitumul is stocky and never smiling in photos. In private, he's funny and loves to compose music and sing. He's also an expert on international criminal law, writing his doctoral dissertation on the International Criminal Court. This knowledge came in handy when he was part of a three-judge panel called to decide two seminal cases: the genocide case against former military strongman Efraín Ríos Montt in 2013, and a 2018 torture and forced disappearance case against the former army chief of staff and the head of military intelligence. The latter case was especially notable because former intelligence head Hector Callejas y Callejas was widely known as a link between sectors of former military intelligence operatives and organized crime.

Xitumul was also no stranger to corruption cases: he had sentenced former Vice President Baldetti in the "magic potion" case involving a fraudulent contract to clean up water pollution in a local lake, which I also discuss in Chapter 3. He told me that the holistic view of reparations in Guatemalan law tracks the broad view in human rights and in international criminal law, and that the cooptation of state institutions for corrupt purposes "not only violates human rights but could in some cases be considered crimes against humanity. In Chinautla, for instance, people were knowingly left without water for weeks at a time due to fraudulent contracts." (I discuss the link between corruption and crimes against humanity in Chapter 9.) For his troubles, Xitumul has been attacked on social media, assaulted, suspended from his job for years on spurious grounds, and at one point had to flee the country to avoid arrest based on his judicial decisions. Meanwhile, Medrano and his accomplices have been appealing their sentences; the plaque is still not installed in Chinautla.

7.1 INTEGRAL REPARATIONS: EXPERIENCES FROM HUMAN RIGHTS CASES

Reparations for harm are potentially available in civil suits, as a beneficiary of administrative proceedings against state officials, as a fine in a criminal case or criminal or civil non-conviction based forfeiture (NCBF) of assets tied to criminal activity, or through participation as a civil complainant or private prosecutor in a criminal case brought by the state (other kinds of constitutional or popular actions can lead to injunctions or declaratory relief, but not monetary reparations). Many victims prefer the criminal route where available, in part because the state bears the costs of investigating and trying the case, and civil suits are subject to short statutes of limitation, payment of a bond, and other procedural obstacles, especially when the defendants are powerful private actors or state officials.

There has been very little in the way of reparations to individual or collective victims in grand corruption cases, despite the language of Article 35 of UNCAC allowing suits for damages. Compensation has occasionally been paid for wrongful death or injury connected to corrupt acts, but the tie to corruption has not been explicit. Occasionally, compensation has been paid to failed bidders on contracts where the winning bid was secured by a bribe, or companies or shareholders where an employee stole the funds, or to the State itself or the state agency that was embezzled.[3] Substantial obstacles to implementing a holistic reparations policy include lack of access to information and lack of expertise in defining, proving, and presenting expert opinions on what damages and broader reparations should entail. Courts dealing with grand corruption cases, in particular, have often rejected calls for compensation, much less other forms of reparation, on grounds that the case is too complex, the victims too numerous or the damages too uncertain.[4] They have a point: These are by definition complex cases, but that's precisely what makes them so harmful to large numbers of people and so important to tackle holistically. And, I will argue, the difficulties have in many cases been exaggerated, and these cases are no more difficult than the kinds of mass tort or structural reform cases that judges confront regularly.

Luckily, we're not starting from the beginning here: considerable lessons can be learned from experiences implementing reparations programs in cases of grave human rights violations. Just as international human rights law has changed the definition and rights of victims, it also changed the way courts and advocates think about reparations. One major change involves shifting from a compensation framework focused exclusively on individual money damages to a much wider and more complex view of what is involved.

The basic human rights instruments, as noted earlier, encompass a "right to a remedy." The Universal Declaration of Human Rights in Article 8 holds that "[e]veryone has the right to an effective remedy by the competent national tribunals for acts violating the fundamental rights granted him by the constitution or by law." The International Covenant on Civil and Political Rights' Article 2(3) requires parties to "ensure that any person whose rights or freedoms as herein recognized are violated shall have an effective remedy, notwithstanding that the violation has been committed by persons acting in an official capacity" and to provide compensation for unlawful detention or wrongful conviction. The European and American Conventions on Human Rights have similar provisions. The American Convention is particularly clear that remedy is broader than simply compensation, calling for the consequences of the breach to be remedied as well as fair compensation paid.[5]

The Inter-American Court of Human Rights pioneered the idea of integral reparations. It has sometimes required states to take specific actions such as dredging up missing bodies or reinstating plaintiffs to their jobs, and more often has ordered the state to investigate violations, prosecute those found to be responsible, and provide redress. It has ordered States to publish the judgement in newspapers or make a movie about it for national TV, publicly apologize, demarcate territory, or change laws or practices. In addition, it has awarded damages for lost earnings, for medical and other expenses, for pain and suffering (also called moral damages) and for the loss of life's project, by which the court means the limitations and changes in life plans and prospects brought about by the violator's actions. Punitive damages are generally not allowed.[6]

The 2005 United Nations Basic Principles on the Right to Redress and Reparation set out an oft-used framework, encompassing access to justice, restitution, rehabilitation, compensation, satisfaction and guarantees of non-repetition.[7] The Principles make it clear that restitution need not be monetary but can also include the restoration of liberty, citizenship, identity, and reputation, or return of property or a job; rehabilitation could include medical, legal or psychosocial measures. Compensation includes payment for physical or mental harm, material and moral damages, costs, and lost opportunities, including employment, education and social benefits. Satisfaction is about the restoration of the dignity of the victim, through apologies or official declarations, and verification and disclosure of the facts, while nonrepetition refers to a wide variety of reform measures. Other work on integral reparations has stressed that they can be both material and symbolic, and both individual and collective.[8] They should also be "victim-centered," and responsive to the expressed needs and desires of collectivities of victims, including fair, gender-sensitive, and inclusive processes. And they should be transformative: as the Inter-American Court put it, "it's not permissible to restitute people to the same situation of structural violence and discrimination."[9]

Most reparations for grave human rights violations have not come through tort-like damages administered by courts. Rather, government administrative programs have focused on acknowledgment, dignification and collective reparations along with limited individual ones.[10] Most surveys indicate that victims want individual compensation. Nonetheless, individual reparations can be difficult to finance, limited in transformative potential and potentially divisive when the harms are widespread or perceived as collective harms. Intra-family disputes, marginalization of women and children in provision of compensation, and the rise of a host of local opportunists and scam artists have accompanied these programs. On the other hand, collective reparations have generally focused on access to educational and health infrastructure and economic development (such as land, electrification, road construction, and market access), leading to debates about whether basic governmental functions can or should be rebranded as "reparations." All these debates are relevant to thinking more creatively about reparations in the grand corruption context. In the following sections, I will follow the framework of the Basic Principles and Guidelines to consider how these categories might be applied in grand corruption cases, and where they shouldn't be.

7.2 RESTITUTION: GIVING IT BACK THROUGH SOCIAL REUSE

What should be done with property confiscated from the Mafia? Italians considered this question in the 1990s, when the Mafia killings of two anti-mafia judges provoked national outrage. Law 109 of March 7, 1996 ("provisions on the management of assets seized or confiscated") created a means to repurpose properties and monies seized from criminal enterprises for social use. The law passed largely due to civil society efforts.

Davida Pati was a university student at the time. Pati is clean-cut, bespectacled and earnest. As he tells it: "For myself, and for many other people of my generation, those years changed something inside ourselves. Because of the massacres, I was looking for an engagement that could create a change in the society and in our culture. I eventually found Libera."

> Libera brought together parishes, cooperatives, university student associations, unions, social groups, magistrates associations, scouts, and others who had existed on a local and regional level, and created a national network. That was the innovation. We collected a million signatures for the law. Working together was, let's say, an evolution, a commitment that the fight against the mafias could not be left only to the police and the judiciary, but needed cultural action.

Pati is now the vice-president of the organization. The law was feasible due to a prior criminal statute that codified illicit association, introduced a broad definition of a "mafia-type organization" that would cover high-level corruption[11] and allowed pretrial confiscation of assets under certain circumstances.[12] According to Pati, "the bill creating social use for confiscated Mafia assets was incomplete, because the part relating to corrupt persons was removed. Not all political forces in Parliament were in favor of extending the confiscation of assets to corrupt people as well."

The confiscated assets are subject to a long judicial process that involves first seizing and freezing the assets and then proving that they are the proceeds of crime. Confiscation attaches to persons based on their involvement in or association with a criminal organization, or the commission of organized crime-related offenses or violation of UN sanctions. It does not require proof that the specific asset is the proceeds of criminal conduct. It also reverses the burden of proof, requiring defendants to prove that their assets are lawfully acquired to avoid confiscation. The European Court of Human Rights has held that these measures contain enough safeguards to be compliant with the rights to property and a fair trial under the European Convention on Human Rights.[13] During the confiscation process, Libera acts as a civil party alongside the victims, and at the end, can receive reparations together with victims of Mafia-related crimes.

The confiscated assets are eventually acquired by the State. As of 2010, the state administers them through a "National Authority for the Administration of The Assets Seized and Confiscated From Organized Crime"[14] The law grants private charitable organizations and social cooperatives the right to apply to the state through a competitive process at the municipal level to convert property and other assets acquired through criminal activities to socially beneficial uses.

Libera serves as a clearinghouse for groups wanting to apply for projects involving confiscated properties. More than 4,500 real estate properties (apartments, villas, and lands), especially in Sicily, Calabria, Campania, Puglia, and Lazio, have been taken over by over 1,000 associations and cooperatives. These are often student-based, and deal with inclusion and services to people, job reintegration, youth training and gathering, urban and cultural regeneration, and supporting victims and their families. There have been a few instances where Mafia-related front organizations have tried to reinsert themselves into the use of the property, but these have been discovered and stopped.

There are continuing pressures to sell confiscated properties to individuals, which Libera has resisted. For other assets such as cars, boats or companies, or where no one wants to adopt a property for social use, the asset can be sold and the money will go into a Justice Fund that can be used to compensate victims. However, according to Pati,

> socially reusing confiscated goods has a distinctive compensatory value for that community. It means compensating a community for the effects of the criminal actions carried out by mafia and corrupt persons .... The reuse of confiscated assets, for us, represents a tool to develop the territory from a cultural and social point of view, but also from an economic and political point of view. There are positive experiences related to the recovery of lands, confiscated domains where many products are grown. Cooperatives were born in these lands, and many young people have honest, clean, regular work – a social, clean economy, also linked to the dignity of people.

Directive 2014/42, issued by the European Parliament and Council, builds on this Italian experience and urges European Union Member States to "consider taking measures allowing confiscated property to be used for public interest or social purposes."[15] The 2024 Directive on Asset Recovery and Confiscation also urges EU states to "allow for the possibility to use confiscated property for public interest or social purposes, […]as State property for justice, law enforcement, public service, social or economic purposes or to transfer such confiscated property to the authorities from the municipality or region where it is located" for this purpose.[16] As of 2021, nineteen out of twenty-seven Member States have updated their laws in this regard, but only seven – Spain, Italy, Netherlands, France, Belgium, Bulgaria, and Romania – have active social reuse programs.[17] Simultaneously, asset management authorities in each country are needed to administer social reuse projects, and to combine such projects with EU Cohesion Funds in order to make them more sustainable. Bulgaria requires at least 30 percent of the value of the property confiscated to be used for social purposes. Cyprus gives confiscated drug-related assets to drug treatment centers. France recently gave an apartment confiscated in collaboration with Italian authorities to an association supporting victims of sexual exploitation. In Romania, confiscated funds are to be used for crime prevention, protection of and assistance to crime victims, legal education, and asset administration. And perhaps most creative of all, the Netherlands repurposed a confiscated boat as a public sailing school.

The idea has also taken off globally as well as in the region. In the 2021 United Nations General Assembly Special Session against Corruption (UNGASS), states pledged to "consider the various possible models of disposal and administration of confiscated proceeds of offences […] including, where feasible, allocating such proceeds to the national revenue fund or the State treasury, reinvesting funds for special purposes and compensating victims of the crime, including through the social reuse of assets for the benefit of communities."[18]

Nor is the trend restricted to Europe. In Colombia, a 2022 law created a Fund for victims of corruption, to be administered by the Procuraduría (state attorney's office) from confiscated assets. While the Fund is still not operational, regulations allow social, community and popular non-profit organizations to administer seized properties. The agency in charge has turned them over to peasant associations, groups assisting the disabled, and local police. According to the head of the SAE, ... "the administration of recovered assets can become a key tool for repairing the social fabric ...".[19]

In a lovely example of civil society transmission of ideas across borders, the Italian organization Libera has been working with a civil society group called Proyecto Bien Restituido to pass a law to implement social reuse in Argentina.[20] According to Clara Lucarella of the group, the practice is not prohibited, but it's rarely used because prosecutors are not required to consider it. Although most lower court judges support social reuse, the Supreme Court (unsurprisingly) prefers its existing wide discretion over the disposal of confiscated properties. In a situation with a growing presence of organized crime and an acute economic crisis, a source of resources for vulnerable groups would be welcome, she argues. In addition, the law on management of seized, impounded and forfeited property needs updating, and due to its shortcomings many such assets are ruined or destroyed while legal proceedings drag on. As of now, the law is pending, despite a consensus in favor among political parties.

7.2.1 *Land Restitution: Examples from Human Rights Cases*

Whether it's stolen by narco-governments, paramilitaries, private resource extraction companies or corrupt officials, land is often at the center of the harms created by grand corruption and its cousin, organized crime. It's often the most valuable thing people own, and attachments go beyond market considerations to heritage, home, and hearth. So land restitution has been a central concern in human rights and atrocity cases, and it is a central issue in grand corruption cases, especially given the increase in land grabs and natural resource-related corruption.

There is an extensive literature on property restitution arising first from Nazi confiscations of Jewish property in the 1940s, and second from the wave of privatizations and restitution that accompanied the fall of the communist governments in Eastern and Central Europe following 1989.[21] In the postcommunist cases, difficulties proving the chain of title and dealing with good faith third-party buyers bedeviled the process. Very little of the compensation was cash; the bulk was paid in either vouchers or government securities, creating a secondary market in such securities. There were enormous administrative problems to identify and inventory property, to find funds to pay compensation, and to mitigate the effects of broad restitution on rents and housing costs.

Postapartheid South Africa created a Commission on Restitution of Land Rights (CRLR) to assist those who had lost their land without compensation after 1913 due to apartheid practices. The Commission investigated claims and prepared them for settlement or adjudication, while a Land Claims Court granted restitution orders and adjudicated disputes. The difficulties of proving rights in land going back generations, where land was often held communally and without written title, were formidable, and the Land Claims Courts used testimony from historians and anthropologists as well as local elders to substantiate claims. Remedies included full ownership, partial rights to the land, rights to equivalent land, or compensation. The present landowners (assuming they purchased in good faith) were compensated by the state at market value; where sellers were unwilling, alternative land or money were the only remedies.

The process eventually led to some 80,000 claims. The CRLR reported in 2007 that 1.5 million hectares of land had been restored, US $562 million had been spent on buying alternative land, and US $475 million had been spent on cash compensation.[22] A great majority of claims were urban, and these were largely settled by cash awards. Rural claims tended to be larger, to be concentrated in the north and east, and to involve communities rather than individuals as well as negotiation over land rather than cash. This created definitional difficulties. What constitutes a "community" eligible for group restitution when people have been dispossessed and dispersed up to a hundred years before? In the *Richtersveld* case, involving a large communal claim by indigenous people, the courts looked to shared language, culture, and land use norms. A subsequent case found that communal forms of land holding in the past, even when formal title was now held by others, were enough to show evidence of community.[23] Courts also found that the dispossession did not have to happen all at once and did not have to be based on force, so long as leaving was involuntary.[24]

It was difficult for restituted communities to succeed as farmers. Even worse, given how long communities had been scattered, there was no guarantee that restoring the land would mean that people would have the skills to farm it. Early evidence indicated that most restored farms were not producing. The government began urging people to enter into "strategic partnerships" with the former agribusiness landholders, where the communities lease the land back to the former owners in exchange for a share of the profits, but do not actually live on or work the land. While this avoided the newly restituted lands becoming unproductive, it was not exactly the "transformative" result originally intended.[25]

The most recent, and largest, land restitution effort stems from the decades-long armed conflict in Colombia that left eight million forcibly displaced people, thousands of whom lost their land and livelihood. Of the displaced, tens of thousands were robbed or forced to give up their land by armed actors, mostly paramilitaries but also the FARC guerrillas and the state. As I recount in Chapter 8, land grabbing and displacement were also economic strategies, pursued by paramilitaries allied with private businesses and corrupt officials for drug-related or agribusiness purposes.[26]

Efforts to return land go back to the 2011 Victims' Law. The law declares that legal and actual return of land that was dispossessed after January 1991, along with post-restitution support, is the goal; only when that goal cannot be met (for example, because of continued lack of security) then equivalent land, or compensation, is to be provided.[27] Land is to be returned to owners, occupiers, or possessors, even if they do not have formal title; tenants, however, are excluded. The definition of dispossession is "an action by which, taking advantage of the situation of violence, a person is arbitrarily deprived of their property, possession or occupation, either in fact, through contract, administrative acts, judicial decision, or through the commission of crimes associated with the situation of violence."

Rather than make the claimant prove that they fit within the definition, the law reverses the burden of proof through the use of presumptions. Once the claimant shows that they lost their land during the relevant time period, there is an absolute presumption that any contract, title transfer or other document, signed by the claimant or his family, with those convicted of belonging to or financing illegal armed groups or drug traffickers or persons extradited on trafficking charges, directly or through intermediaries, was completed under coercion and is therefore void *ab initio*. A rebuttable presumption of invalidity exists when the transaction, even if ratified by administrative act or by the courts, took place in an area where at the time of dispossession or abandonment there were generalized acts of violence, collective forced displacement, or grave human rights violations, or where those dispossessed had asked the state for protection. A similar presumption of illegality applies to lands bordering those in which, subsequent to acts of violence, there was a concentration of ownership or a change in the membership of a cooperative farm, or there were substantial changes in land use, for example, from subsistence agriculture to banana or palm oil monoculture, extensive cattle grazing or industrial mining. A third set of circumstances raising the presumption applies to lands that were sold for less than half their actual value. Any subsequent judicial action is also null and void, and therefore courts are free to reopen the sale.[28] Thus, lawmakers tried to take into account how the actual mechanisms of dispossession worked, not just the formal title.

The law creates a Registry of Dispossessed or Forcibly Abandoned Land and of those who claim it. The Registration Unit verifies and registers the property and is charged with pursuing the restitution proceedings. As of January 2024, 149, 839,437 claimants had attempted to register to reclaim their land, but barely 10 percent of the claims had been adjudicated. That represents some 14,000 parcels, most of them small and rural; 27 collective indigenous and Afro-Colombian claims were also adjudicated. The administrative agency charged with initially registering land claims rejected 63 percent of the claims,[29] most often on grounds that there was insufficient proof of a causal link to the armed conflict. This has led to NGO complaints that the administrative agency is improperly raising the burden of proof and substituting its judgement for the courts, rather than simply opening the proceedings.[30] Other complaints include long delays and high costs for claimants, arbitrary decisions, lack of information and of transparency.[31]

The law allows for alternative land to be granted instead of restitution where the land in question is in the path of a natural disaster, where the house has been destroyed, where there were multiple displacements and the land has already been given back to someone else, or where it is too dangerous for the claimant to go back – certain areas are presumptively too dangerous. Government compensation can also be paid, but only as a last resort; up to 2023, only 15 percent of cases involved compensation rather than restitution. In an attempt to avoid having recently returned lands sold under new economic or security pressures, the law forbids the sale of newly restituted land for two years and requires court approval for leases during that period. To avoid land invasions, potential claimants who move back onto their land before a court order grants it to them can be evicted and lose their rights to restitution.[32]

Corporate entities, as well as individuals (mostly former paramilitary members), have been ordered to return dispossessed lands, among them Drummond Mining (so far, 192 hectares) and the Cattlemens' Fund of Córdoba (260 hectares so far), two of the private parties under investigation in the JEP, as recounted in Chapter 8. Banana exporters, cattle ranchers, real estate outfits, the national oil company as well as banks and financial services companies – 116 companies in all – have been accused of acquiring land unlawfully.[33] Companies have argued that they were simply good faith buyers of property and not at fault, but until recently the courts had required the companies to prove that they did adequate due diligence and were not complicit in the dispossession. In 2023, the Constitutional Court made it easier for companies to argue that they couldn't reasonably have known about the circumstances of dispossession given the passage of time and several intermediate buyers. This is likely to result in more corporate compensation requests for land already restituted to displaced farmers, reducing the already meager budget for restitution.[34]

What lessons can be learned from this brief survey for cases involving grand corruption? The first is to think about restitution as a separate, if complementary, remedy to compensation. Second, restitution can have community development and intangible benefits that can help repair the distrust of government and "the system" created by acts of kleptocracy as well as provide sources of livelihood and civic pride, especially if it has a social use or collective orientation. Third, restitution is not necessarily transformative, since it may return assets to those who already had land and were not among the most vulnerable sectors – such programs, like compensation, must consider gender, ethnic and class aspects of any such program. They are themselves also capable of abuses of power and even corruption, so enormous care is needed with respect to their personnel, procedures and ongoing, independent monitoring. Fourth, the use of presumptions of illegality, based on real-world dynamics of expropriation and hiding assets to overcome otherwise near-impossible evidentiary burdens is well established in human rights-related restitution cases; many of the same principles apply in grand corruption cases. Fifth, restitution might be a particularly appropriate remedy in cases where land use changes are the result of bribes or misappropriation, leading to loss or diminution in value of communal or individual rural land.

7.3 COMPENSATION: MEASURING THE HARMS

This is the traditional heart of civil damages, the money expected to repair such losses as medical bills, legal or funeral expenses, property losses, lost wages, lost opportunities and moral damages (also known in common law systems as pain and suffering). In the corruption context, laws often use the word "indemnification" to refer to the damages or compensation element. Courts, agencies and legislators tend to be most comfortable with this category of reparations, which largely tracks well-known torts or civil injury doctrine.

But it's still hard to get courts to take on measuring compensation.

The kinds of compensation (and other reparations) depend on both the crimes involved and the patterns of corruption. The cases to date have involved one of four main paradigms (which sometimes overlap). First, some cases involve personal injury or property damage where embezzlement or bribery create defective, substandard or dangerous situations. A second category involves a project or program that was only viable because of a bribe or the use of undue influence. Third, planned or proposed projects that could not be completed due to misappropriation of funds. Finally, sometimes bribes, undue influence or abuse of authority lead to overpriced contracts or to kickback schemes even if the planned works are completed. Some types of harm are easier to calculate damages for than others. But none are as hard, or as different from other civil harms, as they seem. I consider them in turn.

7.3.1 *Personal or Property Damage Due to Corrupt Acts*

Some cases involve personal injury or property damage due to embezzlement or bribery creating defective, substandard or dangerous situations. The paradigmatic example is the road, school or bridge that collapses due to inferior building materials or techniques because part of the funds were stolen. For example, the Once case in Argentina, where a train accident was traced to misappropriation of the train maintenance budget, or the IGSS-Pisa case in Guatemala, where a kickback scheme involving public health authorities led to a contract with an unqualified dialysis provider, with hundreds of resulting deaths and injuries. (both discussed in Chapter 5.) Here, damages for the personal injuries (including wrongful death, lost wages and/or medical expenses, and pain and suffering or moral damages) or property loss are clearly due, but the question becomes whether additional damages for the corruption itself that caused the harm are necessary. One could conceptualize these as additional moral damages or emotional distress damages based on the knowledge that the harm to the victim or their family members was not inevitable or accidental but based on deliberate and conscious disregard of others in the service of illicit enrichment. In personal injury law terms, corruption transforms what would otherwise be a negligence claim into a recklessness or intentional harm one, giving rise to dignitary and, in some legal systems, punitive or exemplary damages. In addition, those harmed may have other, non-damages related reasons for wanting to participate in the corruption proceedings.

7.3.2 *Where Bribes or Undue Influence Change Law or Procure Permits*

A second category of cases are those where the project or program has been completed, but it was only viable because of a bribe or the use of undue influence. This may be project-specific, as in the environmental, construction, export or other permits fraudulently obtained to build an otherwise unacceptable dam such as Agua Zarca in Honduras or Belo Monte in Brazil. Deforestation or land-grabbing cases would also fit into this category, as would undue influence or bribery cases where the payment was to influence legislative, regulatory or judicial bodies. Here the best approach would be to construct a counterfactual of what would most likely have happened without the bribe or undue influence. Of course, an alternative future is by definition unknowable, but tort law constructs counterfactuals all the time. Would the successful bidder have more likely than not won without a bribe, or would the contract have gone elsewhere? If there had been no bribe, would the project more likely than not have been built? If not, the loss of livelihood, of individual and collective land, forced displacement and environmental harm created by the project would be part of the damages, along with the amount of the bribe. Here the experience of international financial institutions in responding (however inadequately) to "development" projects gone wrong would provide a useful methodological starting point.[35]

7.3.3 *Loss of Opportunity*

Third, a large category of cases involves a planned or proposed project that was not done or an existing one that was shuttered due to embezzlement or misappropriation of the funds. In these cases, loss of opportunity or lost services might be the right measure of damages. These are the cases where farmers lose their market because the promised road was not built, or the anti-poverty project not funded because the monies were stolen, or the changes in life's path due to corruption.[36] Damages can be calculated here by looking at the benefits foregone and then tracing what the impact of those missing benefits should have been. Often, there will be project or financing documents that will establish the relevant expected benefits, which can be obtained through open contracting[37] or freedom of information requests. And economists, health experts and others can complement these with survey data specifying the projected losses and the universe of frustrated beneficiaries. With these tools, damages can be removed from the realm of speculation and made reasonably certain.

A variant of this methodology was used in Honduras' Pandora case, involving funds intended to aid poor farmers and young mothers that were siphoned off to fund the ruling political parties. Victims' representatives urged that the proper measure of damages for the communities that were the intended beneficiaries of the anti-poverty projects would start with the missing monies and add in the multiplier effects and benefits over time that would have been attributable to the project, as laid out in the project documents. It would center on the lost opportunity for positive change in their lives that was no longer available due to the embezzlement of the funds. Of course, this requires a showing that the development project would have benefited either specific members or segments of the community or the community as a whole, as well as some projection into the future of how lives (for example, increased incomes, fewer medical visits) would have been improved.

As part of their efforts to intervene in the case as private prosecutors, representatives of the victims identified nineteen individuals who were from the target areas and met the project eligibility criteria. They interviewed these potential beneficiaries, documenting both their initial incomes, assets and access to goods and services, and what they expected to change as a result of the promised funds and programs. They also asked a larger group of potential beneficiaries how the loss of funds affected them. In addition to the direct loss of the promised economic and social benefits, the respondents mentioned a set of intangible losses that they connected directly to the stolen funds. These included the frustrated expectations created by promises of help, which when it didn't arrive created distrust and even violence toward community leaders; increased vulnerability to hurricanes and droughts for lack of the promised agricultural improvements; lower prices for their crops because they continue to depend on middlemen rather than the promised direct purchasing centers, and the out-migration of most of the youth, defeated by the lack of local economic opportunity. What's more, follow-on grants never materialized due to donors being scared off by the maladministration of the initial grants.[38]

There is the further question of how to monetize these avoided harms or lost opportunities for the expected beneficiaries. But that is the case with many kinds of forward-looking damages (think about future medical expenses, or the future work trajectory of a college student). Given the success – measured by increased income, health, child nutrition, and so forth – of other rural anti-poverty programs using similar justifications, target populations and evaluation methodologies, it should be possible to estimate the lost opportunities. The case, dismissed by the Honduran courts in 2022, is now on hold pending an appeal of the dismissal of the criminal case against most of the defendants. It may eventually be headed to the Inter-American Human Rights system.

To figure out the damages in the maternal/child nutrition case in Medellin, Colombia discussed in Chapter 5, Juan David Correa, the organizer for complainant organization Todos por Medellín told me that the first thing they did to prove the damages was to talk to the association of victims, made up of the families whose maternal nutrition classes or children's lunch were affected. This let them get information about children who stopped attending school because of the lack of safe, edible food, and the health effects of the diminution in quality of the food on mothers and babies, including low birth weight. They got photos of lunch offerings, looked at school budgets, and the like.

In 2023, the complainants, together with an anti-corruption organization, hired an economist to figure out what concrete damages would look like. The economist first compared year-over-year budgets for the relevant programs, finding that despite the same budget, the number of beneficiaries diminished year over year with no plausible explanation except siphoning of funds. He then compared the type and quantity of interventions – nurse visits, food packages, and the like – that were supposed to be distributed according to government plans with survey data obtained through WhatsApp surveys of 442 beneficiaries. He found that over 40 percent of the beneficiaries received more limited benefits than they were supposed to, including missed home visits, incomplete and poor quality nutrition packages, and shorter time periods for coverage. (Admittedly, the COVID-19 pandemic no doubt accounts for some, but not all, of these findings.)

From there, the economist figured out the value of the lost opportunities that were supposed to be provided to mother and child but weren't. For example, a lactating mother who was supposed to receive group therapy, home visits, checkups due to low birth weight or other problems, and several nutrition packages for her and her child, but did not receive the goods and services due to corruption, would have a lost opportunity cost of $CO2,571, 410 (around US$631). Others, who missed out on fewer services, would have smaller damages. To these numbers, one would have to add the mental anguish involved in seeing one's baby fail to thrive due to lack of adequate nutrition, and the long-term effects on child development and health, including increased medical and educational costs. There are multiple studies connecting low weight, increased medical visits, dropout rates and similar indicators to subsequent earnings, which the organization could also use to establish damages.

A third example might be road construction cases, where the road is never completed due to embezzlement of the funds or the creation of phantom jobs or companies. Here too those who were expected to use the road, or who had started construction on property alongside it, might have a claim based on lost expectations, although an admittedly more tenuous one. In the Colombian Ruta del Sol case (an unfinished highway project linked to the Odebrecht scandal), one of the demands of those affected was that the road be finished as promised. This can be money and time-consuming where the original contract has been voided, and a new one must be bid.

Outside the region, an interesting effort to quantify lost opportunities involving employees and community members involved the purchase by a hedge fund connected to Dan Gertler, an Israeli businessman accused by the US Department of Justice of bribing the president and other high officials in the Democratic Republic of Congo to obtain mining concessions. One of the concessions he wrested away from its Canadian owners was a cobalt mine, known as KMT, acquired by Gertler in 2010 following the bribery-induced revocation of the previous owners' mining license. The license was subsequently given to Gertler's entity for a fraction of its value; the mine was closed, and eventually resold.

Two cases (at least) arose from this set of transactions. First, shareholders in the Canadian corporation that was fraudulently deprived of the ability to develop the mine intervened in the US prosecution of Gertler's company, seeking damages under the Mandatory Victim Restitution Act.[39] According to a helpful summary by Rick Messick, they argued that the corrupt scheme to take the mine away from them damaged them to the tune of the profits they would have made from its development, or at least of the current value of the undeveloped mine. Their expert calculated the expected value lost, based on assumptions about ore prices, potential markets and the like; although both prosecutors and defendants objected, the court found that the lack of certainty in estimating the damages was not enough to defeat a claim based on a reasonable estimate of lost benefit. The court found that neither the convoluted nature of the chain of ownership nor the existence of intervening factors were enough to preclude a claim based on "direct and proximate" harm to their intangible property interests.[40]

A British NGO, RAID, along with Congolese NGO Afrewatch, began looking into the case.[41] They found cited in the DoJ investigation documents from the International Finance Corporation, which had provided extensive loans to the initial Canadian owners of the mine. In exchange, the mine owners had contractually committed themselves to various development projects. Once the mine was closed, all those commitments were left in limbo, and the eventual new owners were slow to implement any projects to help the surrounding communities.

Here, surely, was a textbook example of harm to the community from grand corruption: people had been promised benefits, the benefits didn't materialize, and as a direct result they suffered health and livelihood harms. There was a clear before and after, and a relatively tight causal connection. RAID and Afrewatch came up with two groups of victims, represented by sixteen individuals who asked to intervene in the UK's corruption probe. They alleged harms to 700 workers who lost jobs at the mine, and 32,000 inhabitants of nearby villages who will no longer benefit from the Canadian former owners' promised projects, including clean water, cleanup of toxic air and water pollution of the nearby river, and improved healthcare and education. These harms continued during the nine years the mine was closed, and partially after that since the new owners were slow to implement any community benefits. Moreover, with the change in owners, the IFC's participation ended, and with it any monitoring or accounting for the harms and their mitigation. It should have been relatively simple to compare the benefits of the old ownership – set out in detail in the IFC's loan documents – and what currently exists. Unfortunately, in August 2023 the Serious Fraud Office announced that it was closing the criminal investigation, leaving the victims without remedy.[42]

7.4 SOCIAL HARM AND DIFFUSE OR COLLECTIVE INTERESTS

These examples provide a roadmap for estimating damages based on lost opportunity. The hardest cases involve a project that was done correctly (unlike the first category) and finished (unlike the third category), but bribes, undue influence or abuse of authority led to overpriced or unduly extended contracts or to kickback schemes in which part of the overpricing is returned to the briber. These are the cases where the victims are "indirect"[43] and the harm more diffuse and social.

One could look at the difference in quality or quantity of services rendered compared to a "non-bribe" scenario, or the excess costs or diminution of quality to the consumer and the like.[44] Trade economists in antidumping investigations have developed sophisticated methodologies for comparing what things should have cost to what they actually cost (in the trade case, underpricing rather than overpricing is the issue, but the principles are similar).[45] The amount of the bribe, or even the amount of lost profits or of the project, would be insufficient. At times these cases may look like class or representative actions for consumer protection – small losses for lots of people, which need some aggregation mechanism. In others, the best solution may be to set up a fund or use an existing state institution (like a Procuraduría or Ombudsman/Defensor) or a representative public interest organization to craft a compensatory response. In these cases especially, adequate damages will combine redress for individual harms, collective harm to identifiable groups (like the indigenous Lenca people we saw in Chapter 5), and social harm to diffuse interests.

The violation of diffuse interests affects everyone. Examples of diffuse harm include environmental harm, anti-competition harms, consumer protection, and harm to cultural heritage. Social harm arising from grand corruption might be framed as a loss of trust in government generally or in institutions like the judiciary (leading to self-help, vigilantism or lack of remedy), in the integrity of public administration or financial management, or in the government's reputation as an effective service provider. In cases where bribes or embezzlement led to higher prices or scarcity for consumers, the rules (and, where they exist, specific statutes) on consumer protection should come into play. Moreover, research into trust in public institutions draws connections both to individual well-being and to support for democracy and resistance to illiberal regimes.[46] Social harm might also include the devaluing of contracts, of social bonds, and the fear of wittingly or unwittingly running afoul of powerful corrupt actors by speaking up or blowing the whistle on corrupt acts. It might also be calculated as the opportunity cost to the budget arising from government services that were not provided because the money went into private hands.[47]

An approach used to date in environmental and climate litigation may also hold some promise for recognizing and evaluating social harm. In 1988, Edith Brown Weiss[48] argued that the current generation owes obligations to those who come after us to leave the earth no worse than we found it, including legal obligations. The idea of intergenerational equity was subsequently enshrined in international environmental treaties and soft law.[49] The same principle applies to corruption, especially the grand corruption that saps major resources. By stealing these resources and frittering them away for private use (see, e.g., London mansions and Maseratis) rather than husbanding them for the common good, future generations are deprived of access to these resources and the benefits they would otherwise have provided.

Costa Rica has pioneered an approach to social harm. It recognizes that the same illegal act may create individual harm, collective harm, and diffuse or social harm. While collective harm has identifiable victims or affects an identifiable community (like an indigenous group or a labor union), social harm affects everyone. Article 37 of the Costa Rican Criminal Procedure Code allows victims of a criminal act to intervene in order to obtain restitution or damages.[50] To claim social harms, the Procurator or State Attorney (*Procuraduría*) represents the victims. Article 16 gives the *Procuraduría* the right to intervene in corruption and tax evasion cases and to have the same rights as the prosecutor therein. Article 38 specifically allows the *Procuraduría* to claim social damages for criminal acts that affect collective or diffuse interests, although civic society organizations that work on those interests may also intervene.

These provisions have been applied in several dozen corruption and other types of cases. Among the largest corruption awards, the *Procuraduría* received $9.2 million in social harm damages against former president Calderón and former officials of the social security administration, arising out of a medical supplies contract that was steered to a specific supplier in exchange for bribes, known as the Caja-Fischel case.[51] In the ICE-Alcatel telecommunications bribery case,[52] the defendant agreed to a partial settlement in 2015, paying US$10 million to the *Procuraduría* for social harm.[53] Social harm was defined as the loss of trust in public administration, but also as a violation of the constitutional right to a "healthy environment," which was interpreted to include the social environment as well as the natural world, including the right to a corruption-free environment.[54] To calculate the amount of social harm, the State Attorney hired an economist, who calculated that $30.9 million had been lost in potential investment and another $3.6 million in increased abstentionism in the 2006 elections due to the increased lack of trust in politicians.

Guatemala, as you'll recall, has a broad notion of "integral reparations." That notion was applied in 2018 in a case brought by the prosecutor and CICIG involving nine construction companies who were pressured into bribing then-Minister of Communications and Infrastructure Alejandro Sinibaldi in order to obtain new government roadbuilding contracts. In an abbreviated proceeding after the company heads pled guilty and agreed to negotiate reparations with the prosecutor and the Procurator (State Attorney), Judge Erika Aifán of the High-Risk Court sentenced them to five year suspended sentences, a fine that varied depending on the amount of the bribes and the financial capacity of the defendant, and $5 million in reparations, to be spent on fixing or building specific road sections, building a school and, in one case, buying equipment for the road-fixing department. To determine how to implement the reparations portion, the parties held a series of meetings to hash out which roads were to be built or repaired according to government priorities, social utility and technical difficulty.[55] The amount of roadbuilding and fixing duties allocated to each defendant depended on the amount of the bribes paid, their capacity and experience.

Colombia also uses the mechanism of a Procurator or State Attorney to represent the public interest in cases involving corrupt government officials. In the Ruta del Sol II/Odebrecht case, private companies related to the Brazilian construction company Odebrecht paid off officials to win a road construction contract. In January 2017, the State Attorney filed a "popular action" arguing a violation of the collective interests of administrative morality, defense of public patrimony, and efficient and prompt access to public services.[56] On December 6, 2018, the Administrative Court of Cundinamarca ruled in the complainant's favor, suspending the concession contract and ordering measures aimed at rebidding the fifty road projects, an embargo on the defendants' assets, and the payment of $800,000 in collective damages.[57]

The court considered each type of collective interest. With regard to administrative morality, the court defined it as consisting of two elements: a violation of the duty of a public official to act according to their duty to follow the law and uphold the common good, and the intent to do so in order to obtain personal or private gain for themselves or another. A private entity can be liable for a violation of administrative morality when it takes on state functions, for example, a road concession. This is a particularly egregious action, the court added, since it affects the reputation of the state and the sector, undermining the confidence of the citizenry.

The defense of public patrimony requires public officials to not act negligently or inefficiently to avoid misuse and loss of public funds. It is connected to the efficient and prompt access to public services, including transportation, and the means (like roads) without which the service cannot be provided. Because the contract to build and operate the toll road system at issue here was based on bribery, the completion and operation were delayed when the bribe was discovered, thus creating greater costs for both the state and the potential users of the road, violating the right to efficient and prompt access to services.

The court added that there is also a diffuse interest in free competition, which was violated because there were two other bidders on the road contract who were unable to bid (or their bid was rejected) due to the bribes that ensured that Odebrecht got the contract. This was not only a loss for the losing bidders, but for the society, which was unable to take advantage of competition to get the best terms and conditions. There was no need, therefore, to prove a specific amount of harm to the losing bidders; it was the loss of competition itself that was the harm. As a result of these harms, the court found that those who gave the bribes, as well as those who were beneficiaries of the bribery, were jointly and severally liable. Damages were calculated by adding the amount of the bribe, the amount of overpayment due to taking the highest bidder (comparing the winning bid to an average of the losing ones), and the delays, additional maintenance and costs of preparing and adjudicating a new bid, together with the losses to the state because the original contract had specified that the road (and its toll revenue) would be returned to state administration by a date several years sooner than the date on the new contract. These losses were then subject to a modest multiplier, on grounds that the lost opportunities would have created cascading development benefits.

With regard to the reputational losses, the court ordered nonpecuniary relief: the state agencies involved had to implement more extensive due diligence and monitoring to avoid corruption.

In 2023, an intermediate panel of the appellate administrative law body (known as the Council of State), limited the range of remedies that can be granted in popular action proceedings (holding that the termination of the contract could not be adjudicated in a declaratory action to avoid future harm or compensate past harm). Nonetheless, the appeals panel left largely intact the discussion of diffuse collective harms, although it did not admit damages for free competition because they were tied to the contract terms, and it criticized some of the other damages calculations.[58] The complainants appealed again to the Council, which denied their arguments in August 2024. The complainants had not participated in the early stages of the case because at the time the *Procuraduría* was adequately representing the victims, but then it desisted and victims were left with no recourse. At that point, two civil society groups (Dejusticia and Transparencia por Colombia) tried to pick up the slack, but, according to the court, they were too late to jump into the case in order to allege constitutional violations.[59] Despite this setback, the reparation analysis still stands.

Colombia's 2022 anti-corruption law requires judges to take the impact on society into account in setting damages, which may be monetary or nonmonetary. It creates a Fund, and directs fines from public or private offenders to be deposited there. The Procurator (State Attorney) is to administer the fund, and is to use 40 percent of it to "guarantee the reestablishment of the indivisible collective rights affected by corrupt acts, and for the monetary or nonmonetary integral reparation of the individuals and collectivities affected by acts of corruption."[60] Complainants can apply to the Procurator's office. The rest of the funds are to go to other government agencies to defend collective rights, improve transparency and expand anti-corruption efforts. To date, unfortunately, not much has happened.

The use of the State Attorney's office allows diffuse interests to be represented without a showing that a specific organization has sufficient interests in the subject, and puts state resources to work in favor of recovering assets. However, in states where the entire apparatus of the state is too weak, dysfunctional or captured to operate in the public interest, the State Attorney's office is as much at risk of failure or capture as are prosecutors or judges. The Colombian Ruta del Sol case, discussed above and in Chapter 6, shows how political changes in a State Attorney's office can leave those affected by corrupt contracts without recourse. Moreover, any monies obtained simply go back to the state's coffers, where there is no obligation that they be used to redress the harms alleged; State Attorneys in some human rights-related criminal cases (for example in Chile) were initially reluctant to allow victim compensation in order to save money. Mandated victim participation in negotiations around social harm valuations might mitigate some of these harms. In addition, if victims' agency in demanding an independent role in corruption cases has a symbolic or procedural value, it is not served through the use of the State Attorney mechanism.

7.5 CAUSATION AND THE USE OF PRESUMPTIONS

One of the tricky problems in figuring out compensation is how close a causal connection between the harm and the damage is required. Surely proof of some connection is needed to be fair to defendants and to avoid perceptions of arbitrariness. But the usual problem has been the opposite: judges and prosecutors require too specific (and too difficult) a connection between a defendant's specific crime and the harm, even when that harm is generalized or diffuse or the defendant acted as part of a network or overall scheme. Causation in general requires plaintiffs to imagine the counterfactual – what would have happened without the corrupt act. If the funds hadn't been stolen, would the school have been built; without a bribe, would an honest firm have built the bridge with stronger materials so that it wouldn't collapse? If the Minister hadn't suspiciously changed the permitting process, would the forest have been destroyed, given that there are lots of sources of deforestation? You begin to see the problem.

Of course, life is complicated, and few things have a single cause. Tort and criminal law deal regularly with the threshold showing required, and also with exceptions where the burden of proof shifts, or presumptions apply, in order to make it easier for complainants to get their case into court where defendants are particularly hard to go after. Causation questions also have a temporal dimension: it's more difficult to specify the link to a specific victim or victims when the money is stolen or the bribe paid regarding an overall (education, health, or whatever) budget, where the predominant harm may be social, and easier to see the link further along, when the allocation has already been made to a facility or program in a specific village or to a specific group who have individual or group claims.

Part of the problem the courts face is defining what is meant by a "direct" interest or "direct" harm? Is it a requirement of "but-for" causation, where there needs to be an unbroken chain of cause and effect even if there are many steps in the causal chain? Or is it a requirement of proximate or legal cause, where courts attempt to draw an "uncertain and wavering line"[61] beyond which liability will not extend for policy reasons? As I discuss in Chapter 5, Peru includes in its definition of "aggrieved party" not only those "directly offended" by the crime, but also those adversely affected by its consequences.[62] The Peruvian Supreme Court interpreted this to mean that even though the State is offended by a crime against public administration, those who suffer concrete harm (in this case physical harm) are also entitled to participate in the case alongside the state.[63] Colombia's 2022 Anti-Corruption law allows those individually or collectively affected by corruption to seek redress from a Fund financed by fines and forfeitures.[64]

An example from the United States illustrates a broad view of causation. The US airplane manufacturer Boeing created a new software system and equipped its 737 MAX planes with it. Boeing never told its customers that pilots needed special, expensive training to use the system, fearing that the extra cost would reduce sales. In two air crashes less than five months apart, the software malfunctioned and pilots didn't know how to react. Lion Air Flight 610 crashed in October 2018, killing everyone on board; in March 2019 Ethiopian Airline Fight 302 went down. Altogether, 346 people died. The US Department of Justice, according to the plaintiffs' lawyer, secretly negotiated with Boeing while denying to the victims that it was doing so, and signed a Deferred Prosecution Agreement in which Boeing agreed to a very small fine for conspiring to defraud the US. The families of those killed protested that they had been excluded from the negotiations and that they had rights under the Crime Victims' Rights Act ("CVRA").[65] The district court agreed that they were victims under the Act but held a further hearing on whether they had been "directly and proximately harmed." The crime victim definition "imposes dual requirements of cause in fact and foreseeability," the court found. Direct causation was but for causation and did not require that the crime be the only cause, but merely a causal relation as laypeople would view it. Proximate or legal cause was the same as in US tort law: a reasonably foreseeable result of the defendant's conduct, and not merely fortuitous. Under those rules, the families of the crash victims had standing, since without Boeing's fraud against the US, the crashes would more likely than not have been avoided.[66] If corruption is a violation of human rights, according to Anne Peters the test is whether the harms "were foreseeable for the public official and were in the usual course of things."[67] She further posits that concurrent or cumulative forms of causation are included, as are omissions – even where it cannot be proven that proper preventive action would have eliminated the problem, the omission to act properly still counts as a legal cause.

Where a strict insistence on proving direct causality will create impossible barriers to recovery given the secretive nature of corrupt transactions and the power of most potential defendants, burden-shifting and the use of presumptions can rebalance the scales a bit. These devices are already used in establishing culpability for corruption offenses. For example, the 2016 Swiss Foreign Illicit Assets Act discussed earlier allows a presumption that assets are of illicit origin where the following conditions are fulfilled:

> 1. The wealth of the individual who has the power of disposal over the assets increased inordinately, facilitated by the exercise of a public function by the politically exposed person (PEP), and
> 2. The level of corruption in the country of origin or surrounding the PEP was notoriously high during their term in office.
>
> An increase shall be considered inordinate where there is a significant disproportion, inconsistent with ordinary experience and the prevailing circumstances in the country, between the income legitimately earned by the person with the power of disposal over the assets and the growth in that person's wealth.

The presumption is reversed where it has been demonstrated with "overwhelming probability" that the assets in question were acquired legitimately. A causal link between the "inordinate increase" and the exercise of a public function need not be concretely proved.[68]

This language both sets up presumptions and shifts the burden of proof to the person controlling the assets. France uses similar rebuttable presumptions regarding the origin of funds in money laundering cases, which means that it is unnecessary to tie the funds at issue to a specific initial offense and puts the burden on the asset owner to show that the funds are not from an illicit origin.[69] Another example, prevalent in several countries, concerns asset declarations and unexplained wealth orders. In the UK (and Australia), for instance, the Unexplained Wealth Orders law came into effect in 2018. It shifts the burden of proof to explain the legal provenance of assets inconsistent with the owner's income or where there are reasonable grounds to suspect that the property has been obtained through unlawful conduct. An inability to do so leads to forfeiture. In theory, at least, it provides useful language.

As we've seen, presumptions and burden-shifting are also used to make possible restitution and compensation in human rights cases. The rationale for doing so is similar in corruption cases: the essence of the crime involves secrecy, and forcing prosecutors or complainants to come up with evidence that has been deliberately hidden to protect the wrongdoers is unfair. In forced disappearance cases, for instance, the state abducts the victim and then denies doing so. Courts have not hesitated to use rebuttable inferences, including from pattern and practice of other similar unsolved cases, to find both state and individual responsibility.[70] There is no reason why such devices, with adequate safeguards to allow putative defendants to rebut the presumptions, cannot be more broadly used to ensure adequate compensation.

7.6 SATISFACTION: NONMONETARY RESPONSES AND RESTORATIVE PROCESSES

If you ask people what they want from litigation, you find that the process is as important as the outcome, as Tom Tyler has shown.[71] If you ask survivors of human rights violations, you find that right up there with compensation are demands for truth-telling, acknowledgment, apology, a declaration that what was done was wrong, and justice. And if you ask indigenous peoples what redress means, they talk about consultation, negotiation, and the ability to decide what is done with their land and resources.[72] One of the key insights of recent work on reparations is that these kinds of intangible responses must be part of integral reparations. "Satisfaction" is a venerable international law category, usually used in the settlement of interstate disputes for apologies and the like, but now adapted with a human rights focus. We've seen one example in Guatemala's Chinautla case.

In the Construction and Corruption case involving bribery and road-building contracts in Guatemala, Judge Aifán applied the resolution of the Inter-American Commission on Corruption and Human Rights as well as the human rights jurisprudence of the Inter-American Court and Article 12 of UNCAC to find that integral reparations include compensation, restitution, rehabilitation, satisfaction and guarantees of nonrepetition.[73] Here, the victim was the people in general as represented by the State, since bribery harms public administration, she found. Roadbuilding and school construction "place the population in general in the center of the fight against corruption." "Reparation can be understood basically as a message sent to the victims through symbolic and material means, so to meet its goals the form in which these measures are carried out is equally important." Therefore, she ordered the defendants to publicly apologize, including taking out an ad in the newspapers and placing an explanatory plaque near each road or school built or fixed. As a guarantee of nonrepetition, she ordered the firms to create an anonymous whistleblowing channel, a Code of Ethics, and to hire a compliance officer and implement compliance risk assessments. While the decision is a landmark, the attacks on CICIG (see Chapter 3) and eventual exile of Judge Aifán means that implementation of the judgment has been spotty.

It's not surprising that one of the first attempts to apply the notion of satisfaction in a corruption case comes from Colombia, where restorative justice concepts have been widely disseminated. The Ministry of Technology contracted with a group called Union Temporal Centros Poblados (UTCP) to install high-speed internet in poor, rural areas throughout the country. UTCP was a combination of four other entities, some of them connected to people involved in shady dealings in the past, but because the entities' true ownership was concealed during the contract negotiations, no one in government noticed. The required bank guarantee was apparently forged, and no internet lines ever went up despite payments to UTCP of some US$16.3 million. Eventually, criminal and administrative proceedings were brought against the company and several individuals.[74]

In March 2023, the State Juridical Defense Agency (representing the defrauded government) announced that using the penal code's restorative justice provisions, it had made a deal with two of the main accused in the case. Using a local university as mediator, the state agreed to hold meetings between the accused, prosecutors and the victims to design a new internet project, using funds voluntarily returned to the state by the perpetrators in the course of criminal and administrative proceedings.[75] While the process is still in its initial stages, the explicit recognition of victims, and the effort to redirect resources to them, seem promising. Colombia's 2022 Anti-Corruption Law, in article 4(3), also provides that corporations involved in corruption must, as part of a package of fines and sanctions, publish any judgment against them in a newspaper and on their website.

One way to provide greater satisfaction involves reconceptualizing how punishment and reparations fit together. After years of debates worldwide about punitive versus restorative approaches to mass atrocities, Colombia has embraced the notion of "restorative sanctions" in the context of peace accords with the FARC, also discussed in Chapter 8. The activities involved span the reincorporation of ex-combatants into civilian life, reparations to victims, punishment, and reconciliation. In the restorative sanctions framework, members of the FARC or security forces who committed non-amnestiable crimes in the context of the armed conflict can choose to appear before the Special Jurisdiction for Peace, adequately recount what happened and accept responsibility for the crimes early in the process. They then become eligible for "special sanctions" (called *sanciones propias* in Spanish) that involve a term of years subject to non-custodial sanctions.[76] Noncustodial doesn't mean free – those convicted will be subject to restrictions on movement and residence, will be monitored (it's not clear exactly how) and be on probation. The restriction period is longer for those found "most responsible." Those who decide not to voluntarily appear can be charged in a normal adversarial process and, if convicted, face up to twenty-year prison sentences; they are ineligible for non-custodial sanctions. The system is designed to encourage voluntary participation.

While the sanctions are imposed by a chamber of the court, they come at the end of a "dialogic" process that starts with a proposal from the person seeking special sanctions on how they will make amends through work and restorative activities (known as TOARs from the Spanish acronym). The proposal can come either before proceedings begin or as part of sentencing after a plea deal. The proposed public service work or activities are sent to victims and local NGOs for comment and suggestions; the process can also include voluntary meetings between victims and victimizers. Initially, the agreed-upon areas for possible noncustodial sentences were demining, searching for and locating the disappeared, and environmental restoration. The military officials in the case also agreed voluntarily to pay cemetery expenses for the victims.

Harvey Suárez, the Executive Secretary of the JEP, has thought a lot about how the restorative justice aspects could work. "We need to think about not just the harm done, but how the harm was experienced" he told me. "We accompany the victims, help them take ownership of their history without revictimization, we do something similar with the perpetrators, those who benefited from the violent acts, and with the representatives of both sides, who are used to an adversarial logic."

Assuming that the Colombian experiment is successful (a big assumption, admittedly) would a similar program be possible for perpetrators of financial crime? In addition to paying fines into a fund, those convicted of bribery, embezzlement or influence peddling would agree, in a plea deal or abbreviated proceeding that would avoid a substantial prison term, to fund and personally help repair the specific damage to communities, whether it be by building schools or teaching financial literacy. The symbolic value of having the perpetrators of financial crimes personally accepting responsibility, explaining how fraud was committed, and visibly working alongside community members might go some way to both providing satisfaction and rehabilitating offenders. It also entails risks: sending members of the elite private and public sectors to work off their sins in the countryside could become redolent of the worst of Mao's cultural revolution and might lead to more resentment than reconciliation. Still, the concrete needs of both offenders and victims, and encounters between them, might begin to change cultures of impunity.

7.6.1 *DPAs, Immunities and Amnesties, and Satisfaction*

In cases of grave human rights violations and international crimes, human rights law and international criminal law (especially in the Americas) prohibit blanket (across-the-board) amnesties and restrict the use of statutes of limitations as well as other immunity devices. Nonetheless, under certain circumstances, conditional amnesties that require truth-telling, restitution of stolen assets, and a commitment to not take up arms in exchange for shorter or noncustodial sentences have been acceptable, as in Colombia's Integral System for Truth, Justice, Reparation and Non-Repetition.

Unlike in cases of serious human rights violations or international criminal law, international law to date puts no such limits on amnesties, plea bargains or "abbreviated proceedings," when it comes to grand corruption. Indeed, most corruption cases, especially those involving private actors, settle well before trial through deferred prosecution agreements (DPAs) or their analogs. These agreements generally do not require an admission of wrongdoing, allowing corporate executives, intermediaries or officials to avoid prison time and to pay discounted fines in exchange for giving information to prosecutors (but none to the public). In corporate cases, firms generally agree to implement monitoring and compliance programs of varying stringency. Such plea bargains and DPAs are useful to prosecutors, saving time and investigative resources in light of complex, difficult facts that may not produce enough evidence for conviction. But where grand corruption is concerned, they raise suspicions about favoritism, opacity, and collusion.

From the point of view of satisfaction to victims, this must change. I'm not arguing that every case must go to a full trial, but that settlements, plea bargains and DPAs should include incentives and baseline requirements in exchange for a deal, including public disclosure of the facts, admission of wrongdoing, apology and, in some cases, the ability of victims to address defendants and the court and explain the impact that the corrupt behavior had on them as well as restitution of funds and/or fines. The lack of transparency in these abbreviated proceedings not only deprives victims of satisfaction, it perpetuates suspicions that these are sweetheart deals only available to the rich and powerful.

7.7 GUARANTEES OF NONREPETITION: THE REFORM AGENDA

The fourth category of reparation under the Basic Guidelines and Principles encompasses a vast category of reform measures aimed at avoiding a repeat of the crimes or violations. In the corruption space, this is talked about as the prevention agenda. It's too vast, and also too specific to a country and context, for generalities to be of much use. Having said that, there are a few common agenda points that might be worth considering:

At least nine countries in Latin America – Colombia, Bolivia, El Salvador, Guatemala, Honduras, Mexico, the Dominican Republic, Ecuador, and Panama – have NCBF laws, which allow freezing and eventual confiscation of money, real estate, cars and other assets that are either the proceeds of crime or serve to cover up or are mixed with the proceeds of crime, even without a conviction. These proceedings are focused on a particular property, not a crime or a criminal, with a lower burden of proof, and don't require either a parallel criminal proceeding or a prior conviction. They generally establish due process protections, jurisdictional requirements, and in some cases rules for the management of confiscated assets. Other states in the region allow freezing and eventual forfeiture of assets but require a tie to a specific criminal proceeding or don't pursue or allow the procedure in foreign states. According to the UNCAC Working Group on Asset Recovery, this is the number one problem impeding returning assets.

Courts have considered due process and property deprivation challenges to these laws, but in the region, courts have generally (but not unanimously) found that where the property is acquired illicitly (or through unexplained wealth) no legitimate property right ever attaches, so deprivation of the property is legitimate.[77] Certain due process protections are required: the person(s) affected must be adequately notified, have the ability to contest the alleged illegality, to present arguments and proof, and to appeal an unfavorable result.

Several of these laws provide a whistleblowers' reward for information leading to forfeiture – in Colombia and Guatemala, it's 5%, in Honduras 10%. States vary greatly on how the forfeited funds are to be used. Honduras spells out in detail where they go, including for fighting organized crime, for the municipal governments where the assets are located, and for victims (8 percent of proceeds). Guatemala returns about three-quarters of the funds to prosecutors, police and the judiciary to be used for organized crime or money laundering investigations. Mexico has both a federal law and numerous state laws. It sends recovered funds to a "social cabinet of the presidency" which decides the allocation. Peru, like Colombia, created a separate agency to administer forfeited assets; 40% of the proceeds are supposed to go to prison construction and maintenance, and 20% to pay damages where necessary.[78] The idea of using part of the money for victims is thus already there, even if the percentages are low. A preventative approach might be more proactive in not only seizing assets but in ensuring that forfeited funds are used for the direct benefit of those most harmed.

PART III

A CORRUPTION LENS ON HUMAN RIGHTS-RELATED ISSUES

8

Transitions, Transitional Justice, and Grand Corruption

In the previous chapters, I have looked at how a human rights approach can strengthen and broaden anti-corruption efforts, especially with regard to victims. This chapter, like the next one, flips the telescope to look at how areas of human rights law could benefit from an anti-corruption lens, and how that lens can fill gaps in thinking about justice in transition and in international criminal law.

This chapter considers the links between transitions away from dictatorship or civil war and the emergence of grand corruption in newly transitioned states. Is there something about what is – and isn't – done in the crucial months after a reform-minded or post-armed conflict government assumes power that makes the emergence of organized crime networks tied to corrupt officials and elites more or less likely? Are there ways in which efforts during a transitional moment could better target these emerging networks?

8.1 WHY TRANSITIONS? WHY TRANSITIONAL JUSTICE?

One of the changes in thinking about transitional moments over the last forty years or so is the emergence of transitional justice (also called post-armed conflict justice or *jus post bellum*) as a key element. Transitional justice asks what is necessary to deal with a past of massive atrocity crimes or serious human rights violations, in order to move forward on a different trajectory. Over time – and to a large part due to the influence of examples from Latin America – broad acceptance developed of the need to take action to find out and disseminate facts and testimonies about what happened, do some modicum of justice (including but not limited to criminal justice), repair the harm, and reform institutions and culture so as to break cycles of violence and avoid repetition.[1]

Transitional justice efforts started out focusing just on a small subset of human rights violations, involving attacks on life, freedom, and personal integrity. Early efforts involved official investigative commissions aimed at finding out what had happened to people (especially those who disappeared without a trace) and recommending reforms (sometimes shorthanded as "truth commissions."). Many countries in the region implemented more or less generous reparations programs, provided medical and psychosocial help to victims, and – even though not until many years after the fact – countries such as Argentina, Chile, Guatemala, Peru and Colombia tried and convicted at least some of those responsible.[2] Police forces were modernized and armies reduced in size, but there is only one example of systematic vetting of military officers, in El Salvador. There was little effort to talk about or carry out reforms aimed at deterring corruption as part of this agenda, although there were efforts at modernizing the judiciary and prosecutors' offices.

Eventually, the critique of transitional justice held that it had become too top-down, too much a UN import (and imposition) rather than a grassroots-inspired movement, and too unconnected to everyday lives. Part of the resulting "transformative" agenda involved a move to expand transitional justice processes to include consideration of economic, social, and cultural rights[3] or grand corruption.[4] Truth Commissions in Chad, Liberia, Sierra Leone, Kenya, The Gambia and Tunisia included both corruption and human rights violations in their work.[5] The Liberian commission dedicated an entire volume of its report to economic crimes, while the Kenyan commission, controversially, focused on land appropriation. Trials, as I mentioned in Chapter 1, often featured human rights and corruption on parallel tracks. A debate ensued over whether including corruption within the remit of transitional justice was a necessary corrective and a central pillar of "non-recurrence" or an overambitious overburdening of fragile, temporary mechanisms.[6]

Beyond transitional justice, transitions often involve peacemaking and peacebuilding initiatives, changes in economic strategy, territorial reorganization, and/or constitutional and legal reforms. These too have often downplayed or ignored the underlying power structures inherited from war, civil strife or dictatorship,[7] and sometimes pursued economic policies that exacerbated the risks of state capture and grand corruption. In particular, policies of privatization, decentralization and a focus on resource extraction have made the emergence of profoundly corrupt post-conflict regimes more likely. Against these forces, transitional justice efforts have been insufficient and often beside the point.

I use the examples of South Africa, Tunisia, and Colombia (as well as referring back to Guatemala, considered in Chapter 3) to illuminate some of the processes at work. The countries illustrate different questions. In South Africa, I wanted to know how decisions made during a paradigmatic transition after

1994 led by the early 2000s to what is widely known in the country as state capture. Tunisia is a second-generation transition, part of the 2011–2012 Arab Spring, and I wanted to know what could be learned from Tunisians' efforts to think and deal simultaneously with human rights violations and grand corruption. Finally, I look at ongoing state-of-the-art transitional justice processes in Colombia, asking how the country is addressing the human rights/grand corruption nexus, and how not.

8.2 SOUTH AFRICA: THE ROAD TO STATE CAPTURE

"Revealing is Healing" said the banner over the hearings of the South African Truth and Reconciliation Commission (TRC). The Commissioners, led by Anglican Archbishop Desmond Tutu, convened hearings throughout the country where victims spoke of killings, torture, enforced disappearance, and other terrible crimes under the apartheid regime that had ended with the election of Nelson Mandela in 1994. The TRC's hearings and subsequent report were lauded around the world as an exemplar of transitional justice, dealing with the human rights-related crimes of the past in order to move forward. Free elections, a well-respected Constitutional Court, and a lack of revenge killings; Nelson Mandela's "rainbow nation" would inspire people everywhere. For many people, South Africa is synonymous with a successful transition.

And yet, by 2018 another investigatory commission had convened, this one to delve into how the South African government, then headed by Jacob Zuma, had engaged in, facilitated and turned a blind eye to the widespread high-level corruption that had taken hold in the new South Africa. That corruption, according to the Zondo Commission (named for its chair), amounted to billions of dollars stolen between 2014 and 2017, dollars that translated into scant and shoddy housing for workers, failed and nonexistent "development" projects, schools with no books or roof, and the scandalous enrichment of a family of ANC-tied businessmen and political operatives. Faith in South Africa's democracy was low, and the promise of a postapartheid rainbow nation had been replaced by deep cynicism.[8] What had gone wrong?

Transitional justice focused not on the structural aspects of apartheid, including economic inequality, but on torture, killings and arbitrary detention that were illegal under existing law. The passbooks, limits on marriage and residence, and other pillars of a race-based economic model that systematically impoverished most non-Whites were not part of official truth-telling, although they were formally abolished. The Truth Commission recommended significant reparations for the victims of torture and killing, but the

Mbeki administration demurred, eventually – and begrudgingly – awarded only a minimal onetime payment. The TRC also proposed a "wealth tax" on large businesses to be used for redress, but while the business sector was willing to be charitable, it wanted nothing to do with anything called "reparations." Other proposals by victims' groups to directly address economic inequality went nowhere. There were some land restitutions, but only where applicants could show that their community had been dispossessed by discriminatory acts pre-1994.

The TRC, in addition to holding hearings and presenting a multivolume report, implemented a "truth for amnesty" scheme that exchanged a lack of prosecution for full disclosure of how crimes were committed and where the bodies were buried. The corollary of that scheme was that those who didn't come forward and confess, or whose confessions were found to be false or incomplete, would be prosecuted. But after a disastrous early trial resulted in an acquittal, the prosecution service seemed to give up, and few apartheid-era crimes were ever taken to court.

Part of the reason for the seeming collapse of prosecutions was, as later revealed, the National Prosecution Authority's deliberate slow-walking and abandonment of cases, especially those involving killings, torture, and disappearances during apartheid. The TRC referred 300 cases to the NPA for prosecution, but in the past twenty years, there have only been four known indictments in TRC-related cases, ending in plea bargains and suspended sentences. Despite repeated appeals from the families of murdered activists, the unit in charge of investigating these cases repeatedly suspended, delayed or shut down investigations. The NPA provided no resources for investigation, eventually firing or forcing out the officials in charge.[9]

"The [NPA] does not deny that the executive branch of the state took what one can describe as political steps to manage the conduct of criminal investigations and possible prosecution of the perpetrators of the political murders," Torie Pretorius of the Priority Crimes Litigation Unit said in court papers. According to an internal memorandum written by former NPA head Vusi Pikoli in 2007, Pikoli felt "obstructed from carrying out my functions" and claimed that the Justice Minister was worried that ANC activists would be prosecuted for certain campaigns against the apartheid regime.[10] This concern was played up by police and military groups to discourage investigations. As a result, investigators and attorneys left the NPA, and its budget was cut.[11] As we'll see, the politically motivated inaction regarding anti-apartheid victims and weakening of the institution set the stage for continuing inaction and impunity regarding large-scale corruption and state capture.

The most egregious takeover of the state came during the presidency of Jacob Zuma. Zuma was no stranger to scandal: he had already been indicted for fraud, racketeering and money laundering stemming from bribes by French and British military equipment companies when he was deputy president in the Mbeki government.[12] The case was dropped in 2009 but reopened in 2018 after the courts decided that the decision to drop the charges was irrational. As President, Zuma had control of vast state resources. He allied with the Gupta brothers (Ajay, Atul, and Rajesh), Indian immigrants who had befriended Zuma and his son in the early 2000s, to plunder the state; media reports cite between $3 and $7 billion in losses.[13] Not only did the Guptas get rigged contracts for state-owned mines, trains, energy generation, media and computer companies, they got ministers and officials hired and fired, laws changed, and investigations into their doings quashed. It was a classic example of state capture.

By 2016, the degree of state capture became so extreme that the Public Protector (charged under the constitution with investigating public maladministration), upon complaints by a religious order and the political opposition, began an inquiry into the Guptas' role in appointing government ministers and steering contracts with state entities to Gupta-controlled businesses. Public Protector Thuli Madonsela published an initial State of Capture report, but found that her budget and timeframe were inadequate and recommended a commission of inquiry, with a chair to be chosen by the Chief Justice. The result was the Zondo Commission.

The Commission on State Capture (its official name) was formed to "uncover the extent to which tools and organs of government have been unduly and inappropriately used to enrich and benefit private citizens and individuals, by virtue of them enjoying closeness to political power." Its Chair, then-Deputy and now Chief Justice Raymond Zondo, was the son of a domestic worker who was an expert in labor and corporate law. The Zondo Commission held 429 public, televised hearings with more than 300 witnesses on the scandal between 2018 and 2021 and published its report in 2022. In the words of the *Guardian* newspaper, the State Capture Commission is "a truth and reconciliation commission for our times."[14]

The Commission's hearings and submissions documented the two-pronged nature of state capture. On the one hand, the institutions charged with ensuring probity and accountability were attacked and weakened. The tax agency, the investigative police ("Hawks") and the NPA were defunded and deprived of personnel. Those who investigated grand corruption cases found themselves the subject of leaked allegations of wrongdoing, spurious investigations, and pressure to resign, while the results of their investigations languished or were derailed.[15] The capture of the NPA, as previously detailed, made it equally useless in corruption as it had been in human rights-related cases. On the other hand, the Commission heard about how the Guptas' empire spread: rigged contracts to advertise in Gupta-controlled papers, use Gupta-controlled coal and uranium, change airline routes to suit the Guptas, and even use a poverty-reduction scheme involving dairy farms to benefit the Guptas.

What, then, explains the rise of state capture and grand corruption in post-transition South Africa? The prevailing explanations foreground a history of impunity, the need to protect the electoral predominance of the ANC, and features of the economic model chosen in 1994.

The pre-transition state was marked by control of the military over large swaths of the economy and civilian life, a culture of secrecy, and a total lack of accountability, all rooted, as in Guatemala, in a fear that the anti-apartheid insurgency was on the verge of winning. The apartheid years were great for arms merchants and sanction-busters, mostly military and intelligence service officers and businessmen, who developed ways to circumvent UN and bilateral anti-apartheid sanctions using international banks, arms, oil, ivory, diamond and other natural resource deals,[16] in collusion with governments that looked the other way.

Over time, the old ways permeated the new. The intelligence services "turned into a private resource to serve the political and personal interests of particular individuals."[17] Zuma, who had been the ANC's intelligence chief, transformed the agency into one where agents swore personal loyalty. They then worked to further – and to cover up – the expanding state capture.

In a 2019 book, Hennie van Vuuren, an investigative journalist and cofounder of a group called Open Secrets, argues that "the current struggle against corruption in South Africa is undermined by a basic lack of appreciation of the nature of that corruption and the criminal networks that facilitate it – namely, that they are continuities of a profoundly corrupt system that predates the first democratic election."[18] When I met with van Vuuren, he added that the Truth Commission had not wanted to look deeply into audits revealing illicit sanctions-busting. The legacy of state secrets under apartheid carried over to the state-run enterprises at the heart of the Zuma-era scandals. In an interview, former state auditor Jan van Schalkwyk noted that many problems of state-owned enterprises persist (despite stronger regulations and disclosure requirements) because the company culture never changed, "and this culture is one of a lack of control and management, and a fair amount of freedom around the rules, and not too much concern around what we would nowadays call corruption."[19]

The failure of the TRC to delve into economic crimes, and the lack of criminal investigations, left the image of apartheid and its perpetrators as torturers and assassins, but not corrupt economic actors. The officials and businessmen engaged in sanction-busting to make money and prolong a profoundly unjust system were never held to account. No wonder that later, when allegations of corruption surfaced against post-1994 Black political and economic leaders, they could point to the lack of attention to earlier crimes as evidence of a racist double standard. As a longtime human rights activist told me, "We are unable to shake off a racialized view of corruption and economic crime, supported by a perception that they are new."[20]

South Africa differs from other countries in this book due to the predominance of state-run enterprises. So privatization – a key site of grand corruption in other cases – took a different form here. The auditing function was privatized and state auditors sidelined and attacked. International consultants Bain & Company were brought in to restructure the tax agency, which they did by purging experienced staff and gutting the agency's investigative capacity. The company was eventually banned from South Africa for ten years. KPMG, brought in to audit Gupta's companies, also seemingly saw nothing wrong over a period of fifteen years; its South African leadership eventually resigned and the firm refunded some of the fees it had earned.

The same is true of McKinsey, implicated in questionable transport and energy contracts. To secure a consulting contract with Transnet, McKinsey was required by South African law to work with a Black-owned subcontractor. But instead of thoroughly vetting that subcontractor, McKinsey relied on a recommendation from Transnet that it hire a company called Regiments Capital to help oversee the purchase of a fleet of 1,064 rail locomotives. The locomotives were initially estimated to cost \$2.6 billion, but their price inexplicably rose, almost overnight, by about \$1 billion.[21] McKinsey was criminally charged, along with Transnet executives, in 2022.

Decentralization, as elsewhere, seems to have decentralized and multiplied opportunities for corruption. According to a study by Tom Lodge, "political corruption was enhanced by administrative decentralization."[22] Decentralization was eventually chosen over federalism during the transition to democracy.[23] This left in place the structures of the former "Bantustan" or homeland governments and their notoriously shady practices, and a provincial system of political financing and public contracting that became a new source of patronage. In places like the Free State, a shadow state of informal networks and relationships ensured that the looting was both coordinated and justified as economic transformation.[24]

Ivor Chipkin argues that it was the ANCs analysis of how to effectuate their political project that led to state capture and grand corruption. The limited transitional justice process was part of a larger bargain, to gradually change the concentration of wealth in white hands through creation of Black wealth rather than through expropriation and redistribution. President Mbeki tried to use Black Economic Empowerment and affirmative action to do so, but the strategy had drawbacks. As a *Guardian* investigation put it: "as some freedom fighters went into politics and others went into business, support networks morphed into patronage networks, which in turn became criminal syndicates."[25] Moreover, the backers and main beneficiaries of new Black-led enterprises were often existing white elites.

Under Zuma and his ANC faction, the goal became to use direct state investment to create an African capitalist class and ensure the ANC's continuing political dominance in the face of rising discontent.[26] This meant that monies added onto state contracts could be used for Black capital accumulation, but also to finance the ANC and put its cadre into office. The state was used to maintain and build the party above all – even above the limits imposed by independent courts and oversight mechanisms, which became impediments to this economic strategy in Zuma's eyes.

In the end, Zuma was forced to resign. His refusal to appear before the Commission, and the resulting fifteen-month sentence for contempt, triggered a violent response among his base, including a week of looting and arson that left 354 people dead (in the end, he served only two months of the sentence). Meanwhile, criminal cases against the Guptas have been filed in Germany[27] and the United States imposed financial sanctions against them under the Global Magnitsky Act in 2019. The NPA's extradition request for them to the UAE was denied in March 2023, ostensibly on technical grounds, although a new attempt was announced soon after. The NPA, now under new leadership, brought criminal and asset forfeiture cases against many of the main players. The Zondo Commission's recommendations, including on public contracting, whistle blower protection, and stronger watchdog authorities, are still being debated in the legislature. Meanwhile, Zuma in 2024 formed his own political party to compete against the ANC.[28]

8.3 TUNISIA: A PACKAGE DEAL FALLS APART

Just about fifteen years ago, Tunisia's revolution ushered in a period of enormous hope. In short order, the interim government seized then-dictator Ben Ali's assets and those of his extended family, and set up Commissions on Human Rights, Asset Recovery, and Anti-Corruption. It created a Ministry of Human Rights and Transitional Justice, which engaged in a broad, two-year national dialogue on what Tunisian-style transitional justice should look like and began a constitution drafting process. Soon after, a Truth and Dignity

Commission (TDC) was empaneled. The country was widely celebrated as the only long-term democratic success story of the Arab Spring.

The Tunisian transitional justice design boasted several innovations. It was based on an understanding that corruption was systemic and integral to the regime. It was closely connected to human rights violations of both civil and political and economic, social and cultural rights, creating a mutually reinforcing double impunity. Therefore, the TDC was to look at both civil/political and economic violations, investigate cases involving both, and consider reforms to the system as a whole. At the same time, there was a focus on asset tracing and return of the estimated US$9 billion (some estimates say up to $17 billion) lost between 2000 and 2010 to illicit financial activities and corruption.

Houcine Bouchiba, a slender, chain-smoking man who I met for coffee one evening in Tunis, was a math teacher in the southern town of Tatouine (for Star Wars fans, that's where young Luke Skywalker lived, or at least where the movie scenes were filmed...). The south of Tunisia was a stronghold of opposition to Tunisia's first president, Habib Bourguiba, and was thus systematically neglected and marginalized under his thirty-one-year reign (and beyond). Bouchiba published an essay in a trade union paper against Bourguiba in 1987, and was hauled off to jail, the first of several stints as a political prisoner. Along the way, he became a member of the Ennahda party (he's no longer a member), which got him arrested again, fired from his job, and blacklisted. When the 2011 revolution happened, he became a leader in Karama, an association of former political prisoners.[29]

He explained that from the beginning, the regime had lacked transparency and that state contracts and licenses always favored those close to the regime. When Ben Ali came to power, his in-laws (the Trabelsi clan) became especially good at looting the state, controlling procurement and business licenses and bribing judges. They took over key economic sectors, squashing competition and requiring kickbacks. Even the World Bank was outraged, writing that "[w]e find that the scale of state capture in Tunisia under Ben Ali was extraordinary – by the end of 2010 some 220 firms connected to Ben Ali and his extended family were capturing an astounding 21 percent of all private sector profits annually."[30] Ben Ali also used the police, especially the secret police, to stigmatize, isolate, imprison and torture his perceived political enemies, most of whom were Islamists. So the revolution had twin goals: economic change and an end to repression.

The 2014 Constitution guaranteed rights and liberties, reformed judicial administration, and called for a Constitutional Court to vet legislation and a unicameral Parliament. Notoriously corrupt judges, and those close to Ben Ali, lost their jobs. Regional dialogues aimed to redress imbalances between the coast and the interior. A freewheeling media and multiple political parties (including some banned in the past) cemented a view that Tunisia was on the right track. An inter-ministerial group, meanwhile, pursued the wealth of those close to the Trabelsis within Tunisia and sent requests for cooperation to Switzerland, France, and other European states thought to be holding stolen funds. Youth groups, especially those based in the interior, mobilized to the slogan "We will not forgive." "We were euphoric," recalled Houcine, "dreaming of the best transition ever."

In 2013, as part of a transitional justice law, Parliament created the Truth and Dignity Commission (TDC) to implement truth, accountability, and reparations, and propose institutional reforms.[31] The TDC was to act as a kind of investigative magistrate, compiling files about potential crimes to be transmitted to thirteen Special Judicial Chambers within the regular courts, to be tried for either corruption or human rights-related violations (or both). Article 46 of the TDC Law had an "arbitration" function that, in economic crimes cases, allowed potential defendants to voluntarily come forward, acknowledge guilt and apologize, declare their ill-gotten gains, and accept paying reparations in exchange for an end to legal proceedings against them.

Unfortunately, before much of this could be implemented, the 2014 election marked a turning point. The failure of a draft law on political exclusion allowed the old guard to reinvent itself and become a dominant political force once again, eventually in a coalition with the Islamist Ennahda party. The government, which had been a supporter of a truth-seeking process, was now opposed to anything that might shine an unfavorable light on its members or on the police; collaboration with the nascent TDC ended, including access to documents and service of legal process on those whose files were sent to the Special Judicial Chambers. Adverse media coverage and reports of infighting in the TDC also undermined its legitimacy. The new government quickly proposed an "economic reconciliation" law that would have protected both public and private actors from corruption prosecutions or public scrutiny; after an epic two-year battle, civil society managed to whittle down the law so that it was limited to providing a kind of "superior orders" defense to mid-level public servants who engaged in bribery or other illicit behavior. But a lot of energy was spent on defense.

The TDC published a lengthy final report in 2020.[32] The report has a separate section on corruption, including a chapter on the interplay between corruption and human rights violations. I visited the head of the TDC, a petite, soft-spoken, 60-ish woman named Sihen Bensedrine, at her modest apartment by the beach. She told me that international NGOs advising the Tunisians were mostly unenthusiastic about a focus on corruption, about which they knew little; it was the Tunisian activists who pushed to put human rights and corruption together. Doing so gave rise to a few successes: Ben Ali's son-in-law went before the TDC (and the country) in a televised hearing where he apologized and outlined how corruption took place, although it's doubtful that he (or any other perpetrator) actually paid into a reparations fund as was required. But by and large, the Commission, despite broad powers, was never able to fully carry out its corruption-related mandate.[33]

The Commission took some 60,000 statements, held 14 public hearings, and referred some 200 cases (69 indictments and 131 cases requiring further investigation) to the Special Chambers for prosecution, covering rights violations and financial crimes from 1956 onward. It held only one public hearing on corruption, however, and only a handful of the cases it referred for prosecution were completed corruption investigations. It mostly failed to name names on corruption, or to put together detailed databases, or to use appropriate investigative methodologies.[34]

Its recommendations went far beyond reparations and changes to the police and judiciary to consider reforms of the customs authority, public procurement, audit institutions, and other parts of the administrative state. The TDC adopted the concept of the victim region, focusing on interior areas, especially mining regions, that had been systematically marginalized and neglected since they were labeled as opposition bastions after independence.[35] While there were no public hearings on marginalization, the TDC called for collective reparations to these regions. In a separate letter to the World Bank and IMF asking for reparations, the Commission tied marginalization to international policies of structural adjustment during previous governments.[36] The banks never responded.

The lengthy media attacks, the lack of state cooperation regarding archives, subpoenas and assets, and political divisions within the TDC itself took a toll. The arbitration and prosecution parts of the scheme were unsuccessful. Few people came forward, and civil society groups noted that there was no ability to check whether the asset declarations filed were complete, or truthful. No significant funds were recovered this way. The Special Chambers process, which began in 2018, was similarly unsuccessful. Police unions refused to serve subpoenas, and judges filed no contempt claims when defendants did not appear, stymying hearings. Judges were subject to annual rotations to other judicial posts, which meant that the chambers never developed a dedicated cadre of judges trained in complex criminal or financial investigations. Only eight cases that went to the Chambers involved corruption. The Chambers never issued a single final verdict.

Efforts to reclaim the stolen assets were similarly frustrating. At first, there was progress. On March 14, 2011, the interim government decreed that all the assets of Ben Ali, Leila Trabelsi, and 112 other individuals obtained after 1987 would be considered illegally obtained and automatically confiscated. A Confiscation Committee with representation of various ministries quickly confiscated the assets of this group within Tunisia, including 550 properties, 48 boats and yachts, 40 stock portfolios, 367 bank accounts, and approximately 400 enterprises, with an estimated value of $13 billion.[37] However, the Committee had a lifespan of only four years, and in 2015, with Ben Ali allies back in power, it was not extended or replaced. Its functions reverted to the Prosecuting Authority, which had neither the expertise nor the resources to pursue internationally held funds effectively.

Initially, the EU was quick to impose sanctions on forty-eight members of the Ben Ali-Trabelsi family. In 2013, Lebanon returned USD 28.8 million to Tunisia, while the Swiss government announced a 10-year freeze on 60 million Swiss francs (US$65.6 million), of which $260,000 was returned in 2016 and nearly $4 million in 2019. It's not clear how much more was returned, in part because the government never published any statistics on the issue. It is clear that in at least one case, the government asked Switzerland to release funds back to a Ben Ali family member. It's also clear that the Tunisian authorities had no clear strategy or institutional support for seeking asset recovery abroad, and although they filed dozens of requests, few were adequately documented. In particular, under Swiss law at the time the requesting state had to show that the specific assets were connected to wrongdoing through a domestic conviction against the individual. But Ben Ali and much of his family had been tried in absentia (so there was no final conviction), while others were in hiding or protected and never tried. The Swiss courts found that the evidence and due process protections in Tunisia were too weak to sustain a return of the bulk of the funds.[38]

With the value of hindsight, many of those who had been involved in the process agreed that the fundamental failure was in not dealing more quickly with the economic issues and structural inequities that had prompted the 2011 revolution. The focus on corruption and police as the twin pillars of dictatorship might have been better accomplished in two separate but coordinated entities, which might have diffused rather than concentrated opposition and allowed at least one set of investigations to proceed with fewer headwinds. There was no follow up to the TDC's reform recommendations, and no concerted effort after 2015 to pursue the stolen funds.

The economic bases of the prior system remained in place. Corruption had mostly been dealt with as an individual or familial failing, not a systemic feature that went far beyond Ben Ali and his clan.[39] Parliament failed to effectively dismantle the systems of licenses and permits, procurement and land rents as well as unaccountable police, that kept (and keep) the old elite in command. Farmers continued suffering from high debt and dispossession rates, and job opportunities were few. It was this sense of wheel-spinning and dysfunction, compounded by pandemic-related economic and health crises from 2020 on, that led most Tunisians to applaud on July 25, 2021, when Tunisia's President Kais Saied, a former constitutional law professor, suspended Parliament and affirmed he would rule by decree. As time has gone on, the government has taken on more and more of an authoritarian cast, and its support has dwindled.

Kais Said ignored the recommendations of the TDC, promoting instead a new form of "criminal reconciliation" in corruption cases that would allow those accused or convicted of economic crimes – at any time – to invest in marginalized regions in exchange for immunity or pardons.[40] Most observers agree that Kais Saied himself is not corrupt, and that he was right to insist on changes in an unsustainable status quo. But as of this writing, Tunisia seems to have joined the lengthening list of "illiberal democracies." As Houcine put it "future generations will know that corruption is responsible for human rights violations. But we couldn't muster the political will to change it."

8.4 COLOMBIA: "PARAPOLÍTICA," ECONOMIC ACTORS, AND COMPREHENSIVE TRANSITIONAL JUSTICE

Magistrate Nadiezhda Henríquez of Colombia's Special Jurisdiction for Peace (JEP, its Spanish initials), contemplated the five men appearing before her. The men were former executives of the Cattleman's Fund in northwest Colombia. They described how they had worked with paramilitaries to massively evict local peasants and indigenous communities from their land, how the communities were threatened or forced to turn over deeds or to sell their land for pennies, and how corrupt notaries, cattlemen and palm oil companies then took over the land, making millions. Henriquez nodded as the former governor of the state of Córdoba and manager of the Fund, Benito Osorio, explained how the paramilitaries captured and forcibly disappeared those who resisted.

Henríquez knew that process personally. Her father, Julio Henríquez Santamaría, an environmental activist, was kidnapped in 2001 by paramilitaries. She never saw him alive again. Her family was forced to move away, joining the millions forcibly displaced across the country. His body was found six years later; Nadiezhda and her mother watched the exhumation.

Vivacious, whip-smart and quick to laugh, she became a lawyer, eventually working on land restitution cases. When the JEP opened its doors in 2017 as a result of peace accords with Colombia's largest insurgent group, she applied to become a judge. One of her cases, on armed conflict-related crimes in the Urabá region, implicated landowners in the cattle, palm oil and banana businesses in supporting, financing and participating in the crimes.

Colombia suffered a sixty-year armed conflict with multiple actors, motivations, and phases. The country's conflict confronted state officials, private elites (based in legal and illegal businesses), paramilitary, organized crime and insurgent groups, which morph from one type to another. Colombians have used demobilization processes for paramilitaries and guerrillas, peace accords focused on rural development, alternatives to drug cultivation and victims' rights, and several bouts of official and unofficial truth-seeking including a Truth, Coexistence and Non-recurrence Commission (here called simply the Truth Commission) that issued its report in 2022. According to the Commission, some 450,000 people were killed, almost 100,000 disappeared without a trace, and over 7 million were displaced. It has pioneered several rounds of alternative judicial processes for armed actors, including a Justice and Peace process starting in 2005 mostly aimed at paramilitaries, and the current JEP that covers the FARC guerrillas and security forces, while allowing other actors to opt in. It created institutions for restitution of land and multiple reparations processes. All this in a large, diverse country with marked regional dynamics and a complex and sophisticated justice system and state.

The majority of human rights violations were carried out by paramilitary groups working hand in glove with the military and large landowners. By the 2000s many of the paramilitary groups had coalesced into the United Self-Defense Groups, known as the AUC. According to the Truth Commission report, these groups terrorized the countryside, massacring entire communities thought to support the guerrillas and displacing millions of rural and small town inhabitants, often in order to empty out the territory and seize their lands.[41] "Thus, the counterinsurgency component intertwined with the interest in exterminating and expelling social and political sectors that opposed the paramilitary order, with the aim of expanding drug-related business through the clearing of contraband routes in strategic parts of the national territory."[42] Other income sources included gaining control over state and local government coffers, oil theft, and extortion.[43]

The AUC and other such groups did not just control militarily, but also instituted their own local economies, rough justice, and even development projects (as did the FARC in the areas that they controlled), replacing a largely absent central state. They also coopted the country's electoral politics, starting at the local level. Colombia's 1991 Constitution decentralized considerable power and resources to the municipal level, and it was easy for a coalition of paramilitaries, landowners and organized crime to coerce or coopt their way into local government.[44] These groups then demanded, on pain of death, that the population in areas under their control vote for their preferred candidates.

A 2005 complaint to the Supreme Court asked the Court to investigate public declarations by AUC leaders that they controlled at least 35 percent of Congress and were looking to increase that percentage.[45] The lead Associate Justice investigating on behalf of the Court: Iván Velásquez, the former Medellín prosecutor whom we met leading the CICIG in Guatemala in Chapter 3. Investigation of then President Uribe's ties to the paramilitaries (and thus to drug trafficking) led to investigations of Uribe's cousin and of leaders of his political party and allies, including sixty-five members of Congress, in cases that became known as "*parapolítica*." Threats from the government against Velásquez and his fellow Justices escalated, especially from the military intelligence agency.[46]

Presidents going back to at least 1994 had been accused of ties to drug cartels, but this was a whole new level of interlocking control. As the Truth Commission found: [This control]

> implied as well the infiltration and penetration of public institutions, including the theft of public resources to finance armed groups, businesses or networks of collaborators. This happened with health entities – like several hospitals in the Caribbean region or the indigenous clinic Manexha –, with different NGOs -like Asocomún-, with educational institutions like the University of Córdoba – and in general with a broad range of public bodies, such as municipal secretaries and state-level departments of Finance, Education, Health, and infrastructure contracts, among others. At the same time, assassinations and disappearances took place against those who complained about these things, who were stigmatized as subversives.[47]

The emerging *parapolítica* scandal threatened to engulf the government of President Alvaro Uribe. Uribe, a law and order conservative adamantly opposed to any talks with the FARC guerrillas, proposed a demobilization process for the right-wing paramilitaries. To many observers, this seemed like a clumsy attempt to distance himself from the crimes of his allies and disassociate the military from these crimes. Nonetheless, in 2005 Congress passed a Justice and Peace Law aimed at those paramilitaries who had committed serious crimes. Illegal groups who agreed to demobilize, turn over their ill-gotten gains and any prisoners or underage soldiers, testify fully and truthfully about their activities and foreswear illegal activities going forward could reduce what would otherwise be multi-decade sentences to between five and eight years in prison. The prosecutors' office would investigate the potential crimes, and special chambers within the ordinary court system would pronounce sentence.

In the end, 31,810 people demobilized under Justice and Peace by 2018, but only 4,346 applied for reduced jail time and gave statements. The process was long and drawn out, especially before reforms in 2012 allowed for greater prioritization and consolidation of cases. There were only sixty-five final convictions after fifteen years, according to the Prosecutor's Office. Meanwhile, many of the remaining paramilitaries regrouped into smaller criminal bands. Moreover, the Prosecutors' Office was slow – some said deliberately slow – to follow up on leads to other cases, especially those involving the private sector or public officials' support for the paramilitaries.

The process was especially ineffective at finding and returning stolen assets. In principle, those who signed up for the Justice and Peace process were to declare and return what they had stolen, but of all the reparations paid to the victims of their actions, only 6 percent came from the paramilitaries, with the rest from the state itself. A few paramilitary leaders turned over properties and a few more were found and confiscated, but most of the stolen wealth was hidden under layers of shell companies and fake owners. However, investigations into ill-gotten wealth could continue even after sentencing (or even release) and the pace of confiscations has improved: in 2022 some 329 properties, with a value ten times greater than in the first years of the program, were seized.[48]

Even when property was turned over or found, there was no mechanism in place for the authorities to freeze, register, sell, or transfer the proceeds to the victims. Only in 2013 was a (small) unit dedicated to finding and securing paramilitary assets. What's worse, properties turned over to the state were stripped of value and left abandoned because it wasn't clear who was in charge: for example, paramilitary leader "Cuco" Vanoy built a hospital in Tarazá, which he duly turned over to the state as the proceeds of crime. While the state dithered, the doors, plumbing and even walls were stolen, leaving a useless shell.[49]

The issue of land proved particularly intractable. In many places, paramilitaries had stolen land but the original owners were scattered around the country (and elsewhere). In others, the land belonged to the state, or had been turned over to demobilized paramilitary troops to farm. In 2011, the Victims' Law created a Reparations Fund, and eventually directed paramilitary assets into the fund. It also created an adjudication process for returning land, which I describe in Chapter 7. Magistrate Nadiezhda Henríquez, before her current position, was a judge in the Land Restitution Courts.

The example, and the limitations, of the Justice and Peace process were foremost in the minds of negotiators as they began talks with the leadership of the FARC guerrillas to end the insurgency. The peace accords that followed in 2016 seemed, at least, to focus on some of the conditions that had led to state capture, especially the overwhelming dynamic of the "war on drugs," the links between government and paramilitaries, and the abandonment of rural areas. Colombia's transitional justice package aimed to be comprehensive. In addition to the eleven-member Truth Commission, there was a search commission for the disappeared, and a purpose-built justice system (the JEP) that would try those who had committed crimes that under international law could not be amnestied.

The peace accords, for the first time, envisioned a broad set of anti-corruption measures, arising in part from negotiators' concerns that simply throwing new money at rural areas and demobilization projects without robust transparency and accountability would reproduce, and exacerbate, the penetration of criminal structures into public institutions.[50] The government committed to creating and supporting citizen monitoring and observatories of government spending, especially related to the accords, as well as local complaint mechanisms around corruption, a publicity campaign, and the technical expertise of specialized organizations or universities. It agreed to vet the suitability of public servants for both integrity and competency, to compare their assets to salaries (presumably through asset declarations). And it agreed to sponsor legislation to punish political groupings whose candidates or officials are convicted of ties to criminal groups, including new groups of paramilitaries. For the negotiators, an anti-corruption agenda was part and parcel of "carrying out of the accords, security guarantees in the regions and democratic participation."[51]

The accords created the Special Jurisdiction for Peace, or JEP, where Magistrate Henríquez is one of thirty-eight judges. The JEP's process is convoluted – the case management flowchart looks like a bowl of spaghetti – but it boils down to a sliding scale of full (ordinary), reduced (alternative) or non-custodial (special) potential sanctions, depending on when in the process the demobilized person acknowledged their crimes (if ever) and how high up in the leadership they were when they committed them. Unlike the earlier process, the JEP is a largely self-contained system with its own investigators, prosecutors and judges, created under national law.

The JEP requires demobilized members of the FARC and public security forces involved in war-related crimes to appear, testify about their crimes and the conflict, return ill-gotten gains for the use of victims, and agree to complete their alternative sentences; lying, stonewalling or backsliding sends them to the regular justice system, where long prison sentences await. The JEP started by requesting reports on particularly hard-hit areas and notorious crimes, from the Prosecutors' Office, other government agencies, victims' groups, NGOs, and universities. From that information it synthesized six priority cases (later expanded to eleven), a combination of regional foci, political actors, and indigenous and other vulnerable groups. Rather than wait for prosecutors to investigate the claims of applicants (as in Justice and Peace) the JEP has a database to start from.

At least two of the cases currently before the JEP raise issues of public and private sector corruption. Case 4, described above, focuses on the hard-hit Urabá region of northern Colombia. Case 8, opened in 2022, focuses on the linkages among security forces and other state actors, private actors and paramilitaries in crimes against humanity and war crimes due to, occasioned by or directly or indirectly related to the armed conflict. Unlike earlier cases based on regions or types of crimes, this case looks at specific actors, while trying to prioritize certain areas and avoid overlap with those earlier investigations. It's also big and bulky, and may have to be subdivided or whittled down before trial.

Announcing the opening of the case, the JEP noted two patterns that it intended to investigate: those crimes that were carried out to favor private economic interests, and those aimed at control of the state apparatus.

> [The case] groups together events that were motivated by control of the region's economic interests, its wealth and the takeover of land from rural populations. An important part of the crimes related to the counterinsurgency were useful to legal and illegal economic actors, by allowing the conditions for the extraction of natural resources, the expansion of the agricultural frontier and the incorporation of new lands to the market.
>
> The same actors "sought to capture rents from public administration in order to [...] expand and consolidate paramilitary structures, and broaden their social base by controlling the supply of bureaucratic and electoral services or public contracting. The paramilitaries were supported by security forces, other state agents and private civilians who were their intermediaries in the capture of public functions and institutions."[52]

Early on, the JEP focused on the private sectors' role in financing paramilitary atrocities, as well as the paramilitaries' control of the state. There has been little on how that control translated into state capture per se. When I asked several of the JEP judges why, they pointed to a lack of forensic financial expertise and a reluctance to further expand an already overwhelming workload. Yet without an understanding of how corruption, crime and rights violations were intertwined, the history sketched by these cases will remain incomplete and distorted. As of now, it seems like at least these two cases may move in that direction, but a wholesale investigation into the role of the private sector may create too much pressure on the JEP, forcing it to back off. The Petro administration, unlike its predecessor, strongly supports these efforts, and his period in office may be the best chance the JEP will get.

8.5 COMMONALITIES AND CONCLUSIONS

What can be learned from this sample of emblematic transitions that might forestall or at least ameliorate the tendency for state capture or grand corruption to reemerge after transition? One answer might be that a more concerted, conscious effort is needed to change not just societal attitudes but how transitional governments act against past corrupt actors and seek to prevent new ones from emerging. This has, by and large, not been done.

The parallels between large-scale atrocity crimes and systemic corruption jump out from these stories: both are committed by the powerful, who arrange their own impunity by weakening systems of control or putting their allies in charge. Both feature complex networks rather than isolated crimes, which means they take a long time to unravel. Ordinary justice systems often aren't up to the task – witness the Colombian prosecutors' uneven follow up of Justice and Peace processes, or the Tunisian prosecutor or the South African NPA's reluctance to take on even notorious high-level cases. And in all these cases, the past isn't really past. Just as over the last thirty years, the emerging consensus has been that ignoring atrocity crimes isn't an option, the same is true of the large-scale stealing and sacking of the country's land, resources and governments. Not confronting systemic corruption will sink the transition.

A common theme running through these cases is that inadequate or superficial vetting of current and prospective security or intelligence officials presages their emergence as agents of organized crime or grand corruption. Often only the name of the security body changed, but the methods, selection procedures and even faces remained. Military intelligence especially needs to be carefully pruned and renewed; South Africa's experience (or Guatemala's cautionary tale from Chapter 3) of military intelligence morphing into corrupt networks and organized crime is not unique. Similarly, civil servants need to be vetted for competency rather than simply political affiliation.

Peacebuilding practice established an informal division of labor between transitional justice advocates and economic policymakers, creating a great deal of policy incoherence. In many transitions, especially in the 1990s and 2000s, international economic orthodoxy recommended programs of privatization of state enterprises, infrastructure and resources, and decentralization to the municipal level. Both ideas, while not irrational responses to government dysfunction, in the context of states already captured by shortsighted elites and weakened by conflict ended up accelerating the capture and reconfiguration of the state. They made control of government at both the local and national levels more worthwhile for those intent on looting the newly available resources. The buyers of state-owned resources were usually related (by family, school ties or political affiliation) to those government officials selling off the resources in the name of efficiency. Licenses and permits were used to restrict new entrants, steer official contracts and cover up illegal markets.

Municipalities, now guaranteed a percentage of the national budget, became newly ripe targets. Decentralization, which was supposed to minimize corruption and bring government closer to the people, often ended up making municipal governments more vulnerable to control by organized crime and traditional elites looking for new ways to loot social services and steer jobs and contracts to allies. In the 1990s, the World Bank strongly supported decentralization, although it later became more cautious due to the "risks of elite capture."[53] Decentralization was part of state policy in Colombia starting in 1991. The Truth Commission found that it exacerbated the incursion of paramilitary groups into local government. In Guatemala, decentralization also led to penetration by organized crime and corrupt officials. The same is true in South Africa, especially given the legacy of "Bantustans" and efforts to return power to traditional chiefs. In Bosnia, we know that the heavily decentralized government structure emerging from the 1990s war encouraged rent-seeking behavior and made accountability more difficult.[54]

Going forward, peacebuilders need to incorporate anti-corruption strategies into every element of a transition. In Venezuela, for instance, it is difficult to imagine a genuine transition that does not deal with both human rights violations and grand corruption. This is not a technocratic imperative but a political one: power and money go together, and systems of impunity and self-dealing will not give up without a fight. Any analysis of leverage points and alliances must take this reality into account.

Could some type of transitional justice apply to cases of grand corruption? International law limits amnesties, pardons and statutes of limitation in cases of international crimes, including crimes against humanity, war crimes, and genocide. It also draws a distinction between those most responsible for these crimes and others, allowing more flexibility with regard to lower-ranked or less responsible parties. As we've seen with Colombia, punishment of such crimes does not necessarily involve long prison sentences, although it does require some form of accountability.

There are no such limits with regard to economic crimes, even those that have human rights consequences but do not rise to the level of international crimes. On the contrary, what is needed, as I've argued above, is a more robust approach to victim consultation, participation and remedy, and a focus on reparation and repair. In the case of Venezuela, one scenario for eventual transition involves negotiating the exit of the current leadership in exchange for limits to criminal drug smuggling and corruption charges against them in the United States and elsewhere. This would, of course, still leave open charges at the International Criminal Court for crimes against humanity.

The more complicated question is whether transitional justice approaches might be applied to organized criminal groups, to encourage demobilization and reincorporation into civilian life. Colombian President Gustavo Petro has been attempting a hybrid approach, called "total peace." The initiative covers both insurgent groups that did not sign the Peace Accords as well as "organized high-impact armed criminal structures" whether organized as a network or a vertical hierarchy. The government proposal involves suspending arrest warrants on group members while the group negotiates its demobilization and the terms under which it will face (presumably lessened) criminal charges in the regular courts.[55] The law requires any such policy to take victims' rights into account to the greatest extent possible and to avoid impunity. To date, the attempt is highly controversial and has had limited success.

9

A Corruption Lens on Atrocity Crimes*

Seeing behind the Slaughter

Rodrigo Gonzalez was frustrated. He had been trying for months to get federal authorities to investigate repeated reports of extortion, corruption and violence by top authorities in his home state of Nayarit, on the Pacific coast of Mexico. But the feds would do nothing.

Gonzalez didn't have proof at the time, but the beatings and intimidation were coming directly from the office of the state's public prosecutor (*fiscalía*). As more people came to him with stories about torture, forced disappearances, and extortion coming from high-ranking state authorities, Gonzalez and several others decided that they were going to do their own investigation. In 2016, they formed the Truth Commission of Nayarit as an independent citizens' effort. They began gathering evidence and talking to victims and witnesses; some 2,000 of them told their stories. What they found was a conspiracy from the top of the state government to ally with organized crime, embezzle millions in state funds, steal property and money from the citizenry, and commit a range of atrocities to do so. The corrupt acts and the atrocities were intertwined and fed off each other in what Gonzalez described as a scheme of macrocriminality. For his troubles, in December 2019 González was attacked by three masked gunman when he picked up his daughter from a friend's house, but managed to escape. The would-be assassins tried again a month later, leaving him with a bullet in the neck. Truth Commission members regularly received death threats.

At the center of the conspiracy was Edgar Veytia, the state's public prosecutor from 2011 to 2017. Veytia, whose self-declared nickname was "the Devil," set up a clandestine jail and torture center right in the offices of the public prosecutor. There he and the police and prosecutors under his command would bring landowners whose properties they or their allies coveted. They forced landowners to turn over their holdings, either for nothing or for a pittance. Sometimes police would accompany the victim to his or her house to get the paperwork. Other times, the target would be falsely arrested and jailed until the family turned over the deed. The land sometimes was useful for a landing strip, private road, laboratory, safehouse or other drug-related activities, sometimes it abutted one of the governor's extensive holdings, and sometimes Veytia and his friends knew that upcoming federal projects (like a canal project) would increase the land's value many times. Those who resisted selling were tortured, or their family members were jailed and tortured. In over 1,000 cases, according to the Truth Commission, people were brought in and simply disappeared.

Apparently Veytia "was so corrupt even the crooks who paid him off couldn't trust him" as the Associated Press put it. He started out working for the Beltrán Leiva cartel but then switched to the Jalisco Nueva Generación, ensuring protection for their members but not for rivals, recruiting new members, and enlisting the law enforcement apparatus of the state to facilitate drug movements. Despite the brazenness of his crimes, Veytia was only arrested in March 2017 when he crossed the US border into San Diego, California. The US government tried him for drug trafficking and sentenced him to twenty years imprisonment. The US prosecution, however, ignored Veytia's killings, torture, disappearances and thefts, leaving them to the Mexican authorities. Although with pressure from the Truth Commission and the Mexican Commission to Search for the Disappeared, some cases have been opened in Mexico against Veytia and his associates, many of them are still pending.

9.1 A CORRUPTION LENS

Sometimes acts of grand corruption also involve the commission of atrocity crimes, by which I mean serious human rights violations that can, under certain circumstances, also be considered international crimes such as war crimes, crimes against humanity, widespread ethnic cleansing or torture, or genocide. Although the correspondence between countries with a pattern of atrocity crimes and those with a high rate of grand corruption is notorious, they have been seen as separate phenomena, with their own international and national legal regimes, as well as with their own communities of activists and experts.

This chapter considers how looking at atrocity crimes through a corruption lens – and grand corruption as sharing many characteristics of atrocity crimes – can improve the fight against both. Incorporating corruption-based analysis into the effort to achieve some degree of justice for victims of crimes against humanity provides several benefits. It allows advocates, judges and prosecutors to name the phenomenon as the motivating force behind many atrocity crimes in a way that resonates with ordinary people and constitutes a powerful explanatory narrative. This fulfills the expressive, naming function of criminal law.[1] The fight against corruption contributes to the more general popular demand for public and private accountability. The emphasis on corruption can also serve to unmask a rhetoric of left against right that obscures and confuses, making it clear that such rhetoric is only a ruse to hide the plunder. This broadens the constituency for justice and the fight against impunity.

Conversely, the classification of the facts as constituting war crimes or crimes against humanity could make it easier to combat examples of grand corruption where atrocity crimes are committed at the same time or within the same general course of conduct. Both types of crimes are hard to trace and prosecute. In situations where they overlap, a characterization as international crimes would allow the use of broader universal jurisdiction, limitations on prescription (statutes of limitations) and immunities and more severe penalties than those provided by anti-corruption laws alone. While the evidentiary burdens are considerable for both types of crime, in some circumstances there may be more accessible evidence of atrocities than of corruption-related crimes. That was the case, for example, in Guatemala's Molina-Theissen case involving torture, rape and forced disappearance, where one of the high-ranking military officers convicted[2] was widely known as a key figure in organized crime and corruption, but no corruption case against him was ever forthcoming.

Increasingly, grand corruption crimes share with atrocity crimes the inability of national courts to investigate and prosecute them adequately, due to the degree of state capture giving rise to impunity. Judges are not independent, prosecutors are bought or threatened, witnesses are intimidated or attacked. Alleged perpetrators of grand corruption share with high-level perpetrators of atrocity crimes their access to official resources and structures, which increases their degree of dangerousness. In many parts of the world, the types of crimes that were once considered "ordinary" (murder, rape, forced displacement or torture by organized crime syndicates, gangs or paramilitary groups), are now carried out with the participation, connivance, or acquiescence of state actors, who are participants and partners in vast schemes of state plunder that involve both public and private actors. These changes make national systems inadequate. When these crimes are committed to silence human rights defenders, whistleblowers, rivals or inconvenient witnesses, or to clear or control an area of population and thus facilitate illegal mining, logging or other resource extraction, drug trafficking or smuggling, they should be properly characterized as international crimes.

This chapter develops these arguments using examples from Venezuela and Mexico. I use the definitions of international crimes in the Rome Statute creating the International Criminal Court (ICC) because they have been widely adopted into national law and subsequent international instruments. The ICC starting in 2002 has been the court of last resort for trying international crimes in circumstances when national courts are unable or unwilling to do so, so long as either the state where the crimes took place or the state of the suspects' nationality are parties to the treaty (or have otherwise agreed to jurisdiction).[3] In a few places, the ICC requirements and definitions differ from those of other tribunals, and there I will explain what difference it makes. Other places could be analyzed in similar terms, but I focus on these examples because there is an ICC investigation already open in Venezuela, and there have been repeated efforts to open a preliminary examination in Mexico.

9.2 CRIMES AGAINST HUMANITY AND GRAND CORRUPTION

The two most likely international crimes raised by grand corruption-related acts are the war crime of pillage and several subspecies of crimes against humanity. It is possible to analyze events involving large-scale violent misappropriation as the war crime of "pillage." Pillage and "extensive ... appropriation of property, not justified by military necessity and carried out unlawfully and wantonly" are both prohibited by Article 8 of the Rome Statute. Pillage, long prohibited in the law of war, is understood as a crime against property, which requires that the "perpetrator appropriated certain property" and that the "appropriation was without the consent of the owner." Pillage can be individual or systematic and organized; the property taken need not belong to an "enemy," nor is violence needed. The ICC Elements of Crimes adds a third, more controversial element that the property must be appropriated for private or personal use.[4] Applying the term to events like those described earlier in Nayarit is problematic on several counts. At the most basic level, war crimes only take place in a situation of (international or non-international) armed conflict: no war, no war crime. Many analysts as well as states have been loath to characterize Mexico, much less Venezuela, as engaged in such an armed conflict.[5] The "personal or private use" requirement is also problematic where the stolen property serves to fund a political campaign or the land acquisition of an ally. For these reasons, the rest of this analysis will focus on crimes against humanity.

Article 7 of the statute of the International Criminal Court sets out a list of enumerated acts, including murder, slavery, torture, imprisonment or other severe deprivations of physical liberty, enforced disappearance, persecution or "other inhumane acts" of a similar nature. To qualify as crimes against humanity, these acts must be committed "as part of a widespread or systematic attack directed against a civilian population, with knowledge of the attack." The attack need not be a military attack; rather, an "attack" within the meaning of Article 7 refers to a "campaign or operation carried out against the civilian population."[6] Crimes against humanity occur in times of war as well as peace and can be carried out by private organizations as well as states.

A grand corruption lens on these crimes would help in the analysis of crimes against humanity in at least four ways. It would contribute to characterizing modes of individual responsibility; it would point to the existence (or otherwise) of a state or organizational policy as required under the Rome Statute (although not elsewhere); it would facilitate recognizing and analyzing the widespread or systematic nature of the acts listed in Article 7; and it would help show the existence of patterns of persecution of a group or collectivity under Article 7(h). In the specific case of the ICC, it would also help to analyze complementarity and severity, both required for the ICC to open an investigation.

9.2.1 *Modes of Liability*

One of the characteristics of crimes against humanity is that they are generally collective, not isolated crimes of a single person or a small group. In part, this collective aspect is what gives these crimes their dangerousness and their suppression its moral weight. It also creates specific problems with respect to understanding the connection between the direct perpetrators – triggermen, rapists or baselevel torturers – and those at the top: the indirect, intermediate or intellectual authors, those who plan, allow, order, help or, having the obligation to intervene, refrain from doing so.[7] International criminal law, and national jurisprudence based on this law, solves these problems with the help of specific doctrines such as joint criminal enterprise, indirect perpetration through control of an organized power structure, command responsibility for hierarchical superiors, or extended forms of coauthorship.[8] The exact mode of participation may vary depending on the facts and jurisdiction. The ICC, in particular, applies several forms of individual liability.[9]

To understand how an approach focusing on grand corruption networks can be useful here, we need to go back to Nayarit, Mexico. We already saw how the public prosecutor of the state, Edgar Veytia, sought a mutually beneficial alliance with drug cartels, and used extortion and torture to make millions. It's not hard to draw a line between Veytia and the cops and thugs under his command who carried out those crimes on his behalf, especially since one of his first acts in office was to consolidate local and statewide police forces under him. But once Veytia was arrested in the US, Mexican journalists, victims' families, and US authorities dug further. They found that the entire leadership of the state, starting with then-Governor Roberto Sandoval, was deeply involved in the looting, and necessarily had at least known about and aided and abetted Veytia.

Sandoval, who was born into a family of poor butchers and at one point was a street sweeper in Los Angeles, started his political career as mayor of Tepic, the capital of Nayarit. He appointed Veytia to several posts, helped him control the state police forces and benefited from his extortion and land-grabbing. The two were allies as well as godparents to each other's children. After Veytia was arrested and Sandoval lost his reelection bid in June 2017, a wave of over 300 forced disappearances followed. Eyewitnesses told of the white unmarked cars and masked police agents from the Public Prosecutor's office taking people away; associations of victims' families found clandestine cemeteries with at least 140 bodies. The US Treasury Department imposed Global Magnitsky sanctions (see Chapter 4) on Sandoval in 2019 for misappropriating state assets and receiving bribes,[10] and in 2020 he was finally arrested and jailed in Mexico after months on the run. Since then, several local cases filed against him have gone nowhere or been dismissed; the main charges still pending involve using illicit assets to buy property in the names of family members and businesses. At the time, he and his family owned extensive ranches, 12,000 head of cattle, 350 Spanish broodmares, luxury art objects and equestrian artifacts, and at least 42 bank accounts, totaling more than 1.196 billion Mexican pesos (US$70.5 million).[11] But he has not, to date, been charged for the killings and disappearances.

The criminal network extended beyond Veytia and Sandoval to other high-ranking authorities. Judges like Isidro Avelar Gutiérrez (sanctioned by the US as a drug kingpin) dismissed cases (or not) in exchange for bribes. A leader of the state congress from the PRI party, Carlos Saldate, was Sandoval's operator, helping him and Veytia extort properties by coercing their owners. He was sentenced to thirty-five years in prison in 2023. On the other hand, Sandoval's private secretary, Raymundo García Chavez, was appointed at the end of Sandoval's reign as an anti-corruption judge (!), despite having bought at least fifteen properties and twenty-eight cars for Sandoval.[12] And many of the police and prosecutors who worked for Veytia are still in the Public Prosecutors office.

A corruption lens helps to understand who forms part of these chains of liability. It contributes, for example, to seeing that the governor and prosecutors of Nayarit are part of the same chain as the narcos and hitmen who murder and torture, and the police who surround a targeted property or take the victims to the torture cell. The common purpose is illicit enrichment, which involves the commission of atrocity crimes to control drug routes, lands and/or population, to intimidate possible opponents or to achieve and maintain impunity. Co-commission, complicity and commission through the conduct of others also seem relevant.

9.2.2 *State or Organizational Policy*

A second way in which a grand corruption approach clarifies and, at the same time, complicates international criminal law, has to do with the existence of a policy. The Rome Statute of the ICC, unlike previous international tribunals, requires proof that the criminal acts were carried out in accordance with a state or organizational policy.[13] This language has been controversial and is specific to the Rome Statute, not a general requirement of law. Some commentators argue that it is unnecessary given the already-existing "widespread or systematic" definition of a crime against humanity, while others support it as a necessary boundary that distinguishes international crimes from ordinary crimes of individuals, mobs, mafias or gangs, which are capable of being dealt with by national justice systems.[14]

While I cannot reprise these debates here, it's worth pointing out that the conception of a mafia has changed from 1998 until today. More and more states have been totally or partially captured precisely by mafias of various kinds. If, as commentators have suggested, the concern is to avoid applying international criminal law to crimes capable of being investigated and tried by national jurisdictions, these jurisdictions have shown themselves to have great difficulty holding powerful Mafia-state alliances to account. It may be time to reconsider this debate.

The ICC Trial Chamber in the Bemba case elaborated on the factors that could be taken into consideration for the purpose of establishing the existence of a policy: "[T]he 'policy' need not have been formalized, but an attack which is planned, directed or organized – as opposed to spontaneous or isolated acts of violence – will satisfy this criterion."[15] If they are state actors, the Court finds that "a policy adopted by regional, and even local bodies could satisfy the requirement of a state policy."[16]

The ICC's Pre-Trial Chamber II, in the case on electoral violence in Kenya, had to decide whether the non-state groups carrying out the alleged acts had an organizational policy. The majority decided that they did, since "While some have argued that only organizations similar to States can qualify, the Chamber is of the opinion that the formal character of a group and the level of its organization should not be the defining criterion. Instead, ... one must distinguish whether the group is capable of performing acts that infringe upon basic human values."[17] The dissent argued, instead, that an organization must share at least some characteristics of a state in order to have international responsibility under the Statute.[18]

Nonstate actors still have to meet certain characteristics, which the court summarized as follows:

> [T]he Chamber may consider various elements, such as: "(i) whether the group is under responsible command, or has an established hierarchy; (ii) whether the group possesses in fact the means to carry out a widespread or systematic attack against a civilian population; (iii) whether the group exercises control over part of the territory of a State; (iv) whether the group has criminal activities against the civilian population as a primary purpose; (v) whether the group articulates, explicitly or implicitly, an intention to attack a civilian population; (vi) whether the group is part of a larger group, which satisfies some or all of the above criteria." While these considerations may assist the Chamber in its determination, they do not constitute a rigid legal definition, and need not be met exhaustively.[19]

As we will see below, mapping and understanding corruption as context changes the way we visualize whose policy it is and what policy is implemented. The massacre in the town of Allende, in the State of Coahuila, Mexico, between March 18 and 20, 2011 provides an additional example. At the time, the area was a smuggling crossroads for the Zetas criminal cartel, which controlled the territory and population, and was at odds with other groups. The Zetas suspected that three members of the group had given information to the DEA and considered them traitors. All three fled to the United States. Since they were gone, the Zetas decided to retaliate against their families and others associated with them.[20] They surrounded the village, took over the streets and went from house to house, looking for people with the same surname as the three alleged traitors, or people who had worked with or for them, or who had some other relationship. They took their victims to Finca los Garza, where they killed everyone – including children, the elderly, and babies – and set the bodies on fire, creating smoke visible from miles away.[21] About 300 people lost their lives, but most of the bodies were never found.

Accompanying the Zetas were many police officers from the town, while others were in charge of cordoning off streets; there was no police response to the multiple calls for help. Later, it came to light that the police director and the municipal police commander took bribes to help the Zetas. A few days before the massacre, there was a meeting with the town's mayor and police chief, where they agreed that they would not intervene. In several trials in the United States, where the three former Zetas who fled testified, they claimed that not only local officials, but also those from other towns, from the Coahuila state government (from the governor on down), and a part of the federal police and the armed forces, were active associates of the Zetas. At the very least, they accepted money for not seeing or acting against the group, or for acting against their rivals.[22] The bribes were, in Jimena Reyes' words, "a condition sine qua non of the State's contribution to the enforced disappearances."[23] There has been little effort to investigate the actions of high-level officials in the massacre or in subsequent investigations.[24] In the same area, at the same time, around 150 disappearances were reported in the Piedras Negras Penitentiary, which the government handed over to the Zetas and which served as their center of operations.[25]

Or consider, briefly, the most famous Mexican disappearance case of the last ten years: the September 26, 2014 abduction of forty-three students of the Ayotzinapa Rural Teachers' College in Guerrero. The students were commandeering buses to participate in a protest in Mexico City when they were surrounded by armed men, some were shot, and the rest taken away and never seen again. Mexican authorities initially tried to blame local police for turning the students over to a local organized crime group, and alleged that their remains had been burned. An international fact-finding commission known as GIEI debunked that theory, and over time it came out that federal, state and local police, military officers and local authorities as well as drug traffickers were involved; apparently, one of the commandeered buses was to have been on its way to Chicago, packed chock full of drugs. The unlucky students picked the wrong bus.[26]

When López Obrador became president, he reopened the investigation, and eventually, a special investigative unit headed by the former secretary of the GIEI took it over. Omar Gómez Trejo is young, bearded, and a doting father. After all the obstacles the previous government had placed before the work of the GIEI, he was optimistic that things would now be different. And for a while, they were. But when Gómez Trejo and his team tracked down proof of the Chicago heroin connection of the buses, and started issuing indictments for high-ranking government officials and military officers (including several generals), he was unceremoniously pushed aside. Afraid for his personal safety, he fled, and now lives abroad.[27] "We uncovered the links between organized crime, parts of the military, the police, local government and the prosecutors' office, and that was too much" he told me.

Some authors object that the crimes committed do not constitute crimes against humanity but simple common crimes, or violations of human rights. Jesús Pérez Caballero,[28] for example, doubts that organized crime in Mexico qualifies as an "organization" within the meaning of the Rome Statute. He argues that there is not enough institutional and non-personalistic development in organizations such as the Zetas.[29] He also objects that the massacres and atrocities of the Zetas do not reach the level of "attacks on a civilian population," because there is a lack of a "policy" that unifies each attack committed in a Mexican state. But that is precisely what a grand corruption lens can add to the analysis.

The conceptual difficulty lies in defining where the organization begins and ends, to distinguish whether there was a state or organizational policy. On the one hand, this is not a simple matter of criminal gangs, since the contribution of the state is necessary, conscious and active; but neither is it only that the state acts through paramilitary groups that carry out its "dirty" work. Rather, there is a hybrid with new characteristics that owes its existence, in large part, to corruption and the corruption/organized crime nexus. This hybrid exhibits hierarchical or networked leadership and the knowledge or purpose of attacking civilian populations to intimidate, sow terror, take revenge, appropriate resources and territory, or finance activities. On the other hand, as Ximena Medellín and Jorge Peniche point out in discussing Nayarit, these organizations are much more decentralized than those analyzed in prior ICC cases, and their connections to public and private authorities vary from state to state and even from town to town.[30] They operate as an ever-shifting constellation of alliances of groups of various sizes and configurations, including state and nonstate actors, and it's difficult to shoehorn them into a version of international criminal law that depends on stable, hierarchical organizations where those most responsible for the crimes are easily identifiable.

Old categories that conceptualize nonstate actors only as militias thirsting for state power or ethnic defense do not capture current dynamics. The state as the beneficiary of a monopoly on violence, protector of the population, or repressor of illicit groups doesn't fit either. It is worth asking whether the distinction between state and non-state groups makes sense, and instead positing that these hybrid organizations attack the civilian population to enrich themselves or guarantee their impunity, turning acts that would otherwise be isolated crimes into examples of systematic policy and practice.

9.2.3 *Establishing That Acts Are Widespread or Systematic*

I turn now from *who* is committing crimes against humanity to *how* they do it, using Venezuela under President Maduro as a case study. Here too a corruption lens is useful. There is an open investigation regarding Venezuela in the Office of the ICC Prosecutor that focuses on protesters and political leaders opposed to the government of Nicolas Maduro, at least since April 2017, with emphasis on the crimes against humanity of "imprisonment or other serious deprivation of physical liberty," "torture," "rape and/or other forms of sexual violence" and "persecution of a group or collectivity with its own identity based on political motives" by civilian authorities, the armed forces and government supporters. On March 1, 2024, the ICC Appeals Chamber denied the Venezuelan government's appeal against a Pre-Trial Chamber's approval of the investigation in Venezuela; as of this writing, the investigation continues.[31]

Crimes against humanity, to qualify as such, must be widespread or systematic. Widespread means "massive, frequent, carried out with a considerable seriousness and directed against a multiplicity of victims."[32] Systematic is understood either as "an organized plan, in furtherance of a common policy, which follows a regular pattern and results in a continuous commission of acts," or as "patterns of crimes" such that the crimes constitute a "non-accidental repetition of similar criminal conduct on a regular basis."[33]

An advantage of a corruption lens on these crimes is that it can look at a wider range of victims, not just protesters or opposition figures, and provides the necessary linkage among various types of violations. It clarifies patterns of acts that would otherwise be treated as separate, isolated events, making it easier to understand their widespread or systematic nature. Beyond the technical definitions, it is about changing the narrative, reflecting in criminal prosecutions the scope of these criminal networks, which extend beyond organized crime to their allies in government and the "legal" private sector. These ties are initiated and maintained through acts of grand corruption.

A clear example is the Mining Arc ("Arco del Orinoco") of southern and eastern Venezuela. In order to continue extracting minerals from the area to finance the government and enrich themselves and their allies, military and paramilitary groups (especially Colombian insurgents) have engaged in massacres, attacks, and ill-treatment of miners and indigenous groups in the area.[34] Since 2016, a military-owned corporation known as CAMIMPEG has been in charge of both the commercialization of the resources and access to the area. Extraction and smuggling of gold, diamonds, and coltan (blue gold) as well as drug trafficking headed by military officers in this region[35] has spread violence and amplified social conflicts, in addition to creating serious environmental and social problems. According to a report by the UN High Commissioner for Human Rights,[36]

> The national strategic development zone "Arco Minero del Orinoco" was created by Decree No. 2,248 in February 2016 […] Testimonies documented by OHCHR describe high levels of labour exploitation, trafficking and violence due to the existence of a system of corruption and bribery imposed

by groups that control the mines, whereby these groups pay some military commanders to maintain their presence and their illegal activities.

According to the same report, armed groups use violence to punish disobedience, to control territory, and to extort payment of "rent." Of the 16 violent incidents recorded in or near mines between 2016 and 2020 which resulted in the deaths of approximately 150 people, the report found that in half the incidents "members of the state security forces involved in security operations in the area were involved in some of the deaths," and that in any case, these forces maintained a tight grip on the area, including 25 checkpoints on the road going through it.[37]

Members of the Pemon indigenous community, in the border region with Brazil, have opposed mining in their traditional territories. A Pemon leader was killed by the military in December 2018, and at least twenty-five others were killed when they opposed government incursions into their territory in February 2019. According to Survival International, members of the group have fled into the forest, claiming persecution.[38] Under the Rome Statute, "deportation or forcible transfer of population" means the forcible displacement of the persons concerned, by expulsion or other coercive acts, from the area in which they are lawfully present, without grounds authorized by international law.[39] The forcible transfer of indigenous populations is linked to the activities of both the armed forces and private militias and organized crime groups which control access to areas of illegal mineral extraction and export, a business necessarily facilitated by the corruption of high-ranking officials.[40]

A focus on corruption helps explain the systematic nature of what otherwise appear to be random patterns of high levels of violence. For example, one of the most violent regions of the country, the State of Bolívar, is one of the least populated. Within it, the three most violent cities in the country are located in the mining area: El Callao, with a rate of 511 homicides per 100,000 inhabitants, in 2021; Roscio, with 125 homicides per 100,000 inhabitants, and Sifontes, with 189 victims per 100,000 inhabitants.[41] In September 2017, twenty-one people were killed by the Venezuelan Armed Forces in the city of Piar. In February 2018, eighteen were killed by the Venezuelan Armed Forces in the city of Guacipati. These were presented as combat deaths, as part of the ongoing conflict between miners and the military for control of mining reserves.

Adopting a corruption lens would mean seeing the deaths as struggles for control of resource extraction, for smuggling, or for the enrichment of military leaders (often allied with organized crime). They would become evidence of a strategy to maintain the loyalty of the military brass to the Maduro government, creating a more systemic explanation to the attacks that rejects the official narrative of simple criminal gangs. Under this analysis, some of the unsolved deaths in the area, although reported as clashes with or between criminals, are likely state-sanctioned extrajudicial executions.

With its variants, the situation of the Mining Arc is repeated throughout the continent (and the world). The illicit extraction of natural resources is generally induced and facilitated by corruption in granting permits, licenses, export documents, or in the manner of appropriating the land. The unlawful or coerced appropriation of land for the cultivation of African palm or other "legal" crops or extractive industries, or for marijuana, coca or poppy cultivation or "narco-cattle,"[42] also depends on the actions of corrupt officials and businessmen, legal or illegal. Sometimes, organized crime groups or paramilitaries do the dirty work, but the final beneficiaries are elites deeply rooted in the legal economy. Chapter 8 provides Colombian examples of the actions of companies such as Drummond Mining, local cattle ranchers or Chiquita Banana, which illegally paid violent paramilitary forces to rid them of trade union or rural activists or to provide security for their operations.

Attacks on communities that lose or resist losing their lands and resources have led to dispossession, displacement and forced transfer, massacres, disappearances and, in some cases, the destruction of water and crops while knowing that the population will have no other means to survive. Seeing these facts through a corruption lens helps to unravel the networks of those responsible and connect the dots among what can seem to be random violence. From a more political perspective, it allows linking the anti-corruption and anti-extractivism agendas, as well as corporate accountability, in a way that strengthens all three agendas.

9.2.4 *Specific Acts Listed in Article 7*

In other cases, corruption is not just context, but gives rise to new acts that could constitute crimes against humanity. For example, the creation of a humanitarian emergency to then take advantage of it, as has been done in Venezuela with food distribution for the poor. An AP investigation found that when the military was given control over food distribution in 2016, corruption in the sector increased, including the demand for bribes to allow imports into the country, the use of shell businesses to create fake contracts and invoices, and hugely inflated prices billed for poor-quality imported food, allowing those involved to pocket the excess. Thousands of tons of food rotted on the docks because insufficient bribes were offered.[43] Fake food purchases were used to launder money. Military officers were implicated in smuggling flour into the country for sale on black markets.[44] Food (and medicine) smuggling became lucrative and therefore tightly controlled by the military and its allies.

In a trial for money laundering in the United States, high-level advisors and officials linked to the Venezuelan government were accused of corrupt schemes related to food subsidies; those involved would have received about 1.6 billion dollars, of which at least $180 million was laundered through the US and the rest was held in Antigua, the United Arab Emirates, Panama and elsewhere.[45] Among those indicted were the former governor of Táchira state, along with Colombian businessman Alvaro Pulido, who is a business partner of Maduro financier Álex Saab (and his alleged coconspirator in a separate corruption case involving public housing). Those involved:

> used numerous companies they controlled, for the purpose of entering into contracts with the Venezuelan Government to manufacture and export boxes of food from Mexico [...] to import the boxes [...] and distribute them within Venezuela, to receive money under contracts granted by the Venezuelan Government, in order to bribe Venezuelan Government officials, including those in charge of awarding contracts [...] distributing the fruits of the illegally obtained contracts [...] and concealing the nature and purpose of the fruits of the illegal bribery scheme.[46]

The program, called Local Committees of Supply and Production (CLAP), was supposedly intended to meet the food needs of the poor and vulnerable.[47] The Mexican authorities reported that

> on the occasion of this program [referring to CLAP], as of 2016 [...] a network of companies and individuals, both national and foreign, obtained Venezuelan public resources [...] diverting them from their humanitarian purposes, to [...] acquire food and speculate commercially with it, taking advantage of the food shortage that afflicts Venezuela; through [...] 1) acquiring low-quality products, [and] 2) exporting them to Venezuela at an excessive price.

Moreover, through "[...] the existence of commercial transactions and financial movements in multiple jurisdictions with shell companies and nested correspondent payment accounts, [...] Venezuelan officials involved in awarding the supply contracts would have been the beneficiaries of payments of several million US dollars from CLAP suppliers."[48]

All this occurred at a time when vast swaths of the population were suffering from malnutrition and hunger, and there were even reports of starvation.[49] The government's food policy clearly violated its human rights obligations; however, if the policy was carried out knowing that the main result would be to enrich high-ranking political and military officials and their friends in organized crime and the private sector, and knowing that widespread and severe food shortages among the civilian population would result, and that such food shortages would not only seriously affect the life and health of the poor population but that creating hunger would further enrich those involved, isn't that also the crime against humanity of extermination?

Article 7(2)(b) of the Rome Statute states: "'Extermination' shall include the intentional infliction of conditions of life, *inter alia* the deprivation of access to food or medicine, calculated to bring about the destruction of part of a population." As for the necessary state of mind, Article 30(2)(b) states that it includes consequences where the accused "is aware that it will occur in the ordinary course of events." The systematic nature, the deliberate decision to withhold food to increase bribes and kickbacks, knowing that there will be hunger, malnutrition due to poor quality and even deaths, would seem to bring these corrupt acts of corruption within the scope of Article 7(2)(b). Similarly, in the context of an armed conflict, a deliberate decision to withhold food may constitute the war crime of starvation under Article 8(2)(e)(xix).

There is an additional element: if, as has been reported, the distribution[50] of food (and medicine) depended on showing loyalty by presenting a ruling party identification card, and opponents were denied food by regime supporters marking their houses,[51] then people who were denied food or medicine because of their political views would have suffered, in addition, the crime of persecution under Article 7(h). Persecution is defined as defined in Article 7(2)(g) as: "the intentional and severe deprivation of fundamental rights in contravention of international law by reason of the identity of the group or collectivity." Without a corruption-based lens, these connections can be lost.

9.2.5 *Complementarity and Gravity*

For a case to be heard in the International Criminal Court it must meet certain requirements arising from its governing statute. The crimes at issue have to be within the jurisdiction of the Court with respect to time (after the State of territory or nationality became part of the Court or specially agreed to jurisdiction, except if the UN Security Council refers the case), subject matter (war crimes, crimes against humanity, genocide or aggression) and personal identity (only natural persons, not corporations, can be defendants). In addition, the Prosecutor must show that a case is admissible and in the interests of justice.

Admissibility involves the ideas of complementarity and gravity. The Rome Statute requires the Court to act only when national jurisdictions are unwilling or unable to conduct the investigation or prosecution, a requirement known as "complementarity." If the places where the trial could be carried out in national courts (including under extraterritorial jurisdiction, as we'll see later) are not investigating or prosecuting the same people or the same conduct (even if called something else), complementarity is met. But if there is evidence of a sham trial, an unjustified delay or that the proceedings were (or are) not conducted in an independent or impartial manner, or in a manner compatible with an intention to bring the person concerned to justice, then the Prosecutor (and in some cases a Pre-Trial Chamber of the Court), must decide if the case is admissible.[52] There is a whole jurisprudence on how and when these requirements are met, but justice systems are often infiltrated by corrupt actors who engineer impunity for both acts of grand corruption and serious violations of human rights and crimes against humanity.

This is clearly seen both in Venezuela – where most judges are provisional and independent prosecutors have had to leave the country[53] – and in Mexico – where the public prosecutor's offices (and the former federal PGR) are not independent and state prosecutors and judges have often come under corrupt control (as was the case in Nayarit, among others). This is a common phenomenon in countries where grand corruption prevails. In Guatemala, the US Engels List-sanctioned public prosecutor and her deputies have fired and jailed anti-corruption and human rights prosecutors alike, and dozens of judges and prosecutors have gone into exile due to criminalization, a tale told in Chapters 3 and 4.[54] The seizure of the justice system by grand corruption guarantees its lack of independence and impartiality, and should be an important factor in analyzing cases – current and potential – in national jurisdictions and, therefore, the need for international justice to act.

In addition to demonstrating complementarity, the Policy Document on Preliminary Examinations provides, as a separate step, for consideration of the gravity of the situation under Article 17(1)(d). To establish the gravity of the cases that come before the ICC, the Office of the Prosecutor must consider the scale, nature and means employed for the commission of the crimes, as well as their impact. The means employed measures, among others, the degree of involvement and intent of the perpetrator, systematicity, and abuse of official power or position.[55] The impact of the crime includes "social, economic and environmental damage inflicted on the affected communities."[56] The Pre-Trial Chamber has previously held that the nature, means employed and impact of the attack are critical and must be assessed at a qualitative level and not merely quantitatively.[57]

In a 2016 article, Ester Hava García proposed that the existence of indicators of grand corruption is itself a mark of gravity, since it always indicates abuse of power by the perpetrators, as well as serious harm to the affected population.[58] Thus, in a scenario where grand corruption is present, in a case that otherwise meets the requirements of scale and nature it would automatically meet the gravity threshold. More ambitiously, even if the scale or nature of the crimes are smaller than those seen in other cases, the fact that they were committed within a context of severe corruption and abuse of power could elevate them in importance and indicate sufficient gravity. For example, in the Venezuelan case, even if the number of murders or other crimes is relatively small compared to other ICC investigations, the possibility that such behaviors are systemic and therefore will likely continue to be committed and increase in magnitude – given the perpetrators' impunity and access to resources to sustain a scheme of grand corruption, would meet the requirement of gravity.

9.3 OPERATIONALIZING A CORRUPTION APPROACH IN INTERNATIONAL AND NATIONAL COURTS

What would it look like in practical terms to apply a corruption lens to international crimes? As the scope and seriousness of the problem of grand corruption becomes more obvious, along with the limitations of existing law and practice, a number of proposals have emerged. Some require interpretation of existing law and the use of existing institutions, while others propose a whole new architecture. The discussion here is ongoing, so new ideas may have emerged by the time you read this book.

One way to incorporate grand corruption as an international offense would be to add a new crime to the Rome Statute.[59] This would undoubtedly be a long and uncertain process, requiring an amendment to the statute that would then have to be separately ratified by states. The arguments in favor of creating a new crime within the Rome Statute date back at least to 2015.[60] However, there has been resistance to expanding the universe of recognized international crimes. The underlying concern has always been to distinguish crimes that require international attention from ordinary crimes, no matter how heinous or widespread. In other words, to distinguish crimes that can be adequately dealt with by national courts from those that, for structural reasons, cannot. In addition, those concerned seek to prevent the waste of the limited resources of international tribunals on anything less than the most awful crimes, capable of affecting peace and security.

Efforts to add a new crime to the Rome Statute were strengthened in 2021 by proposals to incorporate the crime of ecocide into the Statute. The first Prosecutor of the International Criminal Court noted that "the Office will give special consideration to the criminal prosecution of crimes [...] that are committed through, or that result in, inter alia, the destruction of the environment, the illegal exploitation of natural resources, or the illegal dispossession of land,"[61] but the statement was repeated but never developed. The arguments for a new crime are similar to those for grand corruption: it is committed by powerful offenders who enjoy impunity and have effects beyond national borders, threatening international peace and security as well as human rights.

An Independent Panel of experts recently sought to resolve some of the problems of causation and intent shared by ecocide and grand corruption. They argued that not all acts of ecological destruction would be the target of the crime, only those that are "serious and/or widespread, or long-lasting." This limit parallels the distinction between grand corruption and other types of corruption more likely to be suppressed at the national level. As for the necessary state of mind, the Panel proposed "knowledge that there is a substantial probability" of harm as sufficient, which would be equally appropriate language for grand corruption crimes given the secrecy with which they are committed. As for causation, the proposal does not require proof that specific harms arising from the crime have already occurred, but only a likelihood of harm to individuals or communities.

The discussion on ecocide is in its infancy and any modifications to the Rome Statute will have to be negotiated and approved by the Assembly of States Parties to the International Criminal Court; however, it facilitates discussion of a parallel crime for acts of grand corruption, either in the International Criminal Court or in an international court dedicated exclusively to crimes constituting grand corruption (discussed in Chapter 10). However, in both cases, discussions on capacity, resources and political will are still pending.

Other authors propose the use of the existing Article 7. One possible solution would be to use Article 7(1)(k), "other inhumane acts." This "catch-all" or residual phrase is meant to leave the definition of crimes against humanity open-ended, since new evils emerge over time. The acts must be similar in gravity and nature to the acts already enumerated in Article 7; examples include mutilation of prisoners, brutal and deplorable living conditions for detainees, or, more broadly, the violation of rights contained in human rights instruments if severe and widespread or systematic.[62] Grand corruption, due to its scale, pervasiveness and systemic nature seriously affects the life and health, in particular, of vulnerable populations and therefore could be considered of a similar nature to other crimes against humanity. The most difficult problem is showing the required intent; negligence is not enough. Here is where the definition of grand corruption (versus non-grand) might help: if the looting is large and obvious enough, and the negative effects on mental or physical health well-known, one could at least prove the "knowledge" demanded by Article 30 of the Rome Statute.[63]

Another use of existing law and institutions, of course, would be to use a "corruption lens" to evaluate the existing elements of Article 7. This is what I've proposed earlier. Other writers have used tests like "shock the conscience" or effects on international peace and security to create a threshold beyond which corruption moves from being an ordinary crime to one of international concern.[64]

Of course, most justice continues to rely on national processes. Another option would be to focus on national courts' ability to freeze, seize and forfeit the assets of those committing grave human rights violations. Most courts have some such ability in cases where freezing is requested, but it has to be requested early enough that the assets are still findable, and the law has to allow for the limited information often available at the beginning of an investigation. For example, when the Pinochet investigation began in Spain in 1996, lawyers for the victims obtained a broad order freezing any assets found to be connected to Pinochet. Several years later, as a result of unrelated US Senate inquiries into Washington, DC-based Riggs Bank, evidence emerged that the bank had helped set up large secret offshore accounts for Pinochet and his family. Since the Spanish case against Pinochet had never been officially closed even though he had long since been returned to Chile, failing to freeze the assets violated Spanish law. In an innovative plea bargain, lawyers for the victims negotiated in 2005 that Spain would drop the charges in exchange for the bank and its owners creating an almost $9 million reparations fund for victims of Pinochet's regime.[65]

Civil forfeiture focuses on the asset, not the wrongdoer, and uses a less demanding standard of proof. In the UK, for instance, assets can be frozen and then confiscated if they are the product of conduct abroad that is unlawful under both state's laws. Conduct is unlawful, among other reasons, if it "constitutes, or is connected with, the commission of a gross human rights abuse or violation." This could solve some of the causation problems getting from killings, torture or the like, as we saw earlier, to the mansion in London or the Rolls-Royce of the defendant. Unfortunately, the definition of "gross human rights abuse or violation" is narrow and idiosyncratic, covering only: (i) a "whistle blower" or "human rights defender"; (ii) who has been subjected to torture or inhumane or degrading treatment; (iii) by, or on behalf of, a public official; (iv) for having sought to obtain, exercise, defend, or promote human rights or expose illegal activity by a public official.[66] Given this limited definition, it's not surprising that the provision has rarely been used; expanding the definition to encompass the wider range of acts considered "gross violations" in general international human rights practice would make the procedure more valuable.

A different problem arises in US law, where federal prosecutors choose to indict perpetrators of human rights abuses who are also organized crime members solely on crimes such as drug trafficking or money laundering. This then makes it more difficult for victims to take part in proceedings since it's harder to argue they were direct or even indirect victims of the drug trafficking or money laundering per se. In a case involving the paramilitary leader responsible for killing Colombian environmental and human rights advocate Julio Henríquez among others, US prosecutors extradited him and others to stand trial for conspiracy to traffic drugs in US court. US prosecutors initially took the position that the families of those massacred or disappeared – including Nadiezhda Henríquez, the JEP judge we met in Chapter 8 and Julio Henríquez' daughter – weren't victims of drug trafficking and therefore could not participate in proceedings under the Crime Victims Rights Act.[67] They also did not make the defendants available to talk to human rights victims or condition plea deals on providing information to them or on giving up assets located in Colombia. Eventually, after a seven-year legal battle, Henríquez' family was able to address the sentencing court as victims about the impact of the crimes and the effect a short sentence would have on them and the hundreds of victims of drug-related human rights crimes.[68] Creating better communication and synergies between organized crime and human rights prosecutors, and clarifying that these are not victimless crimes, would go some way toward broader accountability.

Other options would create new international or hybrid institutions to deal with the phenomenon of grand corruption, on grounds that existing national courts are no longer enough. A new institution could focus on a specific aspect like international support for national prosecutors, as pioneered by the UN in Guatemala and the OAS in Honduras (these efforts are described in Chapter 3). Such initiatives could also help bolster national anti-corruption prosecutors and courts, especially through international attention to prosecutorial capacity, judicial selection and discipline.[69] It could encourage legislation providing for universal jurisdiction over at least the gravest corruption-related crimes, as also discussed in Chapter 4. It could aim to support and share good practices around asset recovery, including creating a global fund through which recovered assets could be inventoried, managed, and repurposed. Or it could become a stand-alone international court, as I discuss in Chapter 10.

10

Conclusions

Where To and What to Watch Out For?

As we've seen throughout this book, the scale, scope and systematic nature of corruption have changed. I have been particularly concerned with the variants of grand corruption, characterized not just by large amounts of assets and perpetrators at high levels of authority, but with the ability to commandeer, co-opt and enlist state and private institutions to facilitate corrupt acts, while also weakening those institutions that provided checks on power and ensuring impunity. I have also been concerned with how the lessons learned by human rights movements, in their many flavors, could be useful to the emerging movement advocating a advocating a human rights-based approach to anti-corruption, as well as how an anti-corruption lens could strengthen specific areas of human rights-related practice.

This final chapter summarizes how responses have changed accordingly, and where they have not changed enough. It considers some of the fundamental limitations of the existing approach in dealing with systemic corruption-related crime, and in particular questions of attribution to the state of behavior at least in part carried out by private parties. It asks whether a proposed International Anti-Corruption Court (IACC) might overcome some of those limitations. It also looks at some of the possible objections to a focus on corruption, both from a human rights perspective and more generally. And it places the convergence among anti-corruption, human rights, development and environment problems (and solutions) within some larger analytical frameworks, including structural inequality, moral breakdown and the rise of global social movements.

10.1 LESSONS LEARNED AND LIMITATIONS OF CURRENT LAW

A change in the nature of the corruption problem means the responses must change too. The current architecture of the UNCAC, in particular, is largely geared to situations where corruption – public and private – is aberrant and where the state is genuinely trying to combat it. But where the entire leadership of the country is at least complicit and the organs of the state have been captured, this architecture is much less useful. The state where assets were stolen is considered the "victim" state for purposes of asset return, but that allows the same people who stole – or at least allowed the money to be stolen – to be in charge of getting it back, or deciding not to. Mutual legal assistance doesn't work for the same reason: if requests for evidence, witnesses or documents come to officials of the same government that stole the money, either they don't answer (as in Venezuela) or they falsify the documents. Too much initiative rests on the requesting states in proceedings for asset recovery and returns; either you need an official mutual legal assistance request after a domestic conviction (unlikely where the judiciary and/or prosecutors are disinclined to indict, much less convict), or a process in the state where the asset is located based on another state's request, also unlikely. Exceptions are generally limited in practice to situations where an offender is dead or has fled or absconded, despite the ability to proceed in "other appropriate cases." All in all, while still a step forward, the UNCAC needs a thorough revision through the lens of grand corruption to bring the language into line with the unfortunate reality.

If the current architecture doesn't deal well with grand corruption, what might help? One set of responses involves enlisting additional actors beyond prosecutors and anti-corruption bodies, especially individuals and civil society organizations, and especially at moments of transition and change. Decentering and adding more sources of information, strategy and monitoring will make it easier to take advantage of openings, however limited, at the national level. Insisting that there are individual and collective victims of corruption, with names and stories and real harms, changes the discourse to recognize these people as rights-holders, opens up possibilities of redress and reparations and harnesses the obligation of governments to respect, ensure and fulfill rights. But only if civic space remains open.

The rise of grand corruption has also meant that anti-corruption strategies are increasingly transnational and focused on the states where stolen assets are parked, given the difficulties inherent in operating in captured institutions at the source of the corruption. Efforts to diversify beyond national prosecutions can use international support for prosecutors, the application of "smart" sanctions, and tapping into human rights and environmental forums and market incentives, among other tactics. The transnational nature of grand corruption also presents opportunities: to look to extraterritorial jurisdiction or jurisdiction based on where assets are located rather than where crimes took place, to further tighten rules on beneficial ownership and public contracting internationally. It means enforcement strategies focused on understanding and dismantling complex networks that span countries and extend beyond criminal kingpins to the politicians, state agents, and business leaders who work with them. And it means that infusing anti-corruption monitoring and evaluation into the practice of human rights bodies, global and regional environment and climate-related agencies and those concerned with consumer protection will help broaden and multiply the opportunities for changing discourse and pressuring recalcitrant states. A focus on practices that involve gross human rights violations like forced disappearances in pursuit of illicit profits might be a starting place.

The transnational nature of grand corruption also focuses new attention on enablers: those accounting, consulting, real estate and law firms, mostly located in Western countries, that facilitate and cover up corruption crimes elsewhere. These are the people who help kleptocrats spirit their funds out of the country or advise them on law reforms that will make it easier to do so. Grand corruption would be more difficult without them, and some governments are considering how to subject them to more oversight. Some enablers are still missing from the discussion: international development banks and aid agencies, in particular, despite extensive microlevel anti-corruption rules, often miss the macro picture.

A final area for consideration might be the pursuit of a wider range of corruption-related remedies. In particular, as we saw in the Colombia Ruta del Sol case, should a contract obtained as a result of bribery be able to be canceled, and who needs to adjudicate the recission? In cases of grand corruption, authorities are obviously implicated, but can subsequent authorities disassociate themselves from their corrupt predecessors? And does cancelling contracts procured as a result of corruption violate international investment law? How much evidence is needed of the bribes? A Luxemburg-based Odebrecht subsidiary (in an apparent fit of extreme chutzpah) sued Peru for annulling a contract that had, according to Peru, been obtained as a result of a bribe.[1] Even if Peru eventually wins, the time and expense involved makes this an area ripe for reform.

One of the interesting trends emerging from this study is how international law migrates not only from international bodies to local courts and other institutions (and back) but across issue areas. We have seen how some Latin American courts are increasingly using the jurisprudence developed out of obligations toward victims of human rights-related crimes, first at the international and regional level and then incorporated into domestic law and jurisprudence. The cases that allow standing and access to victims in anti-corruption actions have been influenced by the decades-long struggle in the region to identify, investigate, and prosecute grave violations of human rights. That struggle has given rise to a rebalancing of the rights and obligations of victims and offenders in criminal trials, with more rights for victims even in adversarial common law systems. Several countries have passed versions of a "victims' law" that have opened up discussions about how broadly these laws apply. It has led to widespread acceptance of a "right to truth" and of "victim-centered justice" that are now finding their way, at least sometimes, into corruption-related cases. Concepts of diffuse or social harm arising from corruption are also borrowed, often from consumer protection or environmental laws. In other words, international law is not just moving into domestic systems, but the precepts developed in one area of law are migrating to others.

This extends to evidentiary issues. The first contentious case before the Inter-American Court of Human Rights concerned a forced disappearance, where a student leader vanished one day and the state argued that there was no proof either that a crime had been committed (because there was no body) nor proof that, in any case, state officials had been involved. The Court held that it could use inferences arising from the pattern and practice of disappearances, and the lack of alternative explanations, to conclude that a forced disappearance had indeed taken place. Human rights courts and expert bodies have developed jurisprudence on the use of patterns, inferences, and presumptions in cases where secrecy and denial are inherent to the offenses. Grand corruption cases usually fit that bill.

Prosecutors and judges in human rights-related cases started out (with a few early exceptions) dealing case by case and incident by incident with crimes against humanity and grave violations such as massacres and forced disappearances. They soon learned that it was impossible to deal with systemic crimes by powerful structures and networks this way. Instead, they needed specialized analytical offices (within prosecutors' offices or elsewhere) that could see connections among cases, find patterns, and target entire networks. In some countries (such as Argentina), this change in paradigm led to so-called mega-cases involving dozens of defendants. These cases made it possible to confront macrocriminality within a reasonable timeframe and respecting the due process rights of defendants. The same kind of network analysis is needed in cases involving grand corruption. In addition, these cases would benefit from specific institutions in charge of dealing with freezing, seizing and managing confiscated property – both to use it for the benefit of victims and to preserve assets so that they don't fall apart.

When elected civilian governments followed military-controlled regimes, amnesties or long-passed statutes of limitations made it difficult to even investigate, much less prosecute massive rights violations. Advocates filed habeas corpus petitions even knowing they would be automatically denied; years later these same petitions formed key pieces of evidence. They brought cases based on narrow exceptions and limitations in otherwise broad amnesty laws, over and over until judicial sentiment slowly changed. They used international law – and its incorporation into constitutional law – to revise unfavorable doctrines. Most of all, they persevered, even in legal systems that seemed closed and unfriendly. Eventually, the tide (albeit slowly and incompletely) turned. The same sort of creativity and perseverance are needed again.

10.2 ATTRIBUTION TO THE STATE: HOW GRAND CORRUPTION CHANGES THE PICTURE

One of the legal problems that arises in using international law, and especially human rights law, to grapple with grand corruption is connecting the state to the unlawful actions in order to establish that the state is legally responsible and thus bound by obligations to prevent, investigate, take action against and repair the harm. This is a threshold question, unlike the causation issue we saw earlier in connection with reparations. Attribution asks "who is liable for the objectionable conduct?" while causation asks "how is the objectionable conduct linked to the harm that resulted?"

As we saw in Chapter 2, states have obligations not just to respect rights, but to protect, ensure and fulfil them. These obligations involve positive duties to regulate and control others, to prevent (through due diligence), investigate, prosecute, and repair the damage. Human rights bodies don't generally reach private conduct directly, but indirectly through these state obligations. This is important in cases where direct evidence as to what happened and whether the state was involved is difficult to get, for example, forced disappearances or paramilitary killings – or grand corruption. It's a useful body of law in grand corruption cases when the state either doesn't have an adequate legal or enforcement framework in place or doesn't adequately investigate, prosecute or repair, whether due to negligence, incapacity or complicity.

The law on state responsibility, going back centuries, decides when states are liable to other states for breaches of international law. As currently interpreted, it establishes a pretty tight test for when private actors' behavior is attributable to the state (not surprisingly since states generally make rules to protect themselves). Courts have used tests ranging from "effective control"[2] by state officials over private conduct, to "overall control" of paramilitary or other organized forces.[3] Under these rules, states are liable even if the conduct of their officials is unauthorized or goes beyond their authority. They are also responsible if their agents are complicit or acquiesce in the actions of private actors, or if "the person or group of persons is in fact exercising elements of the governmental authority in the absence or default of the official authorities and in circumstances such as to call for the exercise of those elements of authority."[4] Moreover, they are responsible for the omissions of state officials in failing to stop or investigate violations where they knew or should have known of the risks and the potential harm of inaction.

Grand corruption, especially the kind that involves macrocriminality and control of territory, challenges the distinctions between states and nonstate actors in new ways. We saw a variant of this issue in Chapter 8, where the usefulness of distinctions between state and nonstate actors in international criminal law has eroded. More generally, one of the objections to applying international law in cases of grand corruption has been that whatever crimes may have been committed, they are crimes under national law by private parties, and so not attributable to the state. But when politicians not only acquiesce but instigate and organize schemes involving organized crime and corporate actors, as in Coahuila or Nayarit, Mexico or in mining operations throughout the continent, how is the state not responsible, even if some of the actors involved are private? Where armed groups in Colombia or Brazil select local officials, coerce the population into voting for them, provide "protection" and jobs, dispense rough justice, and set the rules under which thousands must live, are they not exercising elements of governmental authority in the absence of the state? The change in the nature of the problem should allow for an evolution in doctrine.

A grand-corruption informed notion of what constitute actions or omissions of the state raises difficult problems where only certain organs of the state are captured, while others are incapable of un-capturing them. Police, prosecutors and judges are frequent targets of capture; even a committed executive branch or Congress will find it difficult to combat crime and corruption when these actors are part of the problem; the most dedicated police force will find it hard to act against a captured legislature or executive. And yet the state is technically liable for their actions. This is the situation in Guatemala in 2024, for example. Some form of *force majeure* or other excuse doctrines could let the state off the hook, but in the past state incapacity has been a reason for more international supervision, not less.

10.3 AN INTERNATIONAL ANTI-CORRUPTION COURT?

Grand corruption, almost by definition, implies a lack of independence of the organs of state, including the judiciary. Judiciaries are coopted, selection processes are manipulated, incorruptible judges are sidelined, threatened, or attacked. And yet, judicial action is necessary even if not sufficient to tackle corruption within a country.

This dilemma is not unique to anti-corruption work. Human rights violations and international crimes also confront the impunity of powerful actors. Over the years since the Nuremberg Tribunals after World War II, an ecosystem of transnational, regional, international and hybrid proceedings has grown up to complement and incentivize national prosecutions in situations where national justice is unable or unwilling to do the job. These include civil and criminal cases under various forms of extraterritorial jurisdiction, bespoke and permanent international criminal tribunals, regional courts focused on state responsibility and integral reparations, factfinding bodies connected to the UN or regional organizations, and combinations of these. In the Americas, the Inter-American Court of Human Rights has been key to removing unwarranted obstacles to prosecution and insisting on an end to impunity. Through doctrines of "convention-based control" and related ideas, the Court's jurisprudence has become interwoven with domestic law. The International Criminal Court's doctrine of complementarity (the presumed primacy of national law unless there is a showing that the local courts are unable or unwilling to act) is also aimed at combatting impunity within a framework of sovereignty.

It's not surprising that the increasing prevalence and virulence of grand corruption should send those trying to combat it toward these examples.

Mark Wolf, a bespectacled, avuncular senior trial judge from Massachusetts, proposed in 2014 that just as an international court was needed to deal with atrocity crimes, the same is true of grand corruption. The proposed IACC would investigate and prosecute cases of grand corruption and kleptocracy when national courts are captured and unable to be independent. Such a court, he argued, could either use the crimes already in the UNCAC as a basis or use their domestic counterparts where these exist. Since practically all countries have ratified the UNCAC, this would merely implement existing treaty obligations. It could prosecute people who committed crimes (including money laundering or hiding assets) on the territory of a member state as well as nationals of that state. And it would be able to recover, return, and repurpose illicit assets for the benefit of victims. The problem, he said, wasn't the lack of laws, it was the enforcement lacuna. That could only be filled with an international body that was a modified and improved version of the ICC.[5]

The Colombian government quickly jumped on the bandwagon, followed by Ecuador and Peru. Canada and the Netherlands followed. A group of 100 former government officials, business leaders, and Nobel laureates signed on. A nonprofit called Integrity Initiatives International, headed by Wolf and former international court prosecutor Richard Goldstone, took up the cause, assembling research and preparatory texts for a draft treaty.

Doubts quickly arose.[6] First, why would kleptocrats ever allow their countries to join such a court? Supporters of the proposal countered that you wouldn't need all states, only some 20–25 states if those include major financial centers used to launder funds and other states that are attractive as recipients of stolen funds. Because the proceeds of grand corruption are laundered, stored or invested in financial centers or tax havens, those states would have a form of territorial jurisdiction even if the kleptocrats' own state objected. Moreover, changes of government (not to mention hubris) happen, and a new government might well want to show its anti-corruption bona fides by signing on to the IACC (perhaps only to regret it, as Pinochet did in Chile after signing on to the Torture Convention). On the other hand, such a court could be vulnerable to the "west against the rest" rhetoric that has bedeviled other global efforts, including the ICC.

Second, the ICC and other international court experiences show that state cooperation is necessary to a successful prosecution, or at least makes it a lot easier. While technology makes it much easier to obtain records, recordings, satellite images and other evidence from outside a country, and cooperating witnesses can also often be found outside the country, even an experienced and specialized prosecutor might find it hard to amass sufficient evidence of large-scale, complex financial wrongdoing without access to the state where the crimes allegedly took place – access that is unlikely without a change in regime.

Third, there's the question of cost. International courts are expensive, especially when key personnel are paid international salaries. The ICC has been criticized for the small number of trials given the expense; supporters of the IACC say they can learn from the critiques and fashion a leaner, more streamlined court, perhaps with part-time judges. They also argue that a court with expertise, personnel and techniques in a specialized area is more efficient than expecting multitasking, overworked and under-protected national judges and prosecutors to take on the task. Moreover, justice in general is expensive, but that's not an argument to abandon it. Nonetheless, could the same amount of money be better spent strengthening national anti-corruption efforts? On the other hand, would that money actually be forthcoming without a global focal point? Fourth, criminal prosecution is not the only, or the best, way to deal with kleptocrats. Seizing their stolen assets, some argue, is far more important. This argument has led to proposals for a Civil Chamber of an IACC, or related variations.[7]

There's a more basic disagreement at bottom, I think. International backup of national processes can be done through top-down, state-based institutions-building like the ICC that have the advantage of dedicated staff and budget and varying degrees of state commitment to supporting them. The alternative is much more decentralized and horizontal, a networking rather than an institution-building approach. As I wrote almost twenty years ago about the relative advantages of these approaches in the context of atrocity crimes, "[i]nstitutions of global justice, no matter how noble and well-intentioned … [are] a creature of states, subject to the least-common-denominator politics of state consensus and the power of large states to threaten and bribe where necessary."[8] In contrast, more bottom-up approaches tend to be less controllable by states (especially powerful ones), to encourage victim (and civil society) initiative and imagination, and to be more easily tailored to the cultural and historical particulars of a given place.

What might such alternatives look like, and is there a way of combining top-down and bottom-up approaches? One group of scholars has proposed a focus on asset recovery, through a Transnational Asset Recovery Mechanism that would encourage, assist, mediate, monitor and serve as an escrow-type repository for return of stolen assets.[9] Such a customizable menu of functions would fill a need while keeping costs and ambition low. It might be possible to embed forensic accounting and other financial specialists in international or regional evidence-gathering bodies such as the Independent Investigative Mechanism for Syria or similar bodies created by the UN. Another option might be to focus on changes to national law, including on immunities, statutes of limitation, modes of liability, predicate acts for money laundering, and broad extraterritorial jurisdiction – all needed to combat grand corruption. Transparency International advocated this approach in a 2023 paper.[10] I might add that making it easier for victims of corruption to intervene in different kinds of justice processes would also have a positive effect, as I describe in Chapter 5. Of course, a more integrated approach to looking at atrocity and grand corruption crimes would require increased cooperation among prosecutors and a breaking down of silos among advocates. Both atrocity crimes and grand corruption require extensive analysis of patterns, networks and connections, and well-staffed and independent joint analysis units or information-sharing efforts would facilitate the work of both.

No matter which way the debate comes out, an IACC will entail a long process of discussion, drafting, signature and ratification. Obtaining sufficient ratifications for the ICC was far quicker than anyone had anticipated, but the context was more favorable, and major powers have still refused to sign on. It may be that an "all of the above" strategy is the best, indeed the only option. In adopting such a strategy, advocates can learn from the process of creating an ICC. For several years before and after the 1998 Rome conference that created the Court, the ICC process "sucked all the air from the room" as a colleague said. Few paid attention to national courts or cases, much less noncriminal law-based ways of dealing with atrocities. As the Court's limits became more obvious, it emerged that this had been a mistake. Hopefully, history will not repeat itself with an IACC.

10.4 PITFALLS AND DANGERS

Throughout the preceding chapters, I have advocated for addressing the systematic and transnational phenomenon of grand corruption through an approach that sees it as a violation of a range of human rights and puts victims of corruption at the center of a response. Here I want to take up some of the dangers and limitations in doing so, even though on balance I think they don't invalidate the project. They could be summarized as victimhood, politicization and resources.

10.4.1 *Victimhood*

Throughout the book, I have talked about victims of corruption and the need to put victims at the center. One of the lessons from the human rights movement is that victims themselves are divided about the use of the term. While some see it as recognizing that their rights are at stake and that governments have duties of acknowledgment and repair, for others the word evokes helplessness, powerlessness, and lack of agency. It can also lead to a discourse of "innocent victims" who are deserving of assistance and deference, contrasted to "unworthy victims" who fought back with violence or who arguably contributed to (or failed to oppose) the harm.[11] These critics prefer the words "survivor" or "activist." The victim versus perpetrator dichotomy is also viewed as too rigid and limited in situations where there are many shades of gray, including bystanders, rescuers, and passive beneficiaries of the behavior at issue.[12] What's more, a politics of victimhood can lead to debates over who speaks for victims, especially when politicians and nongovernmental organizations seeking funding lay claim to the mantle of representing victims. It can leave those who take on a victim identity stuck in revisiting past harms, with diminished ability to move forward with their lives.

In the grand corruption context, recognizing individual and collective victims has undeniable advantages in naming the harm, demanding state actions to redress it, and channeling public discontent into concrete action. But in cases where the harms are diffuse or widespread, large numbers of people may see themselves as victims without any hope of receiving individual damages. Indeed, one of the objections to a human rights-based approach to corruption is precisely that innocent taxpayers would be stuck with the bill for damages given to enterprising individuals (and their lawyers) who bring cases on structural harms. Resolving this dilemma requires promoting understanding that victimhood may not necessarily entail individual monetary compensation but may be focused more on ensuring collective and other forms of redress, including reform. And that being a "victim" does not connote helplessness, but on the contrary, is a way of ensuring that those most affected by corruption have a voice and can insist on their rights.

10.4.2 *Politicization and Abuse*

One of the characteristics of grand corruption is that by controlling the levers of accountability, those in charge can use those levers to target and tarnish their critics while deflecting attention from their own misdeeds. It's easy to accuse your political enemies of corruption and ascribe your lack of evidence to the secret nature of the crimes involved. Indeed, there's a long history in Latin America of new leaders accusing their predecessors, rightly or wrongly, of corruption. The result, of course, is to delegitimize the whole enterprise of anti-corruption accountability and, more broadly, of politics. Suspects in corruption cases know this, and routinely proclaim that any investigation is a political vendetta no matter how much evidence is forthcoming.[13] Journalists and advocates routinely face defamation or "SLAPP" suits aimed at shutting down their investigations or bankrupting them.

Sometimes real governmental overreach can undermine an entire investigation, as happened with the Odebrecht case in Brazil, where apparent judicial partiality led not only to the invalidation of charges against then-former (and now current) president Lula da Silva, but a decision by the courts to dismantle the whole edifice of evidence based on the initial plea agreement involving Odebrecht officials, including those clearly involved in bribery.[14]

Moreover, corruption and money laundering charges are often used to silence government critics. For example, Guatemalan journalist José Rubén Zamora edited a muckraking newspaper that investigated many government corruption scandals, which naturally created government antipathy, threats, and pressures. He found himself in 2022 accused of money laundering, a charge with a maximum forty-year penalty. The basis of the charge was a $30,000 donation to the beleaguered paper, which Zamora asked a supposed friend to deposit in the friend's account because the donor didn't want his name to become public. Instead, the "friend," – an ex-banker himself accused of corrupt acts – went to the prosecutor's office, which in turn found a friendly judge; both the prosecutors and the judge have been designated by both the US and EU as corrupt and antidemocratic.[15] Zamora has to date spent over two years imprisoned under harsh conditions, and his paper was forced to close down.

Nor is this an isolated case. In Peru, journalist Gustavo Goritti spent decades writing about grand corruption, and at one point was kidnapped by goons linked to former president Fujimori and then forced into exile. He returned, and continued writing about the latest corruption scandals, even while battling cancer. In 2024, prosecutors close to Fujimori's daughter, a perennial presidential candidate, accused him of bribery in a case the Associated Press called "bizarre."[16]

In a captured justice system (such as Guatemala's or Peru's) how can instrumentalization of anti-corruption laws be avoided? To start with, strong due process protections should ensure that those accused have easy access to an attorney of his or her choice (which Zamora didn't), the right to be heard and present evidence (which Zamora couldn't), to demand evidence of wrongdoing, and to appeal to an independent court. In cases of noncriminal-based forfeiture, courts have relaxed the burden of proof on grounds that these are civil proceedings and no restriction on liberty is contemplated. Even in these proceedings, however, basic protections are needed. Along the same lines, certain anti-corruption-related crimes, like abuse of authority or undue influence, need to be tightly defined, with objective elements, since they are themselves easily subject to abuse. Early in proceedings, prosecutors should be able to publicly explain how the elements of charged crimes are minimally met. Civil society monitoring can also sometimes forestall – or at least denounce – irregularities.

The usual proposed remedy for politicized prosecutions is to ensure that prosecutorial and judicial selection procedures guarantee independence from the executive (and to a lesser extent legislative) branches and to create separate judicial administration and disciplinary bodies that don't keep lower-court judges dependent on higher courts for their jobs and promotions. But under conditions of grand corruption and state capture, independence may mean that selection processes are themselves vitiated and that independence is used to undermine the justice system and protect the powerful (see, again, Guatemala in 2024, where prior efforts to protect a crusading prosecutor led to a change in the law that makes the current corrupt occupant of the job difficult to dislodge).[17] A focus on impartiality rather than simply formal independence might help alleviate these concerns.

Where national justice systems are captured or dysfunctional, advocates often turn to international bodies and standards. This might involve lobbying the peer review mechanisms set up in various anti-corruption bodies (UNCAC, GRECO, OECD, FATF) to investigate and take a stand against politicized use of international anti-corruption standards in specific cases or to ensure that questionable anti-corruption actions do not violate rights to free expression and association. It might also involve demanding some evidence that meets international standards, not just accusations, before people are denied liberty.

At a minimum, international standards should not make it worse. For example, nongovernmental groups long complained that FATF's anti-money laundering and counterterrorism (AML/CTF) standards went overboard in trying to avoid terrorists' use of NGOs and private actors to channel funds. Its 2002 Recommendation 8, intended to avoid private actors serving as conduits or fronts for terrorist groups in the wake of 9/11, required onerous registration, reporting and recordkeeping that could be used by authoritarian or corrupt governments to harass or shut down critics. In response to these complaints, in 2016 the standards were partially revised to clarify that not all NGOs (only a subset to be defined through risk analysis) were subject to these rules, that wholesale disclosure of funders and associates was not required, and that any requirements had to comply with human rights and other obligations.[18] But even the revised standard leaves open the possibility of corrupt judges or authoritarian leaders using the AML/CTF rules to attack independent media or civil society organizations.

Ultimately, no amount of legal language can guard against all efforts to demonize one's political opponents, or draw an adequate line between politicization and putting easy cases at the front of the prosecutorial queue. Nonetheless, safeguards against politicization might include explicit prioritization criteria for prosecutors' offices similar to those used by some prosecutors of international offenses or organized crime to analyze connections and focus on the worst or most emblematic cases first.[19] A publicly known prioritization strategy will allow for checking the worst abuses of prosecutors, at least.

10.4.3 *Resources*

A related objection to an emphasis on anti-corruption in human rights and international criminal law processes, and to human rights in anti-corruption work, is that it overburdens each of these fields.[20] These are difficult investigations, of facts often shrouded in layers of secrecy and obfuscation, of powerful and dangerous individuals and organizations, and requiring expertise (especially financial expertise) that most lawyers and activists lack. As an investigator for the ICC told me a few years ago: "we can barely do what's in our core mandate, we don't have the resources to field and protect people to take on new tasks." Expecting human rights-related bodies to take on, or even to evaluate, grand corruption cases – or anti-corruption bodies to grapple with the subtleties of human rights jurisprudence – may strain already under-resourced mechanisms. This is one of the objections to a new Special Rapporteur on Corruption and Human Rights (see Chapter 2); it has been the objection to many new mandates,[21] which end up having to raise their own funds before they can act, and to minimize their travel. But resources for worthy causes have always been scarce, and there are ways in which greater collaboration and interconnectedness of the anti-corruption, human rights, development and environmental and climate-related agendas may create efficiencies and accumulate power as well as lower costs.

Beyond the specifics, many of my suggestions focus on strengthening and using law and judicial systems. A long-standing argument posits that an emphasis on law individualizes and depoliticizes social problems, disempowers ordinary people (and empowers professionals and experts) in ways that in the end weaken social movements, and even serve as a handmaiden of capitalist expansion. This is a possible outcome, but not a necessary one. The last few decades have seen lots of work on lawyering from below, public interest lawyering and law as only one tool in a multifaceted, multidisciplinary, context-specific toolbox. The opposite problem, an abandonment of law and legal efforts out of a sense that judiciaries and prosecutors are uniformly captured and corrupt, is as big a risk.

10.5 CONVERGENCE WITH OTHER MOVEMENTS: "EVERYTHING, EVERYWHERE, ALL AT ONCE"

As I hope the preceding has made clear, fighting grand corruption and state capture will require tenacity, imagination and the use and combination of different types of laws and forums together with media, political mobilization, and economic strategies. It will demand that anti-corruption, human rights, and environment champions and organizations become fluent in all these areas, able to imagine and use more than one area of law or international mechanism to push back against kleptocracy and to obtain redress. An "everything, everywhere, all at once" strategy will be needed, the ability to go to UN and regional bodies, to use environmental, constitutional, and private law, and to bring evidence to anti-money laundering and anti-corruption prosecutors in multiple countries, in a sequence and combination that will vary. These abilities are already starting to come together in large global organizations. But this breaking down of silos needs to go further: it will take multidisciplinary teams that include social scientists and development and forensic economists and financial analysts, lawyers, community organizers, and media and survey specialists, to pull together strategies that can begin to chip away at kleptocracy.

This convergence of activism and study arises from the convergence of problems that together define our era. The rise of powerful transnational organized crime groups with nearly unlimited funding and a finger in scores of legal, illegal and quasi-legal businesses is usually discussed separately from grand corruption, but in practice the two are deeply entwined – organized crime could not exist without the ability to bribe, co-opt and ally with public officials and private elites, and the funds for bribery multiply exponentially when these alliances hold.

But both draw participants and power from an increasingly lopsided and exclusionary economic system. Waves of privatization, globalization and the "Washington Consensus" of international financial institutions and governments on debt and trade kicked off decades of massive and growing inequality, borne out by statistics that show a greater proportion of GDP gains going to the top income and wealth brackets, while real wages stagnate.[22] As a result, the economic system cannot provide dignified livelihoods for young people in the formal economy, pushing them into illegal markets, extortion of their neighbors, or quasi-legal hustles that depend on corruption. The same is true for corrupt businesspeople or state officials: Increasing concentration of resources and wealth in few hands, monopoly power and barriers to entry for those without connections mean that corruption is left as one of the few ways to get ahead economically. And without attention to grand corruption, efforts to mobilize international finance for development will simply provide more opportunities for looting.

Corruption also has an ethical and cultural dimension. I don't mean this in terms of a timeless "culture of corruption" discourse that tends to come with a neocolonialist tinge. Rather, I agree with many analysts who trace the loss of an already-tenuous sense of the "common good," and its replacement by a "me-first" mentality to the Reagan-Thatcher years (the 1980s) when the rules of politics changed to "win at any cost," while the rules of the economic system abandoned any pretense of obligation to workers and communities, allowing CEOs, Wall Street and investors to extract all financial gains and to rig the economy for their benefit.[23] But it has also been accompanied by a cultural shift to views that paying taxes is for suckers, that cutting corners, skipping or disabling regulations that slow extraction of the earth's resources, skimming a bit off the top, and paying for "favors" are normal business practices necessary to compete, and that the social, environmental and economic consequences of these actions don't matter because they will be felt by unknown actors far away, not by one's own community. This makes it possible, and even inevitable, that the practices underlying corruption at all levels will flourish.

Moreover, while growing inequality and an increasingly harsh version of capitalism co-generate corruption, corruption – especially grand corruption – feeds into the concentration of wealth in a small number of hands seeking continuing control of the state in order to continue accumulating. The result is a vicious cycle of democratic breakdown, extractivist policies on natural resources and labor, a weakening of institutions, rise of anti-regulatory and anti-state "illiberal" populism, and a breakdown of trust in institutions, in democratic checks and balances, in community solidarity and in fellow human beings.

Corruption has a security dimension. As Chayes has written,[24] the rise of radical Islamist movements in much of the world was a reaction to disgust with governments and institutions perceived as irremediably corrupt. After all, the Arab Spring began as an anti-corruption protest in Tunisia, and the rise of the Taliban in Afghanistan during the Russian and US-backed regimes can be traced to perceptions that these regimes were stealing the country blind. Moreover, the link between corruption and war, especially civil conflict, is well-documented.[25]

Grand corruption both causes and is a result of an extractive mentality that sees the natural world simply as resources to be exploited and monetized. Scratch a case of illegal mining, timber trade, fisheries, or wildlife poaching, and you'll find that someone bribed a minister to get the concession, or a congressperson to change the laws, or a local official to issue a license or permit, or an importer to look the other way. Fighting environmental decline and supporting restoration and regeneration require not just environmental law, but a focus on combatting these illegal practices.[26] Similarly, mitigating and adapting to climate change will remain a set of words on paper if issues of corruption in financing, certification schemes, and carbon credit markets monitoring are not confronted.[27]

The fight against grand corruption needs to connect to current debates about emerging technologies, including blockchain, cryptocurrencies and artificial intelligence. These may be useful in identifying and analyzing patterns of corruption (big datasets are already changing how this is done), but also in facilitating rules-free movements of large amounts of capital, to the benefit of kleptocrats of all sorts. Grand corruption blurs the line between legitimate business practices and illicit ones. In areas like agribusiness production of cattle, palm oil or bananas, as we've seen, payments to officials eased the way for corporate entities to obtain fraudulent title on the basis of coercion or deceit. The UN's Guiding Principles on Business and Human Rights require businesses to avoid causing or contributing to adverse human rights impacts in their own operations, and to seek to prevent or mitigate those directly connected to their operations, products or services.[28] To implement the Guiding Principles (or the host of other binding and nonbinding rules that take a similar approach) will require companies to integrate anti-corruption due diligence, monitoring and disclosure alongside other due diligence obligations. That due diligence will need to move beyond identifying venal individuals to consider systemic state capture and organized crime-related issues, and to strengthen compliance programs accordingly.

One reaction to these connections might be to throw up your hands in despair if everything is connected in a downward spiral. I've done that at times, I confess, during the writing of this book. But I think a better response is to see the interwoven nature of the problems as both as a reflection of the limits of law and as an opportunity. Law, by itself, cannot enact lasting social change, however much we lawyers would like to believe otherwise. It can however act to support, protect and mobilize social movements. Social movements have been behind most advances of the last 100 or more years; human rights movements have slowly (and incompletely) changed the narrative around impunity for international crimes and serious rights violations, around the rights of women, children, LGBTQ individuals, indigenous peoples and other minorities, and around the proper role of businesses. Environmental movements have stopped some of the worst forms of pollution, saved the ozone layer and some (but by no means all) threatened species, and increasingly are pushing action to protect the climate to the forefront of government, educational, media and business agendas. Development "beneficiaries" have organized, lobbied and sat down in the streets to stop harmful projects, leading to complaint mechanisms at development banks and withdrawal of financing from some of the worst projects. Consumer boycotts, shareholder activism, investigative journalists and angry citizens have imposed a "social license to operate" on at least some businesses. Imagine if all those movements included an anti-corruption (including political corruption, tax evasion and illicit finance) platform across their work. Imagine if they all worked together …

Epilogue

As this book goes to press, the new Trump administration in the United States has made the fight against grand corruption – at home and abroad – much more difficult. Following the playbook for state capture almost perfectly, it has, in short order, fired 18 Inspectors General (in charge of dealing with fraud in the US federal government), imposed loyalty tests on remaining Department of Justice lawyers and FBI agents, intimidated the press, and tried to dismantle the professional civil service, USAID (a major funder of anti-corruption work around the world) and the Consumer Financial Protection Bureau. The Attorney General declared a half-year pause to enforcement of the Foreign Corrupt Practices Act, leaving corporations able to bribe abroad with impunity in the US. Trump has sent the world's richest man, who has vast government contracts (and wants more, as well as deregulation of his industries) into the bowels of US payment systems, personnel records and private information regarding its citizens. All of this has no authorization from Congress, and most of it is illegal. In a way, it proves my point about the emergence of a virulent new form of top-down, systemic corruption.

It's not clear as I write how far the US administration will go before the courts, an outraged citizenry and/or legislators with a modicum of independence and decency stop the current juggernaut, and how bad the economic, fiscal, social and institutional damage – not to mention the cruelty inflicted on thousands of people – will be. But the trends I describe in this book don't depend on a single administration in a single country, no matter how powerful.

It will take even more persistence, creativity and alliance-building to break through the current barrage, but it can be done. And more than ever, it will take all of us, together.

Notes

1 THE GRAND CORRUPTION PROBLEM

1. Global Expert Group Meeting on Corruption, "Oslo Statement on Corruption Involving Vast Quantities of Assets," United Nations Office on Drugs and Crime, June 14, 2019. www.unodc.org/documents/corruption/meetings/OsloEGM2019/Oslo_Outcome_Statement_on_Corruption_involving_Vast_Quantities_of_Assets_-_FINAL_VERSION.pdf.
2. Transparency International, "Grand Corruption." www.transparency.org/en/our-priorities/grand-corruption.
3. Sarah Chayes, "When Corruption Is the Operating System: The Case of Honduras," Carnegie Endowment for International Peace, May 30, 2017, Introduction.
4. Chayes, "When Corruption Is the Operating System."
5. USAID Anti-Corruption Task Force, "Dekleptification Guide: Seizing Windows of Opportunity to Dismantle Kleptocracy," September 2022, p. 3. www.usaid.gov/sites/default/files/2023-02/USAID-Dekleptification-Guide.pdf.
6. Oliver Bullough, "The Rise of Kleptocracy: The Dark Side of Globalization" (2018) 29 *Journal of Democracy*, 25–38; Oliver Bullough, *Butler to the World: The Book the Oligarchs Don't Want You to Read – How Britain Helps the World's Worst People Launder Money, Commit Crimes, and Get Away with Anything* (New York City: St. Martin's Press, 2022).
7. Joel Hellman and Daniel Kaufmann, "Confronting the Challenge of State Capture in Transition Economies,"(2001) *Finance and Development*, 38(3). www.imf.org/external/pubs/ft/fandd/2001/09/hellman.htm#author.
8. Luis Jorge Garay-Salamanca, Eduardo Salcedo-Albaran and Bernardo Guerrero, *The Capture and Co-opted Reconfiguration of the State in Colombia* (Bogota: Grupo Metodo, 2008), p. 15. www.cels.org.ar/web/wp-content/uploads/2018/01/Captura-y-Reconfiguracion-Cooptada-del-Estado-en-Colombia.pdf.
9. Elizabeth David-Barrett, "State Capture and Inequality," Pathfinder, December 2021. https://s42831.pcdn.co/wp-content/uploads/1662/65/cic_pathfinders_state_capture_inequality-2021.pdf.
10. Jimena Reyes, State Capture through Corruption: How Can Human Rights Help? Harvard Human Rights Program Research Working Paper (June 2019), available at https://hrp.law.harvard.edu/wp-content/uploads/2022/10/JimenaReyes_HRP_19_002.pdf.

11. Garay Salamanca et al., *The Capture*, p. 84.
12. Eduardo Salcedo-Albaran and Luis Jorge Garay-Salamanca, *Super Network of Corruption in Venezuela: Kleptocracy, Nepotism and Human Rights Violation* (St. Petersburg: Vortex Foundation and SciVortex, 2021). www.scivortex.org/_files/ugd/f53019_5483e38181af4cc8bec464bbda9b1a7a.pdf.
13. UN Convention against Transnational Organized Crime (UNTOC), 2000, Art. 2(a), (c).
14. Daniel Vásquez, "Las Redes de Macrocriminalidad: Corrupción, impunidad y delitos empresariales," *Justicia en las Américas*, June 25, 2024, https://dplfblog.com/2024/06/25/las-redes-de-macrominalidad-corrupcion-impunidad-y-delitos-empresariales/.
15. Enrique Desmond Arias, *Criminal Enterprises and Governance in Latin America and the Caribbean* (Cambridge: Cambridge University Press, 2017); Benjamin Lessing, "Conceptualizing Criminal Governance" (2021) 19 *Perspectives on Politics*, 854–873. https://edisciplinas.usp.br/pluginfile.php/5894706/mod_resource/content/1/Lessing%20-%202020%20-%20Conceptualizing%20Criminal%20Governance.pdf.
16. Ugljesa Zvekic, Suncana Roksandic and Bojan Dobovsek, "Organized Corruption: Political Financing in the Western Balkans," Global Initiative, June 23, 2023. https://globalinitiative.net/analysis/organized-corruption-political-financing-western-balkans/.
17. Commission Against Impunity in Guatemala, Informe Final: El Legado de Justicia en Guatemala (2019). www.cicig.org/cicig/informes_cicig/informe-de-labores/informe-final-de-labores/#informe.
18. E. Salcedo-Albaran and L. Garay Salamanca, Super Network of Corruption; Luis Daniel Vazquez Valencia, *State Capture, Macrocriminality and Human Rights* (Ciudad de Mexico: FLACSO Mexico, Fundacion Boll-Mexico and UNAM, Instituto de Investigaciones Juridicas, 2019). https://mx.boell.org/sites/default/files/2019-12/captura%20del%20estado%20-%20interiores%20final.pdf; Harald Waxenecker and La Otra Cooperativa, "Honduras: Undue Networks of Power, Impunity and Enrichment? A Sketch of a Complex Reality," Heinrich Boll Stiftung, July 2016. https://mx.boell.org/es/2016/08/05/honduras-redes-indebidas-de-poder-impunidad-y-enriquecimiento.
19. Venezuela Research Unit, "GameChangers 2022: Maduro Stands as Venezuela's Shadow Underworld Power," InSight Crime, December 27, 2022. https://es.insightcrime.org/noticias/gamechangers-2022-maduro-se-erige-como-el-poder-en-la-sombra-del-hampa-en-venezuela/.
20. Sally Bowen and Jane Holligan, *The Imperfect Spy: The Many Lives of Vladimiro Montesinos* (Peisa, 2003).
21. Naomi Roht-Arriaza, *The Pinochet Effect: Transnational Justice in the Age of Human Rights* (Philadelphia: University of Pennsylvania Press, 2005), pp. 112–113 and pp. 140–149.
22. Joel Millman, "El Salvador's Army: A Force Unto Itself," The New York Times Magazine, December 10, 1989. www.nytimes.com/1989/12/10/magazine/el-salvador-s-army-a-force-unto-itself.html.
23. Michael Smith, Sabrina Valle and Blake Schmidt, "No One Has Ever Made a Corruption Machine Like This One," Bloomberg Businessweek, June 8, 2017. www.bloomberg.com/news/features/2017-06-08/no-one-has-ever-made-a-corruption-machine-like-this-one.

24. Nicolas Campos, Eduardo Engel, Ronald D. Fischer et al., "The Ways of Corruption in Infrastructure: Lessons from the Odebrecht Case" (2021) 35 *The Journal of Economic Perspectives*, 171–190.
25. Jonathan Watts, "Brazil: Insider Claims Rousseff Coalition Took Funds from Belo Monte mega-dam," The Guardian, April 8, 2016. www.theguardian.com/world/2016/apr/08/brazil-rousseff-corruption-belo-monte-dam.
26. Tiffany Higgins, "Belo Monte boondoggle: Brazil's Biggest, Costliest dam May Be Unviable," Mongabay, January 17, 2020. https://news.mongabay.com/2020/01/belo-monte-boondoggle-brazils-biggest-costliest-dam-may-be-unviable/.
27. Pablo Albarenga and Francesc Badia I Dalmases, "Dani Silva: Displaced from Her Home – But Fighting to Save All of Ours," openDemocracy, July 29, 2022. www.opendemocracy.net/en/democraciaabierta/belo-monte-dam-brazil-construction-displaced-ecosystem-flooding-deforestation-feminist-campaign-dani-silva/.
28. Kejal Vyas, "Colombia Charges 60 with Graft in Odebrecht Scandal," Wall Street Journal, August 18, 2023.
29. Matthew Stephenson, "The Incredible Shrinking Scandal? Further Reflections on the Lava Jato Leaks," The Global Anticorruption Blog, June 17, 2019. https://globalanticorruptionblog.com/2019/06/17/the-incredible-shrinking-scandal-further-reflections-on-the-lava-jato-leaks/.
30. Kathryn Sikkink and Margaret Keck, *Activists Beyond Borders* (Ithaca, NY: Cornell University Press, 2014).

2 TREATY LAW ON CORRUPTION AND HUMAN RIGHTS

1. H. Pablo, "When is Corruption Good?," World Bank Blogs, April 19, 2006. https://blogs.worldbank.org/psd/when-is-corruption-good.
2. Group of States against Corruption, "About GRECO Mutual Evaluations," Council of Europe. www.coe.int/en/web/greco/evaluations/about.
3. Ioannis Androulakis and Stefano Betti, "State of Implementation of the United Nations Convention against Corruption: Criminalization, Law Enforcement and International Cooperation," United Nations Office on Drugs and Crime, 2017. www.unodc.org/documents/treaties/UNCAC/COSP/session7/V.17-04679_E-book.pdf.
4. I. Androulakis and S. Betti, "State of Implementation," pp. 265–266. www.unodc.org/documents/treaties/UNCAC/COSP/session7/V.17-04679_E-book.pdf.
5. Aleksi Pursiainen, "The FATF and Evolution of Counterterrorism Asset Freeze Laws in the Nordic Countries: We Fought the Soft Law and the Soft Law Won," in K. Karjalainen, I. Tornberg and A. Pursiainen, *International Actors and the Formation of Laws* (Cham: Springer, 2022). https://doi.org/10.1007/978-3-030-98351-2_7.
6. National Defense Authorization Act § 6304, "Corporate Transparency Act of 2021 passed as part of the National Defense Authorization Act," 2021. Corporate Transparency Act (CTA) | Practical Law (westlaw.com).
7. The Establishing New Authorities for Businesses Laundering and Enabling Risks to Security (ENABLERS) Act passed the US House in 2022 but failed in the Senate. As I write this there is a proposed US Treasury regulation that would require title companies and some others to do due diligence on their clients when selling residential real estate for all cash. H.R.5525 – 117th Congress (2021–2022): ENABLERS Act | Congress.gov | Library of Congress.

8. UN General Assembly, "Our Common Commitment to Effectively Addressing Challenges and Implementing Measures to Prevent and Combat Corruption and Strengthen International Cooperation," A/RES/S-32/1, June 2, 2021. https://ungass2021.unodc.org/ungass2021/index.html.
9. Conference of the State Parties to the United Nations Convention against Corruption, "Follow-up to the Marrakech declaration on the prevention of corruption." "9. *Strongly encourages* States parties, in addition to integrating anti-corruption policies in broader crime prevention and criminal justice reform strategies and public sector reform plans … to undertake similar action with regard to development programmes, strategies and action plans"; Resolution 5/4, November 25–29, 2013.
10. Resolution 6/6 and subsequent years, always tied to the "softer" obligations of education, culture, and prevention.
11. Office on Drugs and Crime, "UNODC Pledge for the Human Rights 75 Initiative," United Nations. www.unodc.org/unodc/en/humanrights/pledge.html.
12. Inter-American Court of Human Rights, "Case of Lagos Del Campo v. Peru, Judgment: Preliminary Objections, Merits, Reparations and Costs," August 31, 2017. www.corteidh.or.cr/docs/casos/articulos/seriec_340_esp.pdf; Advisory Opinion OC- 23/ 17, The Environment and Human Rights, November 15, 2017.
13. Department of Economic and Social Affairs, "Sustainable Development Goal 16, Targets and Indicators: 16.4; 16.5; and 16.10," United Nations. https://sdgs.un.org/goals/goal16#targets_and_indicators.
14. High-Level Panel on International Financial Accountability, Transparency and Integrity (FACTI Panel), "Financial Integrity for Sustainable Development: Report of the High Level Panel on International Financial Accountability, Transparency and Integrity for Achieving the 2030 Agenda," February 2021. https://uploads-ssl.webflow.com/5e0bd9edab846816e263d633/602e91032a209d0601ed4a2c_FACTI_Panel_Report.pdf.
15. Final Report of the Human Rights Council Advisory Committee on the issue of the negative impact of corruption on the enjoyment of human rights, January 5, 2015, A/HRC/28/73, para. 38; Human Rights Council, Resolution: 40/4, "The negative impact of the non-repatriation of funds of illicit origin to the countries of origin on the enjoyment of human rights, and the importance of improving international cooperation," United Nations Human Rights Office of the High Commissioner, April 5, 2019.
16. Human Rights Council, Resolutions on "The Negative Impact of the Non-repatriation of Funds of Illicit Origin to the Countries of Origin on the Enjoyment of Human Rights, and the Importance of Improving International Cooperation," United Nations Human Rights Office of the High Commissioner: 17/23, June 17, 2011; 19/38, March 23, 2012; 22/12, March 21, 2013; 25/9, March 27, 2014; 28/5, March 26, 2015; 31/22, March 24, 2016; 34/11, March 23, 2017; 40/4, March 21, 2019; and 46/11, March 23, 2021;. Resolutions on "The negative impact of corruption on the enjoyment of human rights": Res. 53/17, July 13, 2023, Res. 35/25, June 23, 2017; For an earlier effort, see Christy Mbonu, "Corruption and Its Impact on the Full Enjoyment of Human Rights, in Particular, Economic, Social and Cultural Rights," United Nations Human Rights Office of the High Commissioner, June 22, 2005. UN Doc. E/CN.4/Sub.2/2005/L.24/Rev.1. On good governance, see for

example, Res. 51/5, October 6, 2022; on the SDGs and public service delivery, see for example, Res. 52/8, April 3, 2023.

17. Inter-American Commission on Human Rights, "Resolution: 1/17 Human Rights and the Fight Against Impunity and Corruption," Organization of American States, September 12, 2017. www.oas.org/en/iachr/decisions/pdf/Resolution-1-17-en.pdf; Annual Report 2021, Chapter IV(b), "Guatemala," www.oas.org/en/iachr/docs/annual/2021/chapters/ia2021cap4b.guatemala-en.pdf.
18. Inter-American Commission on Human Rights, "Resolution: 1/18 Corruption and Human Rights," Organization of American States, March 2, 2018. www.oas.org/en/iachr/decisions/pdf/Resolution-1-18-en.pdf.
19. Inter-American Commission on Human Rights, Corruption and Human Rights, December 6, 2019, www.oas.org/en/iachr/reports/pdfs/CorruptionHR.pdf, see especially paras. 250, 270–73.
20. Inter-American Commission on Human Rights, "Report No. 72/15 Case 12.896, Report on Merits, Ramirez Brothers And Family v. Guatemala," Organization of American States, October 28, 2015. www.oas.org/en/iachr/decisions/court/2016/12896FondoEn.pdf?fbclid=IwAR01NDBjHexol2tnoD8TuycwcBk4PTeX90qqJGcswJBNIWC6KX-E5RrVj-I.
21. Inter-American Court of Human Rights, "Case of Ramirez Escobar et al. v. Guatemala, Judgment: Merits, Reparations and Costs," March 9, 2018, para. 241. www.corteidh.or.cr/docs/casos/articulos/resumen_351_esp.pdf.
22. Inter-American Court of Human Rights, "Case of the Kichwa Indigenous People of Sarayaku v. Ecuador, Judgment: Fund and Reparations," Series C No. 245, June 27, 2012, para. 186.
23. Inter-American Court of Human Rights, "Case of Carvajal et al. v. Colombia, Judgment: Merits, Reparations and Costs," Series C No. 352, March 13, 2018, para 177.
24. Inter-American Court of Human Rights, "Case of Luna Lopez v. Honduras, Judgment: Merits, Reparations and Costs," Series C No. 269, October 10, 2013, paras. 122, 125.
25. Inter-American Court of Human Rights, "Caso Viteri Ungaretti y Otros v. Ecuador, Judgment: Merits, Reparations and Cost," Series C No. 510, November 27, 2023.
26. Id., paras. 82–84.
27. Id., paras. 85–89.
28. https://au.int/sites/default/files/treaties/36390-treaty-0011_african_charter_on_human_and_peoples_rights_e.pdf. Id., para. 94.Art. 21(2).
29. African Court of Justice and Human Rights, "Protocol on Amendments to the Protocol on the Statute of the African Court of Justice and Human Rights – Corruption," African Union, July 11, 2000, Art. 28I. https://au.int/sites/default/files/treaties/36398-treaty-0045_-_protocol_on_amendments_to_the_protocol_on_the_statute_of_the_african_court_of_justice_and_human_rights_e-compressed.pdf.
30. Community Court of Justice, "The Registered Trustees of the Socio-economic and Accountability Project (SERAP) v. Nigeria & UBEC," Economic Community of West African States (ECOWAS), November 30, 2010. https://caselaw.ihrda.org/en/document/qrb6wqua4frswtjqwichxgvi?page=1.
31. Council of Europe, "Civil Law Convention on Corruption," November 4, 1999. https://rm.coe.int/168007f3f6.

32. European Court of Human Rights, "Case of Khadija Ismayilova v. Azerbaijan (No. 2), Judgment: Merits and Just Satisfaction," Council of Europe, August 25, 2020.
33. "Case of Rantsev v. Cyprus and Russia," January 7, 2010.
34. European Parliament, "Recommendation to the Council and the Vice-President of the Commission/High Representative of the Union for Foreign Affairs and Security Policy concerning corruption and human rights" (2022) 65 *Official Journal of the European Union*. https://eur-lex.europa.eu/legal-content/EN/TXT/?uri=CELEX:52022IP0042.
35. For example, Australian Human Rights Commission, Human Rights Based Approaches, at https://humanrights.gov.au/our-work/rights-and-freedoms/human-rights-based-approaches.
36. Maeve McDonagh, "The Right to Information in International Human Rights Law" (2013) 13 *Human Rights Law Review*, 25–55. https://ssrn.com/abstract=2446424.
37. Inter-American Court of Human Rights, "Case of Claude Reyes et al v. Chile, Claude Reyes et. al. v. Chile, Merits, reparations and costs," IACHR Series C no 151, IHRL 1535, September 19, 2006.
38. United Nations Conference on Environment and Development, Rio de Janiero, Braz., June 3–14, 1992, Rio Declaration on Environment and Development, U.N. Doc. A/CONF. 151/26/Rev.
39. United Nations Economic Commission for Europe, 1998 Aarhus Convention on Access to Information, Public Participation in Decision-Making and Access to Justice in Environmental Matters, 2161 UNTS 447, 38 ILM 517 (1999).
40. Regional Agreement on Access to Information, Public Participation and Justice in Environmental Matters in Latin America and the Caribbean (Escazú Agreement), March 4, 2018, Art. 7. See Economic Commission for Latin America and the Caribbean (ECLAC), Regional Agreement on Access to Information, Public Participation and Justice in Environmental Matters in Latin America and the Caribbean: implementation guide (LC/TS.2021/221/Rev.2), Santiago, 2023.
41. UNCAC Conference of the Parties, Res. 10/10, para. 1, CAC/COSP/2023/L.14/Rev.1. www.unodc.org/documents/treaties/UNCAC/COSP/session10/resolutions/L-documents/2325384E_L.14_Rev.1.pdf.
42. Human Rights Council, Report of the Independent Expert to Update the Set of Principles to Combat Impunity, Diane Orentlicher, Addendum, E/CN.4/2005/102/Add.1 (February 8, 2005).
43. Human Rights Committee, General Comment 32, CCPR/C/GC/32, August 23, 2007, available at https://docstore.ohchr.org/SelfServices/FilesHandler.ashx?enc=6QkG1d%2FPPRiCAqhKb7yhsrdB0H1l5979OVGGB%2BWPAXhRjoXNTTvKgFHbxAcZSvX1OsJj%2FiyRmVA4IiMvUt2NlGKqqg2nh1qOE2hX5xoGtKE2v2YSQVV1Rv5NitNbSYwp.
44. United Nations Congress on the Prevention of Crime and the Treatment of Offenders, "Basic Principles on the Independence of the Judiciary," UN Human Rights Office of the High Commissioner, September 6, 1985. www.ohchr.org/en/instruments-mechanisms/instruments/basic-principles-independence-judiciary.
45. United Nations Round Table Meeting of Chief Justices, "The Bangalore Principles of Judicial Conduct," UN Office on Drugs and Crime, 2002. www.unodc.org/pdf/crime/corruption/judicial_group/Bangalore_principles.pdf.

46. Special Rapporteur on the independence of judges and lawyers, "International standards," United Nations Human Rights Office of the High Commissioner. www.ohchr.org/en/special-procedures/sr-independence-of-judges-and-lawyers/international-standards.
47. Jessica Schultz, "The UNCAC and Judicial Corruption: Requirements and Avenues for Reform," CMI | U4 Anti-Corruption Resource Centre, September 2009. www.cmi.no/publications/file/3457-the-uncac-and-judicial-corruption.pdf.
48. Lillian Dang and Mary Greer, "Anti-Corruption Approaches in Justice Sector Assistance" CMI | U4 Anti-Corruption Resource Centre, December 19, 2023. www.u4.no/publications/anti-corruption-approaches-in-justice-sector-assistance.
49. See generally Due Process of Law Foundation, Selection of Judicial Authorities. www.dplf.org/en/resources-topics/selection-judicial-authorities.
50. UN Office of High Commissioner for Human Rights, Guiding Principles on Business and Human Rights: Implementing the United Nations "Protect, Respect, and Remedy" Framework (2011). www.ohchr.org/sites/default/files/documents/publications/guidingprinciplesbusinesshr_en.pdf.
51. The latest draft of the treaty can be found at UN Doc. A/HRC/55/59/Add.1. www.ohchr.org/en/hr-bodies/hrc/wg-trans-corp/session10.
52. UNCAC Conference of the Parties, Res. 10/10, para. 1, CAC/COSP/2023/L.14/Rev.1. www.unodc.org/documents/treaties/UNCAC/COSP/session10/resolutions/L-documents/2325384E_L.14_Rev.1.pdf.
53. Regional Agreement on Access to Information, Public Participation and Justice In Environmental Matters in Latin America and the Caribbean (Escazú Agreement) (2018). https://treaties.un.org/doc/Treaties/2018/03/20180312%2003-04%20PM/CTC-XXVII-18.pdf.
54. United Nations General Assembly, "Resolution: 53/144. Declaration on the Right and Responsibility of Individuals, Groups and Organs of Society to Promote and Protect Universally Recognized Human Rights and Fundamental Freedoms," United Nations, March 8, 1999. www.ohchr.org/sites/default/files/Documents/Issues/Defenders/Declaration/declaration.pdf.
55. Elizabeth Abi-Mershed et al., "The Esperanza Protocol: An Effective Response to Threats Against Human Rights Defenders," Center for Justice and International Law, 2021. https://esperanzaprotocol.net/wp-content/uploads/2022/06/Esperanza-Protocol-EN-2.pdf.
56. Human Rights Council Special Rapporteur on the Situation of Human Rights Defenders, A/HRC/49/49: "At the Heart of the Struggle: Human Rights Defenders Working against Corruption," December 28, 2021. www.ohchr.org/en/documents/thematic-reports/ahrc4949-heart-struggle-human-rights-defenders-working-against.
57. Juliet Sorensen, *Human Rights and Corruption* (Edward Elgar, 2019); Julio Bacio-Terracino, "Corruption as a Violation of Human Rights" (2008) *International Council on Human Rights Policy*.
58. Article 30 of UNCAC comes closest, but is a weaker and more contingent set of obligations on states than those of human rights law.
59. Peters, "Corruption as a Violation of International Human Rights" (2018) 29(4) *European Journal of International Law*, 1251–1287, https://doi.org/10.1093/ejil/chy070.

60. Inter-American Court of Human Rights, Advisory Opinion OC-23/17, The Environment and Human Rights, November 15, 2017; Human Rights Council, Res. A/HRC/RES/48/13, October 8, 2021; HRC Res. A/HRC/52/L.7, March 23, 2023.
61. UN General Assembly Res. 76/300, July 28, 2022.
62. Ndiva Kofele-Kale "The Right to a Corruption Free Society as an Individual and Collective Human Right: Elevating Official Corruption to a Crime under International Law" (2000) 34(1) *The International Lawyer*, 149–178; Kolawole Olaniyan, *Ownership of Proceeds of Corruption in International Law* (Oxford University Press, 2023).
63. Anne Peters, Corruption as a Violation.
64. David Kinley, A New Human Right to Freedom from Corruption, February 10, 2014, http://ssrn.com/abstract=2393205.
65. Anita Ramasastry, "Is There a Right to Be Free from Corruption?" (2015) 49 *UC Davis Law Review*, 703–739. https://lawreview.law.ucdavis.edu/sites/g/files/dgvnsk15026/files/media/documents/49-2_Ramasastry.pdf.
66. Armin von Bogdandy and René Urueña, "International Transformative Constitutionalism in Latin America," (2020) 114(3) *American Journal of International Law*, 403–442. doi:10.1017/ajil.2020.27.
67. Estefanía Medina and Adriana Greaves, ¿Existe un derecho a vivir en un ambiente libre de corrupción? [Is there a right to live in a corruption-free environment?], January 21, 2020. https://eljuegodelacorte.nexos.com.mx/existe-un-derecho-a-vivir-en-un-ambiente-libre-de-corrupcion/.
68. Noveno Tribunal Colegiado En Materia Penal Del Primer Circuito, Amparo en revisión 216/2019. October 3, 2019. sec. 3C, p. 9. https://bj.scjn.gob.mx/doc/tesis/2PhwMHYBN_4klb4H9kHf/%22Anticorrupci%C3%B3n%22.
69. Article. 7, Constitution of Baja California; Article 2(40), Constitution of Tabasco.
70. Sala de lo Constitucional de la Corte Suprema, San Salvador, No. 146-2014/107-2017, May 28, 2018, s/ Extinción de Dominio. https://sv.vlex.com/vid/651742597, pp. 9–12.
71. Id., p. 14.
72. Supreme Court of Costa Rica, Constitutional Chamber, decisión 2000-00041, January 4, 2000.
73. For example, Case N° 71-2013, Tribunal Penal del II Circuito Judicial de San José, Costa Rica, Goicoechea, February 19, 2013, see www.cpccs.gob.ec/docs/niceditUploads/tempo/141815866218.%20PANEL%204_COSTA%20RICA_Miguel%20Cort%C7%B8s%20Ch%C7%ADves.pdf.
74. State of Maharashtra Tr.C.B.I v. Balakrishna Dattatrya Kumbhar on October 15, 2012, available at https://indiankanoon.org/doc/92963982/, para. 14.

3 TRANSNATIONAL APPROACHES I

1. Matías Ponce, *CICIG: Misión Posible* (Guatemala City: Saqarik, 2021), pp. 21–22.
2. Commission for Historical Clarification, Guatemala: Memory of Silence, Conclusions and Recommendations (1998). https://hrdag.org/wp-content/uploads/2013/01/CEHreport-english.pdf.
3. REMHI, Guatemala Nunca Mas (1998), available with English explanation at https://spotlight-prod.lib.utexas.edu/spotlight/monsenor-juan-gerardi-guatemala/feature/remhi-historical-memory-recovery-project.

4. See, for example, Naomi Roht-Arriaza, "Guatemala: Lessons for Transitional Justice," in Cheryl Lawther, L. Moffett and D. Jacobs, *Research Handbook on Transitional Justice* (London: Edward Elgar, 2017), pp. 445–465.
5. Suzanne Jonas, *Of Centaurs and Doves: Guatemala's Peace Process* (Boulder, CO: Westview Press, 2000).
6. Rachel A. Schwartz, *Undermining the State from Within: The Institutional Legacies of Civil War in Central America* (Cambridge: Cambridge University Press, 2023), p. 45.
7. Jesse Franzblau, "The Rise and Fall of Guatemala's Most Feared General," Foreign Policy in Focus, September 22, 2015, http://fpif.org/the-rise-and-fall-of-guatemalas-most-feared-general.
8. Schwartz, Undermining the State from Within, p. 94 et seq.
9. US Dept. of Justice, "Former President of Guatemala, Alfonso Portillo, Sentenced In Manhattan Federal Court for Laundering Millions of Dollars Through United States Banks," May 22, 2014. www.justice.gov/usao-sdny/pr/former-president-guatemala-alfonso-portillo-sentenced-manhattan-federal-court.
10. CMI, El padrino de los poderes paralelos: el general Callejas y Callejas (The godfather of informal powers: General Callejas y Callejas), January 26, 2017. https://cmiguate.org/el-padrino-de-los-poderes-paralelos-el-general-callejas-y-callejas/.
11. Prensa Libre, "How does cattle ranching linked to drug trafficking impact Guatemala's Mayan jungle," prensalibre.com, May 29, 2020, www.prensalibre.com/ciudades/peten/como-impacta-la-ganaderia-ligada-al-narcotrafico-en-la-selva-maya-de-guatemala.
12. Kenneth Freed, "Corruption Found at Top of Military, Government," Los Angeles Times, September 19, 1991, www.latimes.com/archives/la-xpm-1991-09-19-mn-3532-story.html; Carlos Enrique Fuentes Sánchez, "Ladrones, Corrupción y Violencia," Gazeta, June 15, 2022. https://gazeta.gt/59196/.
13. "Strengthening of Civilian Power and the Role of the Armed Forces in a Democratic Society," September 1996. www.guatemalaun.org/paz.cfm (in Spanish).
14. Agreement between the United Nations and the State of Guatemala on the Establishment of an International Commission Against Impunity in Guatemala, Art. 2(1), December 12, 2006. www.cicig.org/uploads/documents/mandato/cicig_acuerdo_en.pdf.
15. Open Society Justice Initiative, "Against the Odds: CICIG," Open Society Foundation, p. 34. www.justiceinitiative.org/uploads/88ffafc0-09bf-4998-8ef3-e2a175e3f455/against-odds-cicig-guatemala-20160321.pdf.
16. Naomi Roht-Arriaza, *The Pinochet Effect: Transnational Justice in the Age of Human Rights* (Penn Press, 2005).
17. Centro de Investigaciones Economicas Nacionales, "Juzgados de Mayor Riesgo: Análisis y Retos" (High-Risk Courts: Analysis and Challenges), November 2019. https://cien.org.gt/wp-content/uploads/2019/11/Procesos-Mayor-Riesgo-VF-19.11.19.pdf.
18. OSJI, Against the Odds, p. 92.
19. Martha Soto, Velasquez, El Retador del Poder (Velasquez, The Challenger of Power) (Ed. Intermedio, 2016).
20. CICIG, Final Report: The Legacy of Justice in Guatemala (2019). www.cicig.org/wp-content/uploads/2019/08/InformeLegadoJusticia_SI.pdf.

21. Jovanna García, "CSJ traslada a juez que extinguió propiedades por delitos de corrupción, narcotráfico o lavado de dinero," April 8, 2024. https://epinvestiga.com/actualidad/csj-traslada-a-juez-que-extinguio-propiedades-por-delitos-de-corrupcion-narcotrafico-o-lavado-de-dinero/.
22. CICIG, Communiqué 047, State Cooptation Case, June 2, 2016. www.cicig.org/casos/caso-cooptacion-del-estado-de-guatemala/.
23. CICIG, Communiqué 051, The "Cooperacha" Case, June 11, 2016. www.cicig.org/casos/caso-la-cooperacha/.
24. CICIG, "Encuesta Prodatos: 72% de la población guatemalteca apoya labor de la CICIG" (Prodatos Survey: 72% of Guatemalan population supports CICIG's work), April 5, 2019. www.cicig.org/apoyo-ciudadano/poblacion-guatemalteca-apoya-labor-de-la-cicig/.
25. Department of Political and Peacebuilding Affairs, "Evaluative Exercises: A Summary of Lessons Learned Studies and Evaluations." United Nations, 2019. https://dppa.un.org/sites/default/files/_evaluationsummary_2019_final.pdf.
26. His Excellency Juan Orlando Hernandez Alvarado and Secretary General Luis Almagro, "Agreement Between the Government of the Republic of Honduras and the General Secretariat of the Organization of American States for the Establishment of the Mission to Support the Fight Against Corruption and Impunity in Honduras," Presidency of the Republic of Honduras and Organization of American States, January 19, 2016. www.oas.org/en/spa/dsdsm/docs/maccih_%20agreement_e.pdf.
27. Charles Call, "Fleeting Success: The Legacy of Honduras' International Anti-Corruption Mission," Center for Latin American & Latino Studies, American University, Working Paper Series No. 27, July 7, 2020. https://papers.ssrn.com/sol3/papers.cfm?abstract_id=3633943.
28. Rene Estrada, "'Breaking Points' That Explain Why Honduras Did Not Sign the Memorandum for the Installation of the CICIH," CESPAD | Center for the Study of Democracy, September 27, 2022. https://cespad.org.hn/puntos-de-quiebre-que-explican-por-que-honduras-no-firma-el-memorandum-para-la-instalacion-de-la-cicih/.
29. Loida Martinez Avelar, Karen Moreno and Suchit Chavez, "CICIES Denounced Bukele's Circle for Corruption," FACTum, January 29, 2024. www.revistafactum.com/secretos-cicies/.
30. Guillermo Trejo and Camilo Nieto-Matiz, "Containing Large-Scale Criminal Violence through Internationalized Prosecution: How the Collaboration between the CICIG and Guatemala's Law Enforcement Contributed to a Sustained Reduction in the Murder Rate" (2023) 56 *Comparative Political Studies*, 1328–1364.

4 TRANSNATIONAL APPROACHES II

1. Noura Abughris, "A Brief History of Economic Sanctions," Carter-Ruck. www.carter-ruck.com/insight/a-brief-history-of-economic-sanctions/.
2. Francisco Rodríguez, The Human Consequences of Economic Sanctions (Center for Economic and Policy Research, 2023). www.cepr.net/report/the-human-consequences-of-economic-sanctions/.

3. Richard N. Haass, "Economic Sanctions: Too Much of a Bad Thing," Brookings Institution, June 1, 1998. www.brookings.edu/articles/economic-sanctions-too-much-of-a-bad-thing/.
4. Jane Boulden, and Andrea Charron. "Evaluating UN Sanctions: New Ground, New Dilemmas, and Unintended Consequences." (2009) 65(1) *International Journal*, 1–11. *JSTOR*, www.jstor.org/stable/25681082.
5. Michael A. Weber, "The Global Magnitsky Human Rights Accountability Act," Congressional Research Service, December 3, 2021. https://sgp.fas.org/crs/row/R46981.pdf; Hermitage Capital Management, "Inquiry into Targeted Sanctions to Address Human Rights Abuses, Submission 4, Ref: Australian Magnitsky Act," Scribd.com, January 14, 2020. www.scribd.com/document/485568995/4-Sub-William-Browder-r-4; Human Rights Watch, "The US Global Magnitsky Act: Questions and Answers," hrw.org, September 13, 2017. www.hrw.org/news/2017/09/13/us-global-magnitsky-act.
6. Martin Russell, "Global Human Rights Sanctions Mapping Magnitsky Laws: The US, Canadian, UK and EU Approach," European Parliamentary Research Service, November 2021. www.europarl.europa.eu/RegData/etudes/BRIE/2021/698791/EPRS_BRI(2021)698791_EN.pdf.
7. Weber, "Global Magnitsky," at 2; Dianne E. Rennack and Cory Welt, "U.S. Sanctions on Russia: An Overview," Congressional Research Service In Focus IF10779, September 1, 2021.
8. Julia Ioffe, "Why Does the Kremlin Care So Much about the Magnitsky Act?," The Atlantic, July 27, 2017. www.theatlantic.com/international/archive/2017/07/magnitsky-act-kremlin/535044/.
9. Weber, "Global Magnitsky," at 2, footnote 7.
10. Rep. Christopher H. Smith, "Subcommittee on Africa, Global Health, Global Human Rights, and International Organizations, Committee on Foreign Affairs, The Global Magnitsky Human Rights Accountability Act," House Hearing, 114 Congress U.S., Government Publishing Office, April 29, 2015. www.govinfo.gov/content/pkg/CHRG-114hhrg94388/html/CHRG-114hhrg94388.htm.
11. Representative Christopher Smith, note 27.
12. United States Commission on International Religious Freedom (USCIRF), "USCIRF Applauds Permanent Reauthorization of Global Magnitsky Human Rights Accountability Act," uscirf.gov, April 13, 2022. www.uscirf.gov/news-room/releases-statements/uscirf-applauds-permanent-reauthorization-global-magnitsky-human.
13. Human Rights First, "Global Magnitsky Sanctions Frequently Asked Questions," HumanRightsFirst.org, July 2020. https://humanrightsfirst.org/wp-content/uploads/2022/09/Global-Magnitsky-FAQs.pdf.
14. Human Rights First, "Global Magnitsky Sanctions Frequently Asked Questions."
15. Human Rights First, "Shaming Without Naming: The Limits of Confidential U.S. Visa Sanctions for Accountability," HumanRightsFirst.org, December 2023. https://humanrightsfirst.org/wp-content/uploads/2023/12/Shaming-without-naming_December-2023.pdf.
16. Gisela Salomon, "U.S. Restricts Visas for Guatemalan Congressmen for 'Undermining Democracy,'" The Associated Press, December 11, 2023. https://apnews.com/world-news/general-news-68ad85a88ea8f6d5a20c23853e049de0.

17. Redress, Human Rights First, Open Society Foundations et al., "Evaluating Targeted Sanctions: A Flexible Framework for Impact Analysis," Redress, November 2023. https://redress.org/wp-content/uploads/2023/11/Evaluating-Targeted-Sanctions.pdf.
18. Human Rights First, Open Society Foundation, Raoul Wallenberg Centre for Human Rights et al., "Multilateral Magnitsky Sanctions at Five Years," Redress, p. 4.
19. Senate and House of Commons of Canada, Her Majesty by and with the advice and consent, "Justice for Victims of Corrupt Foreign Officials Act (Sergei Magnitsky Law)," Government of Canada Justice Laws Website, October 18, 2017. https://laws.justice.gc.ca/eng/acts/j-2.3/FullText.html.
20. Redress, Sanction. Confiscate. Compensate: Briefing on Comparative Laws for Confiscating and Repurposing Russian Oligarch Assets, September 2022, p. 7. https://redress.org/wp-content/uploads/2022/09/Briefing-on-Comparative-Laws.pdf.
21. Global Affairs Canada, "Canada Announces Sanctions in Response to Long-standing Human Rights Violations," Government of Canada, December 8, 2023. www.canada.ca/en/global-affairs/news/2023/12/canada-announces-sanctions-in-response-to-long-standing-human-rights-violations.html.
22. Weber, "Global Magnitsky," at 21, footnote 90.
23. Migration and Home Affairs: Policies: Internal Security: Corruption, "EU legislation on anti-corruption," European Commission. https://home-affairs.ec.europa.eu/policies/internal-security/corruption/eu-legislation-anti-corruption_en.
24. UK Statutory Instruments, "The Global Human Rights Sanctions Regulations 2020," 2020 No. 680, Part 3, Regulation 11, Legislation Gov UK. www.legislation.gov.uk/uksi/2020/680/regulation/11/made.
25. UK Statutory Instruments, "The Global Anti-Corruption Sanctions Regulations 2021," 2021 No. 488, Part 1, Regulation 4, Legislation Gov UK. www.legislation.gov.uk/uksi/2021/488/regulation/4/made.
26. The Senate, "Autonomous Sanctions Amendment (Magnitsky-style and Other Thematic Sanctions) Bill 2021," The Parliament of the Commonwealth of Australia. https://parlinfo.aph.gov.au/parlInfo/download/legislation/bills/s1326_aspassed/toc_pdf/2116121.pdf;fileType=application%2Fpdf.
27. Cecily Rose, "Magnitsky Sanctions, Corruption, and Asset Recovery," in Rotberg, R. and Hampson, F.O., Grand Corruption: Curbing Kleptocracy Globally (Routledge, 2023).
28. Redress, Human Rights First, Open Society Foundations et al., "Evaluating Targeted Sanctions: A Flexible Framework for Impact Analysis," HumanRightsFirst.org, November 2023. https://humanrightsfirst.org/wp-content/uploads/2023/11/Evaluating-Targeted-Sanctions-v.4.pdf.
29. Human Rights First, Open Society Foundations, Raoul Wallenberg Centre for Human Rights et al., "Multilateral Magnitsky Sanctions at Five Years," November 2022, p. 14. https://redress.org/wp-content/uploads/2022/11/Multilateral-Magnitsky-Sanctions-at-Five-Years_November-2022.pdf.
30. Jack Haynie, "Working Smarter, Not Harder: Using Secondary Sanctions to Strengthen the Global Magnitsky Act," April 22, 2024. https://globalanticorruptionblog.com/2024/04/22/working-smarter-not-harder-using-secondary-sanctions-to-strengthen-the-global-magnitsky-act/#more-25242.

31. Euractiv.bg, "US Cleans Up Bulgarian Mafia," Euractiv, June 2, 2021. www.euractiv.com/section/politics/short_news/us-cleans-up-bulgarian-mafia/
32. Redress, Human Rights First, Open Society Foundations et al., "Evaluating Targeted Sanctions: A Flexible Framework for Impact Analysis," November 2023, p. 10. https://redress.org/wp-content/uploads/2023/11/Evaluating-Targeted-Sanctions.pdf.
33. Jacobo Garcia, "That's How You Buy a State. How a Russian Mining Company Corrupted All Powers in Guatemala," El País, March 6, 2022. https://elpais.com/internacional/2022-03-06/asi-se-compra-un-estado-como-una-minera-rusa-corrompio-a-todos-los-poderes-en-guatemala.html.
34. Sandra Cuffe, "Guatemala Mine's Ex-security Chief Convicted of Indigenous Leader's Murder," The Guardian, January 7, 2021. www.theguardian.com/global-development/2021/jan/07/guatemala-nickel-mine-death-adolfo-ich.
35. Hector Silva Avalos, "Russia's Dirty Business in Guatemala and Millions of Dollars Wrapped in a Gift Rug for the President," Infobae, March 12, 2022. www.infobae.com/america/mundo/2022/03/12/los-negocios-sucios-de-rusia-en-guatemala-y-millones-de-dolares-envueltos-en-una-alfombra-de-regalo-para-el-presidente/.
36. Inter-American Court of Human Rights, "Case of Maya Q'Eqchi" Agua Caliente Indigenous Community v. Guatemala, Judgment (Merits, Reparations, and Costs), Corteidh.or.cr, May 16, 2023. www.corteidh.or.cr/docs/casos/articulos/seriec_488_esp.pdf.
37. U.S. Embassy Guatemala, "Treasury Targets Russian-Backed Corruption in Guatemala Mining Sector," gt.usembassy.gov, November 18, 2022. https://gt.usembassy.gov/treasury-targets-russian-backed-corruption-in-guatemala-mining-sector/.
38. Colin McClelland, "Ex-FBI Leader Advises Fenix Mine in Guatemala after US Drops Sanctions," Mining.com, December 4, 2023. www.mining.com/ex-fbi-leader-advises-fenix-mine-in-guatemala-after-us-drops-sanctions/.
39. McClelland, "Ex-FBI leader."
40. US Dept. of the Treasury, "Treasury Sanctions Former Guatemalan Official for Engaging in Mining-related Corruption," January 17, 2024. https://home.treasury.gov/news/press-releases/jy2024.
41. Matthew Miller, "Designation of Alejandro Eduardo Giammattei Falla for Involvement in Significant Corruption," U.S. Department of State, January 17, 2024. www.state.gov/designation-of-alejandro-eduardo-giammattei-falla-for-involvement-in-significant-corruption/.
42. Roht-Arriaza, The Pinochet Effect; Maximo Langer and Mackenzie Eason, "The Quiet Expansion of Universal Jurisdiction" (2019) 30 *European Journal of International Law*, 779–817, www.ejil.org/pdfs/30/3/2994.pdf.
43. *See* Mads Andenas and Thomas Weatherall, "International Court of Justice: Questions Relating to the Obligation to Extradite or Prosecute [Belgium v. Senegal] Judgment of 20 July 2012," (2013) 62 *The International and Comparative Law Quarterly*, 753–769
44 Criminal Division and Enforcement Division, "A Resource Guide to the U.S. Foreign Corrupt Practices Act," 2nd Ed., U.S. Department of Justice and U.S. Securities and Exchange Commission, justice.gov, July 2020, www.justice.gov/criminal-fraud/file/1292051/download; 95th United States Congress, "Foreign Corrupt Practices Act of 1977 [15 USC §§78dd-1, et seq.]," justice.gov, December 19, 1977; 18 USC §1956. Laundering of monetary instruments. (f) "There is

extraterritorial jurisdiction over the conduct prohibited by this section if – (1) the conduct is by a United States citizen or, in the case of a non-United States citizen, the conduct occurs in part in the United States;…"

45. Transparencia Venezuela, "Corruptometer: The Inventory of Corruption in Venezuela," corruptometro.org, May 2023, https://corruptometro.org/casos.
46. Office of Public Affairs, "Former Venezuelan National Treasurer and Husband Convicted in International Bribery Scheme," U.S. Department of Justice, December 15, 2022, www.justice.gov/opa/pr/former-venezuelan-national-treasurer-and-husband-convicted-international-bribery-scheme.
47. Joshua Goodman, "Bribery Trial Tests US Cases against Venezuela Kleptocrats," Associated Press, November 29, 2022, https://apnews.com/article/business-crime-venezuela-florida-fort-lauderdale-0a4c17c8f0546d11ecf84473b35744af.
48. Office of Public Affairs, "Nicolas Maduro Moros and 14 Current and Former Venezuelan Officials Charged with Narco-Terrorism, Corruption, Drug Trafficking and Other Criminal Charges," U.S. Department of Justice, March 26, 2020, www.justice.gov/opa/pr/nicol-s-maduro-moros-and-14-current-and-former-venezuelan-officials-charged-narco-terrorism.
49. Financial Action Task Force (FATF), "International Standards on Combating Money Laundering and the Financing of Terrorism & Proliferation," fatf-gafi.org, November 2023, Recommendation 3. Money laundering offence, p. 12, www.fatf-gafi.org/content/dam/fatf-gafi/recommendations/FATF%20Recommendations%202012.pdf.coredownload.inline.pdf.
50. Financial Action Task Force (FATF), "Designated Categories of Offences," fatf-gafi.org, Terms-Definitions, pp. 125–126, www.fatf-gafi.org/content/dam/fatf-gafi/recommendations/FATF%20Recommendations%202012.pdf.coredownload.inline.pdf.
51. National Defense Authorization Act for Fiscal Year 2024, 118th Congress, "section 5101. Prohibition of demand for bribe," congress.gov, www.congress.gov/118/plaws/publ31/PLAW-118publ31.pdf.
52. Riccardo Boffo and Robert Patalano, "ESG Investing: Practices, Progress and Challenges," OECD Paris, 2020, www.oecd.org/finance/ESG-Investing-Practices-Progress-Challenges.pdf.
53. Extractive Industries Transparency Initiative (EITI), "Guidance Note: Addressing Corruption Risks through EITI Implementation," eiti.org, December 1, 2021, https://eiti.org/guidance-notes/addressing-corruption-risks-through-eiti-implementation.
54. Tina Soreide and Aled Williams, "Certified Integrity? Forest Certification and Anti-Corruption," U4 Anti-Corruption Resource Centre | Chr. Michelsen Institute, January 2013, www.u4.no/publications/certified-integrity-forest-certification-and-anti-corruption.pdf.
55. Forest Stewardship Council (FSC), "FSC and Corruption," fsc.org, March 2017, criterion 1.7, p. 6, https://fsc.org/sites/default/files/2019-10/FSC%20and%20corruption%20paper%20final%202017-03-23.pdf.
56. Jonathan Vit, "Greenwashing? RSPO Audits Rife with 'Mistakes and Fraud', Report Finds," news.mongabay.com, November 16, 2015, https://news.mongabay.com/2015/11/greenwashing-rspo-audits-rife-with-mistakes-and-fraud-report-finds.
57. Marie Chene, "Corruption and the International Financial System," Transparency International, September 24, 2009, www.u4.no/publications/corruption-and-the-international-financial-system.pdf.

58. Matthew Jenkins, "Multilateral Development Banks' Integrity Management Systems," u4.no, September 14, 2016, www.u4.no/publications/multilateral-development-banks-integrity-management-systems-2.pdf.
59. Organized Crime and Corruption Reporting Project (OCCRP), "The Dictators' Bank," occrp.org, 2023, www.occrp.org/en/the-dictators-bank.
60. OCCRP, "The Dictators' Bank."
61. International Center for Journalists and Connectas, "World Bank/IFC: The Silent Partner of Corruption in Central America," "No Ficción (Non-Fiction)", August 27, 2018, www.no-ficcion.com/projects/world-bank-ifc-the-silent-partner-of-corruption-in-central-america.
62. International Finance Corporation, "Unique Markets, Responsible Investing: IFC's Integrity Due Diligence Process," ifc.org, 2017, www.ifc.org/content/dam/ifc/doc/2023/202103-ifc-integrity-due-dilligence-process.pdf.

5 FRAUD ON THE RIVER

* An earlier version of this article was published as Naomi Roht-Arriaza, "Empowering Victims of Grand Corruption: An Emerging Trend?" (2021) 37 *Connecticut Journal of International Law*, 27.
1. National Congress of Honduras, "Code of Criminal Procedure, Standard No. 9-99-E," pensamientopenal.com.ar, December 30, 1999, Art. 16, www.pensamientopenal.com.ar/system/files/2014/12/legislacion32343.pdf.
2. Criminal Court with National Jurisdiction in Matters of Corruption (Honduras), "Gualcarque River Fraud Case," March 25, 2019. National Anti-Corruption Penal Court. [Juzgado de Letras de lo Penal con Competencia Nacional en Materia de Corrupción, Honduras Caso Fraude en el Gualcarque] https://v1.cespad.org.hn/wp-content/uploads/2020/01/Caso-Gualcarque-CESPAD2020.pdf.
3. Court of Criminal Appeals with National Jurisdiction in Matters of Corruption (Honduras), "Order s/ Appeal of the Defense, (Exp. 13-2019)," August 28, 2019. Corte de Apelaciones de lo Penal con Competencia Nacional en Materia de Corrupción, 28/8/2019, "Auto s/ Recurso de Apelación de la Defensa," (Exp. 13-2019). Penal nº AP-341-21 de Supreme Court (Honduras), 13 de Enero de 2022 – Jurisprudencia – VLEX 897338572.
4. Council of Europe, "Civil Law Convention on Corruption," coe.int, November 4, 1999, https://rm.coe.int/168007f3f6.
5. United Nations Office on Drugs and Crime, "United Nations Convention against Transnational Organized Crime and the Protocols Thereto," unodc.org, December 2000, www.unodc.org/documents/treaties//Publications/TOC%20Convention/TOCebook-e.pdf.
6. United Nations Office on Drugs and Crime, "United Nations Convention against Corruption," unodc.org, October 31, 2003, Art. 13(1).
7. United Nations Office on Drugs and Crime, "Preparatory Work of the Negotiations for the Elaboration of the United Nations Convention against Corruption," unodc.org, 2012, p. 300, www.unodc.org/documents/treaties/UNCAC/Publications/Travaux/Travaux_Preparatoires_-_UNCAC_E.pdf.

8. United Nations Office on Drugs and Crime, "Preparatory Work," Art. 35, p. 200; *See also* Anita Ramarastry, "Is There a Right to be Free from Corruption" (2015) 49 *UC Davis Law Review* 703.
9. United Nations Office on Drugs and Crime, "Preparatory Work," p. 299.
10. United Nations Office on Drugs and Crime, "Preparatory Work," pp. 319 and 321.
11. Open-ended Intergovernmental Working Group on Asset Recovery, "Good Practices in Identifying the Victims of Corruption and Parameters for their Compensation," unodc.org, August 4, 2016, www.unodc.org/documents/treaties/UNCAC/WorkingGroups/workinggroup2/2016-August-25-26/V1604993e.pdf.
12. Conference of the States Parties to the United Nations Convention against Corruption, "Best Practices for the Identification and Compensation of All Different Types of Victims in Accordance with the Convention, and Third-Party Challenges and Their Impact on Asset Recovery under chapter V," unodc.org, March 22, 2019, www.unodc.org/documents/treaties/UNCAC/WorkingGroups/workinggroup2/2019-May-29-30/V1901853e.pdf.
13. Felipe Freitas Falconi, et al., "Victims of Corruption: Back for Payback," star.worldbank.org, December 5, 2023, https://star.worldbank.org/publications/victims-corruption-back-payback.
14. Lisa Bostwick, et al., "Managing Seized and Confiscated Assets: A Guide for Practitioners," star.worldbank.org, December 7, 2023, https://star.worldbank.org/publications/managing-seized-and-confiscated-assets-guide-practitioners.
15. Conference of the States Parties to the United Nations Convention against Corruption, "Atlanta 2023: Promoting Integrity, Accountability and Transparency in the Fight against Corruption," unodc.org, December 15, 2023, www.unodc.org/documents/treaties/UNCAC/COSP/session10/resolutions/L-documents/2325351E_L.5_Rev.1.pdf. See also note 13 on the paucity of cases where compensation has been paid.
16. Universal Declaration, UNGA Res. 217, UN Doc. A/810 (1949), Art. 8.
17. For example, Article 2(3) of the ICCPR, Articles 8 and 25 of the American Convention on Human Rights, and Article 13 of the European Convention on Fundamental Rights and Freedoms. See also UN Human Rights Committee, General Comment 31, paras. 15, 16.
18. United Nations General Assembly, "Resolution: 40/34. Declaration of Basic Principles of Justice for Victims of Crime and Abuse of Power," ohchr.org, November 29, 1985, www.ohchr.org/en/instruments-mechanisms/instruments/declaration-basic-principles-justice-victims-crime-and-abuse.
19. United Nations, "Resolution: 40/34," A(1).
20. United Nations General Assembly, "Resolution: 60/147. Basic Principles and Guidelines on the Right to a Remedy and Reparation for Victims of Gross Violations of International Human Rights Law and Serious Violations of International Humanitarian Law," ohchr.org, December 16, 2005. I will develop the remedies listed in the Basic Principles in Chapter 7.
21. Inter-American Court of Human Rights, "Rules of Procedure of the Inter-American Court of Human Rights," oas.org, November 16–25, 2000, www.oas.org/36ag/english/doc_referencia/Reglamento_CorteIDH.pdf.
22. Inter-American Court of Human Rights, "Rules of Procedure," Art. 35.
23. Inter-American Court of Human Rights, "Case of the 'Street Children' (Villagran-Morales et al.) v. Guatemala, Judgment, Series C No. 63," November

19, 1999, paras. 174–176; Inter-American Court of Human Rights, "Case of Bamaca-Velasquez v. Guatemala, Judgment, Series C No. 70," November 25, 2000, paras. 163–165.

24. Inter-American Court of Human Rights, "Advisory Opinion OC-22/16" (2016); Diego Mejia-Lemos, "Advisory Opinion OC-22/16" (2016) 111 *American Journal of International Law*, 1000–1006; Organization of American States, "American Convention on Human Rights 'Pact of San Jose, Costa Rica'," oas.org, November 22, 1969, Art. 1(2), in relation to Arts. 1(1), 8, 11(2), 13, 16, 21, 24, 25, 29, 30, 44, 46 and 62(3) (Ownership of rights of legal persons in the inter-American human rights system (interpretation and scope)) XXXVIII Curso de Derecho Internacional 2011 (oas.org); Organization of American States, "Additional Protocol to the American Convention on Human Rights in the Area of Economic, Social and Cultural Rights: 'Protocol of San Salvador'," November 17, 1988, Arts. 8.1(a) and (b).
25. *See, for example*, Grand Chamber, "Case of Roman Zakharov v. Russia, Judgment, Application no. 47143/06," European Court of Human Rights, December 4, 2015, §164 (A number of European countries allow such actions, which give anyone standing to sue based on the public interest.)
26. Grand Chamber, "Case of Vallianatos and Others v. Greece, Judgment, Applications nos. 29381/09 and 32684/09," European Court of Human Rights, November 7, 2013, §47.
27. Grand Chamber, "Case of Vallianatos," §48.
28. European Parliament, "Recommendation T9-0042/2022: concerning corruption and human rights" (2022) C342 *Official Journal of European Union*, February 17, 2022, https://eur-lex.europa.eu/legal-content/EN/TXT/HTML/?uri=CELEX:52022IP0042.
29. European Parliament, "Recommendation T9-0042/2022," Art. 1(s).
30. Paolina Massidda, et al., "Representing Victims before the International Criminal Court: A Manual for legal representatives, Rule 85 of the Rules of Procedure and Evidence," in Sarah Pellet and Anna Bonini (The Hague: Office of Public Counsel for Victims, International Criminal Court, 2019), p. 26, www.icc-cpi.int/sites/default/files/2021.03.01-ENG-5th-Rev-Rev.pdf.
31. International Criminal Court, "Rome Statute of the International Criminal Court, Part 6: The Trial," icc-cpi.int, July 17, 1998, Art. 68(3): Where the personal interests of the victims are affected, the Court shall permit their views and concerns to be presented and considered at stages of the proceedings determined to be appropriate by the Court and in a manner which is not prejudicial to or inconsistent with the rights of the accused and a fair and impartial trial … Such views and concerns may be presented by the legal representatives of the victims where the Court considers it appropriate, in accordance with the Rules of Procedure and Evidence, p. 33.
32. Art. 75. International Criminal Court, "Rome Statute," p. 36.
33. International Criminal Court, "Prosecutor v Lubanga, Decision Establishing the Principles and Procedures to Be Applied to Reparations, ICC-01/04-01/06-2904," icc-cpi.int, August 7, 2012, paras. 176–181, pp. 64–65. CR2012_07872.PDF (icc-cpi.int).
34. Christine Van den Wyngaert, "Victims before International Criminal Courts: Some Views and Concerns of an ICC Trial Judge" (2011) 44 *Case Western Reserve Journal International Law*, 475–496, https://scholarlycommons.law.case.edu/jil/vol44/iss1/22; Mina Rauschenbach and Damien Scalia, "Victims and International

Criminal Justice: A Vexed Question?" (2008) 90 *International Review of the Red Cross*, https://international-review.icrc.org/sites/default/files/irrc-870_15.pdf.

35. *See, for example*, War Crimes Research Office, "The Case-Based Reparations Scheme at the International Criminal Court," American University, Washington College of Law, June 2010, www.wcl.american.edu/impact/initiatives-programs/warcrimes/our-projects/icc-legal-analysis-and-education-project/reports/report-12-the-case-based-reparations-scheme-at-the-international-criminal-court/.
36. Paolina Massidda, et al., "*Representing Victims, Rule 90 of the Rules of Procedure and Evidence*," www.icc-cpi.int/sites/default/files/2021.03.01-ENG-5th-Rev-Rev.pdf (If the victims can't agree, the Registrar of the Court chooses for them.)
37. In the US, *see* United States Code, "Crime Victims' Rights Act 18 U.S.C. §3771," uscode.house.gov, October 30, 2004.; (Canada has a similar law.)
38. Simon Ball, "Who is a 'victim' under French law?," Weightmans.com, January 6, 2023, www.weightmans.com/insights/who-is-a-victim-under-french-law.
39. Government of Canada, "Canadian Victims Bill of Rights S.C. 2015, c. 13, s. 2," laws-lois.justice.gc.ca, April 23, 2015, https://laws-lois.justice.gc.ca/eng/acts/C-23.7/page-1.html#h-76032. The EU definition is similar. See Directive 2012/29/Eu of the European Parliament and of the Council establishing minimum standards on the rights, support, and protection of victims of crime, October 25, 2012.
40. Sarah Cormack, et al., "Quebec Court Tackles Novel Issues during Approval of the Second Remediation Agreement (a.k.a. Deferred Prosecution Agreement) under the Canadian Criminal Code," Davies Ward Phillips & Vineberg LLP, May 24, 2023, www.jdsupra.com/legalnews/quebec-court-tackles-novel-issues-8235755.
41. Directive of the European Parliament and of the Council on Asset Recovery and Confiscation, April 3, 2024. https://data.consilium.europa.eu/doc/document/PE-3-2024-INIT/en/pdf, para. 37 and Article 18.
42. Sentencing Council, "Fraud, Bribery and Money Laundering Offences: Definitive Guideline," sentencingcouncil.org.uk, 2014, p. 42, www.sentencingcouncil.org.uk/wp-content/uploads/Fraud_bribery_and_money_laundering_offences_-_Definitive_guideline.pdf, *cited in* Corruption Watch, "Compensating Victims for the Harm of Overseas Corruption: Discussion Paper," June 2018, https://islp.org/wp-content/uploads/2018/06/compensation-discussion-paper-final-amended.pdf.
43. Spotlight on Corruption, Written Evidence, June, 2022. https://committees.parliament.uk/writtenevidence/109307/pdf/.
44. Id., quoting R v. Kenneth Donovan (1981) 3 Cr App R (S) 192 and R v. Ben Stapylton [2012] EWCA Crim 728. See also R v Smith, Smith and Smith & Ouzman Ltd (January 7, 2016): https://docs.wixstatic.com/ugd/54261c_9dabc24c7c134274ba0a96c3cd7e6c52.pdf.
45. Helen Taylor, "Guest Post: U.K. Court Refuses to Compensate Victims of Foreign Bribery," Global Anticorruption Blog, November 9, 2022. https://globalanticorruptionblog.com/2022/11/09/guest-post-u-k-court-refuses-to-compensate-victims-of-foreign-bribery/.
46. Constitutional Chamber, "Writ of Criminal Protection SCO 0974-2019," Supreme Court of Justice Honduras, August 10, 2021. https://copinh.org/wp-content/uploads/2021/08/AMPARO.-COPINH.GUALCARQUE.pdf.

47. Honduras, Constitutional Chamber, "Writ of Criminal Protection," Recital 18, p. 20.
48. Honduras, National Sentencing Tribunal for Organized Crime and Corruption (Tribunal de Sentencia con Competencia Nacional en Materia de Criminalidad Organizada y Corrupción), Case 0801-2019-8-01 TS/CNMC, May 3, 2024.
49. Federal Criminal Court 2, "Judgment, CFP 1188/2013/TO1," Judicial Branch of the Nation (Argentina), December 29, 2015, Equipo Nizkor – Judgment in the Once case. (derechos.org) TRIBUNAL ORAL EN LO CRIMINAL FEDERAL 2 CFP 1188/2013/TO1; Federal Criminal Court 2, "Marco Antonio, et al., Case no. 2127/2186 s/ inf. Arts. 196, inc. 1 and 2 and 173, inc.7° in function of Article 174 of the CP', Record of Judgments No. 1753," Judicial Branch of the Nation (Argentina), March 30, 2016. TOCF nro. 2, causa nro. 2127/2186 CÓRDOBA, Marco Antonio y otros s/inf.arts.196,inc.1 y 2 y 173,inc.7°in function of Article 174 of the CP, Registry of judgmentsnr.1753 (March 30, 2016). See also https://poderciudadano.org/en-un-fallo-sin-precedente-la-justicia-permitio-a-poder-ciudadano-ser-querellante-en-causa-de-corrupcion/.
50. Nomad, "Pisa's Payment to IGSS Survivors Seems Like a Human Gesture, But It's about Something More," nomada.gt, February 27, 2018, https://nomada.gt/pais/la-corrupcion-no-es-normal/el-pago-de-pisa-a-los-sobrevivientes-del-igss-parece-un-gesto-humano-pero-busca-algo-mas.
51. Mattia Fossati, Mark Wilson and Olivia de Gaudemar, "IGSS-PISSA: And Impunity for All," No Ficcion, December 1, 2021, www.no-ficcion.com/projects/igsss-pissa-impunidad-todos.
52. Digital Press, "UFECIC Presents 'Pandora' Case Involving 38 Officials and Deputies in Corruption," proceso.hn, June 13, 2018, https://proceso.hn/ufecic-mp-presenta-caso-pandora-que-involucra-a-38-funcionarios-y-diputados-en-corrupcion.
53. Digital Press, "The Status of the MP-Maccih Cases," proceso.hn, December 6, 2020, https://proceso.hn/el-estatus-de-los-casos-mp-maccih.
54. Ruben Escobar, "The Pandora Case and the Amparo That Could Mean a New Opportunity to Bring Justice to Hondurans," CESPAD | Center for the Study of Democracy, May 15, 2023, https://cespad.org.hn/el-caso-pandora-y-el-amparo-que-podria-significar-una-nueva-oportunidad-de-hacer-justicia-a-los-hondurenos.
55. La Silla Vacia, "The Same Old Theft of Health Comes Due with the Coronavirus," Apr. 28, 2020, www.lasillavacia.com/silla-nacional/el-robo-de-siempre-a-la-salud-pasa-factura-con-coronavirus/.
56. Congress of the Union, "General Law on Victims," United Mexican States, January 9, 2013, Art. 4, www.gob.mx/cms/uploads/attachment/file/112957/Ley_General_de_Victimas.pdf.
57. 31 de mayo de 2019 por el juez Sexto de Distrito de Amparo en Materia Penal en la Ciudad de México dentro del juicio de amparo 22/2019: (Sixth District Judge of Injunctions in Criminal Matters issued a ruling in Constitutional Injunction trial).
58. Id., p. 16.
59. Id., p. 24.
60. First Chamber, "Amparo in Review 104/2020, Eighth Collegiate Court in Criminal Matters of the First Circuit," Supreme Court of Justice of the Nation (Mexico), January 14, 2021. https://bj.scjn.gob.mx/doc/sentencias_pub/ACMs3XgB_UqKst8ofKHP/%22Delitos%20financieros%22.

61. Id., p. 77.
62. Id., p. 83.
63. Second Chamber, Supreme Court of Justice of the Nation (Mexico), "Case 29993 Contradiction of Thesis 253/2020 (QUINTO)," Mexican Federal Judicial Weekly, August 6, 2021, https://sjf.scjn.gob.mx/SJFSem/Paginas/DetalleGeneralScroll.aspx?id=29993&Clase=DetalleTesisEjecutorias Undécima Época, Semanario Judicial de la Federación, caso 29993, Corte Suprema de Justicia de la Nación (Mexico), Segunda Sala, CONTRADICCIÓN DE TESIS 253/2020 (QUINTO), August 6, 2021.
64. Edilberto Aldan, "Ratified the Status of Citizens as Victims of Corruption," lja.mx, May 8, 2023, www.lja.mx/2023/05/ratifican-la-calidad-de-victima-de-la-corrupcion-de-los-ciudadanos.
65. First Chamber, "Injunction in Review 162/2022," Supreme Court of Justice of the Nation (Mexico), scjn.gob.mx, February 8, 2023, www.scjn.gob.mx/sites/default/files/listas/documento_dos/2022-11/221107-AR-162-2022.pdf.
66. Coparmex, Reformas presentadas a la Ley de Amparo violan los Derechos Humanos y permitirían el abuso de autoridad, April 10, 2024. https://coparmex.org.mx/reformas-presentadas-a-la-ley-de-amparo-violan-los-derechos-humanos-y-permitirian-el-abuso-de-autoridad/.
67. "Code of Criminal Procedure Brazil," www.wipo.int, October 3, 1941, Art. 37.; "Code of Criminal Procedure Bolivia," www.wipo.int, March 25, 1999, Arts. 76(4) and 78.; "Code of Criminal Procedure Costa Rica," www.wipo.int, April 10, 1996, Art. 70 et seq.; "Code of Criminal Procedure El Salvador," www.asamblea.gob.sv, December 4, 1996, Arts. 12(4) and 302.; "Code of Criminal Procedure Guatemala," www.oas.org, January 1, 1992, Arts. 117(4) and 302.; "Code of Criminal Procedure Paraguay," www.wipo.int, October 16, 1997, Art. 70.; "Code of Criminal Procedure Bolivian Republic of Venezuela," www.wipo.int, October 2, 2001, Arts. 118 and 301.; "Code of Criminal Procedure Peru," www.wipo.int, July 22, 2004, Art. 94.; "General Procedural Code of Uruguay, Art. 42"; *See also* Civil Association for Equality and Justice, "Towards the Recognition of the Collective Grievance in Causes of Corruption: The Situation of Impunity for Corruption," acij.org.ar, 2018, https://acij.org.ar/wp-content/uploads/2018/12/Hacia-el-reconocimiento-de-la-querella-colectiva-en-causas-de-corrupcion.pdf.
68. The Netherlands, Portugal, Spain, Estonia, and Slovenia apply versions of this principle. Civil Association, Towards the recognition, at 37.
69. George Pring and Catherine Pring, *Greening Justice: Creating and Improving Environmental Courts and Tribunals*, (Washington DC: The Access Initiative/World Resources Institute, 2009), pp. 3–6, https://perma.cc/YB2H-U45Y (Environmental harm has been the classic example of a diffuse harm.) (Some courts (and commentators) conflate collective and diffuse interests, while others insist that the difference resides in the inability to identify the members of the collective in cases of diffuse interests.)
70. United Nations Economic Commission for Europe, "Convention on Access to Information, Public Participation in Decision-Making and Access to Justice in Environmental Matters (The Aarhus Convention)," unece.org, June 25, 1998, https://unece.org/DAM/env/pp/documents/cep43e.pdf; United Nations Economic

Commission for Latin America and the Caribbean, "Regional Agreement on Access to Information, Public Participation and Justice in Environmental Matters in Latin America and the Caribbean," cepal.org, March 4, 2018, www.cepal.org/en/escazuagreement

71. *See, for example,* David Takacs, "We Are the River" (2021) 2 *University of Illinois Law Review*, 545–606.
72. Bundesverfassungsgericht, "Constitutional Complaints against the Federal Climate Change Act Partially Successful," bundesverfassungsgericht.de, April 29, 2021, www.bundesverfassungsgericht.de/SharedDocs/Pressemitteilungen/EN/2021/bvg21-031.html.
73. Margaret Barry and Maria Antonia Tigre, "January 2024 Updates to the Climate Case Charts," Sabin Center for Climate Change Law, January 11, 2024, https://climate.law.columbia.edu/news/january-2024-updates-climate-case-charts.
74. European Court of Human Rights, "Case of Gorraiz Lizarraga and Others v. Spain, Application no. 62543/00, Judgment (Merits)," hudoc.echr.coe.int, April 27, 2004, §35.
75. ECHR, Grand Chamber, Case of Verein Klimaseniorinnen Schweiz and Others v. Switzerland, Judgment of April 9, 2024, para. 524.
76. Criminal Law Chamber, "Case Association Transparence International France, No. 09-88-272," Court of Cassation France, November 9, 2010, §1.
77. Associated Press, "Equatorial Guinea Sues France at UN Court over Paris Mansion," apnews.com, September 30, 2022, https://apnews.com/article/africa-france-paris-united-nations-e40715ae4c171cfd7c474e2478bc4b6f (At one point, Obiang argued that his mansion was actually diplomatic property. France disagreed, and the case ended up at the International Court of Justice, which found for France (although in 2023 Equatorial Guinea tried again))
78. Stanis Bujakera, et al., "Congo Says It Won't Renew Contract with Passport Maker Semlex," Reuters, May 19, 2020, www.reuters.com/article/idUSKBN22U2R8.
79. Mercedes de Freitas, et al., "Report of the International Meeting on Corruption and Human Rights in Venezuela, Panel 7: Strategic Litigation and the Problems Arising from Litigation in Different Jurisdictions," transparenciave.org, April 18–19, 2023, https://transparenciave.org/wp-content/uploads/2023/06/Report-of-the-International-Meeting-on-Corruption-and-Human-Rights-in-Venezuela-01.pdf.
80. Mercedes de Freitas, et al., "Report of the International Meeting," April 18–19, 2023, https://transparenciave.org/wp-content/uploads/2023/06/Report-of-the-International-Meeting-on-Corruption-and-Human-Rights-in-Venezuela-01.pdf.
81. UNAL Periodical, "What Makes the School Feeding Program So Vulnerable to Corruption?," National University of Colombia, April 8, 2022, https://periodico.unal.edu.co/ABC/programa-de-alimentacion-escolar-que-lo-hace-tan-vulnerable-a-la-corrupcion.
82. Criminal Cassation Chamber, "Interlocutory Order: VICTIMS – Concept and Requirements for Their Recognition," Supreme Court of Justice, Republic of Colombia, July 6, 2011, www.cortesuprema.gov.co/corte/wp-content/uploads/relatorias/pe/spa/VICTIMAS/CONCEPTO/CONCEPTO.docx. Constitutional Court, Judgment C-228/02, sec. 3.

83. Constitutional Court, judgment T-293 of 2013.
84. Constitutional Court, "Court Ruling: Complaint of Unconstitutionality, C-228/02," corteconstitucional.gov, April 3, 2002, www.corteconstitucional.gov.co/relatoria/2002/c-228-02.htm.
85. The Congress of Colombia, "Statutory Law 1757 of 2015 on the Promotion and Protection of the Right to Democratic Participation," funcionpublica.gov.co, July 6, 2015, Arts. 62 and 68, www.funcionpublica.gov.co/eva/gestornormativo/norma.php?i=65335.
86. National Federal Criminal and Correctional Court No. 3, "Cantarero Emilio, et al., s/bribery, Cause 9900/00," Judicial Branch of the Nation (Argentina), February 1, 2006 (The specific ruling regarding NGO access is *at* http://cipce.org.ar/sites/default/files/2016/11/casos2198_7.pdf).
87. Art. 82 bis. – Intereses colectivos. Las asociaciones o fundaciones, registradas conforme a la ley, podrán constituirse en parte querellante en procesos en los que se investiguen crímenes de lesa humanidad o graves violaciones a los derechos humanos siempre que su objeto estatutario se vincule directamente con la defensa de los derechos que se consideren lesionados. (Collective interests. Associations or foundations, duly legally registered, may become civil parties in criminal cases investigating crimes against humanity or grave human rights violations, so long as their stated goal is directly related to the defense of the rights at stake.)
88. Second Chamber, "Incident of Lack of Action, Case No. CFP 6089/2016/4 (Reg. Int. 9543)," Federal Court of La Plata (Argentina), November 1, 2018. *See also* Citizen Power, "In an Unprecedented Ruling, the Courts Allowed Citizen Power to Be a Plaintiff in the Corruption Case," poderciudadano.org, November 6, 2018, https://poderciudadano.org/en-un-fallo-sin-precedente-la-justicia-permitio-a-poder-ciudadano-ser-querellante-en-causa-de-corrupcion.
89. Poder Ciudadano será querellante en la causa contra Insaurralde y Clerici por enriquecimiento y lavado," La Nación, Nov. 7, 2023, www.lanacion.com.ar/politica/la-fundacion-poder-ciudadano-sera-querellante-en-la-causa-contra-insaurralde-y-clerici-por-nid07112023/.
90. Economic Criminal Court 6, "Certificate of Notification," Judicial Branch of the Nation (Argentina), May 2022, https://poderciudadano.org/wp-content/uploads/2022/07/resolucion-judicial.pdf.
91. Chamber of Deputies, "Law 19696 Establishes Code of Criminal Procedure," National Congress of Chile, September 29, 2000, Art. 111, www.bcn.cl/leychile/navegar?idNorma=176595&idParte=8646651.
92. Press Release, "Intelligent Citizen Foundation's Lawsuit against Senator Orpis for Corpesca Payments is Accepted," biobiochile.cl, August 18, 2015, www.biobiochile.cl/noticias/2015/08/18/acogen-querella-de-fundacion-ciudadano-inteligente-contra-senador-orpis-por-pagos-de-corpesca.shtml; *see also* https://issuu.com/jorgemolinasanhueza/docs/querlla_corpesca_final?utm_medium=referral&utm_source=www.theclinic.cl (Corpesca Complaint).
93. Juan Pablo Andrews, "Corpesca: Jaime Orpis Sentenced to Serve Effective Imprisonment for Tax Fraud and Bribery," latercera.com, April 16, 2021, www.latercera.com/nacional/noticia/corpesca-condenan-a-jaime-orpis-a-cumplir-carcel-efectiva-por-fraude-al-fisco-y-cohecho/3YHXBURUVRHAPDDMAQ4BELBYWQ

94. Supreme Court, Permanent Penal Chamber, Casación 596-2021/Junín, March 11, 2022, https://img.lpderecho.pe/wp-content/uploads/2022/04/Casacion-596-2021-Junin-LPDerecho.pdf.
95. "Code of Criminal Procedure Peru," wipo.int, July 22, 2004, Art. 94, www.wipo.int/wipolex/en/text/202824.
96. Juan Carlos Ruiz Molleda, "La protección jurisdiccional de los intereses difusos," Enfoque Derecho, January 15, 2020. https://enfoquederecho.com/la-proteccion-jurisdiccional-de-los-intereses-difusos/#_ftn6.
97. Transcription of Oral Argument and Decision, Exp. N° 396-2023-1, Incidente sobre tutela de derechos, Fifth Criminal Appellate Chamber of the Specialized Superior National Court, August 19, 2024.
98. Congress of the Union, "General Law on Victims," United Mexican States, January 9, 2013, www.diputados.gob.mx/LeyesBiblio/pdf/LGV.pdf.
99. Seventh Tribunal, First Circuit Collegiate Court in Criminal Matters of Mexico City, "Documents: Case 159/2019, Criminal Review, Indirect Amparo Proceeding," Victims of Corruption, January 16, 2020, https://victimasdecorrupcion.wordpress.com/documentos.
100. Inter-American Commission on Human Rights, "Reconsideration of Original Petition," Victims of Corruption, January 22, 2021, https://victimasdecorrupcion.files.wordpress.com/2021/03/recurso-cidh-caso-duarte_-22_01_2021-vf-1.pdf (As of January 2021, the case had been submitted for reconsideration.)
101. Arturo Angel, "Financial Intelligence Asks Judge to Recognize NGO as a Victim in Lozoya Case and Give It Access to the Process," Animal Politico, April 17, 2021, www.animalpolitico.com/2021/04/lozoya-uif-ong-corrupcion-victima.
102. French Republic, "Code of Criminal Procedure Arts. 2-23, Law No. 2016-1547 on the Modernization of Justice in the 21st Century," November 18, 2016, Art. 43. LOI n° 2016-1547 du 18 novembre 2016 de modernisation de la justice du XXIe siècle (1) – Légifrance (legifrance.gouv.fr); Constitutional Council, "Decision No. 2016-739," conseil-constitutionnel.fr, November 17, 2016.
103. Corruption & Human Rights Initiative, "Statement: A missed opportunity – France's Return of Gulnara Karimova's Illegally Acquired Assets," corruptionandhumanrights.org, May 21, 2020, https://corruptionandhumanrights.org/publications/statement-a-missed-opportunity-frances-return-of-gulnara-karimovas-illegally-acquired-assets
104. ECHR, Grand Chamber, Case of Verein Klimaseniorinnen Schweiz and Others v. Switzerland, Judgment of April 9, 2024, para. 502.
105. National Congress, "Art. 5 of Law No. 7,347 on Public Civil Action," Federal Republic of Brazil, July 24, 1985, §4, www.jusbrasil.com.br/topicos/11269621/artigo-5-da-lei-n-7347-de-24-de-julho-de-1985 (The (1 year) pre-constitution requirement maybe waived by the judge, when there is a manifest social interest evidenced by the dimension or characteristic of the damage, or by the relevance of the legal interest to be protected. (Included by Law No. 8,078, dated 9.11.1990)).
106. *See, for example*, Dr. Juanita Olaya Garcia, "Dealing with the Consequences: Repairing the Social Damage Caused by Corruption," SSRN, January 15, 2016, https://ssrn.com/abstract=3475453.

6 GIVING IT BACK

1. Basel Institute on Governance, "Basel Institute Congratulates Peruvian Authorities for USD 19.5 Million Recovery Linked to Odebrecht Case," baselgovernance .org, May 23, 2019. https://baselgovernance.org/news/basel-institute-congratulates-peruvian-authorities-usd-195-million-recovery-linked-odebrecht.
2. SWI, "Switzerland Hands CHF365m Petrobras-Odebrecht Assets to Brazil," swissinfo.ch, April 9, 2019. www.swissinfo.ch/eng/business/illicit-funds_switzerland-hands-chf365m-petrobras-odebrecht-assets-to-brazil/44884118.
3. United States Attorney's Office, Eastern District of New York, "Justice Department Will Return Approximately $686,000 in Forfeited Corruption Proceeds to the Republic of Peru," justice.gov, August 31, 2022. www.justice.gov/usao-edny/pr/justice-department-will-return-approximately-686000-forfeited-corruption-proceeds.
4. Ruben Carranza, "Transitional Justice, Corruption and Mutually Reinforcing Accountability: What the Global South Can Learn from the Philippines," in Leigh A. Payne, Laura Bernal-Bermudez and Gabriel Pereira, *Economic Actors and the Limits of Transitional Justice* (London: British Academy, 2022), pp. 236–264.
5. Open-ended Intergovernmental Working Group on Asset Recovery, "Foreign Illicit Assets Act (FIAA) of December 18, 2015," Federal Department of Foreign Affairs, Swiss Confederation, August 16, 2016. www.unodc .org/documents/treaties/UNCAC/WorkingGroups/workinggroup2/2016-August-25-26/V1605154e.pdf.
6. Working Group on Bribery in International Business Transactions, "Recommendation of the Council for Further Combating Bribery of Foreign Public Officials in International Business Transactions," OECD, November 26, 2009, XIII(i).
7. United Nations Office on Drugs and Crime, "Confiscated Asset Returns and the United Nations Convention against Corruption: A Net for All Fish" (2023). www .unodc.org/documents/corruption/Publications/2023/UNODC_Confiscated_Asset_Returns_and_UNCAC_-_A_Net_for_All_Fish_2023.pdf.
8. Conference of the States Parties to the United Nations Convention against Corruption, "Progress in implementing the mandates of the Open-ended Intergovernmental Working Group on Asset Recovery," unodc.org, June 26, 2023. www.unodc.org/documents/treaties/UNCAC/WorkingGroups/workinggroup2/2023-September-4-8/CAC-COSP-WG.2-2023-2/CAC-COSP-WG.2-2023-2_E.pdf.
9. Conference of the States Parties to the United Nations Convention against Corruption, "Progress in implementing the mandates of the Open-ended Intergovernmental Working Group on Asset Recovery," unodc.org, October 11, 2021. www.unodc.org/documents/treaties/UNCAC/COSP/session9/CAC-COSP-2021-6/V2107584_E.pdf.
10. United Nations Office on Drugs and Crime, "A Net for All Fish, UNCAC Interpretative Notes, art. 57, para. 3," "It was agreed that…," p. 13.
11. United Nations Office on Drugs and Crime, "A Net for All Fish," pp. 54–55. See UNCAC Art. 54(1)(b).
12. International Consortium of Investigative Journalists, "The Panama Papers: Exposing the Rogue Offshore Finance Industry," icij.org, April 3, 2016. www.icij .org/investigations/panama-papers/.
13. Charlie Cooper, "Anti-Corruption Summit 2016: Cameron Facing Calls to Reform Offshore Tax Havens as World Leaders Arrive in London," Independent.co.uk, May 12, 2016. www.independent.co.uk/news/world/politics/

anticorruption-summit-2016-cameron-facing-calls-to-reform-offshore-tax-havens-as-world-leaders-arrive-in-london-a7025106.html.

14. Prime Minister's Office, The Rt. Hon. Lord Cameron, "Anti-Corruption Summit 2016: PM's closing remarks," gov.uk, May 12, 2016. www.gov.uk/government/speeches/anti-corruption-summit-2016-pms-closing-remarks.
15. Global Forum on Asset Recovery, "GFAR Principles for Disposition and Transfer of Confiscated Stolen Assets in Corruption Cases," star.worldbank.org, December 2017. https://star.worldbank.org/sites/star/files/the-gfar-principles.pdf.
16. Laure Brillaud and Matilde Manzi, "Stop Kleptocrats: The EU Must Not Be a Vault For The World's Stolen Assets," Transparency International EU, December 15, 2020, Annex B. https://transparency.eu/wp-content/uploads/2021/01/Asset-Recovery_Policy_Report_2020.pdf.
17. Executive Council, African Union, "Common African Position on Asset Recovery (CAPAR): 4.4.1(e)," au.int, February 6–7, 2020, p. 11. https://au.int/sites/default/files/documents/42297-doc-COMMON-AFRICAN-POSITION-ON-ASSEST-RECOVERY-ENGLISH-NEWLY-PROOFREAD-1.pdf.
18. United Nations Human Rights Office of the High Commissioner, "OHCHR Recommended Principles on Human Rights and Asset Recovery," ohchr.org, March 2022. www.ohchr.org/sites/default/files/2022-03/OHCHR-RecommendedPrinciplesHumanRightsAssetRecovery_0.pdf.
19. Attiya Waris, "Practical Guidelines for Efficient Asset Recovery: Report of Independent Expert on debt, other international financial obligations and human rights," United Nations Human Rights Special Procedures A/HRC/52/45, December 30, 2022. www.ohchr.org/sites/default/files/documents/issues/iedebt/A-HRC-52-45-userfriendlyversion.pdf.
20. UK Serious Fraud Office, Compensation Principles to Victims outside the UK (June 1, 2018). www.sfo.gov.uk/publications/information-victims-witnesses-whistleblowers/compensation-principles-to-victims-outside-the-uk/.
21. Home Office, "Policy Paper: Framework for Transparent and Accountable Asset Return," gov.uk, January 13, 2022, para. 40. www.gov.uk/government/publications/framework-for-transparent-and-accountable-asset-return/framework-for-transparent-and-accountable-asset-return.
22. Spotlight on Corruption, Response to Parliament, June 2022. https://committees.parliament.uk/writtenevidence/109307/pdf/.
23. Proceeds of Crime Act 2002, c. 29, available at www.legislation.gov.uk/ukpga/2002/29/contents.
24. Natalia Kubesch, "The UK Is Failing to Recoup Ill-gotten Gains Linked to the Syrian Regime," Just Security, April 1, 2024, available at www.justsecurity.org/94080/uk-recoup-syrian-regime-assets/. For further discussion, see David Ireland, "Deterring Corruption Through Asset Seizure, "in Rothberg and Hampson, eds., Grand Corruption, pp. 193–207.
25. The Minister for Europe and Foreign Affairs, For the Government of the French Republic, "Re. Mechanism for the Return of Illicit Assets," diplomatie.gouv.fr, November 22, 2022. www.diplomatie.gouv.fr/IMG/pdf/22-5209-circulaire_n6379-sg_du_22_nov._22_en_anglais__cle8fac62.pdf.
26. Redress, "Sanction. Confiscate. Compensate. Briefing: Comparative Laws for Confiscating and Repurposing Russian Oligarch Assets," September 2022, p. 10. https://redress.org/wp-content/uploads/2022/09/Briefing-on-Comparative-Laws.pdf.

National Assembly and the Senate, Republic of France, "Title I: Art. 2 of the Law on Programming Relating to the Inclusive Development and the Fight against Global Inequalities," legifrance.gouv.fr, August 4, 2021. www.legifrance.gouv.fr/jorf/id/JORFTEXT000043898536/.

27. The Minister for Europe, "Re. Mechanism," p. 4. www.diplomatie.gouv.fr/IMG/pdf/22-5209-circulaire_n6379-sg_du_22_nov._22_en_anglais__cle8fac62.pdf.
28. Directive of the European Parliament and of the Council on Asset Recovery and Confiscation, April 3, 2024. https://data.consilium.europa.eu/doc/document/PE-3-2024-INIT/en/pdf.
29. Directive on Asset Recovery and Confiscation, Arts. 4 and 11.
30. "Criminal organisation" means a structured association (i.e., not randomly formed, but not requiring formally defined roles or continuity of membership), established over a period of time, of more than two persons acting in concert [to commit crimes punishable with at least 4 years imprisonment] to obtain, directly or indirectly, a financial or other material benefit. Council Framework Decision 2008/841/JHA on the fight against organised crime, October 24, 2008, Art. 1. https://eur-lex.europa.eu/legal-content/EN/TXT/HTML/?uri=CELEX:32008F0841.
31. Open-ended Intergovernmental Working Group on Asset Recovery, "Foreign Illicit Assets," Arts. 17–18, pp. 9–10. www.unodc.org/documents/treaties/UNCAC/WorkingGroups/workinggroup2/2016-August-25-26/V1605154e.pdf.
32. Federal Assembly of the Swiss Confederation, "196.1 Federal Act of December 18, 2015 on the Freezing and the Restitution of Illicit Assets held by Foreign Politically Exposed Persons (Foreign Illicit Assets Act, FIAA)," July 1, 2016, Arts. 3 and 4. www.fedlex.admin.ch/eli/cc/2016/322/en.
33. Federal Assembly, "196.1 Federal Act," Art. 15.
34. Federal Assembly, "196.1 Federal Act," Art. 17.
35. United Nations Office on Drugs and Crime, "A Net for All Fish," p. 28. www.unodc.org/documents/corruption/Publications/2023/UNODC_Confiscated_Asset_Returns_and_UNCAC_-_A_Net_for_All_Fish_2023.pdf.
36. United States Code, "Civil forfeiture 18 USC § 981," uscode.house.gov, January 2, 2001; United States Code, "Laundering of Monetary Instruments 18 USC § 1956(a)(2)," govinfo.gov, January 3, 2012; U.S. Department of Justice, Criminal Division, Money Laundering and Asset Recovery Section, "Asset Forfeiture Policy Manual 2023," 129 (2021) www.justice.gov/criminal-afmls/file/839521/download; see generally Michael J. Biondi, "Building Trust(s): Rethinking Asset Return in Kleptocracy Forfeitures" (2023) 72 *Duke Law Journal*, 1080–1122. https://scholarship.law.duke.edu/cgi/viewcontent.cgi?article=4151&context=dlj; Pablo J. Davis, "'To Return the Funds at All': Global Anticorruption, Forfeiture, and Legal Frameworks for Asset Return" (2016) 47 *The University of Memphis Law Review*, 291.
37. 18 USC sec. 981(i)(1). See UNODC, note 32, at 28.
38. www.justice.gov/jm/jm-9-119000-asset-forfeiture-approval-consultation-and-notification-requirements.
39. Joseph R. Biden Jr., The White House, "Memorandum on Establishing the Fight against Corruption as a Core United States National Security Interest," whitehouse.gov, June 3, 2021, Sec. 2(c). www.whitehouse.gov/briefing-room/presidential-actions/2021/06/03/memorandum-on-establishing-the-fight-against-corruption-as-a-core-united-states-national-security-interest/.

40. United Nations Office on Drugs and Crime, "A Net for All Fish," p. 28. www.unodc.org/documents/corruption/Publications/2023/UNODC_Confiscated_Asset_Returns_and_UNCAC_-_A_Net_for_All_Fish_2023.pdf; Annabel Oromoni, "Feds introduce amendments to seize and redistribute assets of sanctioned Russians," Canadian Lawyer, May 23, 2022. www.canadianlawyermag.com/news/general/feds-introduce-amendments-to-seize-and-redistribute-assets-of-sanctioned-russians/366851.
41. Dr. A. Neil Campbell, William Pellerin, Philip Kariam, et al., "Canada Expands Sanctions on Russia and Proposes Broad Legislative Changes to Its Sanctions Regime," McMillan International Trade Law Bulletin, June 1, 2022. https://mcmillan.ca/insights/canada-expands-sanctions-on-russia-and-proposes-broad-legislative-changes-to-its-sanctions-regime/.
42. Simon Lock, "How Roman Abramovich Became the Face of Russian Wealth," Bureau of Investigative Journalism, November 15, 2023. www.thebureauinvestigates.com/stories/2023-11-15/how-roman-abramovich-became-the-face-of-russian-wealth/.
43. OECD, "Resolving Foreign Bribery Cases with Non-Trial Resolutions: Settlements and Non-Trial Agreements by Parties to the Anti-Bribery Convention," oecd.org, 2019, p. 128.
44. Claudia Baez-Camargo, Gretta Fenner and Saba Kassa, "It Takes Two to Tango: Decision-Making Processes on Asset Return," Basel Institute on Governance, International Centre for Asset Recovery, October 2017. https://baselgovernance.org/sites/default/files/2019-06/WP%2024%20web.pdf.
45. Aaron Bornstein, The Bota Foundation: A Model for the Safe Return of Stolen Assets? East-West Management Institute, 2016. https://ewmi.org/sites/default/files/docs/Bota-Foundation-PtP%20Case-Study%201-15-17_0.pdf; IREX and Save the Children, "The BOTA Foundation: Final Summative Report," irex.org, February 12, 2015. www.irex.org/sites/default/files/node/resource/bota-foundation-final-report.pdf.
46. U.S. Department of Justice, "Case 2:07-cv-03559-LAP Attachment A: The BOTA Foundation: Final Summative Report," justice.gov, December 9, 2015. www.justice.gov/opa/file/798316/download.
47. U.S. Department of Justice, "Case 2:07-cv-03559-LAP." www.justice.gov/opa/file/798316/download; Fred Merttens, Ian MacAuslan and Marta Marzi, "Evaluating the BOTA Foundation's Social Sector Programmes in Kazakhstan," Oxford Policy Management, 2011. www.opml.co.uk/projects/evaluating-bota-foundation-social-sector-programmes-kazakhstan; Clare O'Brien, Oxford Policy Management, "The Impact of the BOTA Foundation's Conditional Cash Transfer Programme for Pre-school Children in Kazakhstan," International Policy Centre for Inclusive Growth, February 2016. https://socialprotection.org/discover/publications/impact-bota-foundation%E2%80%99s-conditional-cash-transferprogramme-pre-school.
48. Amanda Wheat, "West Africa: The BP Oil Spill Spells Disaster for Region," MediaGlobal, June 18, 2010.
49. Adeyemi Dipeolu, et al., "Illicit Financial Flows: Report of the High Level Panel on Illicit Financial Flows from Africa," au.int, January 2015. https://au.int/sites/default/files/documents/40545-doc-IFFs_REPORT.pdf.
50. William Clowes, "U.S. Opposes Nigeria Plan to Hand Looted Funds to Governor," Bloomberg, February 21, 2020. www.bloomberg.com/news/articles/2020-02-21/u-s-opposes-nigeria-plan-to-hand-looted-funds-to-state-governor#xj4y7vzkg.

51. Sara Brimbeuf and Rahima Zitoumbi, "Handbook for Asset Restitution: Good Practices and Recommendations for the Responsible Return of Stolen Assets," Transparency International France, p. 74. https://transparency-france.org/wp-content/uploads/2022/06/Handbook-for-asset-restitution_Transparency-France_230622.pdf; Soji Apampa, et al., "Utilization of Repatriated Abacha Loot," World Bank and Federal Ministry of Finance Nigeria, documents.worldbank.org, December 1, 2006. https://documents1.worldbank.org/curated/en/629531468775591807/pdf/393900v10UNI0A11Monitoring01PUBLIC1.pdf.
52. British High Commission Abuja, "Immigration Minister Signs Agreement with Nigeria on Returning Stolen Criminal Assets," gov.uk, September 1, 2016. www.gov.uk/government/news/immigration-minister-signs-agreement-with-nigeria-on-returning-stolen-criminal-assets--2.
53. Rachael Hanna, "The Trilateral Nigeria-US-Jersey Agreement to Return Nigerian Dictator Abacha's Assets: A Preliminary Assessment," GAB | The Global Anticorruption Blog, April 24, 2020. https://globalanticorruptionblog.com/2020/04/24/the-trilateral-nigeria-us-jersey-agreement-to-return-nigerian-dictator-abachas-assets-a-preliminary-assessment/.
54. ANEEJ, Monitoring Return of Returned Assets in Nigeria (2021), p. 5. www.aneej.org/asset-recovery-mantra/.
55. Foreign, Commonwealth & Development Office, Serious Fraud Office and Vicky Ford MP, "UK Aid Supports Vulnerable People in Chad Using Millions of Pounds Recovered during Corruption Case," gov.uk, November 29, 2021. www.gov.uk/government/news/uk-aid-supports-vulnerable-people-in-chad-using-millions-of-pounds-recovered-during-corruption-case.
56. Catherine Putz, "Swiss Agree to Return $131 Million to Uzbekistan Via UN Trust Fund," The Diplomat, August 17, 2022. https://thediplomat.com/2022/08/swiss-agree-to-return-131-million-to-uzbekistan-via-un-trust-fund/.
57. The Swiss Confederation and the Republic of Uzbekistan, "Agreement between the Swiss Confederation and the Republic of Uzbekistan on the Modalities for the Return of Illegally Acquired Assets Forfeited in the Swiss Confederation to the Benefit of the Population of the Republic of Uzbekistan," August 16, 2022. www.newsd.admin.ch/newsd/message/attachments/73095.pdf.
58. ISHONSH, 2022 Annual Report for the Uzbekistan Vision 2030 Multi-Partner Trust Fund for August 16 to December 31, 2022.
59. Stolen Asset Recovery Initiative, The World Bank, United Nations Office on Drugs and Crime, "Alexander Yakovlev and Vladimir Kuznetsov (United Nations Oil-for-Food Programme)," star.worldbank.org, August 16, 2023. https://star.worldbank.org/asset-recovery-watch-database/alexander-yakovlev-and-vladimir-kuznetsov-united-nations-oil-food.
60. Mukesh Kapila, "Scandal shakes the UN and gives us lessons in how to reform it," The National, May 19, 2022. www.thenationalnews.com/opinion/comment/2022/05/20/scandal-shakes-the-un-and-gives-us-lessons-in-how-to-reform-it/. See generally www.u4.no/publications/corruption-cases-within-multilateral-organisations.
61. Umida Niyazova, et al., "Call for Transparency and Inclusion in the Return of Gulnara Karimova's ill-gotten Assets to Uzbekistan by the Swiss Government," Uzbek Forum for Human Rights, July 8, 2021. www.uzbekforum.org/call-for-transparency-and-inclusion-in-the-return-of-gulnara-karimovas-ill-gotten-

assets-to-uzbekistan-by-the-swiss-government/; S. Brimbeuf and R. Zitoumbi, "Handbook for Asset Restitution," p. 43. https://transparency-france.org/wp-content/uploads/2022/06/Handbook-for-asset-restitution_Transparency-France_230622.pdf.

62. Daley Birkett, "Asset Recovery at International(ised) Criminal Tribunals: Fines, Forfeiture, and Orders for Reparations," pp. 3–4, in Nina HB Jorgensen, *The International Criminal Responsibility of War's Funders and Profiteers* (Cambridge: Cambridge University Press, 2020), pp. 455–480. https://ssrn.com/abstract=4411249.
63. International Criminal Court, "Rome Statute, Part 7: Penalties," icc-cpi.int, Art. 77(2)(b).
64. International Criminal Court, "Rome Statute," Art. 93(1)(k).; International Criminal Court, "Rome Statute," Art. 57(3)(e).; D. Birkett, "Asset Recovery," pp. 8–9.
65. International Criminal Court, "Case: The Prosecutor v. Jean-Pierre Bemba Gombo, et al.,: Decision Re-sentencing Mr Jean-Pierre Bemba Gombo, Mr Aime Kilolo Musamba and Mr Jean-Jacques Mangenda Kabongo ICC-01/05-01/13-2312," September 17, 2018, para. 128.
66. Daniela Mohor, "EXCLUSIVE: UN Greenlights Massive New Humanitarian Fund for Venezuelans," October 17, 2023. www.thenewhumanitarian.org/news-feature/2023/10/17/united-nations-greenlights-humanitarian-fund-venezuela.
67. Senate of the United States, "S. 1417 (117th): PANA Act 117th Congress 1st Session, Bill to create a Venezuela Restoration Act," govtrack.us, April 28, 2021. H.R. 6539 (117th) 2nd Sess, February 1, 2022, Text of H.R. 6539 (117th): PANA Act (Introduced version) – GovTrack.us.; INRAV, "Venezuela Asset Recovery Initiative," inrav.org, 2020. www.inrav.org/en.
68. Maria Alejandra, E-mail exchange, February 26, 2024.
69. R. Yewdall Jennings, "Some International Law Aspects of the Refugee Question" (1939) 20 *The British Yearbook of International Law*, pp. 98–114; Guy S. Goodwin-Gil and Selim Can Sazak, "Footing the Bill: Refugee-Creating States" Responsibility to Pay, *Foreign Affairs*, July 29, 2015.

7 REPARATIONS FOR VICTIMS OF GRAND CORRUPTION

1. Code of Criminal Procedure (Guatemala), "Decree No. 7-2011 of the Congress of the Republic of Guatemala, Art. 124 of the Constitution," p. 6, http://ww2.oj.gob.gt/camarapenal/media/kunena/attachments/62/DECRETO_07_2011.pdf (Right to dignified reparation).
2. Arnoldo Medrano et.al., Case C-01081-2012-00364 OF. 2do. First Sentencing Tribunal for Crimes, Drug-Related and Environmental Offenses, High Risk Court C, Department of Guatemala, August 20, 2020.
3. See, for example, Richard Messick, "Recovering Damages for Corruption – Bribery Victims," Global Anticorruption Blog, April 21, 2021. https://globalanticorruptionblog.com/2021/04/21/recovering-damages-for-corruption-bribery-victims/.
4. See Transparency International, Exporting Corruption (2020). https://files.transparencycdn.org/images/A-slim-version-of-Exporting-Corruption-2020.pdf. See also discussion of the UK Glencore case in Chapter 6.

5. American Convention on Human Rights, Art. 63. See generally Dinah Shelton, *Remedies in International Human Rights Law* (Oxford: Oxford University Press, 2015).
6. For more on reparations in the Inter-American system, *see* Claudio Grossman, Agustina del Campo and Mina A. Trudeau, *International Law and Reparations: The Inter-American System*. (Atlanta: Clarity Press, 2018); Dinah Shelton, *Remedies in International Human Rights Law* (Oxford University Press, 2015).
7. United Nations Human Rights Office of the High Commissioner, "General Assembly Resolution 60/147, Basic Principles and Guidelines on the Right to a Remedy and Reparation for Victims of Gross Violations of International Human Rights Law and Serious Violations of International Humanitarian Law," United Nations, December 2005.
8. *See, for example*, Naomi Roht-Arriaza, "Reparations Decisions and Dilemmas" (2004) 27 *Hastings Int'l & Comp. L. Rev*, 157.; Pablo de Greiff, *The Handbook of Reparations*. (Oxford: Oxford University Press, 2006).
9. Inter-American Court of Human Rights, "Case of Gonzalez et al. ('Cotton Field') v. Mexico, Judgment," refworld.org, November 16, 2009, www.refworld.org/jurisprudence/caselaw/iacrthr/2009/en/107991 (Accessed April 22, 2024.)
10. Pablo de Greiff, "Introduction Repairing the Past: Compensation for Victims of Human Rights Violations," in Pablo de Greiff, *The Handbook of Reparations* (Oxford: Oxford University Press, 2006), pp. 4, 10, 12, 13, 15, 17.
11. Code of Criminal Procedure (Italy), "Law Rognoni-La Torre," September 13th, 1982, n.646, *see* especially Art. 416-bis, p. 106. https://legislationline.org/sites/default/files/2023-09/criminal%20code%20of%20Italy.pdf.
12. Redress, "SANCTION. CONFISCATE. COMPENSATE. Briefing: Comparative Laws for Confiscating and Repurposing Russian Oligarch Assets," redress.org, September 2022. https://redress.org/wp-content/uploads/2022/09/Briefing-on-Comparative-Laws.pdf
13. Redress, "SANCTION," p. 4.
14. Legislative decree of February 4, 2010, converted into Law No. 50 of March 31, 2010; *See* also The Italian Republic, "Code of Anti-Mafia Laws and Prevention Measures, Legislative Decree No. 159," normattiva.it, September 6, 2011.
15. The European Parliament and the Council of the European Union, "Directive 2014/42/EU of the European Parliament and of the Council of April 3, 2014 on the Freezing and Confiscation of Instrumentalities and Proceeds of Crime in the European Union" (2014) L127 *Official Journal of the European Union*, especially Art. 10, 39–50 at 49, https://eur-lex.europa.eu/eli/dir/2014/42/oj.
16. Directive of the European Parliament and of the Council on Asset Recovery and Confiscation, April 3, 2024. https://data.consilium.europa.eu/doc/document/PE-3-2024-INIT/en/pdf, para. 38 and Art. 19.
17. Giulia Baruzzo, Tatiana Giannone and Giulia Pasinato, "The Social Re-Use of Confiscated Assets in Europe: A First Mapping," Good(s) Monitoring Europe!, July 2021, available *at* www.confiscatibene.it/sites/default/files/blog-upload/The%20social%20re-use%20of%20confiscated%20assets%20in%20Europe_a%20first%20mapping.pdf.
18. UN General Assembly, "Our Common Commitment to Effectively Addressing Challenges and Implementing Measures to Prevent and Combat Corruption and Strengthen International Cooperation," A/RES/S-32/1, June 2, 2021. https://ungass2021.unodc.org/ungass2021/index.html, para. 49.

19. "The SAE and the Food Bank give 16.5 tons of food to vulnerable families in Colombia," Jan. 10, 2025, www.saesas.gov.co/sala_prensa/noticias/la_sae_banco_alimentos_entregan_16_133712. See also Law 1708 of 2014.
20. Proyecto Bien Restituido, "Para el desmantelamiento patrimonial del crimen organizado y el fortalecimiento de la sociedad civil," (Project Well Restored, "For the dismantling of the assets of Organized Crime and Strengthening of civil society,") www.bienrestituido.org.ar.
21. Mark Landler, "German Company Pays Jewish Family for Nazi-era Confiscation," The New York Times, March 30, 2007.
22. Ruth Hall, "Reconciling the Past, Present, and Future: The Parameters and Practices of Land Restitution in South Africa," in Cherryl Walker, et al, *Land, Memory, Reconstruction, and Justice: Perspectives on Land Claims in South Africa* (Athens: Ohio University Press, 2010), pp. 18–19.
23. Hanri Mostert, "Change through Jurisprudence: The Role of the Courts in Broadening the Scope of Restitution," in Cherryl Walker, et al., *Land, Memory, Reconstruction, and Justice: Perspectives on Land Claims in South Africa* (Athens: Ohio University Press, 2010), pp. 64–68.
24. Mostert, "Change through Jurisprudence," pp. 65–74.
25. Bill Derman, Edward Lahiff and Espen Sjaastad, "Strategic Questions about Strategic Partners Challenges and Pitfalls in South Africa's New Model of Land Restitution," in Cherryl Walker, et al., *Land, Memory, Reconstruction, and Justice: Perspectives on Land Claims in South Africa* (Athens: Ohio University Press, 2010), pp. 306–324.
26. Colombia, Truth Commission, Legacy: Land Dispossession (Comisión de la Verdad, Legado: Despojo de Tierras) (2022). www.comisiondelaverdad.co/violacion-derechos-humanos-y-derecho-internacional-humanitario/despojo-y-memoria-de-la-tierra.
27. The Congress of the Republic (Colombia), "Victims and Land Restitution Law, Law 1448 of 2011," unidadvictimas.gov.co, June 10, 2011, available *at* www.unidadvictimas.gov.co/es/documentos_bibliotec/ley-1448-de-2011-2.
28. Colombia, "Victims and Land Restitution Law," Art. 77, pp. 26–28.
29. Forging Futures Foundation, "Analysis of Restitutions in the Country," forjandofuturos.org, April 30, 2023, www.forjandofuturos.org/wp-content/uploads/2024/12/INFOGRAFIA-ENERO-2024-1.pdf.
30. Aaron Alfredo Acosta and Nelson Camilo Sanchez, *Insurmountable Barriers: An Analysis of the Administrative Stage of the Land Restitution Process*. (Bogota: Editorial Dejusticia, 2021), www.dejusticia.org/wp-content/uploads/2021/12/Doc75_Web-1.pdf.
31. Rutas del Conflicto, The Obstacles to Restitution (Los Obstáculos de la Restitución) (2022). https://rutasdelconflicto.com/notas/los-obstaculos-la-restitucion.
32. Victims and Land Restitution Law, Art. 207.
33. Jorge L. Esquirol, "The Presumptions and Burdens of Land Restitution in Colombia" (2021) 31 *Transnational Law & Contemporary Problems*, 93–119, https://tlcp.law.uiowa.edu/sites/tlcp.law.uiowa.edu/files/7._esquirol_-_the_presumptions_of_land_restitution_final.pdf.
34. Paula Andrea Valencia Cortes, "The Court's Decision that Puts Land Restitution at Risk," Dejusticia, February 23, 2024, www.dejusticia.org/column/la-decision-de-la-corte-que-pone-en-riesgo-la-restitucion-de-tierras.
35. *See, for example,* the work of groups like Accountability Counsel, www.accountabilitycounsel.org.

36. See, for example, the Inter-American Court of Human Rights discussion of damage to the project of life of the victim in Case of Loayza Tamayo v. Peru, Judgment of November 27, 1998, www.corteidh.or.cr/docs/casos/articulos/seriec_42_ing.pdf ("options, in themselves, have an important existential value") para. 148.
37. Open Contracting Partnership, www.open-contracting.org/what-is-open-contracting.
38. Interview with one of the lawyers present, December 2023.
39. Richard Messick, "A Breakthrough in Recognizing Who is a Corruption Victim," GAB | The Global Anticorruption Blog, December 17, 2020, https://globalanticorruptionblog.com/2020/12/17/a-breaththrough-in-recognizing-who-is-a-corruption-victim.
40. United States District Court Eastern District of New York, "United States v. OZ Africa Mgmt. GP, LLC, 16-CR-515 (NGG)," August 28, 2019, https://casetext.com/case/united-states-v-oz-africa-mgmt-gp-llc.
41. RAID and AFREWATCH, "Democratic Republic of Congo: Congo's Victims of Corruption," raid-uk.org, January 2020, www.raid-uk.org/sites/default/files/raid-congosvictimsofcorruptionfullreportfinal.pdf.
42. RAID, "Statement by UK Corporate Watchdog RAID Following the UK Serious Fraud Office Announcement to Close the Corruption Investigation into Mining Giant ENRC," raid-uk.org, August 25, 2023, https://raid-uk.org/raid-statement-following-the-uk-sfo-announcement-to-close-the-corruption-investigation-into-mining-giant-enrc.
43. Samuel J. Hickey, "Remediation in Foreign Bribery Settlements: The Foundations of a New Approach" (2021) 21 *Chicago Journal of International Law*, 367–418, *at* https://cjil.uchicago.edu/print-archive/remediation-foreign-bribery-settlements-foundations-new-approach.
44. OECD and The World Bank, "Identification and Quantification of the Proceeds of Bribery," star.worldbank.org, November 11, 2011, p. 33. (A 2012 StAR report notes that: "[…] in cases of bribery, […] courts often quantify the difference between the price or the quality of goods and services provided by the briber and the price or quality that the customer would have accepted if its agent had not taken the bribe.")
45. CFI, "Anti-Dumping Duty," https://corporatefinanceinstitute.com/resources/economics/anti-dumping-duty.
46. Eduardo Salcedo-Albaran, et al., "Victims of Corruption: Integral Reparation and Institutional Trust as Cores of Anticorruption Strategies," SSRN, August 3, 2021, https://ssrn.com/abstract=3898710; Eric M. Uslaner, "Trust and Corruption Revisited: How and Why Trust and Corruption Shape Each Other" (2013) 47 *Quality & Quantity*, 3603–3608.
47. Dr. Juanita Olaya Garcia, "Dealing With the Consequences: Repairing the Social Damage Caused by Corruption," SSRN, January 15, 2016, p. 21, *at* https://ssrn.com/abstract=3475453.
48. Edith Brown Weiss, *In Fairness to Future Generations: International Law, Common Patrimony, and Intergenerational Equity*. (Tokyo, Japan: United Nations University, 1989), pp. xxix, 385.
49. These include the United Nations Framework Convention on Climate Change (UNFCCC), Art. 3; the Convention on Biological Diversity, Preamble, Art. 2; the World Heritage Convention, Art. 4; and the United Nations Economic

Commission for Europe (UNECE) Water Convention, Art. 2.5 explicitly reference obligations to future generations. The principle also appears, inter alia, in the Stockholm Declaration, Principles 1, 2, and the Rio Declaration, Principle 3.

50. Office of the Attorney General of the Republic of Costa Rica, "Jurisprudence on Social Damage," www.pgr.go.cr/servicios/procuraduria-de-la-etica-publica-pep/temas-de-interes-pep/dano-social/jurisprudencia-sobre-dano-social.
51. Third Chamber of the Supreme Court of Justice (Costa Rica), "Judgment No. 00499," Ref. No. 04-005356-0042-PE, vlex.co.cr, May 11, 2011.
52. Third Chamber of the Supreme Court of Justice (Costa Rica), "Ref. No. 04-006835-0647-PE," vlex.co.cr.
53. Carlos Cordero Perez, "Alcatel Lucent Indemnifies ICE with $10 Million in Damages," El Financiero, August 4, 2015, www.elfinancierocr.com/tecnologia/alcatel-lucent-indemniza-al-ice-con-10-millones-por-danos-y-perjuicios/UXKPPC46UVGVPCJHNOUY5LDDOU/story.
54. Dr. Juanita Olaya Garcia, Kodjo Attisso and Anja Roth, "Repairing Social Damage Out of Corruption Cases: Opportunities and Challenges as Illustrated in the Alcatel Case in Costa Rica," SSRN, December 6, 2010, https://ssrn.com/abstract=1779834.
55. Lorena Escobar de Guerrero, Reparación Digna para el Estado (Guatemala, ASIES, July 2022). http://asies.org.gt/pdf/reparacion_digna_del_estado.pdf.
56. Ministry of Trade, Industry and Tourism, "Res. No. 5216," Republic of Colombia, February 16, 2017, §5.1, www.sic.gov.co/sites/default/files/normatividad/052017/Resolucion_5216.pdf (the response to the State Attorney's action can be found in the precautionary measures decision).
57. Administrative Court of Cundinamarca, s. 1, subs. "A," "Office of the Attorney General of the Nation v. Concessionaire Ruta del Sol S.A.S, et al., Exp. No. 25000234100020170083-00, Means of control for the protection of collective rights and interests, Sentence," December 6, 2018, *at* www.consejodeestado.gov.co/documentos/biblioteca/libros/2019pr/Tomo2/25000-23-41-000-2017-00083-00S.pdf, especially pp. 125–138.
58. Council of State, Third Administrative Litigation Section, "Office of the Attorney General of the Nation v. Concessionaire Ruta del Sol S.A.S, et al., Popular Action 25000234100020170008302 (64048)" Republic of Colombia, July 27, 2023. https://apps.procuraduria.gov.co/relatoria/media/file/flas_juridico/4102_CE-RAD-2017-00083-02.pdf.
59. Council of State (Colombia), Contentious Administrative Chamber, 4th Section, Constitutional (Tutela) Action 11001-03-15-000-2024-01500-01, August 30, 2024.
60. The Congress of the Republic (Colombia), "Law No. 2195 of 2022 measures in matters related to transparency, prevention, and the fight against corruption, Civil Service," January 18, 2022, www.funcionpublica.gov.co/eva/gestornormativo/norma_pdf.php?i=175606.
61. Court of Appeals of the State of New York, "Palsgraf v. Long Island RR Co., 248 N.Y. 339," 1928. (Justice Andrews, dissenting).
62. Code of Criminal Procedure (Peru), "Legislative Decree No. 957," July 22, 2004, Art. 94, www.wipo.int/wipolex/en/text/202824.
63. Supreme Court of Justice of the Republic, Permanent Criminal Chamber (Peru), "Crime of violence against authority. Civil Actor. Constitution, Judgment

of Cassation, Appeal No. 596-2021/JUNIN," img.lpderecho.pe, April 18, 2022, https://img.lpderecho.pe/wp-content/uploads/2022/04/Casacion-596-2021-Junin-LPDerecho.pdf.

64. Law 2195 of 2022, Art. 62, www.funcionpublica.gov.co/eva/gestornormativo/norma.php?i=175606.
65. United States Code, "Crime Victims' Rights Act 18 USC § 3771," uscode.house.gov, October 30, 2004.
66. United States District Court, Northern District of Texas, "United States v. The Boeing Co., Second Memorandum Opinion & Order, Criminal Action No. 4:21-cr-5-O," govinfo.gov, October 21, 2022.
67. Anne Peters, "Corruption as a Violation of International Human Rights" (2018) 29 *European Journal of International Law*, s. H(1), 1267–1269, *at* https://doi.org/10.1093/ejil/chy070.
68. Federal Assembly, "Federal Act on the Freezing and the Restitution of Illicit Assets held by Foreign Politically Exposed Persons," Swiss Confederation, December 18, 2015, Art. 15, https://fedlex.data.admin.ch/filestore/fedlex.data.admin.ch/eli/cc/2016/322/20160701/en/pdf-a/fedlex-data-admin-ch-eli-cc-2016-322-20160701-en-pdf-a-1.pdf.
69. Code of Criminal Procedure (France), Art. 324-1-1, 2013, www.legifrance.gouv.fr/codes/article_lc/LEGIARTI000028285954.
70. E.g. Inter-American Court of Human Rights, Velasquez-Rodriguez v. Honduras, ACHR Series C No 4, [1988] IACHR 1, (1989) 28 ILM 291, (1988).
71. *See, for example*, Tom R. Tyler, "Procedural Justice and the Courts" (2007) 44 *Court Review: The Journal of the American Judges Association*, 26–31, https://digitalcommons.unl.edu/cgi/viewcontent.cgi?article=1254&context=ajacourtreview.
72. Lieselotte Viaene, "Life Is Priceless: Mayan Q'eqchi' Voices on the Guatemalan National Reparations Program" (2010) 4 *International Journal of Transitional Justice*, 4–25, https://doi.org/10.1093/ijtj/ijp024.
73. Caso Construcción y Corrupción, Juzgado de Primera Instancia Penal, Narcoactividad y Delitos contra el Ambiente, por procesos de Mayor Riesgo grupo D. (April 14, 2018), para. 226–238.
74. Transparency for Colombia and Global Financial Integrity, "Case Study #3, Temporary Union of Population Centers: Following the money trail to building a business sector more transparent," transparenciacolombia.org, 2022, https://transparenciacolombia.org.co/wp-content/uploads/2022/12/Estudio-de-Caso-Centros-Poblados.pdf.
75. Natalia Chacon, "Population Centers: Emilio Tapia Will Try Again to Bring Internet to Rural Areas," W Radio, March 30, 2023, www.wradio.com.co/2023/03/30/centros-poblados-emilio-tapia-intentara-de-nuevo-llevar-internet-a-zonas-rurales.
76. For a fuller discussion of this regime, *see* Clara Sandoval, Hobeth Martinez-Carrillo and Michael Cruz-Rodriguez, "The Challenges of Implementing Special Sanctions (*Sanciones Propias*) in Colombia and Providing Retribution, Reparation, Participation and Reincorporation" (2022) 14 *Journal of Human Rights Practice*, 478, *at* https://academic.oup.com/jhrp/article/14/2/478/6659909. (For more on the Special Jurisdiction (known as JEP)).
77. *See, for example*, Constitutional Chamber, "Constitutionality of forfeiture of ownership in El Salvador," Ruling: 146-2014/107-2017, Supreme Court of Justice (El Salvador), May 28, 2018; Emilio J. Urbina Mendoza, "Constitutional Justice

and the Forfeiture of Property in Latin America. An Important Lesson for its Configuration in Venezuela, Considering Judgment 315 of 28-04-2023 of the Constitutional Chamber of the Supreme Court of Justice" (2023) 173–174 *Public Law Review*, 361, https://revistadederechopublico.com/wp-content/uploads/2023/09/La_justicia_constitucional_y_la_extincion_de_dominio_en_America_Latina._Una_alta_leccion_su_configuracion_en_Venezuela._Emilio_Urbina.pdf.

78. Victor Soto Martinez and Juan Pablo Cavada, "Domain forfeiture and Confiscation to Confront Organized Crime in International Law, Latin American and Chilean Law," Library of the National Congress of Chile, May 25, 2023, https://obtienearchivo.bcn.cl/obtienearchivo?id=repositorio/10221/34342/1/Estudio_N_06_23_Extincion_de_dominio_y_crimen_organizado.pdf.

8 TRANSITIONS, TRANSITIONAL JUSTICE, AND GRAND CORRUPTION

1. See, for example, UN Commission on Human Rights, Updated Set of principles for the protection and promotion of human rights through action to combat impunity, E/CN.4/2005/102/Add.1, February 8, 2005. For a summary of transitional justice efforts and contributions in Latin America, see, N. Roht-Arriaza, "Transitional Justice in Latin America," in Jens Meierhenrich et al., *The Oxford Handbook of Transitional Justice* (2023). https://doi.org/10.1093/oxfordhb/9780198704355.013.10.
2. I tell this story in Naomi Roht-Arriaza, "After Amnesties: Latin American National Courts and the New Contours of the Fight Against Impunity" (2015) 37 *Human Rights Quarterly* 341.
3. Zinaida Miller, "Effects of Invisibility: In Search of the 'Economic' in Transitional Justice" (2008) 2 *International Journal of Transitional Justice*, 10.1093/ijtj/ijn022 (2008); Dustin Sharp, *Justice and Economic Violence in Transition* (New York: Springer Books, 2013); Paul Gready and Simon Robins, *From Transitional to Transformative Justice* (Cambridge University Press, 2019).
4. Ruben Carranza, "Plunder and Pain: Should Transitional Justice Engage with Corruption and Economic Crimes?" (2008) 2 *International Journal of Transitional Justice*, 310.
5. Alexander Segovia, "The Relationship between Transitional Justice and Corruption: Current State of the Discussion and Proposal for a Research Agenda," September 2023. www.ohchr.org/sites/default/files/documents/issues/transitionaljustice/sg-guidance-note/SG-GuidanceNote-TJ-Corruption-digital.pdf.
6. Pablo De Greiff, "Articulating the links between transitional justice and development: Justice and social integration" in De Greiff and Duthie, *Transitional Justice and Development: Making Connections* (2009), p. 29.
7. For discussion of links between corruption and armed conflict, see Martine Boersma, *Corruption: A Violation of Human Rights and a Crime Under International Law?* (Cambridge: Larcier-Intersentia, 2012); Philippe Le Billon, "Buying Peace or Fuelling War: The Role of Corruption in Armed Conflicts" (2003) 15 *Journal of International Development*, 413–426.
8. See, for example, Lynsey Chutel, "South Africa's Young Democracy Leaves its Young Voters Disillusioned," May 28, 2024. www.nytimes.com/2024/05/28/world/africa/south-africa-election-youth-vote.html?searchResultPosition=9.

9. High Court of South Africa, "Affidavit of Anton Roussouw Ackermann, National Director of Public Prosecutions," May 7, 2015, available *at* www.opensecrets.org.za/wp-content/uploads/2022/09/Anton-Ackermann-Affidavit.pdf.
10. Ra'eesa Pather, "Apartheid Victims Ask Zondo to Probe NPA Capture," New Frame Archives, May 14, 2019, https://newframe.org/apartheid-victims-ask-zondo-to-probe-npa-capture.
11. Ra'eesa Pather and Tabitha Paine, "Bad Cops Bad Lawyers: The Officials at the NPA and Hawks Delaying Justice for State Capture Crimes," Open Secrets, August 2022, www.opensecrets.org.za/investigation-bad-cops-bad-lawyers.
12. Shadow World Investigations (SWI), "The State Capture Project," https://shadowworldinvestigations.org/projects-and-publications/the-state-capture-project
13. Karan Mahajan, "'State Capture': How the Gupta Brothers Hijacked South Africa Using Bribes Instead of Bullets," March 3, 2019, www.vanityfair.com/news/2019/03/how-the-gupta-brothers-hijacked-south-africa-corruption-bribes (The State Capture Project estimated $3 billion in losses.)
14. Mark Gevisser, "'State Capture': The Corruption Investigation that has Shaken South Africa," July 11, 2019. www.theguardian.com/news/2019/jul/11/state-capture-corruption-investigation-that-has-shaken-south-africa.
15. Ferial Haffajee and Ivor Chipkin, *Days of Zondo: The Fight for Freedom from Corruption*. (South Africa: Maverick 451, 2022).
16. Tom Lodge, "Political Corruption in South Africa" (1998) 97 *African Affairs*, 157–187, p. 166.
17. Hennie van Vuuren, *Apartheid Guns and Money: A tale of profit*. (Oxford: Oxford University Press, 2019).
18. van Vuuren, *Apartheid Guns and Money*, p. 507.
19. van Vuuren, *Apartheid Guns and Money*, p. 38.
20. Interview, South African human rights activist, 2023.
21. Michael Forsythe and Walt Bogdanich, "McKinsey Charged in South African Corruption Case," September 30, 2022, www.nytimes.com/2022/09/30/world/africa/mckinsey-corruption-case-south-africa.html.
22. Lodge, "Political Corruption," 157–187 at 187.
23. Richard Humphries and Thabo Rapoo, *Governing the Provinces: Proceedings of Two Conferences Convened by the Centre for Policy Studies on Forming New Governments and Administrations in South Africa's Regions* (Doornfontein: Centre for Policy Studies, 1994); Nico Steytler and Johann Mettler, "Federal Arrangements as a Peacemaking Device during South Africa's Transition to Democracy" (2001) 31 *Publius: The Journal of Federalism*, 93–106; Richard Simeon and Christina Murray, "Multi-sphere Governance in South Africa: An Interim Assessment" (2001) 31 *Publius: The Journal of Federalism*, 65–92.
24. Ivor Chipkin, et al., *Shadow State: The Politics of State Capture* (Johannesburg: Wits University Press, 2018).
25. Mark Gevisser, "State capture," July 11, 2019.
26. Ferial Haffajee and Ivor Chipkin, *Days of Zondo: The Fight for Freedom from Corruption* (South Africa: Maverick 451, 2022), pp. 319–330.
27. SWI, "The State Capture Project," https://shadowworldinvestigations.org/projects-and-publications/the-state-capture-project.

28. Lynsey Chutel, "Jacob Zuma, Once Leader of the A.N.C., Becomes Its Political Rival," May 10, 2024. www.nytimes.com/2024/05/10/world/africa/south-africa-zuma-election.html.
29. *See also* Simon Robins and Paul Gready, *Transitional Justice in Tunisia: Innovations, Continuities, Challenges* (London: Routledge, 2022).
30. World Bank Group, "The Unfinished Revolution: Bringing Opportunity, Good Jobs And Greater Wealth To All Tunisians," worldbank.org, May 2014, pp. 15–16, www.worldbank.org/content/dam/Worldbank/document/MNA/tunisia_report/tunisia_report_the_unfinished_revolution_eng_synthesis.pdf.
31. Republic of Tunisia, "Organic Law No. 53-2013 Establishing and Organizing Transitional Justice, Unofficial Translation," International Center for Transitional Justice, 2013, www.ohchr.org/sites/default/files/Documents/Countries/TN/TransitionalJusticeTunisia.pdf.
32. Truth & Dignity Commission (IVD) and Avocats Sans Frontieres, "The Final Comprehensive Report: Executive Summary," ivd.tn, May 2019, www.ivd.tn/rapport/doc/TDC_executive_summary_report.pdf.
33. Ruben Carranza, Mohamed Azer Zouari and Ichraq Ghdiri, "The Truth about Corruption: Reviewing the Tunisia Truth and Dignity Commission's Report on Corruption Under Dictatorship," (ICTJ, 2024). www.ictj.org/sites/default/files/2024-02/ictj_briefing_tunisia_corruption_en_web_0.pdf.
34. Carranza et al., The Truth about Corruption.
35. Simon Robins, et al., "Transitional Justice from the Margins: Collective Reparations and Tunisia's Truth and Dignity Commission" (2022) 94 *Political Geography*, www.sciencedirect.com/science/article/pii/S0962629821002250.
36. Olfa Belhassine, "Tunisia's Truth Commission vs France, the IMF and World Bank," September 8, 2019. www.cadtm.org/Tunisia-s-Truth-Commission-vs-France-the-IMF-and-World-Bank.
37. Francesca Ebel, "The Tunisia Heist," New Lines Magazine, May 7, 2021, https://newlinesmag.com/reportage/the-tunisia-heist
38. Mohamed Afif Jaidi, "Recovering Ben Ali's Stolen Funds: The Squandered Right," The Legal Agenda, March 31, 2020, https://english.legal-agenda.com/recovering-ben-alis-stolen-funds-the-squandered-right.
39. Taygeti Michalakea, "Anticorruption and Transitional Justice: A Distinction without a Difference" (2022) 22(2) *Human Rights Law Review*, https://doi.org/10.1093/hrlr/ngac014.
40. Tunis Afrique Presse, "Tunisia: Presidential Decree On Penal Reconciliation Issued in Official Gazette," allafrica.com, March 21, 2022, https://allafrica.com/stories/202203220453.html.
41. Comisión de la Verdad, Hay Futuro si Hay Verdad, Hallazgos y Recomendaciones (2022) p. 274. www.comisiondelaverdad.co/hallazgos-y-recomendaciones-1. The Executive Summary is available in English at www.abcolombia.org.uk/wp-content/uploads/2022/07/ENV1.pdf.
42. Comisión de la Verdad, p. 269.
43. Comisión de la Verdad, p. 308.
44. Gustavo Duncan, *More than Silver or Lead: The Political Power of Drug Trafficking in Colombia and Mexico* (Mexico: Debate, 2015), p. 282.

45. Maria McFarland Sanchez-Moreno, *There Are No Dead Here: A Story of Murder and Denial in Colombia* (New York: Bold Type Books, 2018), p. 126.
46. Americas Division, Human Rights Watch, "Breaking the Grip? Obstacles to Justice for Paramilitary Mafias in Colombia," hrw.org, October 2008, www.hrw.org/report/2008/10/16/breaking-grip/obstacles-justice-paramilitary-mafias-colombia.
47. Comisión de la Verdad, p. 292.
48. Infobae, "Almost 400 Billion Pesos were Given by the Attorney General's Office to the Victims' Reparation Fund: The Highest Amount since the Implementation of the Justice and Peace Law," infobae.com, December 26, 2022, www.infobae.com/america/colombia/2022/12/26/casi-400-mil-millones-de-pesos-entrego-la-fiscalia-al-fondo-de-reparacion-de-victimas-la-mayor-cifra-desde-la-implementacion-de-la-ley-de-justicia-y-paz.
49. Verdad Abierta, "Justice and Peace: Where Is the Money Hidden Behind the War?," verdadabierta.com, October 4, 2015, https://verdadabierta.com/justicia-y-paz-donde-esta-la-plata-que-se-esconde-tras-la-guerra.
50. Colombia/FARC-EP, "Final Agreement for the Termination of the Conflict and the Construction of a Stable and Lasting Peace," p. 43, www.comisiondelaverdad.co/sites/default/files/descargables/2022-11/02_acuerdo-final-firmado-escaneado.pdf.
51. Colombia/FARC-EP, "Final Agreement," pp. 95–97.
52. Special Jurisdiction for Peace, "JEP Opens Case 08 that will Investigate Crimes Committed by Members of the Security Forces, other State Agents, in Association with Paramilitary Groups or Civilian Third Parties," jep.gov.co, August 30, 2022, www.jep.gov.co/Sala-de-Prensa/Paginas/JEP-abre-Caso-08-investigara-crimenes-cometidos-fuerza-publica-otros-agentes-de-estado.aspx.
53. Independent Evaluation Group, "Decentralization in Client Countries: An Evaluation of World Bank Support, 1990–2007" The International Bank for Reconstruction and Development and The World Bank, 2008, https://ieg.worldbankgroup.org/sites/default/files/Data/reports/decentralization_eval.pdf.
54. Roberto Belloni and Francesco Strazzari, "Corruption in Post-conflict Bosnia-Herzegovina and Kosovo: A Deal Among Friends" (2014) 35 *Third World Quarterly*, 855–871, *also* in *Corruption in the Aftermath of War* (London: Routledge, 2016); *See also* Melissa T. Labonte, "From Patronage to Peacebuilding? Elite Capture and Governance from below in Sierra Leone" (2012) 111 *African Affairs*, 90–115, https://academic.oup.com/afraf/article/111/442/90/31687.
55. Law 2272 of November 4, 2022, www.funcionpublica.gov.co/eva/gestornormativo/norma.php?i=197883.

9 A CORRUPTION LENS ON ATROCITY CRIMES

* Parts of this chapter were published in earlier versions as Naomi Roht-Arriaza and Santiago Martinez, "Grand Corruption and the International Criminal Court in the 'Venezuela Situation'" (2019) 17 *Journal of International Criminal Justice*, 1057–1082, https://doi.org/10.1093/jicj/mqz038 and *as* Naomi Roht-Arriaza, "Gran Corrupción y Crímenes Atroces en América Latina" (Grand Corruption and Atrocity Crimes in Latin America)" (2022) 13 *Juridica Ibero*, 19–48.

1. Diane Marie Amann, "Group Mentality, Expressivism, and Genocide" (2002) 2.2 *International Criminal Law Review*, 93–143; Mark A. Drumbl, *Atrocity, Punishment, and International Law*. (Cambridge: Cambridge University Press, 2007); Saira Mohamed, "Deviance, Aspiration, and the Stories We Tell: Reconciling Mass Atrocity and the Criminal Law" (2015) 124 *The Yale Law Journal*, 1628–1689.
2. UN Special Procedures, Nota informativa, Sentencia del Tribunal con Competencia en Casos de Mayor Riesgo Grupo "C" de Guatemala en el caso Molina Theissen. (Informative Note, Molina Theissen case). www.ohchr.org/sites/default/files/Documents/Issues/Truth/NotaInformativaGuatemala_SP.doc.
3. International Criminal Court, "Rome Statute of the International Criminal Court," icc-cpi.int, July 17, 1998, www.icc-cpi.int/sites/default/files/RS-Eng.pdf.
4. Yulia Nuzban, "'For Private or Personal Use': The Meaning of the Special Intent Requirement in the War Crime of Pillage under the Rome Statute of the International Criminal Court" (2020) 102 *International Review of the Red Cross*, 1249–1272, https://international-review.icrc.org/articles/for-private-or-personal-use-special-intent-requirement-pillage-rome-statute-icc-915.
5. Insight Crime, "Will the International Criminal Court Investigate Mexico's 'Drug War'?," November 5, 2014. https://insightcrime.org/news/analysis/international-criminal-court-mexico-drug-war/.
6. Trial Chamber III, "The Prosecutor v. Jean-Pierre Bemba Gombo, Case No. ICC-01/05-01/08-3343, Judgment pursuant to Article 74 of the Statute," International Criminal Court, March 21, 2016, para. 149.
7. Jerome de Hemptinne, et al., *Modes of Liability in International Criminal Law*. (Cambridge: Cambridge University Press, 2019), www.cambridge.org/core/books/modes-of-liability-in-international-criminal-law/D088C1218D467E848733767EC71E5586#fndtn-information.
8. Ximena Medellin Urquiaga, "Digest of Latin American Jurisprudence on International Crimes," Due Process of Law Foundation, 2010, www.dplf.org/sites/default/files/1285861527.pdf.
9. International Criminal Court, "Rome Statute," Art. 25(3), p. 14.
10. U.S. Department of the Treasury, "Treasury Works with Government of Mexico against Perpetrators of Corruption and their Networks," home.treasury.gov, May 17, 2019, https://home.treasury.gov/news/press-releases/sm692.
11. FIDH and IDHEAS, "Mexico: Criminal Structure Within the Public Prosecutor's Office of the State of Nayarit and Crimes against Humanity," fidh.org, June 2021, pp. 32–33, www.fidh.org/IMG/pdf/fidh-idheas_-_nayarit_report_english_.pdf.
12. NMas, "Video: Nayarit Anti-Corruption Magistrate Investigated for Enrichment," facebook.com, www.facebook.com/nmas.com.mx/videos/corrupci%C3%B3n-de-funcionarios-relacionados-con-roberto-sandoval/939265543488363/?locale=ms_MY.
13. International Criminal Court, "Rome Statute," Art. 7(2)(a) states "Attack directed against any civilian population" means a course of conduct involving the multiple commission of acts referred to in paragraph 1 against any civilian population, *pursuant to or in furtherance of a State or organizational policy* to commit such attack. (emphasis added), p. 4.
14. For more on these debates, *see* Matt Halling, "Push the Envelope – Watch It Bend: Removing the Policy Requirement and Extending Crimes against Humanity" (2010)

23 *Leiden Journal of International Law*, 827; William A. Schabas, "Prosecuting Dr Strangelove, Goldfinger, and the Joker at the International Criminal Court: Closing the Loopholes" (2010) 23 *Leiden Journal of International Law*, 847; Tilman Rodenhauser, "The 'State or Organizational Policy' Requirement for Crimes against Humanity under the Rome Statute of the International Criminal Court," in *Organizing Rebellion: Non-State Armed Groups under International Humanitarian Law, Human Rights Law, and International Criminal Law* (Oxford: Oxford Academic, 2018), pp. 250–281.

15. *See* Pre-Trial Chamber II, "Decision Pursuant to Art. 61(7)(a) and (b) of the Rome Statute on the Charges of the Prosecutor against Jean-Pierre Bemba Gombo, Case No. ICC-01/05-01/08-424," International Criminal Court, June 15, 2009, para. 81, p. 28; *see also* Trial Chamber II, "Case: The Prosecutor v. Germain Katanga, Judgment pursuant to article 74 of the Statute, Case No. ICC-01/04-01/07-3436-tENG," March 7, 2014, para. 1109, p. 419.
16. Pre-Trial Chamber II, Situation in the Republic of Kenya, Decision Pursuant to Art. 15, March 31, 2010, para. 89.
17. Situation in the Republic of Kenya, para. 90.
18. "Dissenting opinion of Judge Kaul, Pre-Trial Chamber II, Situation in the Republic of Kenya," Decision Pursuant to Art. 15, March 31, 2010, para. 51.
19. Situation in the Republic of Kenya, para. 93.
20. Vázquez Valencia, Captura del Estado, Macrocriminalidad y Derechos Humanos (State Capture, Macrocriminality and Human Rights) (FLACSO, Mex., 2019), p. 113. https://mx.boell.org/sites/default/files/2019-12/captura%20del%20estado%20-%20interiores%20final.pdf; Open Society Justice Initiative, et al., "Corruption That Kills: Why Mexico Needs an International Mechanism to Combat Impunity," Open Society Foundations, 2018, www.justiceinitiative.org/uploads/5071ab37-003f-46b1-9e1f-700bbdae34a3/corruption-that-kills-en-20180502.pdf.
21. *See* Ginger Thompson, "Anatomy of a Massacre: The story of the deadly assault on a Mexican town near the Texas border. And the U.S. anti-drug operation that triggered it.," Propublica, June 12, 2017, www.propublica.org/article/allende-zetas-cartel-masacre-y-la-dea; see also Vazquez Valencia, *State Capture*, p. 139 et seq.
22. Human Rights Clinic, "'Control Over the Entire State of Coahuila' An analysis of testimonies in trials against Zetas members in San Antonio, Austin, and Del Rio, Texas," The University of Texas School of Law, November 2017, available *at* https://law.utexas.edu/wp-content/uploads/sites/11/2017/11/2017-HRC-coahuilareport-EN.pdf.
23. Jimena Reyes, "State Capture Through Corruption: How Can Human Rights Help?," Human Rights Program, Harvard Law School, June 2019, p. 23, https://hrp.law.harvard.edu/wp-content/uploads/2022/10/JimenaReyes_HRP_19_002.pdf.
24. Armando Rios, "The Allende Massacre, 10 Years of Impunity, 'Apologies Have Not Been Enough,'" BorderHub, March 17, 2021, www.borderhub.org/noticias/la-masacre-de-allende-a-10-anos-de-impunidad-disculpas-no-han-sido-suficientes.
25. Open Society Justice Initiative, "Corruption That Kills," pp. 32, 39–44.
26. *See, for example*, Carlos Martin Beristain, *The Time of Ayotiznapa*. (Mexico City: Ediciones Akal, 2016); John Gibler, *I Couldn't Even Imagine That They Would Kill Us: An Oral History of the Attacks against the Students of Ayotzinapa*. (San Francisco: City Lights, 2017).

27. John Gibler, "'The government dynamited the investigation of the Ayotzinapa case': former prosecutor denounces," Animal Político, September 26, 2023, https://animalpolitico.com/sociedad/caso-ayotzinapa-investigacion-exfiscal-denuncia.
28. Jesus Perez Caballero, *The Political Element in Crimes against Humanity*. (Madrid: Dykinson, 2015).
29. Perez Caballero, The Political Element, pp. 240–241.
30. Ximena Medellin Urquiaga and Jorge Carlos Peniche Baqueiro, "Individual Criminal Responsibility for the Perpetration of Heinous Crimes: Perspectives from the Core and the Periphery" (2022) 13 *Jurídica Ibero*, 49, 80–82.
31. ICC, Appeals Chamber, Judgment on the appeal of the Bolivarian Republic of Venezuela against Pre-Trial Chamber I's "Decision authorising the resumption of the investigation pursuant to article 18(2) of the Statute", 1 March 2024, www.icc-cpi.int/sites/default/files/CourtRecords/0902ebd1807927f1.pdf.
32. Trial Chamber III, "Situation in the Central African Republic in the Case of the Prosecutor v. Jean-Pierre Bemba Gombo, Judgment pursuant to Article 74 of the Statute, ICC-01/05-01/08," International Criminal Court, March 21, 2016, www.icc-cpi.int/CourtRecords/CR2016_02238.PDF.
33. Pre-Trial Chamber I, "Situation in the Democratic Republic of the Congo in the Case of the Prosecutor v. Germain Katanga and Mathieu Ngudjolo Chui, Public Redacted Version, Decision on the confirmation of charges, ICC-01/04-01/07," International Criminal Court, September 30, 2008, www.icc-cpi.int/CourtRecords/CR2008_05172.PDF.
34. Emiliano Teran Mantovani, Predatory Mining in Venezuela: the Orinoco Mining Arc, enclave economies and the National Mining Plan, WRM Bulletin 254, March 9, 2021. www.wrm.org.uy/bulletin-articles/predatory-mining-in-venezuela-the-orinoco-mining-arc-enclave-economies-and-the-national-mining-plan.
35. Antonio Maria Delgado and Valentina Lares, "Huge cyber leak offers new proof of how Maduro has turned Venezuela into a narco-state," Miami Herald, November 6, 2023, www.miamiherald.com/news/nation-world/world/americas/article281178108.html?utm_source=substack&utm_medium=email.
36. United Nations Office of the High Commissioner for Human Rights, "Independence of the justice system and access to justice in the Bolivarian Republic of Venezuela, including for violations of economic and social rights, and the situation of human rights in the Arco Minero del Orinoco region, A/HRC/44/54," ohchr.org, para. 41, available *at* https://documents.un.org/doc/undoc/gen/g20/242/31/pdf/g2024231.pdf?token=HZ433WBpbuRYec7Q3p&fe=true.
37. UNOHCHR, "Independence of the justice system," paras. 51–54.
38. Sonia Osorio, "Murder of 25 Venezuelan Indians Condemned During Entry of Humanitarian Aid," The New Herald, February 27, 2019, www.elnuevoherald.com/noticias/mundo/america-latina/venezuela-es/article226873574.html; VIVO play, "Video File: Parliament denounces the murder of at least 25 Pemon Indians," YouTube, February 27, 2019, retrieved *from* www.youtube.com/watch?v=Nm4FPBawsz4.
39. International Criminal Court, "Rome Statute," Art. 7(2)(d), p. 4.
40. International Crisis Group, "Gold and Grief in Venezuela's Violent South," crisisgroup.org, February 28, 2019, www.crisisgroup.org/latin-america-caribbean/andes/venezuela/073-gold-and-grief-venezuelas-violent-south.

41. Venezuelan Observatory of Violence, "Annual Report on Violence 2021," para. 29, https://observatoriodeviolencia.org.ve/news/informe-anual-de-violencia-2021
42. *See, for example,* Helen Montoya, "Terror in the Honduran Jungle where Drug Traffickers Fatten Cattle," InSight Crime, May 18, 2022, https://es.insightcrime.org/investigaciónes/narco-ganaderia-mosquitia-honduras (This phenomenon is not limited to Honduras.)
43. Hanna Dreier and Joshua Goodman, "Venezuela's Army Traffics Food in Time of Hunger," The Associated Press, December 27, 2016, https://apnews.com/45b25be7186f4dbb95b637181ob62d8a.
44. Venezuela Investigative Unit and Colombian Observatory of Organized Crime, "Venezuela: A Mafia State? Venezuela has Become a Hub of Organized Crime in the Region," InSight Crime, 2018, www.insightcrime.org/wp-content/uploads/2018/05/Venezuela-a-Mafia-State-InSight-Crime-2018.pdf.
45. Office of Public Affairs, "Five Individuals Charged with Money Laundering in Connection with Alleged Venezuela Bribery Scheme," U.S. Department of Justice, October 21, 2021, www.justice.gov/opa/pr/five-individuals-charged-money-laundering-connection-alleged-venezuela-bribery-scheme.
46. Jan-Michael Simon, "Foreign Accountability for Venezuelan State Corruption (Part I): Accountability to U.S. Justice," Due Process of Law Foundation, Justice in the Americas, December 21, 2021, https://dplfblog.com/2021/12/21/rendicion-de-cuentas-en-el-extranjero-por-corrupcion-del-estado-venezolano-parte-i-blanqueo-de-capitales-provenientes-de-corrupcion-ante-la-justicia-de-los-ee-uu.
47. Venezuela Investigative Unit, "Venezuela 'Kingpin' Skimmed Millions from State Food Program: Report," InSight Crime, February 22, 2017, https://insightcrime.org/news/brief/venezuela-kingpin-skimmed-millions-state-food-program-report.
48. Jan-Michael Simon, "Foreign Accountability for Venezuelan State Corruption (Part III): The Business Scheme in the 'Food for Venezuela' Case and the Response of Mexican Authorities," Due Process of Law Foundation, Justice in the Americas, April 21, 2022, https://dplfblog.com/2022/04/21/rendicion-de-cuentas-en-el-extranjero-por-corrupcion-del-estado-venezolano-parte-iii-el-esquema-de-negocios-en-el-caso-alimentos-para-venezuela-y-la-respuesta-de-las-autoridades-mexicanas.
49. Jan-Michael Simon, "Accountability Abroad for Venezuelan State Corruption (Part IV): The Weight of the 'Food for Venezuela' Business on Food Insecurity, Hunger, and Malnutrition," Due Process of Law Foundation, Justice in the Americas, May 31, 2022, https://dplfblog.com/2022/05/31/rendicion-de-cuentas-en-el-extranjero-por-corrupcion-del-estado-venezolano-parte-ivel-peso-del-negocio-alimentos-para-venezuela-en-la-inseguridad-alimentaria-el-hambre-y-la-desnu.
50. Nicholas Casey, "'It Is Unspeakable': How Maduro Used Cuban Doctors to Coerce Venezuela Voters," The New York Times, March 17, 2019, www.nytimes.com/2019/03/17/world/americas/venezuela-cuban-doctors.html.
51. Guillermo Perez, "The Local Supply and Production Committees under the Human Rights Based Approach" (2019) 5 *Journal of Public Policy Studies*, 81, https://revistaestudiospoliticaspublicas.uchile.cl/index.php/REPP/article/view/52575; Examples of political discrimination can be found *in* Edgar Lopez, "Special | CLAPs: 7 Signs of Political Discrimination," *PROVEA*, November 4, 2016, https://provea.org/trabajos-especiales/los-clap-7-indicios-de-discriminacion-politica;

See also Christopher Hernandez-Roy, et al., "Report of the General Secretariat of the Organization of American States and the Panel of Independent International Experts on the Possible Commission of Crimes against Humanity in Venezuela, Second ed.," Organization of American States, March 2021, p. 499, www.oas.org/documents/eng/press/Informe-Panel-Independiente-Venezuela-EN.pdf.

52. International Criminal Court, "Rome Statute," Art. 17, pp. 10–11. For the ICC Prosecutor's most recent views on complementarity, see The Office of the Prosecutor, "Policy on Complementarity and Cooperation," International Criminal Court, April 2024, www.icc-cpi.int/sites/default/files/2024-04/2024-comp-policy-eng.pdf.
53. *See* Pre-Trial Chamber I, "Situation in the Bolivarian Republic of Venezuela I: Prosecution request to resume the investigation into the situation in the Bolivarian Republic of Venezuela I pursuant to article 18(2),"' November 1, 2022, www.icc-cpi.int/sites/default/files/CourtRecords/CR2022_06554.PDF.
54. Jonathan Blitzer, "The Exile of Guatemala's Anti-Corruption Efforts," The New Yorker, April 29, 2022.
55. The Office of the Prosecutor, "Policy Paper on Preliminary Examinations," International Criminal Court, November 2013, www.icc-cpi.int/sites/default/files/iccdocs/otp/OTP-Policy_Paper_Preliminary_Examinations_2013-ENG.pdf, para. 64.
56. The Office of the Prosecutor, "Policy Paper," para. 65. See also similar language in The Office of the Prosecutor, "Policy Paper on Case Selection and Prioritisation," International Criminal Court, Sept. 15, 2016, www.icc-cpi.int/sites/default/files/itemsDocuments/20160915_OTP-Policy_Case-Selection_Eng.pdf.
57. Pre-Trial Chamber I, "In the Case of the Prosecutor v. Bahar Idriss Abu Garda: Decision on the Confirmation of Charges, ICC 02/05-02/09-243-Red," February 8, 2010, para. 31, p. 16.
58. Esther Hava Garcia, "Grand Corruption: Strategies to Avoid International Impunity" (2016) 12 *New Penal Forum*, https://doi.org/10.17230/nfp.12.87.2
59. Paul D. Ocheje, "Refocusing International Law on the Quest for Accountability in Africa: The Case Against the 'Other' Impunity" (2002) 15 *Leiden Journal of International Law*, 749–779.
60. Second International Congress on Universal Jurisdiction, FIBGAR, September 2015, https://fibgar.es/portfolio-item/ii-congreso-internacional-de-jurisdiccion-universal/#.
61. The Office of the Prosecutor, "Policy Paper on Case Selection and Prioritisation," International Criminal Court, September 15, 2016, para. 41, p. 14, www.icc-cpi.int/sites/default/files/itemsDocuments/20160915_OTP-Policy_Case-Selection_Eng.pdf.
62 Trial Chamber II, "The Prosecutor v. Zoran Kupreskic, et al., Case No.: IT- 95-16-T, Judgment," International Criminal Tribunal for the Former Yugoslavia, January 14, 2000, para. 566, p. 226.
63. International Criminal Court, "Rome Statute," Art. 30, p. 16, *states* "'knowledge' means awareness that a circumstance exists or a consequence will occur in the ordinary course of events." (There is debate as to whether this allows for a form of *dolus eventualis* [in common law: recklessness], which I cannot cover here.)

64. Sonja Starr, "Extraordinary Crimes at Ordinary Times: International Justice Beyond Crisis Situations" (2007) 101 *Northwestern University Law Review*, 1257; Angela Barkhouse, "Can the ICC Prosecute Grand Corruption as A Crime against Humanity Under Article 7 of the Rome Statute," Academia.edu, 2014, www.academia.edu/29676635/Can_the_ICC_Prosecute_Grand_Corruption_as_A_Crime_Against_Humanity_Under_Article_7_of_the_Rome_Statute?email_work_card=view-paper; Ilias Bantekas, "Corruption as an International Crime and Crime against Humanity: An Outline of Supplementary Criminal Justice Policies" (2006) 4 *Journal of International Criminal Justice*, 466–484. *See also* Chile Eboe-Osuji, "Kleptocracy: a Desired Subject of International Criminal Law that is in Dire Need of Prosecution by Universal Jurisdiction," in Evelyn A. Ankumah and Edward K. Kwakwa, *African Perspectives on International Criminal Justice* (The Hague: Africa Legal Aid, 2005), p. 121.
65. BBC, "Bank Payout to Pinochet Victims," February 26, 2005. http://news.bbc.co.uk/2/hi/business/4300841.stm.
66. Natalia Kubesch, "The UK Is Failing to Recoup Ill-gotten Gains Linked to the Syrian Regime," Just Security, April 1, 2024, www.justsecurity.org/94080/uk-recoup-syrian-regime-assets; UK Public General Acts, "Proceeds of Crime Act 2002," legislation.gov.uk, §241 and §241A, www.legislation.gov.uk/ukpga/2002/29/part/5/chapter/1; Criminal Finance Act 2017, Ch. 3.
67. Sibylla Brodzinsky, "Families of Victims of Colombia's Paramilitaries Get Their Day in US court," March 2, 2017, www.theguardian.com/world/2017/mar/02/colombia-paramilitaries-victims-us-court.
68. Alice Speri, "U.S. Court Issues Landmark Ruling on Paramilitary Violence in Colombia," November 24, 2021. https://theintercept.com/2021/11/24/colombia-macaco-carlos-jimenez-paramilitary-ruling/.
69. Matthew Stephenson and Sophie Arjon Schütte, "An International Anti-Corruption Court? A Synopsis of the Debate," U4 Anti-Corruption Resource Center (2019). www.u4.no/publications/an-international-anti-corruption-court-a-synopsis-of-the-debate.pdf.

10 CONCLUSIONS

1. Odebrecht Latinvest S.à.r.l. v. Republic of Peru (ICSID Case No. ARB/20/4). https://icsid.worldbank.org/cases/case-database/case-detail?CaseNo=ARB/20/4.
2. Case Concerning Military and Paramilitary Activities in and against Nicaragua (Nicaragua v. United States of America); Merits, -, International Court of Justice (ICJ), June 27, 1986, www.refworld.org/jurisprudence/caselaw/icj/1986/en/26087.
3. *Prosecutor* v. *Dusko Tadic* aka "Dule" (Opinion and Judgment), IT-94-1-T, International Criminal Tribunal for the former Yugoslavia (ICTY), May 7, 1997.
4. United Nations International Law Commission, Draft Articles on Responsibility of States for Internationally Wrongful Acts, with Commentaries (2001), https://legal.un.org/ilc/texts/instruments/english/commentaries/9_6_2001.pdf.
5. Mark L. Wolf, "The World Needs an International Anti-Corruption Court" (2018) 147 *Daedalus*, 144–156; Ministry of Foreign Affairs, "Colombia Proposes an International Anti-Corruption Court," Government of Colombia, January 24, 2019. www.cancilleria

.gov.co/newsroom/news/colombia-propone-corte-internacional-anticorrupcion; Ian J. Lynch and Susana Malcorra, "An International Anti-Corruption Tribunal Is Needed to Prevent Kleptocracy," esglobal, October 13, 2021. www.esglobal.org/para-impedir-la-cleptocracia-es-necesario-un-tribunal-internacional-anticorrupcion.

6. Stephenson and Schütte, An IACC?; Juanita Olaya Garcia, "Why an International Anti-Corruption Court is Not the Answer," UNCAC Coalition, December 6, 2022. https://uncaccoalition.org/why-an-international-anti-corruption-court-is-not-the-answer. See also Sabine E. Nölke, "Strengthening Existing International Anti-Corruption Frameworks and Institutions," in Rotberg and Hampson, Grand Corruption, pp. 244–265.
7. see, e.g. Allan Rock, "The Nature and Functions of a Civil Chamber for the IACC," in Rotberg and Hampson, Grand Corruption, pp. 285-294.
8. N. Roht-Arriaza, The Pinochet Effect, pp. 202–205.
9. Laurence R. Helfer, Cecily Rose and Rachel Brewster, "Flexible Institution Building in the International Anti-Corruption Regime: Proposing a Transnational Asset Recovery Mechanism" (2023) 117 *American Journal of International Law*, 560–600. www.cambridge.org/core/journals/american-journal-of-international-law/article/flexible-institution-building-in-the-international-anticorruption-regime-proposing-a-transnational-asset-recovery-mechanism/0F5B45914CEF6935D485F90B5F6133CC.
10. Transparency International, "Tackling Grand Corruption Impunity: Proposal for a Definition and Special Measures," Transparency.org, September 6, 2023, www.transparency.org/en/publications/tackling-grand-corruption-impunity-proposals-for-definition-and-special-measures.
11. Cheryl Lawther, "The Construction and Politicisation of Victimhood," in Lynch O and Argomaniz J, *Victims of Terrorism: A Comparative and Interdisciplinary Study* (London: Routledge, 2014), pp. 10–30.
12. Laurel Fletcher, "Refracted Justice: The Imagined Victim and the International Criminal Court," in De Vos C, Kendall S and Stahn C, *Contested Justice: The Politics and Practice of International Criminal Court Interventions* (Cambridge: Cambridge University Press, 2015), pp. 302–325.
13. Stephen Collinson, "Trump Conviction Heralds a Somber and Volatile Moment in American History," May 31, 2024, www.cnn.com/2024/05/31/politics/trump-conviction-consequences-analysis/index.html.
14. Gregory Michener and B. Cerqueira, "Guest Post: The Judicial Annulment of the Odebrecht Settlement Evidence in Brazil, and Its Implications," Global Anticorruption Blog, September 19, 2023. https://globalanticorruptionblog.com/2023/09/19/guest-post-the-judicial-annulment-of-the-odebrecht-settlement-in-brazil-and-its-implications/.
15. Julie López, The Case Against Journalist José Ruben Zamora was Built in 72 Hours, El Faro, Aug. 17, 2022, https://elfaro.net/en/202208/centroamerica/26331/The-Case-against-Journalist-Jos%C3%A9-Rub%C3%A9n-Zamora-Was-Built-in-72-Hours.htm.
16. Frank Bajak, "Renowned Peruvian Investigative Reporter Battles Criminalized Smear Campaign – and Cancer," April 27, 2024. https://apnews.com/article/peru-gustavo-gorriti-corruption-journalist-4fcc84fdc3d37b76c64c9988f299c77b.
17. Douglas Cuevas, "Diputados del Congreso iniciarán con la discusión de las reformas a la Ley del Ministerio Público," January 24, 2024. www.prensalibre.com/guatemala/politica/diputados-del-congreso-iniciaran-con-la-discusion-de-las-reformas-a-la-ley-del-ministerio-publico/.

18. www.fatf-gafi.org/content/dam/fatf-gafi/fsrb-mer/CFATF-Mutual-Evaluation-Venezuela.pdf.coredownload.inline.pdf, recommendation 8.
19. For example, www.fiscalia.gov.co/colombia/wp-content/uploads/2013/03/Priorizaci%C3%B3n.pdf; www.corteidh.or.cr/tablas/r25829.pdf.
20. For example, Cecily Rose, "The Limitations of a Human Rights Approach to Corruption" (2016) 65 *The International & Comparative Law Quarterly*, 405; *see also* Kevin E. Davis, "Corruption as a Violation of International Human Rights: A Reply to Anne Peters" (2018) 29 *European Journal of International Law*, 1289, 1294.
21. Alston, Philip. "Conjuring up New Human Rights: A Proposal for Quality Control" (1984) 78(3) *The American Journal of International Law*, 607–621. https://doi.org/10.2307/2202599.
22. In the United States, see Inequality.org, "Income Inequality in the United States," (2024). https://inequality.org/facts/income-inequality/. Globally, see World Bank, *2023 in Nine Charts: A Growing Inequality* (Washington DC: The World Bank, 2023). www.worldbank.org/en/news/feature/2023/12/18/2023-in-nine-charts-a-growing-inequality.
23. Robert Reich, *The Common Good* (Knopf, 2018) p. 90.
24. Sarah Chayes, *Thieves of State: Why Corruption Threatens Global Security* (Norton Books: 2015).
25. Martine Boersma; Corruption: A Violation of Human Rights and a Crime under International Law? (Intersentia, 2012); Christine J. Wade, *Captured Peace: Elites and Peacebuilding in El Salvador* (Ohio University Press, 2016).
26. See, for example, UNODC, "Explainer: What are Crimes that Affect the Environment?," (2024). www.unodc.org/unodc/en/frontpage/2024/April/explainer_-what-are-crimes-that-affect-the-environment.html.
27. See Transparency International, Topic Guide: Corruption and Climate Finance (2017). https://knowledgehub.transparency.org/guide/topic-guide-corruption-and-climate-finance/4089.
28. UN Guiding Principles on Business and Human Rights (2011), www.ohchr.org/sites/default/files/documents/publications/guidingprinciplesbusinesshr_en.pdf, Principle 13.

Index

Printed by Integrated Books International,
United States of America